FIRST LIGHT

FIRST LIGHT

Kanaka ʻŌiwi Resistance to
Settler Science at Mauna a Wākea

Iokepa Casumbal-Salazar

University of Minnesota Press
Minneapolis | London

Portions of the text are adapted from "'Where Are Your Sacred Temples?' Notes on the Struggle for Mauna a Wākea," in *Detours: A Decolonial Guide to Hawai'i*, edited by Hōkūlani K. Aikau and Vernadette Vicuña Gonzalez (Duke University Press, 2019), reprinted by permission of the copyright holder, Duke University Press. Portions of chapter 6 are adapted from "A Fictive Kinship: Making 'Modernity,' 'Ancient' Hawaiians, and Telescopes on Mauna Kea," *Native American and Indigenous Studies Journal* 4, no. 2 (University of Minnesota Press, 2017).

Published by the University of Minnesota Press
111 Third Avenue South, Suite 290
Minneapolis, MN 55401-2520
http://www.upress.umn.edu

ISBN 978-1-5179-0245-2 (hc)
ISBN 978-1-5179-0246-9 (pb)

A Cataloging-in-Publication record for this book is available from the Library of Congress.

Printed in the United States of America on acid-free paper

The University of Minnesota is an equal-opportunity educator and employer.

UMP BmB 2025

Dedicated to the many kiaʻi whose stand for
Mauna a Wākea is a testament to the resilience of
our lāhui and shines bright on our path toward a
decolonial future for Hawaiʻi

CONTENTS

.

ACKNOWLEDGMENTS

If this book has any value, it is because of the aloha 'āina, the land defenders, and the freedom fighters who paved a path of resistance for me to follow, in my attempt to compose a moʻolelo of Hawaiʻi, our beloved lāhui, and Mauna a Wākea. Indeed, this book is a result of the lessons and mentorship offered by kumu who so generously accepted me as their haumāna. These kumu are my friends, family, and found family. They are the artists and educators, activists and organizers, comrades and cousins, kiaʻi and kūpuna, and sources of knowledge and inspiration to whom I wish to always be accountable; and if not for their moʻolelo and experiences, their ʻike, their time and labor, and the generosity they've shown to me, this book would not exist. I honor them throughout but devote these first words to celebrating them by expressing my gratitude. At its core, this book is about relationality, so it is appropriate to start by sharing something about the relations that produced it and me. I cherish these relations even if I fail to name them all. Any omissions are unintentional. All mistakes are mine alone.

Whose book are you reading?

I am an able-bodied, light-skinned, ambiguously mixed-race, cis-masculine person and son of working-class parents. I can talk, but I'm mostly a private person. When a time comes that I cannot *not* speak out on behalf of vulnerable people, particularly *my people*, I do, often at some social or professional risk. I was taught to own my love, a value that informs my commitment to being a good relative. Through my father, Joe Anthony Salazar, I am a grandchild of Joe Salazar and Shirley Lanihuli Rowe-Baker Salazar. Through Grandma Shirley, I descend from Nalikolauokalani and Kapuniai; the parents of Haiakeawe who, with Hoʻopiokalani, were the parents of Rebecca Waianuenue Kahalelepo Kahuli Hale, who was the mother of Margaret Maunalei Rowe, my Tūtū Shirley's mother. Our ʻohana hail from Kaupō, Maui; Puna, Moku o Keawe; and Kona, Oʻahu, among other wahi kupuna. Most of Grandma's twelve siblings were raised in Kalihi, but she was raised by her father's parents in the Kapahulu neighborhood on the slopes of Lēʻahi. Of all the gifts I've ever received, knowledge of our relations—from our ʻohana to our moʻokūʻauhau, and our lāhui—is most precious to me.

Being, as we were, a mixed-race family in California living on the ancestral lands of the Chumash, it was difficult for our family to *be Hawaiian* away from Hawaiʻi. I knew nothing about being Native, diasporan, or a settler on other Native peoples' territories. My mother is white and was adopted into a small working-class family. My father is Mexican Hawaiian, also of a working class, but much larger family. As a kid I was taught to play sports but never prepared for college. In Santa Maria, where I was born and raised until I was seventeen, you'd have made it if you joined the Army. Grandma Shirley was adamant that I not only embrace *being* Hawaiian but also know *how to be* Hawaiian. For this, she would introduce me to our ʻohana and her one hānau when I was fifteen on one of the few return visits she made back to Hawaiʻi in her lifetime, since she left at seventeen years of age. If not for her encouragement, I would never have pursued higher education. She planted in me the seed of an idea: "go college in Hawaiʻi and apply for a Kamehameha scholarship." I had no idea what a scholarship was, let alone this thing "Kamehameha," but after high school graduation, I went. For the next twenty years, I studied our language, culture, and history, and co-raised our son in Hawaiʻi. By 2015, I'd received four degrees, thanks to the funding opportunities of numerous Native Hawaiian scholarship programs, primary among them being Kamehameha Schools.

While at the University of Hawaiʻi, I became politicized and educated about the history of our people and the legacies of imperialism, military occupation, and settler racial capitalism. And it was at UH—amidst the horrors of Bush's neoconservative global "War on Terror" following the blowback of 9/11—that I began learning from a long line of aloha ʻāina and antiwar activists *another way of being Hawaiian*. Soon, I joined what has been called the contemporary Hawaiian movement, just as I began to research and write what would become the scaffolding of this book. So, I attribute my path to becoming a kiaʻi ʻāina and, in many ways, *this book*, to Grandma Shirley, whose gift was knowledge that I am a member of a

Native people indigenous to such a wonderous, storied, and sacred place that all my heroes have fought and fight to defend. This gift comes with a kuleana that I hope my telling of this mo'olelo of Mauna a Wākea honors.

I thank my family in California for their love and the many lessons they gave me in my first seventeen years. Your laughter, generosity, and commitment to each other have made me playful, thankful, and vigilant participating in this struggle. Thank you also for teaching me to ask questions, check my facts, keep my receipts, listen before I speak, and to fight alongside the weakest and downtrodden among us.

I also thank my 'ohana in Hawai'i for nurturing me in my next twenty years. Your care and aloha for me and my sister when our immediate family was so far away remains another cherished gift. In many ways, I learned much of what it is to be Hawaiian from the model of aloha that you share so generously, which has pointed me time and again toward aloha 'āina.

To my best friend, my confidant, and my love—the one I turn to when I am overjoyed, terrified, or conflicted—my dearest Melisa, I thank you most deeply for your support and confidence in times that I questioned myself. Mahalo for braving my incessant rambling about this project over the years. Mahalo for talking me down when the stress took hold. You remind me to practice gratitude daily and to speak truth to power unapologetically. You are my best friend and closest comrade in struggle. I am eternally grateful for you.

My sister, Micki, also my best friend, mahalo for our weekly conversations, for (mostly) always taking my side, and for humoring my "political analyses" of the world. Having a sibling in my corner through uncertain times makes me feel that anything is possible.

My son, Koa Moea, I admire and mahalo you for your kindness, your warmth, your generosity, your playful spirit, and your friendship. Mahalo *for allowing me to force you* to surf with me and to go mauka, to work in the lo'i and the loko i'a, to help set up tents at Lā Ho'iho'i Ea, and to join the fight to protect the mauna over the years. It is one of my greatest joys in life to see you grow to become a confident aloha 'āina. I am proud of you. So is Great-Grandma Shirley, Grandpa A, and all your 'ohana, in Hawai'i and California.

Mom, Cara, Uncle Leonard, Mama Terri, my brothers James, Dominic, and Shinji, my cousins Chad, Danielle, Kel, and Mavisanne, Uncle Allen and Aunt Cindy, Cousin Bonnie, and Cousin Lelemia: I mahalo you for always being there for me, especially in moments of need, no questions asked. You have my deepest gratitude.

Noenoe Silva—my first champion and longtime advisor, mahalo for reading my steady stream of *very bad* manuscript drafts. You truly have an adventurous spirit! While my own family has always taught me *to punch up*, it was your first Indigenous Politics course that taught me *who exactly deserved those punches*. Mahalo for encouraging me to apply to grad school. Mahalo for encouraging me to focus my anger about the injustices against our people through research and writing, but to also show up and be counted. Mahalo for your fierce support of my work from the very start. Your mentorship and friendship over these past twenty-five years has been the greatest of many gifts you've shared. Mahalo nui.

I recall first meeting Aunty Terri Kekoʻolani and Kyle Kajihiro at an Easter morning sunrise ceremony in Mākua Valley around 2000. Your demilitarization organizing continues to inspire me. Mahalo to you both. For your teachings that found their way into this book, I also thank Cecilia Akim, Kaleo Akim, Uncle Kekuni Blaisdell, Aunty Gwen Kim, Lynette Cruz, and the ʻōlohe of Pā Kuʻu A Lua.

A sincere mahalo goes to the fierce collective of kiaʻi who defended the mauna before the mass movement that followed: Mahalo to Pua Case, E. Kalani Flores, Kealoha Pisciotta, and Keomailani Von Gogh of Mauna Kea Anaina Hou, Clarence Kūkauakahi Ching, Deborah Ward, Fred Stone, Nelson Ho, John and Ruth Ota, Marti Townsend, and Bianca Isaki for sharing your time, and moʻolelo, and your ʻike about the mauna; but especially for doing the tedious and often thankless legal work that is required to fight this fight. I have learned how to aloha ʻāina through your teachings and your courageous and selfless organizing.

My heartfelt appreciation also goes to folks I was privileged to interview for this book, particularly for sharing your time and ʻike with me, including Leslie Lindsey-Kaʻapuni, Lea Hong, Shelly and Lauren Muneoka, Ikaika Hussey, Candace Fujikane, Lehua Kauhane, Uncle Maka, Kalikolehua Kanaele, Pualani Kanakaʻole Kanahele, Kalei Nuʻuhiwa, Noelani Goodyear-Kaʻōpua, ʻIlima Long, Noʻeau Peralto, Haley Kailiehu, April Drexel, Carl Pao, Marata Tamaira, Franco Salmoiraghi, Kahoʻokahi Kanuha, Mehana Kihoi, Krista Savio, Ala Savio, Billy Freitas, and Kuʻuipo Freitas. I'm also incredibly grateful to Paul Coleman, Larry Kimura, Chad Kalepa Baybayan, Kaʻiu Kimura, Stephanie Nagata, and numerous others who, despite our differing

views on the TMT, were generous enough to share experiences and expertise with me as well.

Candace Fujikane and Krista Savio, I'm extremely appreciative of
your last-minute support in helping to identify kūpuna in several photographs included in my Introduction. I also cannot thank Joy Enomoto,
Ryan Gonzalez, and Kamaoli Kuwada enough for helping me to connect
with the photographers whose photographs now grace the pages ahead. To
the artists Cody-Fay Corbett, Cory Lum, and Antonio Agosto especially,
mahalo piha for your generosity in sharing images and for documenting
the movement so beautifully.

I am forever grateful to the many kumu who, while I attended univer-
sity, contributed to my learning about Kānaka Maoli, social movements,
and power—kumu who included Haunani-Kay Trask, Jon Osorio, Kanalu
Young, April Drexel, Levon Ohai, Lilikalā Kameʻeleihiwa, Keanu Sai, Noelani
Goodyear-Kaʻōpua, Hōkū Aikau, Jon Goldberg-Hiller, Sankaran Krishna,
Charusheela, Mike Shapiro, Jodi Byrd, Ty Kāwika Tengan, Ibrahim Aoude,
Jonathan Okamura, Katerina Teaiwa, Vicky Holt Takamine, Keawe Lopes,
Kahikina de Silva, Lalepa Koga, and Kāwika Napoleon. A special mahalo
goes to my kumu hula and kumu ʻŌlelo Hawaiʻi, Leilani Basham, for teaching
me how to use my leo—as well to my hula siblings of Hālau Kupukupu Ke
Aloha: Malia, Kaliko, Luʻukia, Keoki, Kahikina, Lehua, Lokelia, and Leilani.

I was a young parent when I came to UH before starting this project.
To my friends and comrades who modeled for me how decolonial work
must be a life practice, I mahalo Darlene Rodrigues, Grace Alvaro Caligtan
and Paul Tran, Kalawaiʻa Moore and Sonya Zabala, Jesse Lipman and
Cristina Valenzuela, Joy Enomoto and Kim Compoc, Johanna Almiron
and Anthony Johnson, Kalama Niheu, Cindy Ramirez, Pete Doktor and
Monique Yuen, Chris Lipat, Eri Oura, Gordon Walker, and Hina Kneubuhl.
Ideas formed in our days together talking story and honoring chosen
familia at our many weekend pāʻina, which I hope are reflected in these
pages. To my grad school pals—Willy Kauai, Ron Williams, Sydney Iaukea,
Bianca Isaki, Mary Lee, Duane Henry, Melly Wilson, Jacky Lasky, ʻUmi
Perkins, Sue Haglund, Brianne Gallagher, Ben Schrader, Rohan Kalyan,
Noah Viernes, Lorenzo Rinelli, Sam Opondo, Tuti Baker, Ali Musleh, Sami
Raza, Ponipate Rokolekutu, and Akta Rao—you and our post-seminar gath-
erings and writing groups helped me to better distill my arguments and
think more deeply.

Early stages of this book were completed under the generous financial support of Kamehameha Schools (particularly the ʻImi Naʻauao and Nā Hoʻokama programs), the Ford Foundation Fellowship Program, and the Mellon-Kohala Center Doctoral Fellowship Program. Without these opportunities, I would likely have never finished college, and this book would not exist. I want to mahalo my Mellon-Hawaiʻi Fellowship cohort in particular: Nālani McDougall, Punihei Lipe, Eomailani Kukahiko, and Bryan Kamaoli Kuwada. Your friendship and model of scholarship motivated me to read and write *better*, and during our time together I learned the importance of honoring our ancestral knowledges in our work.

To my comrades and colleagues at the University of Victoria, where I was blessed to have my first teaching experience after graduate school—including Jeff Ganohalidoh Corntassel, Jarrett Martineau, Erynne Gilpin, Peruzzo Andrade, and Carol Bilson—I remain inspired by your work and commitment to intersectional decolonization and solidarity in their many forms.

My first substantial draft of this book was completed while on University of California President's Postdoctoral Fellowship Program funding, for which I extend my warm appreciation to Kimberly Adkinson and Mark Lawson, as well as special thanks to my dear fellows: Robin Gray, Jenny Kelly, Alicia Carol, Liza Williams, Leanne Wang, and Julianne Anesi.

My thanks to Mishuana Goeman and Sharon Traweek, whose professional mentorship during that postdoc taught me how to navigate the academy and to resist institutional capture. Many thanks also to Randy Akee, Keith Camacho, Michelle Erai, and Jessica Cattelino for the generous mentorship and local tips you shared during my time at UCLA.

To my editor Jason Weidemann, thank you for sticking with me and this project, even when I could not seem to resist adding more words! To my manuscript reviewers, kuʻualoha hoʻomanawanui, Dean Saranillio, Emalani Case, and three others who remained anonymous, I am genuinely indebted to you for such generous critical feedback across my various drafts. The book is infinitely better because of your reviews. My utmost gratitude goes to former University of Minnesota Press editor Richard Morrison, who, after hearing a presentation I gave in Kona in 2013, encouraged me to submit a book proposal after finishing my Ph.D.; and texted me out of the blue months later to encourage me to apply for a UC President's Postdoctoral Fellowship. I pursued both suggestions, and both have profoundly shaped my career as a result. Jordan Gonzales and Ākea Kahikina, mahalo for your close reviews and clutch copyediting in the final moments of this book's production.

Several friends in the NAISA community have always show such warm and wonderful kindness and mentorship, including Kealani Cook, Vince Diaz, Robert Warrior, Kēhaulani Kauanui, Maile Arvin, David Chang, Kēhaulani Natsuko Vaughn, and Uahikea Maile—you have my gratitude.

It was an honor to join the faculty at Ithaca College, my first academic appointment, in 2017. While in Ithaca, I learned to teach young people how to turn outrage into analysis from my brilliant colleagues and comrades Belisa González, Nicole Horsely, Paula Ionide, Sue-Je Gage, Scott and Nicole Eversley Bradwell, Nia Nunn, Enrique Gonzalez-Conty, Pam Sertzen, Patricia Rodriguez, Gustavo Licón, Naeem Inayatullah, Shobhana Xavier, Shehnaz Haqqani, and John Blackshire. Likewise, I am profoundly grateful to the Indigenous communities who welcomed me during my time living on the ancestral homelands of the Cayuga Nation, including Sachem Sam George, Debbie George, Lisa Kahaleole Hall, Meredith Alberta Palmer, Theresa Rocha Beardall, Tony Richardson, Jolene Rickard, and Ms. Audrey Cooper.

When the world shut down in 2020, I found new gratitude for the faculty in NAIS and anthropology, who welcomed me to the University of Texas at Austin. Circe Sturm, Kelly McDonough, Luis Cárcamo-Huechante, Hiʻilei Hobart, Craig Campbell, Polly Strong, Tony Di Fiore, Aaron Sandel, Sofian Merabet, Celina de Sá, Maria Franklin, Jason Cons, Kamran Ali, Thomas Fawcett, Chris McNett, and Katie Foster—I cannot thank you enough for your friendship, mentorship, and routine support through natural and unnatural disasters. To our RadFac collective (that is, "Radical Faculty" of color organizing group)—including Mónica Jiménez, Roger Reeves, Ashley Reese, Ana Schwartz, and Ashley Farmer—I survived the Texas Winter Storm and institutional violence of UT in solidarity and mutual aid organizing with you.

Finally, I wish to recognize that I am writing these first words on the unceded ancestral homelands of the Awaswas-speaking Uypi Tribe, where the enduring sovereignty of the Amah Mutsun Tribal Band persists in its people, their continued practice of traditions, and stewardship of the land. My colleagues here in Critical Race and Ethnic Studies at UCSC have shown me a generosity and kindness that I'm learning is matched only by their fierce commitment to social justice and decolonization, both in and outside the classroom. For this I extend my gratitude to Christine Hong, Felicity Amaya Schaeffer, Nick Mitchell, Jenny Kelly, Marisol LeBrón, Fuifuilupe Niumeitolu, Kriti Sharma, Sophia Azeb, Jennifer Mogannam, micha cárdenas, Tsim Schneider, Amy Lonetree, and Angel Riotutar.

These paths and relations have been both fulfilling and sometimes fleeting. I am a reluctant academic with deep ambivalence about the institution. This work has me living once again away from our ancestral homeland, though I do what I can to join in the collective fight against oppression wherever I may live. I embrace the contradictions that continue to make me who I am, and I keep warm the relationships that allow me to practice my commitments to movements for freedom and liberation of all peoples. While I do this work off-island, I've found there is struggle everywhere. As we know, the freedom and liberation of my own people are connected to that of those wherever oppression persists. And I am so grateful to find community among those who do this work. Mahalo nui nā akua, nā ʻaumākua, nā kūpuna, a me nā mākua a pau. I mahalo our ancestors every day for these gifts and relations.

Introduction

PUʻUHULUHULU

A Sanctuary and Struggle

E iho ana o luna
E piʻi ana o lalo
E hui ana nā moku
E kū ana ka paia

That which is above shall fall
That which is below will rise
The islands will unite
The walls will rise

—Mele attributed to Kapihe

On July 15, 2019, I watched a grainy stream from my laptop some six thousand miles away as eight fearless Kānaka ʻŌiwi chained themselves to a cattle guard on the Summit Access Road near the base of Mauna a Wākea. As they lay on the ground in the predawn chill (Figure 1), and later in the scorching sun for twelve hours (Figure 2) in a selfless demonstration of aloha ʻāina—organized to stop work crews from beginning construction of the Thirty Meter Telescope—I watched and wept.[1] Two days later, as thirty-nine activists, most of whom were kūpuna, had their hands bound with zip ties and were carried away, stowed into police vans, arrested, and charged with "obstructing government operations," I wept.[2] As I bore witness to kapu aloha, the code of disciplined conduct that governed the direct actions at Puʻuhuluhulu, I watched and wept. As police in riot gear equipped with batons, sidearms, rubber bullets, pepper spray, tear gas, and an LRAD,[3] or "sound cannon," lined the road and prepared to crack skulls—some with tears in their own eyes as many were also Kānaka Maoli[4]—again, I wept.

Before a third round of vans could be loaded, several dozen kiaʻi wahine emerged to shield kūpuna from the police.[5] With arms locked, the line began

1

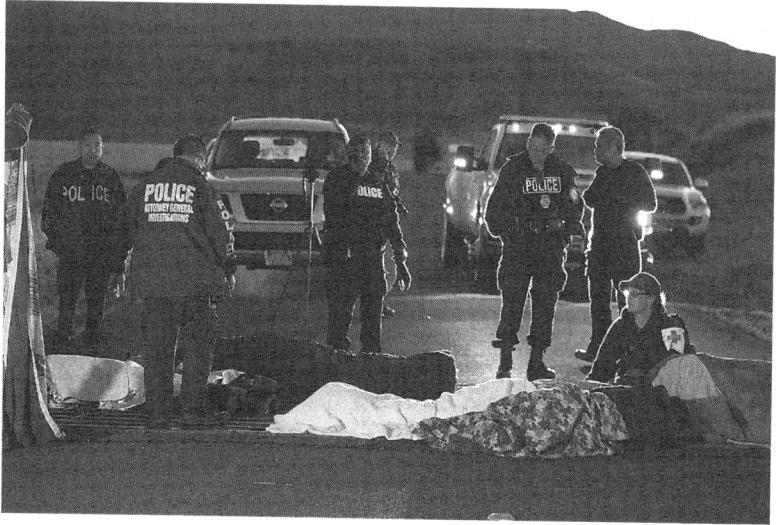

Figure 1. At dawn, State Police find kiaʻi chained to a cattle guard at the Mauna Kea Summit Access Road. July 15, 2019. Photograph by Cory Lum.

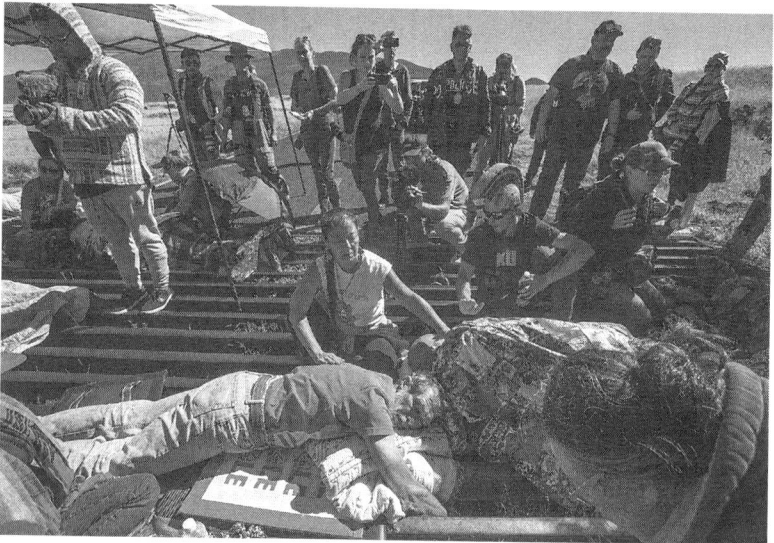

Figure 2. Press and police surround kiaʻi as they provide comfort to those chained to the cattle grate. July 15, 2019. Photograph by Cindy Ellen Russell; courtesy of *Honolulu Star-Advertiser.*

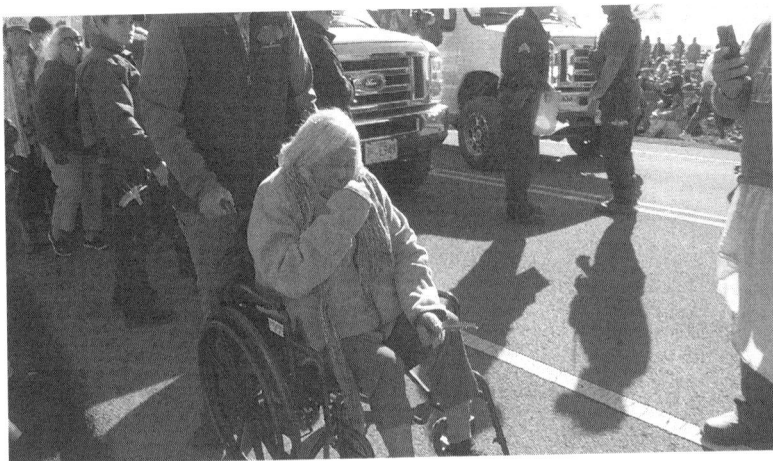

Figure 3. Genevieve "Genny" Kinney of Panaewa, filmed in civil disobedience during her arrest defending the Mauna. July 17, 2019. Photograph courtesy of the Mauna Media Team.

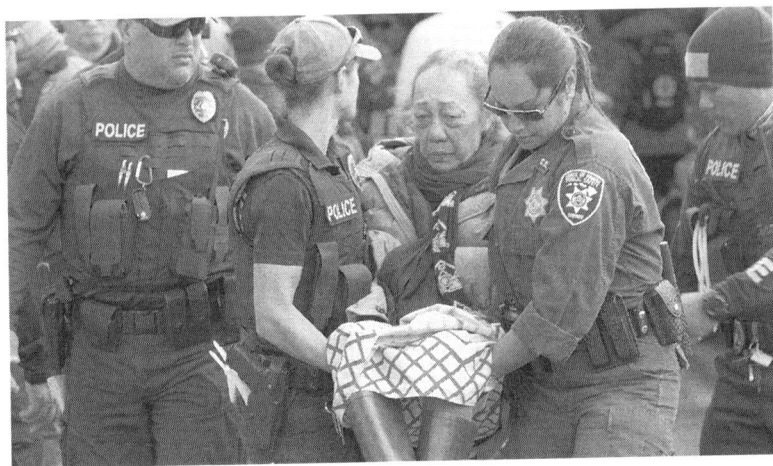

Figure 4. Nohea Kalima of the Kalima family of Keaukaha, in kūʻē for the Mauna, carried away by police. July 17, 2019. Photograph courtesy of the Mauna Media Team.

to oli—fiercely chanting their aloha ʻāina and denouncing the State's willingness to use excessive force against nonviolent protestors.[6] Governor David Ige claimed his "government operations" were about "public safety" and the "rule of law." The deployment of armed police officers from five different agencies across four of the major Hawaiian Islands, however, suggests the excessive display of force and threat of physical coercion was about the settler state's commitment to capitalist development and protecting its $3 billion investment in a monument to Western scientific achievement.[7] The escalation to militarized force also embodied the reality that techno-scientific development and settler capitalism are co-constituted in the U.S. imperial project in Hawaiʻi and the Pacific. In these scenes of uprising, the State's obedience to multinational corporate industrialists fixated on building the next "world's largest telescope"—on lands made available only by virtue of military invasion and illegal occupation—also indicates how Hawaiʻi's prevailing multicultural hegemony requires the latent, and sometimes explicit, threat of physical violence to maintain its order. Rationalized through a liberal rhetoric of progress "for all humanity," the TMT campaign evokes anachronistic civilizational tropes about Native peoples as opposed to science, or simply irrational and inferior, which serve ultimately

Figure 5. Police in riot gear stand ready for orders. One officer appears to wipe away tears. July 17, 2019. Photograph by Cody-Fay Corbett.

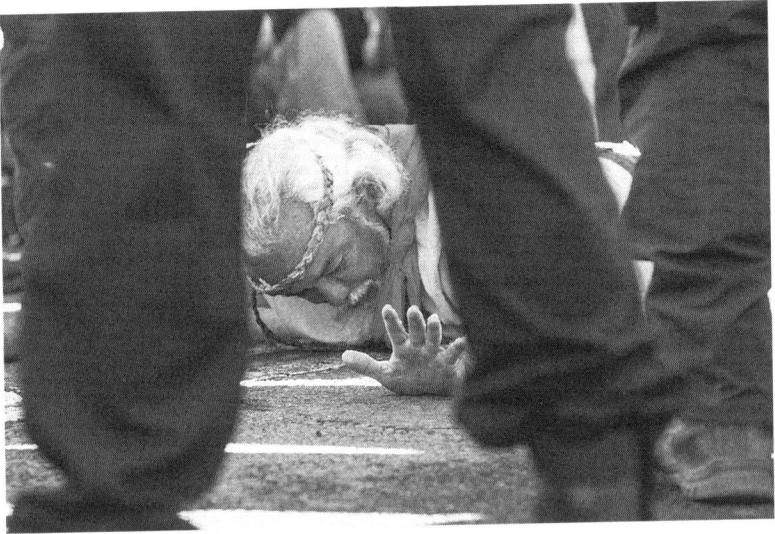

Figure 6. Uncle Billy Freitas in civil disobedience at Puʻuhonua o Puʻuhuluhulu. July 17, 2019. Photograph by Hollyn Johnson; courtesy of *Hawaii Tribune-Herald.*

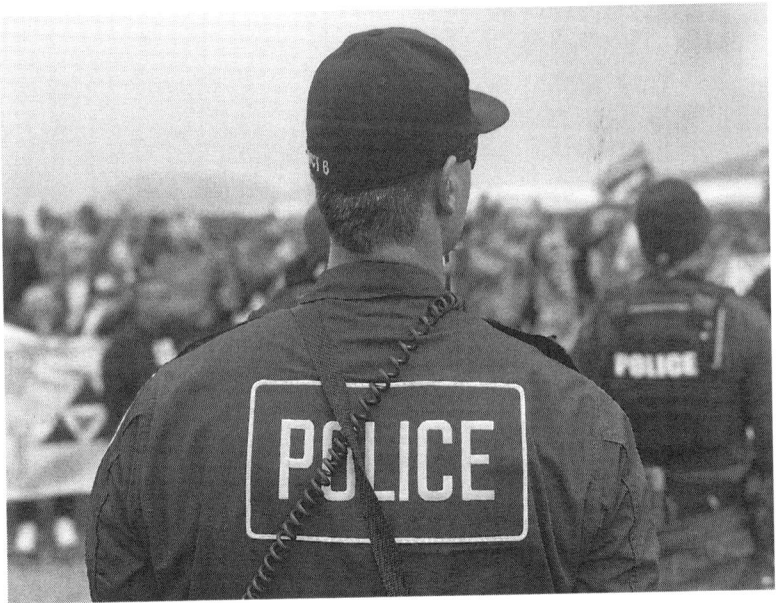

Figure 7. Officers and kiaʻi look on as kūpuna are arrested at the Mauna Kea Summit Access Road. July 17, 2019. Photo by Jonathan Saupe; courtesy of *Hawaii News Now.*

to contain Kanaka alterity and the inherent threat it poses to settler authority. As Kanaka Maoli organizer and kiaʻi ʻIlima Long recognized, Igeʻs deployment was effectively "the largest law enforcement operation in the history of Hawaiʻi, to come down on Hawaiians, short of the U.S. military actually landing Navy and Marine officers to overthrow our government" in 1893.[8]

In their activism, these kiaʻi, or land defenders,[9] were being accused of violating social norms that, upon interrogation, had little to do with law but everything to do with a consistent practice of resistance that began over a century ago. It also revealed an arbitrary legal amalgam designed to reproduce a proprietary authority over Hawaiian people, on whom the Maunakea observatory depends. The kiaʻi had violated a social mandate under settler colonialism to behave according to standards of white liberal respectability, itself derivative of earlier Christian morality. However, *this refusal to behave* was distorted by Governor Ige who immediately launched a smear campaign to vilify the kiaʻi as a small but dangerous group of hooligans, falsely claiming alcohol and drugs were rampant and the demonstration presented a threat to the public. It was clear to many, though, that instead of obstructing government operations, the kiaʻi had disrupted the conventional touristic gaze that dominates representations of Hawaiʻi and Hawaiians: a foreign pleasure in looking and misrecognizing the Native subject to foreclose any possibility of thinking Hawaiian self-determination through a substantive reckoning with history, law, territoriality, and restorative justice. This sort of scopophilia has, since the early nineteenth century, imagined Polynesian women as alluring, exotic, and hospitable objects of Anglo-masculine desire and Native men as impulsive, militant, and insubordinate savages unfit to self-govern. A litany of stereotypes underpins the State's economic control over land and life—a hegemony that also requires an obedient Native subject whose radical alterity must be neutralized at every turn. However, while Ige's rhetoric sought to justify physical violence, on this day, in defiance of settler authority and its distortions, a wave of wāhine (women) refused to allow one more kupuna to be carried off. In a display of fierce mana wahine (women's power), dozens of women rose and locked arms, standing in kapu aloha and taking part in unapologetic civil disobedience. This act forced the police to stand down for the day.

After hours of arrests, an exhausting standoff, and facing what had become an untenable public relations catastrophe for the governor, the police dispersed. Many local people viewing the livestreams had dropped

Figure 8. Arms-locked, kiaʻi brace for police aggression. July 17, 2019. Photograph by Cody-Fay Corbett.

Figure 9. Kiaʻi wahine lock arms in defiance of further arrests of kūpuna. July 17, 2019. Photograph by Antonio J. Agosto.

everything and went to Puʻuhuluhulu to stand in solidarity and kapu aloha against police repression of a nonviolent direct-action protest. Hundreds of spectators now filled the area, many of whom would become long-term kiaʻi, others only politicized that morning. For the governor, the police, and the TMT, the optics of armored soldiers manhandling elders was bad enough, but a sweep of women in prayerful defiance would only make things worse for them. Indeed, the crackdown had undermined the TMT's premise of a noble and benign science at Mauna a Kea.[10] It also undercut the State's image as a protectorate of Native Hawaiian rights, public lands, and the rule of law. In these moments, the law, represented by the police, appeared less concerned with public safety than with protecting the narrow interests of an already privileged astronomy community and its wealthy nonlocal, non-Hawaiian investors. In other words, these direct actions exposed the state's indifference toward Hawaiians and the reality of our condition as a subjugated people. It also introduced many to the reality of an intimate relationship between big science, settler law, and militarist logics. It revealed how science and the state transit Indigenous lands armed with weapons of war and a claim to a monopoly on right and reason.

On Tuesday, July 16, 2019, the day after the cattle guard action, the day before the kupuna arrests, police tried at first to coax the kiaʻi into leaving, but quickly turned to threats of violence if they didn't disperse. They refused, but the daylong standoff ended with no arrests. When it was apparent that law enforcement were leaving, one kūpuna shouted, "The Mauna is safe for one more day!" As the clouds cleared and the sun shone down, the gathering of several hundred erupted into song, rejoicing in Uncle Liko Martin's beloved anthem, "Hawaiʻi Loa, Kūlike Kākou."

This mele lāhui was appropriate, as it calls on all land and water protectors to "Pane mai kō leo aloha ʻāina / Hawaiʻi loa kūlike kākou"—that is, "to answer with your voice of aloha ʻāina / All Hawaiʻi stand together," and remain steadfast in one's aloha and defense of ancestral places until victory is won.[11] After the trauma of mass arrests the very next day, the lāhui (people, nation) answered this call when some four thousand people from across the islands arrived at Puʻuhonua o Puʻuhuluhulu the following weekend to join in this demonstration of unyielding aloha ʻāina. The movement grew in numbers by the hundreds every week that summer.

This aloha ʻāina, embodied in the resilience of Kānaka ʻŌiwi and allies together in resistance, I argue, should be recognized as an iteration of a long-sustained practice of resistance that might be located within a broader

Figure 10. Kūpuna and kiaʻi rejoice in song as police disband. July 16, 2019. Photograph by Hollyn Johnson; courtesy of *Hawaii Tribune-Herald*.

continuum of struggle against myriad forms of colonial domination manifest as liberal multiculturalism, racial and settler capitalism, and U.S. militarism across our islands. This book engages and theorizes the concept and practice of aloha ʻāina as it contextualizes the resistance to industrial astronomy on Mauna a Wākea, just as it instantiates Kanaka indigeneity, resurgence, and relationality to our lands, waters, and each other more broadly. Examining Hawaiian social movements for life, land, and ea,[12] as well as Kanaka ʻŌiwi articulations of ceremony to struggle against structures of domination, this book analyzes ways in which the resistance at Mauna a Wākea over the last half century emerged within a legacy of Indigenous political thought and action organized to protect storied and sacred places, as well as cultural practices, against the backdrop of U.S. occupation and its ongoing subjection of our people.

2019 at the Puʻuhonua

Days prior to the cattle guard action and the arrest of kūpuna and kiaʻi, organizers had chosen to stage a direct action at Puʻuhonua o Puʻuhuluhulu for practical and symbolic reasons that invoke a collective kuleana; a concept signifying a deeply held sense of responsibility. Puʻuhuluhulu was declared a puʻuhonua, or "place of refuge," from the start of the action and, for the next nine months, it would become a "sanctuary" of peace and safety and a kīpuka, that is, an area that has been spared from the destruction of volcanic lava flows and where often ecologically rare native plant and animal life persist as a result. Puʻuhuluhulu is surrounded by miles of dense lava fields that have hardened into an expanse of dark porous rock where it can sometimes take generations for new growth to emerge. A protected space where life was nurtured and ancestral knowledge sustained a movement in what would become almost a yearlong roadblock and protest encampment, this kīpuka became an answer to state repression, police violence, and the gaslighting of settler technoscience. Leon Noʻeau Peralto expands on Davianna McGregor's concept of "cultural kīpuka" to theorize "kīpuka of aloha ʻāina," or sites of great aloha for the ancestral places that have not necessarily been "bypassed by major historic forces of economic, political, and social change in Hawaiʻi," but nevertheless emerge as important spaces "in which ʻŌiwi have maintained their aloha for and kuleana to ʻāina continuously since time immemorial, and from which ʻŌiwi ʻculture

Figure 11. Kiaʻi stage roadblock at the crosswalk near Hale Pōhaku, April 2015. Photograph by Cory Lum.

can be regenerated and revitalized in the setting of contemporary Hawai'i."[13] This kuleana was affirmed and renewed by kia'i in the fight to protect a sacred ancestral place, while the pu'uhonua in turn protected and nourished the kia'i within a constellation of reciprocity and relationality that cohered in struggle.

These scenes of kū'ē (resistance) appeared less than five years after another important sustained civil disobedience demonstration and road-block that resulted in a six-month encampment protest along the Summit Access Road near the Onizuka Visitor Center, also known as Hale Pōhaku, at an elevation of nine thousand feet. During the summer of 2015, when the TMT International Observatory, LLC (or TIO) deployed work crews to begin construction on the summit, and law enforcement officers were deployed to escort them, they were confronted by kia'i. Police arrested thirty on April 2, 2015, inciting kia'i to build an encampment near the cross-walk to the visitor center parking lot, where they would monitor the road for attempts to haul heavy equipment to the summit. Another twelve were arrested on June 24, when approximately 750 kia'i arrived to join the pro-test. Several dozen kia'i had organized themselves into "lines" of arm-locked groups at various intervals ascending the Summit Access Road, each line

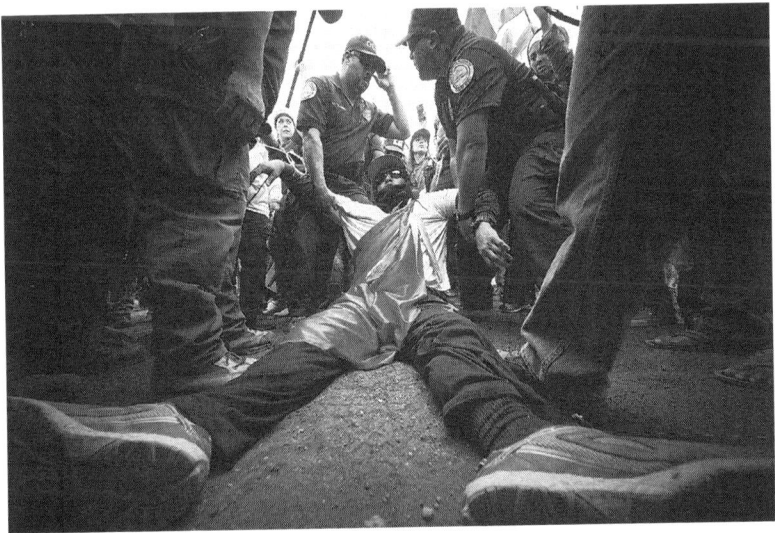

Figure 12. Kaleikoa Ka'eo in civil disobedience defending Mauna a Kea. June 24, 2015. Photograph by Cory Lum.

just out of sight of the previous one, which effectively overwhelmed law enforcement who were unprepared to make so many arrests.

After hours of confrontation livestreamed on social media, police efforts were eventually thwarted, as they were forced to remove not only more bodies than they could handle but also large pōhaku, or rocks, that had been moved from the banks onto the unpaved road. For many bearing witness that day, while the pōhaku would protect the Mauna, they held a special significance for their kaona (or hidden meanings). As one famous mele lāhui called "Kaulana Nā Pua" characterizes pōhaku as "ka ʻai kamahaʻo o ka ʻāina," or *the wonderous food of the land,* the aloha ʻāina who composed its lyrics and scored its music used the metaphor in protest to express their preference to eat stones rather than bend to threats or accept foreign rule and U.S. occupation.[14] By the time police were called off, Lilinoe—the akua of mists that frequently shroud the summit—had arrived, making the operation untenable.

The 2015 direct actions inspired thousands of otherwise nonpolitically active Hawaiians to rethink their positions and commitments as well as the stakes involved in protecting sites like Maunakea. It also forced a legal review of a State Land Board decision to issue a permit for the University of Hawaiʻi (UH) to sublease summit lands for the TMT, which resulted in a State Supreme Court decision to halt construction until a second contested case hearing could be held. While the victory was short-lived— as another permit was issued less than two years later—the momentum of the 2015 actions allowed kiaʻi to build a powerful coalition of cultural practitioners, seasoned activists, and non-Hawaiians from across the islands, many of whom had been indifferent to politics but now identified with the call to action.

Puʻuhuluhulu catalyzed the energy of 2015 into what would become known alternately as the "Kū Kiaʻi Mauna Movement," the "Protect Mauna Kea Movement," or simply the "Mauna Movement."[15] People quickly became educated on the politics and history of not only Maunakea astronomy but the reasons the mountain is sacred to Kānaka ʻŌiwi and, therefore, in need of protection.[16] This combination of the political and the cultural was a potent mixture because it warmed people to the idea of community activism. However, it is also just as Kānaka ʻŌiwi have always done. When the State government proves indifferent to the concerns of Kānaka ʻŌiwi and venues of legal participation in decision making processes available to

Figure 13. Lilinoe envelops. Pōhaku and kiaʻi stand guard. The press bear witness. June 24, 2015. Photograph by Cory Lum.

Figure 14. Kiaʻi stand firm and oli as the mist surrounds and police depart. June 24, 2015. Photograph by Cory Lum.

Kānaka prove insufficient for protecting storied ancestral places from industrial development, be it for tourism or militarism, direct political action rooted in ʻike kupuna—that is, Kanaka ʻŌiwi knowledges, practices, and epistemologies—becomes urgent and necessary. At Mauna a Kea, it was this ʻike kupuna in combination with direct action that revealed how the settler state's claim to the Mauna hinges on its monopoly on the use of force. The number of kiaʻi in 2019 had multiplied because of the media exposure the mass 2015 demonstrations made possible, just as 2015 was the result of decades of aloha ʻāina activism in the courtroom and the streets. The movement highlighted the myriad ways settler colonial governance is not only incapable of adjudicating any meaningful or sustained practice of conservation of rare and fragile ecosystems and culturally significant sites but also unable to account for any knowledge systems beyond the exploitative and extractive logics of global capitalism and a form of science that is implicated in U.S. empire. As the settler state failed to abide its own laws, and those laws no longer concealed the State's fidelity to big science, kiaʻi took to the Mauna.[17]

Puʻuhonua o Puʻuhuluhulu sits at the crossroad of the Mauna Kea Access Road and Hawaiʻi State Route 200, or Saddle Road,[18] which bisects the island east to west and connects Kona to Hilo. Anyone on Hawaiʻi Island can find their way to this intersection, a brilliant decision by the organizers that made it easy for anyone to join the action. When day visitors arrived at the camp, they saw for themselves how Ige's moral panic was a ruse to justify state violence. Day-trippers experienced instead a culturally grounded, nonviolent, and well-organized, if ad-hoc, village-like system, which empowered onlookers to identify with the people-centered, land-based, and Native-led movement. It was nonviolent, and it was a story of an underdog "punching up." At an altitude of six thousand feet, the puʻuhonua is also easier on the body than the encampment of 2015 at nine thousand feet, making Puʻuhuluhulu more accessible to a larger number of participants, including older kiaʻi, children, and those with health issues. Should work crews return, they were well positioned to act quickly.

For close to a year, this kūlanakauhale of sorts, or village, at Puʻuhonua o Puʻuhuluhulu was visited by tens of thousands of supporters that included Indigenous relations from across Oceania and Turtle Island but also around the world.[19] Land and water protectors made the journey to offer a solidarity characteristic of the generosity many colonized communities have always

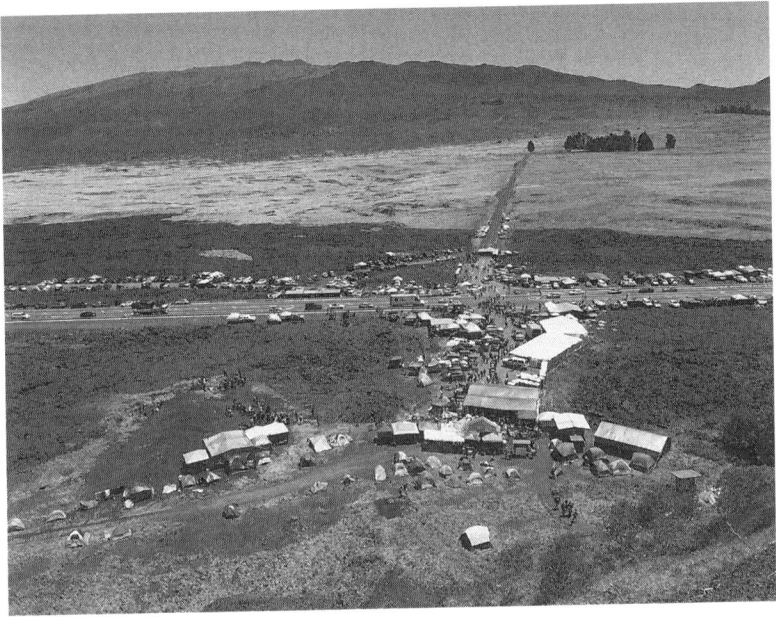

Figure 15. View of the kūlanakauhale from atop Puʻuhuluhulu, Mauna a Wākea in the distance. July 23, 2019. Photograph by the author.

shown one another. Through mass political mobilization grounded in the cultural milieu of aloha ʻāina, the mutual recognition, displays of care, and comradery exhibited at Puʻuhuluhulu signaled a continuity of Indigenous peoples' relationality to their sacred ancestral lands, to each other, and to distant cousins beyond our shores. This kind of mutual aid reflects what Sharon Holland and Tiz Giordano describe as a sustainable communal reclamation of a justice consistently deferred under settler racial capitalism,[20] or "what love looks like in public."[21]

Pilina and Resurgence

One ʻōlelo noʻeau, or poetical saying, speaks to the fact that Kānaka ʻŌiwi, like other Indigenous peoples, have always treated the natural world as a genealogical and kinship relation that is inseverable—he pilina wehena ʻole.[22] This pilina, or relationality, is constituted in networks of care and accountability to the living world as much as to one another, and not the

Figure 16. Visitors along the Kūpuna during midday protocol ceremonies. Puʻuhuluhulu in the background. July 23, 2019. Photograph by the author.

state, which will leave both for dead to protect the interests of capital. Puʻuhuluhulu was a reminder of the *responsibility to ʻāina* that Kānaka ʻŌiwi have, which exceeds the Western proprietary notion of *dominion over land* as property, resource, and commodity. And while Hawaiians can neither be reduced to our colonial subjectivity nor defined by it, Kanaka indigeneity is constituted in pilina to ʻāina[23] and all life, functioning as, what Jamaica Heolimeleikalani Osorio calls, "a counterepistemology of Western nationalism" to which "patriarchy is neither required nor useful."[24] It is a connection to kūpuna o ka pō (ancestors who have passed) that many Kānaka ʻŌiwi today continue to celebrate and nurture as a familial bond that joins one to the other and both to ancestral places. Moreover, it is a familial bond that is distinctly Kanaka ʻŌiwi: neither hierarchical nor heteronormative, but expansive and counterhegemonic.[25] The demonstrations at Puʻuhuluhulu affirmed that pilina as a sacred relationship: one articulated through aloha ʻāina—the organizing principle around which traditional life was structured in generations past and the eco-genealogical knowledges and values of contemporary Kanaka ʻŌiwi life and land defense continue to be practiced today. An enduring, inseverable love for one's homeland, aloha ʻāina is a constant throughout Kānaka ʻŌiwi culture, political thought, and praxis. A constitutive aspect of our indigeneity, aloha ʻāina is ontological, relational, and familial.[26] I discuss aloha ʻāina later in the book, but a provisional way of thinking about the concept is that it informs ways Kānaka ʻŌiwi produce knowledge about the world and mutual obligations to ʻāina and each other through distinct conceptions of time, space, and being that celebrate a pono (good, correct, and balanced) relationality, rather than a hierarchical one. At its core, this book is an exploration of these ways of knowing and being that underpin our conceptions of difference, care, and governance.

Though not defined by subjugation and resistance, these pilina do offer a critique of systems of gender, racial, and colonial oppression, if for no other reason than because they embody an alterity that exceeds social relations structured in hierarchy and domination. Kanaka relationality, thus, is about living in pono *with* more-than-human life, rather than dominion *over* life. In other words, it is more capacious and imaginative than our contemporary hegemonic orientation toward difference, or what has been constituted under imperialism and capitalism as "nature" and the "environment." Granted, the kiaʻi had barricaded the Summit Access Road to stop the Thirty Meter Telescope, but these actions were not only about another telescope. They also cannot be reduced to mere protest. The struggle for Mauna a Wākea is about meaning and its making; about being and becoming. It is about the struggle to restore pono to our islands and communities on our terms. Indeed, the kiaʻi view themselves not as *protestors* but as *protectors*: a parallactic shift that decenters the human to acknowledge the subjectivity of ʻāina as relation instead of resource, and the importance of self-definition when confronting state violence deployed on behalf of big science. When Kānaka ʻŌiwi obstruct bulldozers and defy militarized police in defense of ancestral places, those actions are part of a continuum of embodied genealogical pilina to ʻāina, the living world, and the kūpuna i ka pō.[27] It is also world making in real time. Kānaka ʻŌiwi understand that we are descendants, not heirs, of the land. Confirmed in the countless moʻolelo (stories, histories), mele (songs), moʻokūʻauhau (genealogical successions), and narrative and oratory practices that convey our ʻike kupuna (ancestral knowledges)[28] across generations, the ʻāina and kānaka, the land and people, are connected through genealogy and obligation. This is not some romantic plea for sympathy but is instead the substance of a long-standing communal ethos, habitus, and commitment that many Kānaka 'Ōiwi cherish and pass along from one generation to the next. For this reason, it is said "he ali'i ka 'āina, he kauwā ke kanaka" ("the land is chief, the human is a servant").[29] Our kuleana to the source of all life stems from this commitment to protect our lands and waters in a material sense. As such, the resistance at Mauna a Wākea should be understood as a contemporary iteration of the broader struggle for ea—the life, breath, sovereignty, and independence of Hawai'i and Hawaiians—which is intentional and unapologetic in the articulation of culture to politics and ceremony to struggle. Acknowledging the complex and contradictory reality of that resistance is to understand how much more is at stake than just another telescope.[30]

Gina Starblanket explains, "The land-based orientation of resurgence has immense liberatory potential for Indigenous peoples as it advances a vision of freedom and autonomy that is grounded in our relationships with the living Earth, looks to creation as a source of knowledge and education, draws upon localized cultural archives and provides individuals with the potential to embody certain (but not all) types of politics."[31] The "types of politics" against which land-based resurgence in Hawai'i is distinguished include liberal models of engagement, whereby structural forms of inclusion become the means by which to alienate Native peoples from land and to disavow Indigenous claims to knowledge, authority, place, and space. Self-determined Indigenous relationality thus inherently threatens the settler state because it exceeds the terms of legibility and control by which its own dubious authority has been conjured and justified.

Glen Coulthard describes the constitutive relationality as "grounded normativity," arguing that indigeneity emerges from "the modalities of Indigenous land-connected practices and longstanding experiential knowledge that inform and structure our ethical engagements with the world and our relationships with human and nonhuman others over time."[32] In contrast to liberal models of recognition, which seek to control the prior claims of Indigenous communities to life and land by containing Indigenous alterity within settler logics of inclusion and possession, grounded normativity centers Indigenous ontologies and relationality to the natural and living worlds. Jodi Byrd, Alyosha Goldstein, Jodi Melamed, and Chandan Reddy argue that Glen Coulthard and Audra Simpson's explorations of grounded normativity provide "an ethical way of knowing and being that is more expansive than those ontologies that prioritize the human as exceptional, and it is a placement that extends memory through vast kinship networks that assume life, vibrancy, and agency beyond the limits of enlightenment notions of self, liberty, and property."[33] While these categories have "inflected our understanding of nature, memory, and history through the production of archives and certain kinds of knowledge production that favor hegemonic white possession,"[34] a grounded normativity resurgence model decenters the human to "reorient knowledge and power within and through Indigenous returns to land, philosophy, diplomacy, activism, and kinship."[35] While "the loss of land is not just a loss of property, territoriality, power, nation, or sovereignty; it is the loss of those philosophies that derive from the relationships the land itself activates, fosters, and nourishes."[36] Such a reorientation was observed at Puʻuhuluhulu, where Hawaiian ways of knowing, learning, and valuing shaped the form that direct action would take and not the other way around. A counterhegemonic expression of life, agency, and vibrancy, Kanaka resurgence at the puʻuhonua exceeded the limits of European Enlightenment–derived notions of good governance and rationality. Attention to the grounded normativity of that resurgence may expose the contradictions of liberal democracy under settler occupation and alternatives for imagining a better future.

The Kūlanakauhale

For nine months,[37] where the Saddle Road Highway meets the Mauna Kea Summit Access Road at six thousand feet, the self-sustaining kūlanakauhale at Puʻuhonua o Puʻuhuluhulu emerged as a model of sustainability in struggle; a volunteer-based and community-centered economy of cooperation, instead of competition. Although there were fault lines that emerged over the span of the demonstration,[38] it was successful for inciting people to action and reshaping the narrative away from "angry protesters" to courageous "land and water protectors." While there were smaller communities within the community, and that diversity meant the kūlanakauhale was far from utopic, it was unified in kapu aloha and struggle for the Mauna.

In many ways, the encampment prioritized a communal ethos and praxis of care, as new arrivals could receive meals during their stay, warm clothes, and camping supplies and contribute in ways not already established. They could also access a variety of services from education to health care and childcare, including volunteer-operated rides to and from Kona, Waimea, and Hilo. Repayment for access to provisions and services generally came in the form of volunteer labor, although no expectation of compensation was made explicit. Instead, an economy of reciprocity and noncapitalist exchange prevailed. Volunteers would cook, clean, and serve food in the kitchen under the donated giant circus-style tent, while licensed physicians and nurses—fashioned as the "Mauna Medics"—were stationed beside a "Mauna Media" team that monitored messaging and liaised between commercial media and movement organizers. At the entrance to the camp, volunteers at an information table would point new arrivals to task delegation coordinators. There was a supplies tent, a donation drop-off center, and recycling and composting stations. While folks organized children's activities and free silkscreen printing, others offered direct-action training workshops. Rooted in cultural pilina, a hale mana wahine and hale mana māhū functioned as a trusted space where Native queer and māhū, nonbinary, gender-fluid, and trans folks could hold space and find community within community.[39] Everyone, from day visitors to long-term kia'i also made use

Figure 17. Kaho'okahi Kanuha teaching at Pu'uhuluhulu University. July 24, 2019. Photograph by the author.

of what would become a tuition-free, open-access field school. Organized by UH Hawaiian language instructor Presley Keʻalaanuhea Ah Mook Sang, the sessions held on a smooth pāhoehoe lava rock plateau came to be known as "Puʻuhuluhulu University."

At its peak, over a dozen courses were taught daily by experts—from both academic and local and familial traditions—across ʻŌiwi knowledge and experience, from culture and history to language, law, politics, arts, and sciences. In the absence of an explicit mandate or governing body, hundreds took daily individual responsibility to contribute in myriad ways to meet the collective needs of the whole—breathing ea into the kūlanakauhale and the lāhui. The indispensable labor required to keep the puʻuhonua operating smoothly also served as evidence of worlds imagined and organized beyond capitalism and in tune with the elements. While the camp facilitated a sustained communal protest to capitalist imperialism in the form of industrial astronomy on contested lands, it also expressed Kanaka resurgence and relationality, a physical embodiment of Kanaka ʻŌiwi self-determination.

Flanked by rows of flags where kāhili had first been ceremonially gifted to kūpuna and kiaʻi by local Kānaka ʻŌiwi, cultural hui (groups), and families, and where other hoʻokupu (offerings, gifts) and aloha were given by members of various Indigenous and tribal nations and other supporters from around the world visiting in solidarity, a small strip at the start of the Mauna Kea Access Road was renamed by Pua Case and remains known today as the Ala Hulu Kūpuna.[40] At one end of this strip was the Kupuna Tent, where the elders spent most days on the ready should police or work crews return, and where cultural protocols were staged. The ala began across from Puʻuhuluhulu near the intersection at Saddle Road and the Mauna Kea Access Road to the south, stretching up toward the Kupuna Tent and ending before the cattle guard to the north. The police showed its authority by staging a much smaller day camp just mauka (upland), where they regulated access to the summit. However, in a symbolic reversal of authority, a makeshift bamboo checkpoint was created by the kiaʻi beside the Kupuna Tent, which forced observatory employees, State Park rangers, DOCARE and county police, and others to be admitted. The dueling checkpoints signaled the competing claims to space, with police enforcement of the settler colonial state on one side of a threshold, kiaʻi on the other.

Celebrities, including Dwayne "The Rock" Johnson, Jason Momoa, and Damien Marley, visited the Mauna, using their platforms to bring attention to the struggle. On a given day, upward of one thousand to five thousand people arrived at Puʻuhuluhulu to volunteer or drop off food and donations or to camp or spend the day, each bearing witness to what was sure to become a historic movement. While Governor David Ige and UH President David Lassner both made appearances—efforts at damage control after the excessive police deployment weeks prior—beloved and esteemed visitors also made pilgrimages, like Dakota-Lakota historian and genealogist LaDonna Tamakawastewin Brave Bull Allard, who shared stories of the direct actions at Standing Rock that lasted seven months in 2016 to stop the Dakota Access Pipeline, making explicit the connection Indigenous communities on Turtle Island have always had with Indigenous Oceania in a shared struggle against capitalism, militarism, imperialism, and patriarchy.

The Mauna Media team was a skilled and diverse group of local media creatives, filmmakers, and artists whose regular social media posts, viral videos, and mini-documentaries garnered virtual allies from afar. As mentioned above, in the first days of the kūlanakauhale, Governor David Ige held

Figure 18. Dakota-Lakota historian and genealogist LaDonna Tamakawastewin Brave Bull Allard speaks at sunset protocol ceremony. July 23, 2019. Photograph by the author.

a press conference in which he attempted to portray the camp as a drug den where criminal activity pervaded, invoking late nineteenth- and early twentieth-century political campaigns to delegitimize Native Hawaiian efforts to retain a degree of self-governance, which portrayed Native lawmakers as monkeys, which suggested our political actions are performative and that Hawaiians are by nature uncivilized, undisciplined, and dysfunctional. Seeking to control the narrative by defaming the kiaʻi as rioters and squatters—which it was hoped might justify the use of physical force—Ige had announced an official "emergency proclamation," indicating that, like hurricanes, floods, and wildfires, the kiaʻi were to be treated as a threat to public health and safety. The proclamation also triggered Ige's legal authority to call on several hundred National Guard troops to sweep the camp.[41] However, upon even a brief survey of the camp, it was clear there were no drugs, deviants, or threats to public safety, but instead, only a clean, safe, and well-organized camp. Recording a series of press conferences in which Maunakea Movement leaders dismantled each of the governor's lies, the kiaʻi welcomed the public to the puʻuhonua to see for themselves. Reclaiming the narrative and their public image, the media team also exposed the underlying objectives behind the governor's attempts to malign the kiaʻi as an act of desperation to quell dissent and evade responsibility for violating conservation district laws and the State constitutional obligations to Native Hawaiians.[42]

The 2015 Actions and Kapu Aloha

Puʻuhuluhulu was exceptional in many ways but was possible only because of the 2015 actions, which opened Maunakea as a site of new possibility for the lāhui. Maunakea, in turn, opened many in the lāhui to the significance of organized grassroots collective action as a viable alternative to liberal state policy and discourse, which were being exposed as serving the narrow private interests of corporate industrial development on sacred lands at the expense of Kānaka ʻŌiwi. By 2015, it had become clear the State was no longer indifferent to the TMT but had now become hostile toward it, even if the explicit use of physical aggression had not been exercised. This contempt had developed since 2005, when a Keck Outrigger Telescope project collapsed under the pressure of public interventions, an unsympathetic Hawaiʻi Supreme Court ruling, and NASA's decision to pull funding. Discourse shifted from expanding an already contested observatory to constructing the next "world's biggest telescope," the Thirty Meter Telescope. At that time, DLNR and UH held empty "consultations" in lieu of seeking consent of the people to build the TMT, and communities grew increasingly vocal, first questioning and later outright challenging the project. Many had been calling for a moratorium on new construction, citing concerns about overdevelopment, violations of State conservation law, the flawed permitting process, and a list of broken agreements where limits to the number of telescopes on the Mauna were ignored throughout the 1970s, '80s, and '90s. With no other recourse, a coalition of concerned residents, environmental and Native Hawaiian organizations, activists, and educators organized and went to battle in the courts, showing up at hearings, writing testimony, and filing reports and legal briefs, all of which I document in chapters ahead.

When it became clear that even those methods and venues were wholly inadequate for the protection of Mauna a Wākea, a small group of Hawaiʻi Island Kānaka ʻŌiwi—mostly young people in their twenties and thirties, many fluent in Hawaiian language, and relatively new to activism but staunch in their kūʻē and grounded in cultural practice—began to organize a grassroots campaign to stop the TMT. The first demonstration was an ad-hoc disruption of a groundbreaking ceremony in October of 2014 that ended in a televised spectacle of negative press for UH, project investors, and the TIO leadership.[43] The following April, these kiaʻi would initiate the first blockade at the visitor center crosswalk near Hale Pōhaku. The call to action first voiced by Hāwane Rios, "kū kiaʻi mauna," began to appear on signs, stickers, and T-shirts. As the slogan caught on, people were incited to *stand and defend the mountain,* and soon rallied under the hashtags #ProtectMaunaKea, #TMTShutDown, #AoleTMT, and #KuKiaiMauna.

Since 2015, kapu aloha has been the guiding principle of the Mauna Movement. A collective commitment to disciplined pono behavior, kapu aloha instructs kiaʻi on how to act when participating in direct action or in any space that is part of these efforts. Noelani Goodyear-Kaʻōpua describes kapu aloha as a "philosophy and practice of non-violent engagement."[44] Citing the teachings of movement leader and kumu hula (master hula teacher), Pua Case, Goodyear-Kaʻōpua writes, "The kapu aloha requires the discipline of empathy, even and especially for those with whom one may disagree."[45] Much more than moralistic virtue signaling or a mere compliance

Figure 19. Joshua Lanakila Mangauil condemns attendees of the TMT "groundbreaking ceremony" before a live streaming audience. October 7, 2014. *Big Island Video News.* Video still by the author.

with notions of respectability, kapu aloha is about interpersonal accountability for the sake of the movement. Jamaica Heolimeleikalani Osorio explains that kapu aloha is about "balance with each other as kiaʻi and with our natural relations."[46] On a practical level, kapu aloha protected kiaʻi from being forced out of their discipline or goaded into providing State police any reason to justify physical violence against the kiaʻi. On a strategic level, it invited skeptics or newcomers to learn more about the grievances of Kānaka ʻOiwi with the State, the university, and many astronomers. Kapu aloha thereby grew the movement's base by refuting misrepresentations, appealing to social media followers not yet activated, and creating space for new recruitment, even among scientific communities.

Kapu aloha also grounded direct action within the epistemologies and praxis of Kānaka ʻŌiwi cultural traditions. Three times a day every day, on the kūpuna, kumu hula Pualani Kanakaʻole Kanahele, members of Hālau o Kekuhi, and other kumu hula (master teachers of Hawaiian song and dance) and their haumāna (students) would lead kiaʻi in observing protocols. Four times daily, ceremony included pule (prayer), oli (chants), and mele (songs), offered to our many akua (gods), ʻaumākua (deities), and kūpuna o ka pō (ancestors). The rituals served as a foundation for the spiritual and mental health and well-being of the kiaʻi, the kūlanakauhale, the Mauna, and the movement. Everyone was welcome, young and old, and if one did not already know the mele, there were opportunities to learn. A shared vocabulary took shape as the repertoire of pule, oli, mele, hula, and rallying call-and-response chants throughout the days grew into a collection of communal speech acts expressing a distinctly Indigenous brand of resistance that would be practiced at other sites of community direct action that followed elsewhere. In this way, these events, the principles, and the affective and sensory activities practiced at Puʻuhuluhulu might be understood as forming a body of knowledge that resonates with and builds off earlier Hawaiian social movements and will guide Kānaka ʻŌiwi in mass demonstrations for political self-determination for years to come. These are grammars of resistance and resurgence, and they reflect a shared commitment to aloha ʻāina and Kanaka-led efforts to restore pono and heal the lāhui and all our relations.

My Positionality

Between 2011 and 2015, I conducted interviews with folks whose perspectives on the TMT and Maunakea astronomy cover a spectrum of views ranging from unequivocal support to staunch opposition. I spoke with many people who were involved in earlier legal cases and some who would emerge as key organizers in the direct actions that came to be known as the Protect Maunakea Movement. I traveled to the summit on numerous occasions and participated in both actions at Hale Pōhaku in 2015 and Puʻuhuluhulu in 2019, conducting follow-up and new interviews. I interviewed haole[47] and local administrators, astronomers, physicists, professors, and other supporters of industrial astronomy, and Kānaka ʻŌiwi whose views varied along the spectrum of support and opposition. I was especially keen to analyze the ways Hawaiians who support building the TMT articulate their views. I also interviewed all but one of the petitioners of the first TMT permit in the original 2011 contested case. During this time, the strategies, concerns, and activities of this small hui (group) of land defenders, most but not all of whom are Kānaka ʻŌiwi, went underreported or ignored completely in mainstream media. However, the impact of their work was massive: it ultimately educated the lāhui about the importance of protecting a place like Mauna a Wākea and how law is an ambivalent tool. These are the folks who had been engaged in legal battles since the 1990s, when the movement was confined to the highly controlled spaces of the state's legal authority.

Throughout the book, I refer to them simply as "the Mauna Kea Hui."[48] As I would learn, efforts to protect the Mauna from further development in the uneven playing field of settler law meant that members were forced to become part-time legal scholars simply to navigate the legal processes. However, unlike law students, the hui did not have the benefit of a formal education in law or major institutional financial support, which made the agency of their work and the sacrifices required so striking to me as a researcher of Kānaka ʻŌiwi social movements and settler colonial discourse. The hui found themselves at a disadvantage, disqualified and ineffectual within the legal processes that were originally designed to register their concerns but ultimately to do nothing about them. The hui would be written off as religious fundamentalists or irrational and out of touch with reality; as self-indulgent provocateurs who protest merely *for the sake of protest itself.* I wanted to study and highlight their knowledge, experiences, philosophies, and stories in this project. Though unable to stop the TMT permit in the Hawaiʻi State Supreme Court in 2015, their work is the foundation on which the grassroots activism and direct actions for Mauna a Wākea are built.

Learning from this diversity of views has helped to shape my own politics concerning Maunakea as well, but also Hawaiʻi more broadly. These lessons inform the conversations that I stage in this book. Similarly, my own history and positionality has also informed my analysis of power, as well as my decision to feature the voices of Kānaka ʻŌiwi on their terms; our terms. While I was raised in the small and mostly Mexican American agricultural city of Santa Maria, California, in the 1980s and 1990s, just after high school I moved to Hawaiʻi, where I came to know my grandmother's family—my cousins. For over twenty years, I lived on Oʻahu, where I studied and was part of a loving and affirming community of friends and chosen family, many of whom are lifetime activists. In an extended stepfamily, I coparented our son along with his mother, as well as my current partner and our found family. It was also in that time that I learned to love our language, culture, and history, which inspired me to become a scholar, activist, and educator. My subject position as someone who might be read as "local" but not immediately as Kānaka Maoli or Pacifika, often feeling never quite "Hawaiian," or "Mexican," or "white" enough, I have always occupied a liminal space somewhere between insider and outsider. Where I was raised, we were taught to root for the underdog, to give people without means the benefit of the doubt, to ask questions before making accusations, and to find the courage to speak when you have no other choice. Joining the chorus of voices speaking out on behalf of our people and our islands made sense, but I am still discovering how the resilience of our people, the vibrance of our culture, and the untold trauma of our history as a lāhui make Kānaka ʻŌiwi a beautifully messy, but principled community. These and many other experiences inform how I approached my research and the Mauna. I carry them and my intellectual and familial genealogy with me as I engage with my interlocutors and research on this very sensitive topic. These lessons have encouraged me to proceed with care, humility, compassion, patience, and a commitment to decolonial struggle. And that approach has taught me accountability to our lāhui, our islands and waters, and our ancestral places.

The Struggle, the Movement

The struggle over Mauna a Wākea has never been only about another telescope but instead, as it is emblematic of the broader struggle over Hawaiʻi, it is about the future of Kānaka ʻŌiwi—our humanity and our liberation from imperial occupation. Thus, our social movements are neither arbitrary nor indulgent but instead rooted in historically situated grievances, as well as our claims to life, land, and ea. At stake for Kānaka ʻŌiwi in this struggle is the meaning to be ascribed to place and space, the implications of which have material consequences for a people whose indigeneity is routinely trivialized and attacked by law and science, our history of colonization disavowed, and our lives and bodies alienated from our lands, waters, and ancestral ways of being. The movement is therefore much bigger than just a protest against the TMT.

The Maunakea Movement is the largest collective resistance in Hawaiʻi in recent memory, but it was preceded by others, including the movement to stop the forty years of test bombings on Kahoʻolawe by the U.S. Navy from the 1970s to the 1990s, which continues to inform contemporary political thought and praxis where direct action is needed. It was influenced also by acts of resistance against mass evictions, water diversions, militarism, tourism, pollution, and desecration of innumerable sites across all the islands, including such well-documented struggles as those associated with Kalama Valley, Waiāhole, Mākua, Hālawa Valley, Waimānalo, Anahola, Naue, Niumalu, Nāwiliwili, Molokaʻi Ranch, Nā Wai ʻEhā, East

Maui, Haleakalā, Hilo Airport, Wao Kele o Puna, Pōhakuloa, and myriad others where ʻāina (land), wai (waters), and ʻŌiwi ways of life are threatened.[49] Conversely, the Movement for Mauna a Wākea has also influenced every high-profile conflict since Puʻuhuluhulu, including community protest actions against giant wind turbine development in Kahuku in 2019, the U.S. military's jet fuel storage tank leaks at Kapūkakī, or Red Hill, that poisoned Honolulu residents and Oʻahu's largest aquifer in 2021, as well as the State's governance failures that have created perpetual economic, water, and housing crises that were exacerbated by the Lāhainā wildfires in 2023. Recognizing the genealogies of the contemporary Hawaiian movement allows for a more nuanced analysis of Mauna a Wākea and the TMT. More to the point, this recognition restores the humanity of a people dehumanized by settler racial capitalism and a distorted histography about Hawaiʻi and ʻŌiwi people. As the book argues, the Maunakea Movement exists in a continuum of struggle for ancestral places. These interconnected struggles are generational and ongoing, complex, and contradictory. Yet, while they emerge in response to and defiance of white patriarchal settler capitalism and U.S. military occupation, our movements, like our people, *are not defined by them.*

In 2015 and 2019, kiaʻi had barricaded a road to halt an offensive, ecologically destructive, and self-congratulating monument of Western science—a phallus of settler dominion and domination—through which beneficiaries of U.S. empire enjoy the spoils of conquest, gazing into space, searching for life beyond the stars, and seeking the origins of the universe and *all of us* in it. However, Kānaka ʻŌiwi have our own stories, not of creation or evolution, but of *emergence*, arrival, care, and cooperation. These are stories less concerned with the colonizing imaginaries of otherworldly discovery, cosmic frontier adventure, or a singular originary event, than with constellations of becoming, which substantiate the meanings inscribed in our ways of being and inform our contemporary political thought and action. Hawaiians are known to search for truth and explore other worlds as much as anyone. Yet, while our universe is equally infinite, our beloved and storied places need not be bulldozed and irreparably damaged in the process of finding the truth of our existence in the universe. The challenge that Maunakea presents is this: At what cost do we pursue a single universal truth? At what cost do we ignore the violence of our actions in pursuit of bigger and better science, or telescopes, especially in such a place as Hawaiʻi and in a context of U.S. imperialism? If ever was a body of knowledge suited to confront our ecological, climate, and social crises, it is that of the world's Indigenous peoples. Paying attention opens space to find deeper meaning.

To that end, this book examines the politics and poetics of struggle for Mauna a Wākea and the historical context of the conflict over the proposed construction of the Thirty Meter Telescope: a development project that threatens not only rare and fragile ecosystems with industrial astronomy but also the dynamic myriad relations between Kānaka ʻŌiwi and our ʻāina.

Introduction to the Chapters

Through juxtaposition of two visits to the summit I made in 2012 and the competing valuations of Maunakea they embody, chapter 1 examines how ancestral knowledge about the Mauna and Kanaka relationality establishes some of the ways in which Mauna a Wākea becomes understood as sacred. Against this I contrast celebrations of industrial astronomy and summit tourism to argue settler colonialism under U.S. military occupation has conditioned the TMT, just as it has the broader struggle for Hawaiʻi.

Chapter 2 maps a timeline of telescope development to locate the TMT within the history of settler land grabs. Tracing the shifting legal designations of Maunakea that replace Kanaka relations to ʻāina with neoliberal conceptions of land as possession, I analyze the biopolitics of settler environmental conservation that reinscribe a colonial hierarchy of being and trivializes Indigenous claims to life and land. I argue that to understand the politics of Maunakea one must understand the historical context of settler occupation and ways in which indigeneity remains a substantive threat to settler hegemony and U.S. imperialism in Hawaiʻi.

Chapter 3 examines how liberal multiculturalism operationalizes settler colonialism in Hawaiʻi, facilitates a settler nativism that rationalizes leisure and scientific tourism, disavows Kanaka relationality to ʻāina, and reproduces a hegemony of white ascending settler subjectivity. Through discursive analysis of the ʻImiloa Astronomy Center, I examine how notions of mitigation, compromise, and coexistence invoke liberal multicultural mythologies to undermine Indigenous self-governance, upholding a status quo to which Kanaka indigeneity represents a radical alterity that must be managed.

Situating the #KūKia'iMauna Movement in a continuum of anticolonial struggle since 1893, chapter 4 examines historical moments of resistance that demonstrate how the articulation of cultural-spiritual praxis to direct political action signals an Indigenous politics: one that is neither fraudulent nor irrational but rather is evidence of an ontological reclamation of Indigenous presence and self-determination. My interview with Terrilee Nāpua Keko'olani-Raymond illustrates this articulation and politics.

Chapter 5 examines articulations of the sacred to the contemporary struggle for Mauna a Wākea by drawing on examples found in several key mele, oli, and mo'okū'auhau. Drawing on my interview with Pualani Kanaka'ole Kanahele, I argue that these intellectual traditions offer insights into Kanaka ontologies that speak to the urgency to develop a more accurate account of Kanaka relationality to 'āina and conceptions of pilina and kuleana to place, in order to understand the reasons kia'i are willing to place their bodies in front of bulldozers to protect sacred places. I argue that it is through compositions of nature and articulations of the sacred that Kanaka relationality is substantiated and the struggle for life, land, and ea is rooted.

Through an analysis of legal and popular narratives about the TMT that reproduce exigencies of Western science as universal and Native dispossession as settler inheritance, chapter 6 deconstructs several moves to innocence by which settlers seek absolution from guilt and implication in past and ongoing colonial violence and by which Kānaka 'Ōiwi are cast as obsolete antecedents of modern astronomy. In these imaginaries, the state's claim to legal authority is conflated with scientific objectivity and Kanaka 'Ōiwi claims to land and indigeneity become contained to the past and thus violable in the present. At stake for Kānaka 'Ōiwi is not only our legal rights but our very subjectivity as fully human.

Finally, chapter 7 concludes with an analysis of my interviews with three Kānaka Maoli who support and two non-Hawaiians who oppose the TMT, a paradox that I argue reflects how settler coloniality under U.S. occupation requires a sustained critical analysis of colonial power, not only to understand the politics of Maunakea but to combat the hierarchies of knowledge and being by which Kānaka 'Ōiwi are subjected within states of perpetual legal and scientific disqualification. I argue that, while Kānaka 'Ōiwi are as complex and contradictory as any other community, our contemporary struggle for Mauna a Wākea and social movements for life, land, and ea are no less legitimate for that reason. Indeed, it is only in sifting through the noise of conventional historiographic and contemporary settler discourses invested in the U.S. imperial project in Hawai'i that such paradoxes reveal what is at stake in Kānaka 'Ōiwi resistance and direct political action. Our struggle for Mauna a Wākea becomes legible only through a decolonial critique of power, which requires neither Hawaiian ancestry nor a degree in astrophysics but rather an analysis of struggle and solidarity that centers Indigenous voices as well as critical self-reflection, humility, and a willingness to proceed slowly.[50]

IN CEREMONY

Kū Kilakila ka Mauna

So, there's that sacredness that is totally natural, that totally
belongs to the elements and our elemental deities. We have
nothing to do with shaping it. And we have nothing to do with it
being a benefit to us. But it is beneficial for us. We have nothing to
do with the snow that falls up there and the water that it gathers.
So, it's out of man's realm. That's the whole idea to me of the
sacredness of Mauna Kea.

—PUALANI KANAKA'OLE KANAHELE, interview by the author

(The TMT) will move forward. There will be no more obstruction
from someone who found their cultural roots six minutes ago.

—NEIL ABERCROMBIE, *West Hawai'i Today*

Pi'i ka Lewa

On the road to the summit, our caravan of three four-wheel-drive vehicles
stopped at Hale Pōhaku, the midlevel visitor center, where we must break
for an hour to acclimatize before proceeding to the summit. If we don't,
altitude sickness is likely. Long ago, the only way to the summit was by foot
or horseback, a trek taking several days across desert and rocks into the
dry bitter cold of an environment unlike any other in all of ka pae 'āina o
Hawai'i (the archipelago of Hawai'i). Routes to the summit were known only
to a few—usually designated members of families living on Maunakea's
lowlands, entrusted with this coveted knowledge. From Saddle Road, our
journey in late September 2012 is about an hour. We find ourselves amid
tourists from around the world who have arrived early to view what promises to be a stunning sunrise. On most nights, visitors travel by chartered
buses and rental cars to congregate around mobile telescopes and stargaze,

pointing lasers, conversing, and enjoying the guided tours of the night's sky. The strip of stars called Hōkūnohoaupuni, what Western astronomy calls the "Milky Way," spreads itself like a blanket from horizon to zenith, enveloping the Mauna and all of us.[1] The stars seem close enough to touch. At this altitude where oxygen is low and air pressure drops, dizziness, headaches, and difficulty breathing are common. One's thinking may feel slowed and the body fatigued. Some faint, others vomit, or worse. My stomach rumbled that morning, and my heart pumped fast, even while I remained still. I imagine that the reverence early Kānaka ʻŌiwi held for the Mauna was not only a consequence of its beauty but also a testament to the physical risks associated with the arduous journey and the effects it has on the body.

Of Knowledge and Being

The colonial mythology of a hierarchy of peoples and knowledges has long been used to rationalize the subjugation of Indigenous peoples, often in the name of science, religion, or some ostensibly universal reality.[2] Operating as teleological justification for social relations structured in dominance, the mythology presumes a linear temporality and racialized conception of human evolution that suggests subhuman primitivism has given way to fully human subjectivity.[3] In the context of Mauna a Wākea[4] and within this prevailing order of colonial domination under U.S. settler military occupation, Kānaka ʻŌiwi and our knowledge systems and forms of relating to the living world have come to be treated as subordinate concerns to those of technoscientific institutions. Efforts to maintain Hawaiian knowledges and lifeways are often marginalized by settler capitalism, State governance, and corporate media and seen as distractions from the real order of business that is, for example, proper science and economic growth. These Indigenous knowledge systems are then dismissed as opportunistic or as calculated political strategy, which suggests the expression and practice of traditional Kānaka ʻŌiwi epistemologies are disingenuous, fraudulent, or nefarious in some way. In this context, mainstream discourses on Maunakea and the TMT reproduce a hegemonic social order that disqualifies Kanaka ʻŌiwi knowledge and subjectivity through this mythology of hierarchized being and self-authorizes settler subjectivity, the imperial state, and big science.

Many scientific practices are co-constituted in legacies of power and control, particularly the ambitious large-scale technological projects that involve a nexus of multidisciplinary and multinational scientific research and development, including mass labor, major corporate and philanthropic investment, design and engineering innovation, and international manufacture and financial coordination, all of which comprise what science and technology studies and historians of science call "big science."[5] Relying also on resource extraction of rare minerals and unfettered access to contested physical-geographical spaces secured through violent means—both historical and ongoing—big science has always been implicated in colonialism and imperialism. Ideologies of naturally hierarchized peoples have also long benefitted big science, providing justification for the continued displacement of Native peoples on whose lands big science projects depend, be it to mine, experiment, or station. As such, imperialism and science have become fellow travelers, both operating under a certainty that there is a single universal reality: the Native subject, decidedly inferior, is simply in the way of human progress. Like the imperial state and settler science, the fields of mathematics and physics are also based on a certainty that universal laws can be ascertained.[6] It is the conviction in universality itself that validates the TMT—a validation Kānaka ʻŌiwi do not enjoy under U.S. military occupation and settler racial capitalism. As a universal system of knowledge, big science assumes a responsibility to advance the "common good." Perceived as exemplary of rational thought and human potential in the modern era, and unquestionably beneficial to all of humanity, this very specific type of scientific practice becomes normalized, even sanctified. However, the collateral damage visited upon Indigenous communities and other subjugated peoples is rarely acknowledged in the celebration of this often extractive, exploitive, and indifferent scientific practice. I argue that this is how science is instrumentalized to provide cover and redemption for imperialist regimes built upon conquest of peoples whose exile to inferiority rationalizes elimination of Native people and expropriation of Native lands.

In an example of these hegemonic formations, one astronomer I interviewed argued that astronomy offers "basic human knowledge that everyone should know," like "human anatomy." This universalizing rhetoric treats the presumed hierarchy of human knowledges and human beings as self-evident. As Alexander Weheliye explains, hierarchized "genres of the human" hinge on racializing assemblages that function to produce modern selfhood where "a conglomerate of sociopolitical relations . . . disciplines humanity into full humans, not-quite-humans, and nonhumans."[7] Such a taxonomy presupposes and justifies the continued violability of specific bodies and lands in the name of a "greater good" that conjures a humanity from which Kānaka 'Ōiwi are ideologically and discursively alienated.

As the TMT debate is performed under conditions of U.S. military occupation, every iteration of humanity employed to convey the urgency of another telescope—particularly through invocations of the rational, the modern, and the universal—carries an echo of the Scientific Revolution and European Enlightenment, which presumed a natural hierarchy of knowledges and peoples and disciplined bodies accordingly. While that "revolution" and "enlightenment" would be used to rationalize recursive episodes of genocide and slavery in both the Old and New Worlds, their reverberation today carries the trace of those originary practices of violence.[8] Articulations of humanity, rationality, and modernity in settler colonial contexts have never simply named a universal reality so much as they have enforced the reality preferred by those privileged within these ideological and structured hierarchies. Rather than describing universal laws or the world as it exists, scientific practice that is indifferent to its conditions of possibility—that is, colonialism, imperialism, capitalism, and patriarchy—remakes a world disciplined into hierarchical relations structured in dominance. This can be observed in even the most casual of speech acts within the state and its ideological apparatuses.

For example, in Joan Lander and Puhipau's 2005 documentary *Mauna Kea: Temple Under Siege,* former Institute for Astronomy director Rolf-Peter Kudritzki states, "You can just look at the scientific record of what has been accomplished with these telescopes. They have written the history of modern astronomy on Mauna Kea."[9] The comment trades in discourses of erasure of prior knowledges that settler states require to reproduce their monopolies on the exercise of violence, themselves built on the violence of claims to a single all-encompassing "scientific record," referenced here as mere "history." In conflating "modern astronomy" with Western methodological practices and philosophies of industrial technoscience *as a universal imperative*, alternative knowledges are contained, and a specific conception of modernity itself is normalized. Maunakea is, thus, key to an historical record in which Kānaka 'Ōiwi are peripheral or precursory at best, expired or extraneous at worst. The discursive move situates technoscience as a harbinger of universal knowledge rather than a product of historically situated imperial enforcements of a specific orientation to knowledge and knowledge production that are dependent on logics of Native elimination that underpin settler claims to land, jurisdiction, and political and scientific authority. These logics, embedded within the pro-TMT rhetoric, were hardly obscured in Neil Abercrombie's comments in a 2011 speech given before the Kona-Kohala Chamber of Commerce in which Hawaiʻi's then-governor addressed a probusiness, antiunion audience and sought to dismiss broad opposition to the TMT, by arguing the project "will move forward. There will be no more obstruction from someone who found their cultural roots six minutes ago."[10] Abercrombie makes explicit what Kudritzki presumes is self-evident: that alternative, often counterhegemonic, knowledge systems are not only irrelevant but suspect, if not fraudulent.

Conversely, Pua Kanakaʻole Kanahele speaks from a position within such an alternative knowledge system, one free of ideological debt or attachment to colonial, racial, or imperial conquest, or a presumed hierarchy of knowledge and being. As indicated in the epigraph, Kumu Pua emphasizes interconnected relationality. In contrast to the dominant logic of capitalist use value, Kanakaʻole Kanahele argues that a knowledge of the natural world is only as *universally* beneficial as that system of knowledge that also exists *in balance* with the elemental energies it purports to describe. Implied is a rejection of Enlightenment conceptions of hierarchized difference in which relationality is structured in dominance over the more-than-human world and its elemental forms. In other words, the Mauna benefits humans because of its intrinsic value, regardless of what humans might gain from it. Mauna a Wākea is but one site to witness such a worldview in action, and Kānaka ʻŌiwi are not unique in this. Indigenous peoples everywhere share such perspectives about places, whether they are held in reverence or meant to be left alone. Unlike imperial sciences or any hierarchized knowledge system enforcing supposed universal laws, Kanakaʻole Kanahele teaches a social milieu that prioritizes an ethos and habitus of accountability to each other, the elemental world, and our more-than-human relatives. This speaks to the concept of pono,[11] in which a commitment to balance across difference stands in contrast to hierarchical relationality. Cultivating such a knowledge system and pono relationality is central to the ceremonies that Kānaka ʻŌiwi continue to practice on the Mauna.

As Manulani Meyer observes, the conflict over Mauna a Wākea is "a perfect example of clashing cosmologies."[12] It is also a story of power, and power is always accompanied by resistance. Understanding the violence of industrial astronomy on the Mauna requires attention to politics; that is, politics understood as relations of power. While many characterize the clash as one of religion versus science, at its core it is a contest over meaning and its making. How we understand science, religion, the cosmos, and knowledge stems from how we understand the cultural authority of scientists and how we understand modernity's others and humanity's foil: the Indigenous subject. Reflecting a continuum of struggle against Native subjugation to foreign desires, the movement for Maunakea hangs on a capacity to identify the political within narrative practices and understand relations of power forged under conditions of imperial dominance in Hawaiʻi. Without a critique of power, the struggle for Mauna a Wākea makes little sense.

This chapter introduces several key interventions by juxtaposing two huakaʻi (journeys) that I made to the summit at the start of my interview research in 2012 to illustrate a key difference in relationality to space and place that I argue is at the heart of the TMT controversy. Directing our attention to the reasons and ways in which Kānaka ʻŌiwi articulate aloha for Mauna a Wākea to our methods of resistance, though often puzzling to the settler state, nevertheless can reveal layers of meaning that situate the struggle for all ʻāina in a continuum of land defense, or aloha ʻāina (love of the land and for one's country); a fierce multifaceted aloha that contests the United States' claims to Hawaiʻi while continuing to ground Kanaka relationality and indigeneity in anticolonial and decolonial collective direct action as much as Indigenous epistemology. I will show how the difference between scientific use and recreational tourism on the one hand and Kanaka ʻŌiwi cultural practice linked to political expression on the other signifies a broader tension that, without a critical analysis of power in Hawaiʻi, is simply illegible. The difference in relationality to Mauna a Wākea speaks to how the grievances Kānaka ʻŌiwi attribute to the TMT are linked to broader grievances—both historical and ongoing, as the two are always connected—which animates other community activism beyond the Mauna. These differences and their contradictions require a sustained and nuanced critique of settler law, capitalism, and empire to find meaning. Such analysis may also open space to consider the ways in which difference in relationality can either be used *to uphold or to disrupt* technoscientific industrial development on Maunakea and the myth of a natural hierarchy of the world's peoples and knowledges through which the violence of big science and empire are co-constitued. To that end, I examine an episode of telescope tourism and another of cultural resurgence. I argue that without a politics of colonialism, it is difficult to understand the debate surrounding the TMT, let alone the reasons kiaʻi are willing to put their bodies on the line to stop its construction.

E Ala Ē, Ka Lā i ka Hikina

Our journey began an hour before dawn at Uncle Paul Neves's hale (house) in Keaukaha.[13] A kumu hula[14] (hula teacher) and Aliʻi Noʻeau Loa (high chief) of the Royal Order of Kamehameha I, Neves has been an advocate for justice for Kānaka ʻŌiwi for over thirty years. With just under twenty in our group, we have gathered to hold ceremony in observance of the Polohiwa. The evening begins with oli (chants) and members of Neves's hālau (hula school) and family dance several mele (songs) before we set out. In response to my request for an interview, Kealoha Pisciotta has invited me to join them for this huakaʻi (trip/voyage) made four times a year for the solstices and equinoxes. Pisciotta is a land defender, water protector, and cultural practitioner whose political and spiritual commitments are interwoven with every aspect of her daily life. Founder of Mauna Kea Anaina Hou, Pisciotta is also an environmental activist, former telescope operator on the James Clerk Maxwell Telescope, and a colleague to whom I was introduced through connections at the Hawaiian-Environmental Alliance (KAHEA), where I volunteered during this time. She and others in the group are some of the Kanaka who have been involved in the legal struggle to protect Mauna a Wākea from telescope development expansion for over twenty years. In this regard, she is also an untrained, unsupported, part-time legal scholar with an intimate knowledge of and relationship to State land use and resource management policy. Earlier in the day, she and a friend took me with them to a native forest along the slopes of Kīlauea. There, we picked ʻōhiʻa lehua, koa, palapalai,[15] and other lāʻau (plants) to be made into pūʻolo (bundles) for hoʻokupu (offerings), which we would later use in the Polohiwa ceremony at the summit of Mauna a Wākea.

We traveled through the night, departing from Keaukaha at 10 p.m. and stopping along the way to visit several culturally important wahi pana (storied places) and ahu (stone altars, shrines), where we hold ceremony, leaving hoʻokupu and reciting pule (prayers), talking story, and observing the protocols for healing ourselves and setting intentions to heal the mountain.

On this evening, I am a participant observer and researcher, but I am also Kanaka ʻŌiwi. The experience fills me with a deep sense of kuleana (responsibility, privilege) to learn what it means to aloha ʻāina through, not civil disobedience direct action, monkeywrenching, or mass protest, but through ceremony.[16] Though I wanted to talk more about the broader context of the TMT, for our caravan on this evening, Pisciotta reminded me that our focus was *not* on politics. Instead, we were there to reconnect, remember, and to heal.

We arrive at Hale Pōhaku around 4 a.m. The sun will rise at 6:20 a.m., so we time our hike to reach the puʻu (cinder cone) of Kūkahauʻula around 5:45 a.m. While we wait for our bodies to adjust, Pisciotta explains to me the significance of our journey to witness the rising sun on this particular morning. This was a rare opportunity to experience just how Kānaka ʻŌiwi are spiritual and scientific, maintaining what can accurately be understood as traditions of scientific practice despite the epistemological difference in methods and nomenclature. These knowledges refuse to masquerade as universal, objective, and transcendent truth, although they endeavor to understand, find meaning, and improve the human condition. Kanaka ʻŌiwi knowledge systems are grounded in epistemological traditions of storytelling whereby a Kanaka sense of being and belonging is about being in good relation to ancestral places, elemental forms, and to one another in ontogenealogical and cosmogonic relationality. This is why many know and care for ʻāina as an embodiment of one's ancestors.

Ka Lewa Nuʻu

Polohiwa, or "glistening black," refers to the celestial path of the sun's transit between solstices. An example is ke ala polohiwa a Kāne (the black shining road of Kāne, a major akua associated with sunlight, among other elements), which is marked by the sun's annual motion between the celestial equator and its northern limit, spanning from roughly late March to late September. The southern guiding star, Newe, is out of view from Hawaiʻi during ke ala polohiwa a Kāne. The other half of the year is that of ke ala polohiwa a Kanaloa (the black shining road of Kanaloa, a major akua associated with the ocean, among other elements); the period wherein the sun transits from the celestial equator to its southern limit, at which point the

North Star, Hōkūpaʻa, moves out of view. We have arrived on September 22 for the vernal equinox, when the sun begins its journey south along ke ala polohiwa a Kanaloa.[17]

A Guided Tour, a Kanaka Astronomer, a Gaggle of Boy Scouts

At the start of my research in 2013, I was invited to visit Mauna a Wākea by the late astronomer and University of Hawaiʻi professor Dr. Paul Coleman, who had arranged to give a group of Oʻahu Boy Scouts a tour of the Keck Observatory.[18] Six months after my first visit to the summit, I was very much a malihini (foreigner). On our two-hour drive mauka (upland), I used the time to interview Coleman in hopes of learning more about his unique position as a Native Hawaiian and an astronomer. He was characteristically generous in entertaining my questions.[19] While I wanted to better understand the ways astronomers value Maunakea, I was also keen to explore how someone who is Kanaka ʻŌiwi might also come to support the Thirty Meter Telescope. There are so few Kanaka astronomers, and his positionality seemed counterintuitive. Why would anyone who is Hawaiian support the project? Some of his responses challenged my assumptions about why people support the TMT, but others reflected a popular skepticism about Indigenous ideologies of the sacred and how they lead to anti-TMT activism.

Coleman gave me a wonderful history of astronomy at Maunakea, and it was clear he was passionate about his work and his relationships with various communities on both sides of the controversy. Many of his views about the importance of Maunakea to the field of astronomy echoed the popular opinions circulating among what was then a mainstream and therefore sympathetic view of the Thirty Meter Telescope, which often aligns with a posture that is also protourism and prodevelopment. But his views also revealed his own experiences of overcoming racism in a field that is predominantly occupied and controlled by white men. As a Native person (of color) having conducted research at some of the world's most renowned observatories, Coleman had also experienced structural and interpersonal racism throughout his career.

Traveling with Coleman to the summit helped me to see a rather unexpected side of the Hawaiian community. Despite my own politics, through the course of our day together, I began to understand that Coleman is just as complex and contradictory as any other Kanaka. Yet, likely because I study colonization and empire, what I read as his indifference to the political history of Hawai'i and Kānaka 'Ōiwi points to something that is often removed from mainstream conversations about the TMT: power. Few people seem to think critically about the ideologies underpinning the legal and political structures of contemporary Hawai'i or the political and economic justifications for building the TMT in terms of power and ways discourse may challenge or reify hierarchical social relations. Even fewer consider seriously the ongoing reality that Kānaka 'Ōiwi are a colonized people. Be it indifference or ignorance, the lack of attention is also a mark of power.

Coleman repeated the talking points used in PR promotions touting the merits of the TMT: its promise of jobs and economic stimulus, scientific discoveries, and universal benefit to humanity. He also expressed the idea that TMT is a modern analog to ancient Hawaiian practices of long-distance open-ocean voyaging by star navigation, arguing that what makes someone Hawaiian is that one of their "ancestors came here in a canoe led by an astronomer." He shared his ideas about the perceived benefits of astronomy but was critical of protestors and people fighting in the courts to stop the TMT, suggesting that many people dutifully follow activists as a "knee-jerk reaction," assuming they are right just because they are Hawaiian. Others, he argued, protest for the sake of protesting. No matter how illogical their position, "You're never going to be able to change some people's minds."[20] He was also dismissive of "colonialism":

> Unfortunately, there's this whole colonialism thing going on, and so, you have to somehow, get past that. It's kind of easy for us [astronomers] to get past that because I don't feel like a colonial person . . . I feel like I'm one of the slaves! . . . But it's not like . . . I feel like I'm going to dominate anybody, you know?[21]

In this comment, although Coleman identifies as an astronomer, he does not feel like "a colonial person" but instead, somehow feels like "one of the slaves," a paradox that begs the question: To whom exactly are astronomers enslaved? Does participation in the institutions indebted to colonial relations of power render one "a colonial person?" While the material conditions of a group's oppression are not defined by whether an individual *feels* one way or another, the idea of "getting past" colonialism implies the activity of analyzing power is a distraction or anachronistic.

Coleman expressed great aloha for Maunakea and his work. However, while aloha for the Mauna is why the kia'i oppose the TMT, his aloha was the reason for his support. He had adopted the perspective that competent State regulations combined with the University of Hawai'i's Comprehensive Management Plan (CMP) would be adequate to protect what the State identifies as the cultural and natural "resources" of the Mauna. He also conveyed how fortunate he was to be able to do astronomy in Hawai'i, since it is only the observatories on Maunakea that make this possible. Generally, one of the greatest challenges Kanaka astronomers face is that when they graduate and enter the field, in order to do astronomy, they often must leave their home and move to where the top programs, institutions, funding, and observatories are located. For many burgeoning Kanaka astronomers, the TMT promises new opportunities to practice Western astronomy and practice it at home. Even as some feel ambivalence toward the question of overdevelopment on Maunakea, the opportunities outweigh the harm to Maunakea it is anticipated the TMT will cause.

Coleman also observed protocols he learned as a haumāna (student) of the revered kumu hula John Lake. On our drive, we pulled off of Saddle Road to visit Pu'uhonua o Pu'uhuluhulu and Kanakaleonui, an ahu (altar, shrine) constructed years ago so kūpuna unable to travel to the summit would have a place to hold ceremony. Coleman and I left ho'okupu, and he offered an oli (chant) and pule (prayer). Absorbing what I was learning about Coleman—that he is at once a Kanaka Maoli who embraces his culture and someone who finds no contradiction between his spiritual practice and his advocacy for astronomy expansion on the Mauna—my takeaway was that simply being Hawaiian does not lead one to a critique of power.

During the tour, it became clear the Boy Scouts would be a mischievous bunch. All high schoolers, these adolescent boys were boisterous, irreverent, and difficult to be around. As we stood along the southeast ridge peering out over the telescopes across the summit plateau in the afternoon sun, Coleman described the history of the telescopes to the group. He shared anecdotes about their construction, the early development of the technologies involved, and how these telescopes have contributed to the knowledge we all take for granted about the universe. "Where's the bathroom?!" asked one of the boys, interrupting Coleman.

Most of the kids were paying little to no attention to Coleman, and even the parent chaperones seemed distracted and impatient—several remained in their cars during the Keck tour. Aside from myself, only one leader and one scout seemed even remotely interested in Coleman's stories. I read this as disrespect, but the general attitude of these visitors from Honolulu was not unlike any of the three hundred other daily visitors who drive to the summit for recreational tourism.

Another difficult situation for me came when, after a nice conversation with the scout leader, we walked back to the group and found the boys posing shirtless for selfies. Parading in front of the iconic Pu'u o Kūkahau'ula and the ahu lele (a type of altar), where months before I had just visited with the group of kia'i for the Polohiwa ceremony, the kids were flexing their skinny arms, climbing on each other, laughing, and snapping photos, all while their amused parents watched. I was reminded of the space between settlers and Natives and the ways in which we all come to value and inhabit Hawai'i differently. The significance of the boys' unselfconscious frolic, to me, is that it symbolized the broader multicultural order of settler Hawai'i. Just as Hawai'i has become a playground for tourists, capitalists, and the military—facilitated by an enfranchised settler State of Hawai'i on behalf of U.S. Pacific imperialism—Mauna a Wākea has become a playground for astronomers and, by extension, also for day trippers.

On the drive back to Hilo that evening, our conversation was limited to the TMT's altruism and promise to humanity and economic benefit to Hawai'i. Coleman expressed some dismay about the Boy Scouts "hamming it up," but he seemed less bothered by it than I was. When I asked Coleman about the possible negative impacts of the TMT, he addressed only what I saw as the more trivial concerns like the issue of tourists who stack rock piles and take two-wheel drive vehicles on the dirt road to the summit. Frustrated, he reasoned, "If they get stuck, the burden falls on taxpayers to pay for their rescue. It's also a bad idea because they'll have to spend way more money to get a tow all the way up there."[22] While critical of law enforcement's shortcomings in dealing with rock-piling tourists, he only expressed hope that the matter would be resolved by hiring more rangers, which the TMT's anticipated revenue stream would make possible. In this moment of scrutiny, I asked about the (then) $1.4 billion (now $2.6 billion) price tag and 18-story, 8-acre footprint the TMT would create and its consequences for Native cultural practitioners. He responded not by talking about TMT politics but the seemingly mundane aspects of lesser concern to kiaʻi. Self-conscious of being pushy or contrary, I kept the rest of my questions superficial for the remainder of the drive. But reflecting on that day, I wonder, what should I have expected? My ideas are a bit outside the scope of what generally concerns astronomers. I found it disappointing but unsurprising that one of the TMT's most influential public advocates, though also Hawaiian, could not speak to U.S. militarism or settler capitalism's impacts on the finite space of these islands. The TMT only makes sense if we depoliticize it and ignore history. In the absence of critical analysis of power, any opposition appears excessive and irrational. This is the gap between advocates and opponents of astronomy expansion.

The Polohiwa

My first huakaʻi to Maunakea was dramatically different from the tour of the Keck Observatory with Paul Coleman and the Boy Scouts. While politics hardly figured into conversations throughout the Polohiwa ceremony, it was for very different reasons. Our huakaʻi that evening was but one of many individual acts of everyday resurgence that constitute the contemporary Hawaiian movement today.[23] Kānaka ʻŌiwi have always journeyed to the mountain summit to renew familial and genealogical relations to the Mauna, the akua (gods), and our kūpuna o ka pō (those who have passed into the realm of pō, or ancestors). In the context of a pending decision on the TMT's first permit, and after a lengthy and exhausting contested case hearing that left my hosts on this evening in need of healing, the purpose of our huakaʻi was to find balance in the struggle through ceremony and aloha ʻāina.

The Polohiwa ceremony was fascinating to me because, in its specificity, everything has meaning, and these meanings are layered, expansive, *and* scientific. Just consider how the ceremony required that we position ourselves—spiritually and physically—to be on the tallest peak in Oceania, at a specific time of a particular day, and according to an annual cycle that has been observed by Kānaka ʻŌiwi for generations, so that we may witness this specific rising sun at this exact point along its ecliptic. The celestial equator, which splits the two polohiwa, is known as the piko of Wākea, or ke alanui i ka piko o Wākea (the path at the navel of Wākea,[24] also ke alanui a ke Kuʻukuʻu—the "road of the spider"). The stars within ke alanui i ka piko o Wākea were directly overhead on that night.[25] This belt of stars, which is conceived of as dividing time and space, as in the northern and southern celestial hemispheres, is named after the deified ancestor, Wākea, just as the mountain itself honors this beloved kupuna (ancestor) in our cosmogonic genealogies, or moʻokūʻauhau.[26]

The vocabulary of Mauna a Wākea embodies the temporal and spatial worlds of the kūpuna (ancestors), akua (gods), and Kānaka (Native people) and renews their bonds to each other and to ʻāina. These relations emerged across generations as identity formations and were developed through patient observations of the interconnections between Kānaka and the natural world. And they were nurtured through grammars of kinship relationality. As Katrina-Ann R. Kapāʻanaokalāokeola Nākoa Oliveira explains, within Kanaka ʻŌiwi geographies, nomenclature around various topographical and atmospheric strata can be distinguished as "heavenscapes" and "landscapes."[27] Many know the mountain summit as located within the wao akua, or "realm of the gods," but the Mauna is also in the kuahea, a region between lani (skies) and ʻāina (land) known as "ka lewa,"[28] which is a liminal space of emergence and possibility between "'ka paʻa i luna' (the firmament above)" and "'ka paʻa i lalo' (the solid below)."[29] In this tradition of knowledge, Mauna a Wākea connects the heavenscape to the landscape where the highest "mountainous regions of the mauna and kuahiwi" descend all the way to wao kanaka below the tree line, where the makaʻāinana (the populace) generally live. According to this geography, wao kanaka is the part of the landscape immediately below wao akua, which extends through wao maʻukele, wao ʻeiwa, wao lipo, wao nahele, and ascends toward the kuamauna (mountaintop), where the highest region is the kuahea.[30] These naming practices mapped centuries of observation to catalog patterns from ʻāina to lani. These forms of knowledge production are no less scientific than contemporary practices. However, a key difference is how they inform people's kuleana (responsibilities) to these places.

All ancestral places impart specific kuleana to those who visit them. Pualani Kanakaʻole Kanahele explained to me that, historically, most makaʻāinana understood there were some places that did not require human presence. Should you have reason to travel someplace like the kuahea, it was with reverence and humility. You would never arrive without hoʻokupu or first seeking permission. It was advised to never wear out one's welcome. These kuleana signify a relationality that undermines hierarchy with the elemental world and our more-than-human relatives, who could not be reduced to "natural resources" or "property." Indeed, this relationality is not about *dominion over* so much as *balance with*. Through ceremony like the Polohiwa, a continuity of kuleana from ka wā kahiko (old times) to the present is affirmed, allowing Hawaiians to renew these values and relations with every return. In our twelve-hour journey, we honored Mauna a Wākea as home of numerous akua and kupua (deities) to whom our cultural practice allowed us to fulfill a kuleana.

In the Kumulipo, the great genealogy from which it is said all Kānaka 'Ōiwi descend, Hawai'i Island is the hiapo, or first of the island children of Wākea, birthed by his wahine (spouse, mate) Papahānaumoku (Papa who births islands).[31] Pualani Kanaka'ole Kanahele describes the genealogy and the importance of firsts in this way:

> Maunakea is the first born to us. That's where our roots start. That's where our island begins. That's where the first rain from Wākea hits, is our mountain. That's where the first sunlight that rises every morning hits. That mountain is the first for everything that we have and so because Maunakea is the first born, we need to mālama Maunakea.[32]

The mountain is the tallest peak in the entire archipelago, a major aquifer of Hawai'i Island, and, to many Kānaka 'Ōiwi, an elder sibling and an ancestor. It is also considered a piko. The word *piko* may be translated as "summit," but its kaona (obscured, deeper meaning)[33] points to several additional ideas. To Kānaka 'Ōiwi water is sacred because, of course, without it there can be no life, but historically, the mountain was also known as a kumu (source) of the island's *cleanest* wai (fresh water). Like the first rays of sun, the first rain to touch Hawai'i Island first touches Mauna a Kea. It is said that the purest water is rain caught in the piko of a kalo (taro) leaf— at the junction of petiole and blade—because it has not yet touched the soil. As such, it was reserved for the mō'ī (sovereign, monarch). As a piko, Mauna a Wākea also signified political legitimacy, spiritual emergence, and a source of knowledge.[34] Because the value of wai was well understood, its proper management was a fundamental criterion of one's right to rule. Any mō'ī who failed to manage wai in equitable and sustainable ways would be swiftly removed. Rain caught by Mauna a Wākea is viewed with similar reverence. Wai at the piko—which is embodied by the mist, rain, snow, the alpine lake near its summit, and the permafrost—is sacred because it has not yet entered the streams that eventually feed the maka'āinana below.

The idea of nourishment is implied in another translation of piko, that is "umbilicus." Providing water to at least fifty ahupuaʻa in three of Hawaiʻi Island's largest moku,[35] the mountain is, in a very material sense, a source of life that feeds kānaka as a makua (parent) does their keiki (child). Hence, Mauna a Wākea is known also as "ka piko kaulana o ka ʻāina"—*the famous piko of the land.*

Maunakea is frequently translated as "white mountain," but the name signifies much more. While "kea" certainly does indicate the color white in reference to its snowcapped peaks, the word's kaona refers also to "seed," or "the seed of Wākea,"[36] in acknowledging this as the firstborn mountain on the firstborn island child of Papa (Earth Mother) and Wākea (Sky Father). Historically the Mauna was also described as "the ʻaha hoʻowili moʻo (the genealogical cord) that ties earth to the heavens."[37] Kalani Flores explains how unlike any other mountain in the Pacific, this child of Papa and Wākea "pierces above the clouds in(to) the realm of Wākea."[38] Rising to above 40 percent of Earth's atmosphere where conditions can induce nausea, vomiting, or death, it was clear the human body does not naturally belong at this altitude. Pua Kanakaʻole Kanahele explains that in addition to the extreme cold and the grueling journey across harsh terrain to ascend the mountain, this was no place for Kānaka; it is wao akua, "the realm of the gods."[39]

The Mauna's namesake, Wākea, is itself a constellation of temporal and spatial interconnections.[40] Wākea translates to "expanse of the sky," but colloquially, "Sky Father." The first word in the name, "wā," can refer to either time or space. For example, it might indicate an interval between moments, as in the phrase "mai kēia wā aku," "from this time forth," or a space between objects, as in "kōwā" and "wā," terms for "channel." Its temporal meaning indicates an epoch or an era but may also refer to a specific stretch of time, such as "ka wā kahiko," meaning "the old times," or "wā kamaliʻi," meaning "childhood."[41] Wā is also important to Kanaka ʻŌiwi knowledge systems of astronomy, ocean navigation, planting and farming, and fishing.[42] And within the mele koʻihonua (cosmogonical chant) known as the Kumulipo, wā is an organizing principle. Spanning sixteen wā, or eras, the Kumulipo is a sequence of emergence describing all life through one epic genealogy that begins in the time of pō (darkness, night) and extends to that of human genealogies in the time of ao (light, day). As Brandy Nālani McDougall explains, the Kumulipo "shows how we are inseparably a part of the universe and intimately a part of the land and ocean surrounding us," connected in a familial relationship that constitutes a shared kuleana (responsibility) to care for the ʻāina.[43] Part taxonomy and part moʻokūʻaukau, the Kumulipo names and documents all observable life, from the smallest of living organisms to swimmers, fliers, and four-leggeds all the way through eight hundred generations of aliʻi (rulers, royals), including Wākea and Papahānaumoku, or Papa, also "Earth Mother." In this cosmogeny, all life is interconnected through genealogy. Even the most seemingly insignificant species are at once our kin and our ancestors. Such a classification system and praxis carries with it an environmentalist ethic and a cultural ethos of care. This is significant because the activism to protect Mauna a Wākea has been organized around such a kuleana to protect ʻāina as one would protect their own grandparents. We do not disrespect, harm, or neglect our grandparents, so why would we treat our lands and waters—our relatives—any differently? The cosmogonic genealogy, the nomenclature of the Mauna and its namesake, and the lessons they teach remind us of that kuleana. Likewise, the ceremony and struggle at Mauna a Wākea functions as a collective re-membering of these temporal and spatial interconnections that link people to place in a sacred kinship with specific responsibilities.[44] Just as colonization is not a thing of the past, this cultural pilina (relation), these genealogies, and these kinship obligations also continue.

I ka Hikina, Aia ka Lā

While acclimatizing at Hale Pōhaku, I walked around the premises of the visitor center and noticed the State DLNR[45] sign that reads, PLEASE LEAVE THE LANDSCAPE AS YOU FOUND IT. DO NOT REARRANGE STONES, BUILD ROCK PILES, OR OTHERWISE DISTURB THE TERRAIN. The irony of this warning amidst thirteen observatories littering the summit is that these giant dome structures do just that: "disturb the terrain."

As a grad student and activist, though quite enchanted by the whole scene on my first visit to such a wondrous place, this sign pulled me out of the moment. I thought, "Who are these rock-pilers who threaten to disturb Mauna a Wākea?" The sign pointed to a rather trivial threat that Paul Coleman had also cited as an offense: "rock piles." But Hawaiians do not pile rocks, they build ahu, or dry-stacked stone altars. How could ahu possibly be a threat to anything? Indeed, tourists building small rock piles along the road around the visitor center has become a problem, but implicit in the warning to tourists is another to Kānaka ʻŌiwi that this is no longer the sacred space where cultural practice is welcome. As instruction, the sign asserts settler state authority—to surveil and to discipline. As a claim to jurisdiction, it is also productive.

Like most other nights throughout the year, on this evening there were hundreds of visitors who arrived in tour buses to stargaze through the portable telescopes made available by the visitor center. Our presence, even if only in some small symbolic way, undermined the recreational and touristic use of the summit as commercial entitlement. A small hui (group) of mostly Kānaka ʻŌiwi re-membering cultural identity, our very presence was a response to exploitive and extractive management policy, viewed by kiaʻi as desecration. The Polohiwa offered another reality in its radical alterity: an embodiment of ancestral connection to the Mauna in a way that exceeds liberal democracy under racial capitalism and U.S. settler occupation. The observance of kuleana through ceremony—however complex and contradictory these practices may be—was powerful because it enacts the creative potential of Indigenous resurgence *as resistance*. If the settler scientific vision of Maunakea as "the world's premier astronomy observatory" is threatened by so-called rock piles, the continued cultural practices of Kānaka ʻŌiwi, who have a different vision for the Mauna, leave them terrified. Unlike astronomers, however, it is Kānaka ʻŌiwi who leave the landscape as they found it and not the other way around.

Once acclimatized, we silently gathered everyone and caravanned to the summit. We were advised to enter the space quietly and with reverence. We parked alongside the British telescope, crossed the two-lane road, and silently filed into a line to begin a fifteen-minute walk that felt like an hour hike to the top of Kūkahauʻula (Kū of the red tinted snow).[46]

Kūkahauʻula was translated as "the pink tinted snow god" by Emma Ahuʻena Taylor, "a Hawaiian historian of royal lineage" who in 1931 published an account that was cited by Kepā Maly and Onaona Maly, which describes "the sacred nature of Poliʻahu, and . . . the various attributes of Waiau, Lilinoe, and Kūkahauʻula."[47] Puʻu o Kūkahauʻula, "is the traditional name of the summit cluster of cones," or puʻu, on Maunakea, which refers to its rose hue at sunrise and sunset. It is said that Kūkahauʻula's love for Poliʻahu was thwarted by Lilinoe (find mist rain), Lihau (chilling frost),

Figure 20. Dawn at Kūkahauʻula, Mauna a Wākea, September 22, 2012. Photograph by the author.

and Kipuʻupuʻu (the hail), Poliʻahu's attendants who "drove him from the mountain."[48] Poliʻahu "of the snow white bosom," also translated as "cloaked bosom," is associated with the mountain when covered in snow. While the two lovers were kept from one another, during periods of snow when the sun shines, generally at sunrise and sunset, the rare occurrence is evidence of their lasting embrace. Maly and Maly explain how since the 1960s and the development of the observatory, the recent names of Puʻu Wekiu, Puʻu Hauʻoki, and Puʻu Haukea "have displaced the significant spiritual and cultural values and sense of place associated with the traditional name, Puʻu o Kūkahauʻula."[49] At the top of the puʻu, we left our hoʻokupu and the pūʻolo at an ahu that is routinely dismantled by park rangers. Once settled, from this perch and without direction, we began to oli "E Ala Ē."

E ala ē
Ka lā i ka hikina
I ka moana
I ka moana hohonu
Piʻi ka lewa
Ka lewa nuʻu

I ka hikina
Aia ka lā
E ala ē!

Awaken/Arise
The sun in the east
From the ocean
The ocean deep
Climbing (to) the heaven
The heaven highest
In the east
There is the sun
Awake![50]

It was a beautiful sight: pitch blackness beyond and below gradually giving way to the view of a thick cloud layer covering all we could see, from Hāmākua to Puna. The light of the sun slowly changed the skies from black, to gray, to blue; then a single shot of light pierced the horizon with a glowing but gently emerging white dot. I was overwhelmed by such beauty. We all chanted in unison, and tears followed. I turned to look at the others. Some

Figure 21. First light of sunrise on Mauna a Wākea on the autumnal equinox. From Kūkahau'ula, Maunakea, September 22, 2012. Photograph by the author.

were crying, some stared intently, a few had eyes closed and hands raised; several were holding each other, and all of us were filled with gratitude and reverence. I noticed the shadow that Maunakea casts in its image on the clouds to the west just behind us: an inverted "v," miles away, an illusion of another peak floating in the sky. The Mauna is sacred.

We gathered in a circle. Kealoha Pisciotta and Kaliko Kanaele, a musician, artist, and another longtime kia'i of Mauna a Kea, both offered pule and mana'o (thoughts) about the purpose and significance of the Polohiwa. After some joyful conversation, we headed back to the road.

Several hours later, we descended the summit, driving in silence to the Saddle Road. This was a period of quiet reflection and, for me, a lot to take in. The ceremony was formally pau (concluded) once we turned off the Summit Access Road. I struck up a conversation with another grad student from Harvard also doing research. Kū Ching shared his 'ike about the current efforts to protect the Mauna. Before 2015, whatever might be called "the movement" was mainly confined to courtrooms and hearings, as well as the discursive spaces where written testimony or amicus briefs are received and "community input" is collated, logged, and frequently lost to oblivion. Resistance to telescope development through direct action did not yet exist

Figure 22: Shadow of Kūkahau'ula cast against Hualālai in the western sky at sunrise of the fall equinox. Photograph by the author.

in 2012. As this was several years before the Maunakea Movement would cohere as such, to experience a group whose aloha for the Mauna was manifest through spiritual connection, unencumbered by the casual bureaucratic gaslighting and racism so common in state-sanctioned space, was powerful and empowering. The Polohiwa confirmed in my mind that ceremonial practices conducted on Maunakea are not signs of invented traditions manufactured for the irrational mission of stopping progress and scientific research. They are instead part of a continuum of Kanaka 'Ōiwi relationality to space and place, and to each other.

This, my first visit to the summit, was a learning experience. It also exposed me to what Indigenous resurgence looks like. However, reflecting on the larger struggle with the settler state, big science, and all the money behind the TMT, my feelings of exhilaration were tempered by ambivalence. Here is a hui that drives to the summit at least every three months for the solstices and equinoxes to remind the State they have a kuleana to protect the Mauna because the Mauna cannot defend itself, at least not from industrial development. They bore the expense of fighting the TMT—specifically, the University of Hawai'i and the TMT International Observatory LLC (or TIO)—with far fewer resources and through legal processes designed to alienate them, and to protect the interests of capital and the state. In the courts and at the hearings, the Mauna Kea Hui, of which some in our group were members, had to shapeshift, spending countless hours and energy preparing legal briefs, filing suits, submitting appeals, researching laws and precedence, and building a case: all while holding regular forty-hour-a-week jobs. Yet, they perform these kuleana selflessly. On this huaka'i, I began to understand cultural pilina and praxis is not for the faint of heart or the half-committed but for kia'i whose aloha 'āina runs deep. I also began to understand how these telescopes cannot be understood without some knowledge of their historical context and the relations of power that condition their possibility.

E Ala Ē: The Struggle

Kanaka resistance to telescope expansion is not simply a political theater where cultural nationalists harbor irrational contempt for settlers, government, and economics. The longtime kia'i who fight to protect Mauna a Wākea are defending a very different ontological relationality and knowledge of self, place, and space. It must be understood as a collective response to a long history of settler colonization and U.S. military occupation but also one that is not defined by that history of subjection. The nuances of this Indigenous-led resistance will only become legible through such a lens. Our kū'ē (resistance) emerges as a response to domination and control over our bodies and lands, and the legal and scientific disqualification of Kānaka 'Ōiwi and our knowledge systems. These are not petty grievances or desperate attempts to stop "progress," although these are charges frequently leveled against kia'i. Nor are these selfish and unreasonable reactions disguised as cultural practices. Rather, they are logical responses to the structures of settler colonial governance and economic domination. It is from such an understanding we can make sense of the movement to stop the TMT and recognize how it is just another in a series of injuries. If we are to fully grasp the reasons Kānaka 'Ōiwi are willing to put their bodies on the line to stop another telescope, we must understand the stakes involved for an already subjugated Indigenous people.

Before 2015, the history of violence by which the U.S. acquired Hawai'i and continues to occupy our country was not part of mainstream conversations about Maunakea astronomy. The direct actions on the Mauna and the six-month encampment that blocked construction of the Thirty Meter Telescope in 2015 changed everything. At the time I had completed most of the research for this book, none of the discourses that emerged after the protest camp at Hale Pōhaku[51] and then quickly proliferated existed before 2015. There were no roadblocks, encampments, or sustained critical conversation in popular discourse at all. There were no hashtags or celebrity visits to the Mauna and no chorus of activists focused so intently on Maunakea. What we have seen since 2015 is something of a reawakening of the kū'ē our ancestors in the nineteenth century enacted to stop two attempts by the U.S. to annex Hawai'i.[52] Since 2015 there has been an exponential increase in young people—fluent in our language, culture, and history of struggle— "taking to the streets," or to the Mauna, to demand an end to new telescope development. However, since Maunakea, the movement for life, land, and ea[53] has grown enormously as well because of the Mauna Movement.

The unsettled historical and rightful claims to Hawai'i that Kānaka 'Ōiwi maintain cast a shadow over every conversation regarding land use and resource management in our islands. Likewise, the continued disavowal of Kanaka knowledge systems, which value a different relationality to the summit, has prevailed in the conventional narratives about Maunakea. The ongoing dispossessions and desecrations appear only as minor obstacles in what is imagined as an inevitable march toward "progress." However, this conception of progress would leave Hawaiians for dead, while our stories, language, culture, history, and image are appropriated for the tourist industry and our people alienated from their lands so hotels and golf courses can be built. Because narratives of progress require the absence of alternative realities, our stories of struggle and resistance are central to our future survival.

The astronomy community and supporters of the TMT tout the observatory's potential to answer the oldest existential questions about the origins of the universe and all of us in it—answers that will benefit all humankind. But if Hawaiians are ancient and astronomers are modern, what sort of modernity—what sort of humanity—is this? While imperial science is conflated with modernity and technoscientific achievement imagined as a measure of human worth, in my view the knowledges and lifeways of Kānaka 'Ōiwi emerge as not obstructions to "progress" but as essential to living in better balance.

In many ways, the struggle for Maunakea is also part of a global struggle for freedom from oppression. Though regionally and historically distinct, these movements resonate because of the nature of the violence they confront: from military invasion to settler occupation, extractive and racial capitalism to colonialism and imperialism, forced removals, conquest, slavery, and genocide. These movements speak to one another, look to one another, and often explicitly stand in solidarity with one another across oceans and regional and historical specificity. They reach from Wet'suwet'en to Standing Rock, Kenosha to Bolivia, Syria to Western Sahara, Yemen to Palestine, Amazonia to Rohingya, and beyond. The militarized police response to Kanaka 'Ōiwi land and water defenders may not have led to the disappearances or mass executions endured by other Indigenous communities and land-based, decolonial, and anticolonial movements elsewhere, but these struggles are not entirely disconnected either. The point is not that they are identical or in competition with one another but that movements centering Native and colonized peoples' rights to life, land, freedom, self-determination, and return look to and learn from one another—and in this we can find our way to solidarity. One theme shared across these movements is the desire to protect ancestral places and Indigenous relations to space and community; however, to do this, another shared goal is to live free from oppression, violence, and structures of domination. In

Hawai'i, Maunakea is only part of a broader movement for life, land, and ea. And because of that larger context, Mauna a Wākea has looked toward and resonates with the Oceti Ŝakowiŋ struggle against the Dakota Access Pipeline in 2016, the Black Lives Matter Movement since 2013 and the feminist abolitionist struggle against racial capitalism and its surveillance and carceral oppressions, the long-standing Palestinian liberation struggle for their right to return and to end the Israeli occupation and settler colonial apartheid violence, and the many other resistance and internationalist movements around the world.

My Intervention and Methods

In the chapters that follow, I examine the politics of Maunakea telescopes and the subjectivities, subjugations, and struggles that contextualize the conflict. I argue the forms of power that operate in permitting astronomy expansion on the Mauna are emblematic of the broader context of settler colonialism in Hawai'i.

I anticipate this work will likely be challenged for not treating Kānaka 'Ōiwi with the same degree of scrutiny as astronomy expansionists or the campaign to build the TMT. However, I would contend that there is no shortage of scrutiny of Hawaiians, our politics, and our understanding of stewardship of these islands. Indeed, in popular discourse and corporate media, particularly around the issue of telescope expansion on the Mauna, it has become common to frame these politics in ways that invoke tropes about Kanaka indigeneity and political praxis that suggest Native-led direct action is illegitimate, inauthentic, and unreasonable, or simply "political" and, therefore, disingenuous. The only way to understand Kanaka indigeneity and our relationships to ancestral places—and the reasons we struggle in their defense—is to understand why our ancestral knowledges become articulated to our politics through collective action. In chapter 7, however, I do critique the narratives of three Kānaka, *not because* they are Kanaka, but because the rhetoric that animates their advocacy for the project sanitizes or trades in colonial ideologies that underpin settler state land use and policy and the legal alienation of Kanaka from 'āina. Indeed, Kānaka 'Ōiwi are not a monolith, and I certainly do not speak on behalf of all of us. However, this work tells a story of 'Ōiwi struggle under settler colonialism and U.S. imperial occupation on which the TMT is predicated.

Therefore, my analysis in the pages ahead employs an anticolonial critique that takes seriously Indigenous knowledges. While they are no less rational, rigorous, dynamic, contradictory, or incomplete than any other, the legitimacy of Indigenous articulations of being, belonging, and liberation must be measured not by the standards of European Enlightenment and Western science, or the economic imperatives of settler racial capitalism. Instead, 'Ōiwi politics must be understood according to 'Ōiwi knowledge systems, epistemologies, and legacies of resistance. To this end, the book examines narrative practices and discourses of settler science, law, and capital that operationalize the ongoing colonization of Hawai'i and Hawaiians, as well as the expansive ways kia'i imagine a future beyond white heteropatriarchal imperial settler racial capitalism.

Every discourse on Mauna a Wākea is always already political simply by virtue of the fact they are conditioned on the material reality of settler colonization under U.S. occupation. It is not that Kānaka 'Ōiwi are suddenly using Hawaiian culture to obstruct "progress" but that the ideologies and institutional state apparatuses they confront have rendered the continuation of any Indigenous thought and praxis *a political act.* In other words, the structures that hierarchize difference according to logics of possession, extraction, and dominion over life are not natural or inevitable but instead require constant violence. They are made and remade.

For example, in an episode of the *Viceland* docuseries on global indigeneities called *Rise,* one Kanaka TMT supporter, Kristin Kahaloa, echoes the idea, however inadvertently, that 'Ōiwi knowledge is unscientific. By repeating a conception of "coexistence" that is historically enmeshed with the ideological binary that presumes science exists outside of culture, Kahaloa responds to a question about Hawaiians who believe the TMT would desecrate the Mauna. She reasons that

> Maunakea is definitely sacred. All Native Hawaiians believe that, but I also think we believe that science and culture can co-exist—that the mountain won't be desecrated. It's—yes, something *is being* built there, but it is for *science.* If a hotel was going up on the mountain, then, of course, I would agree that that would be desecration of the mountain.[54]

For some, there is only one proper science, what critical STS scholars distinguish as capital-S "Science"—a form of science presented as neutral, disinterested, value free, and benign, but that is indebted to imperialism and dominion over life in accordance to patriarchal and capitalist hierarchies of difference and being. The implied critique of this rhetoric is that *some* Hawaiians cannot accept the possibility of coexistence of science and culture. They cannot be reasoned with, for they are unreasonable; lacking a capacity for reason. This notion of "coexistence" also suggests science and culture are wholly discrete categories; as if scientists do not reflect the cultures within which they practice their science. I might instead argue that the precolonial lifeways of Kānaka Hawaiʻi (what often is reduced to "culture") *were inherently scientific.* At the very least, they unquestionably honored coexistence, but this conception of coexistence was not conditioned on a tolerance of degrees of destruction, as is the coexistence required of the TMT. How else might our ancestors have cared for these islands and so generously preserved them for the sake of future generations, if not through *coexisting with the more-than-human world?* The problem with pro-TMT advocacy that rationalizes the privilege with which scientific communities are afforded today is that any preexisting notion of coexistence fundamentally threatens that very privilege, and therefore the hierarchies of being on which it depends must be ignored. Put simply, a precolonial conception of coexistence is not the type of coexistence that benefits industrial astronomy on Maunakea.

The conventional rhetoric of coexistence suggests there is a proper science, which derives from white histories alone insofar as it descends exclusively from a European experience. This is an idealistic, imperial science, or Science, however, that is neither weighed down by culture nor accountable to questions of colonial history, let alone social equity. Indeed, it is a science thought to exist independently of culture and history. This Science exists *outside of culture*, a perfectly timeless, apolitical instrument. The implication of this science suggests that *what Hawaiians do* is not science but something inferior. Such a distinction, however, only makes sense when big science is fetishized and Kanaka ʻŌiwi epistemologies are trivialized. This science feigns neutrality. The world simply exists *out there.* Scientists doing proper science, or Science—like astronomers on Maunakea—are merely observing the world around us. I argue, however, the narrative and discursive practices of this form of science do not simply reveal the world as it exists but instead endeavor to shape the world according to the cultural imperatives of the scientific settler state. Likewise, the ideologies it conceals, abides, and reproduces seek to discipline the world according to a single universal reality to which Science alone has access.

In the name of "coexistence," industrial development gets a pass. We are gaslighted at every turn. While its terms are left invisible and unnamed, like the air we breathe, the expectation to "coexist" in my view functions as a reentrenchment of liberal multicultural egalitarianism: it disciplines difference such that white heteropatriarchal settler capitalism and imperialism are treated as self-evident and contemporary expressions of Kanaka indigeneity articulated to political action toward collective liberation is recast as self-indulgent, self-righteous, and excessive. In other words, understanding this liberal multicultural notion of coexistence requires we ask: On whose terms are we to coexist? As the term is manipulated to diminish our ability to recognize social relations of power, Hawaiians become interpellated as obstructions to not only science but also to modernity and humanity itself.[55]

In our interview, kumu hula, educator, and longtime kiaʻi, Pua Case, explained the position she, her ʻohana, and the other petitioners in the contested case hearing took in their fight against the TMT permit in 2011. She makes the point that "we're not anti-science, we're anti-another building. It could be a hospital up there: that's not the point."[56] The problem *is not just* that they want to build another telescope but that they want to build *anything* on the summit. The kiaʻi view any form of development on the Mauna to be a desecration, an act of violence against Kānaka ʻŌiwi and a violation of the environmental ethic and cultural ethos of care and kuleana. I asked about the now-popular claims made by many in public statements, testimonies, TMT promotional materials, and news media that the TMT is in Hawaiians' collective interest. The argument suggests that if Hawaiians *really knew* their own history, they would appreciate the connections between "ancient Hawaiians" and "modern astronomers," forsake their petty jealousies, and lend their support to the TMT. It also follows that because of a presumed shared practice of star knowledge, the TMT is not only a common benefit but is also *very Hawaiian*. Case addresses the violence of such an argument:

You know?! No use our kūpuna for your ends. Our kūpuna would never destroy, in order to advance—destroy their environment like that . . . I think the parts that make me sad is when they say things about how they know the mountain is sacred to us, or important and significant—that they realize there is cultural significance and how much they *love* that mountain. And in the next breath, [they say] 'but we're still going to build on it.[57]

Case also expressed the pain felt when the university invokes the culture-versus-science binary and the feigned appreciation for Kanaka relationality to the Mauna in the contested case:

When you talk to two sides like that, that makes me sad because it's then I know that we still have a long way to go. Because usually, if you gonna say all that, you gonna follow that with, "so therefore you're right, we cannot do that. Because it is a temple. It is sacred." A lot of them will say this. It's in their brochures. But when you say all that and in the next breath, you say, "ooh, but on top of that place, we still gonna do this [build the Thirty Meter Telescope]." That makes me know that we are still going to be going on for the long haul.[58]

The simultaneous recognition and disavowal of Indigenous knowledge characteristic of the violence inherent to multicultural liberalism incites Pua Case's activism. For many kiaʻi, the TMT represents just another violation in a long list of encroachments by military, capitalist, and state interests, invasions that have defined the last 130 years of U.S. occupation.

As mentioned briefly in the introduction, the research process for this project has helped shape my analysis of settler coloniality and power in Hawaiʻi beyond Mauna a Wākea. As a Kanaka ʻŌiwi researcher, writer, and teacher, the process has also strengthened my commitments to the struggle of our lāhui for the betterment of our people, the health of our ancestral lands, and the independence of our country.

This book is the culmination of over a decade of research that involved participant observation, oral history interviews, archival data collection, and discourse analysis of key events, social structures, and relationships that inform the Maunakea Movement as well as the broader history of Kanaka struggles for life, land, and ea. In researching this book, I conducted several dozen informal interviews and forty formal interviews. I offer textual analyses of them as well as oral histories of kamaʻāina to Maunakea, telescope management plans, environmental impact statements, written testimonies, the State legislative audits of the University of Hawaiʻi's management of the summit, transcripts of hearings and meetings, and various mele (songs) and moʻolelo (stories) that speak to the ways in which Kanaka relations to kūpuna o ka pō and places, and a range of obligations come to frame Mauna a Wākea as "sacred." I decided early on to limit the scope of this project to focus my interviews mainly on Kānaka ʻŌiwi, though from a range of positions on the Maunakea observatory, including those who support the TMT project. One lesson I gleaned from this seeming contradiction that we don't all oppose the TMT is that Kānaka ʻŌiwi are anything but monolithic. It is important not to think of our communities as homogenous or unified in resistance, not only because it is inaccurate but also because all stereotypes function according to dehumanizing logics by leveling difference. I find that confronting our contradictions reveals not our flaws but our strengths, as well as a deeper understanding of the stakes of our politics. While I have been studying Maunakea since about 2009 and Kānaka Maoli resistance to settler colonial occupation and militarism for close to thirty years, I am no expert. However, I have interviewed experts— the kiaʻi whose lives are intwined with the Mauna. I have recorded their words and ideas, and presented them with a commitment to accuracy and care but also with a sustained critical analysis of power.

To this end, I am not concerned with the personal character of my interlocutors, but I am interested in their narrative practices and the ideologies they reflect and replicate. How do the knowledge and belief systems we take most for granted *question* or *reproduce* the social relations of power that structure our lives? Under what circumstances might they do both? In my view, the answers point to the urgency for us, as Kānaka ʻŌiwi, to hold each other *and ourselves* accountable while maintaining a critical posture toward power that is principled and unapologetic.

For now, my scholarship is how I am best able to express my commitment to movements for liberation and decolonization. In my view, it is our very humanity, our ancestral homeland, and our future generations that are at stake. Indeed, too few of us have access to a platform from which to write ourselves back into history as fully realized modern subjects. In conducting this research, I have learned that I cannot *not* take a stance. When writing about knowledge and social relations of power that structure Kanaka subjugation, there are no *two sides*. In considering the colonial logics of Native elimination, there is no *fair and balanced* reporting. While I embrace and aspire to the principles of academic objectivity, I also recognize objectivity is only ever aspirational. To stage a conversation that disrupts power is to think critically about the oppressive terms of legibility that render Kānaka 'Ōiwi suspect and disqualified. To this end, I endeavor to compose a sustained and self-reflexive critical analysis of the interlocking forms of power that subject our people but that are nevertheless always met with resistance. Admittedly, it won't be for everybody. I do not feign neutrality nor claim omniscience, but I do critique power. To be a member of a community that continues to be treated as inferior under white heteropatriarchal settler capitalism and U.S. imperialism is to be always already a politicized subject. From this position I examine and celebrate the aloha 'āina movement for its determined commitment to liberation and decolonization by reclaiming our collective voice and our humanity.

Therefore, I also engage a complex and paradoxical reality that not all Kānaka 'Ōiwi are unified against the TMT, and not all non-Hawaiians endorse industrial astronomy on Maunakea, which I discuss in chapter 7. While the book explores Indigenous thought and praxis, it also rejects the settler demand to render our indigeneity legible to everyone—an expectation that often functions as a mode of control. In this regard, it also seeks to disrupt colonial discourses that assert authority to set conditions of future possibility for Kānaka 'Ōiwi, particularly in ways that certain knowledges are determined legitimate and others targeted for deletion. As such, the book also seeks an audience with the patience to consider the alterity, testimony, and ambivalence of Kānaka 'Ōiwi, and to proceed with care. It may be unsurprising that many Hawaiians identify proudly as "American," despite what I have said already about U.S. empire. However, this book is for anyone interested in thinking deeply through such contradictions and discourses about power, indigeneity, and resistance in Hawai'i. It is an invitation to anyone skeptical or curious about the Maunakea Movement. It is for those who are down to lock arms to block bulldozers. However, it is also for anyone with aloha for Kānaka 'Ōiwi and Indigenous lifeways, particularly those with a commitment to models of coexistence that presuppose consensual relationality, rather than a hierarchy of humanity.

Just as Kanaka 'Ōiwi cultural praxis and political activism are always interwoven, kia'i articulate Indigenous epistemologies and ceremony to decolonial struggle as an expression of our critical relationality to Mauna a Wākea that looks to the past as much as the future. In this way, the movement is about protection of place and space as a means of assuring future possibility. As cultural practices are always already complex and contradictory, but no less legitimate or rational for that reason, Indigenous spiritual praxis must be understood on its own terms. Kānaka ʻŌiwi indigeneity, relationality, and subjectivities are fluid and political, not because they are invented or inauthentic—or grasping for legitimacy through contrived invocations of the past—but because the structures of domination within which Kanaka alterity becomes a threat to settler hegemony have conditioned social relations as hierarchical and oppressive. In response to these hierarchies and oppressions, Kānaka ʻŌiwi are composing our relationality to the natural world as an act of self-determination and radical resurgence, just as our ancestors have always done.

2

NEOLIBERAL ENVIRONMENTALITIES AND MONUMENTS TO SCIENCE

The Myth of Conservation

In Hawaiʻi, a history of contradictory land designations and patchwork state policies around land use, conservation, and Native rights have left the summit of Maunakea irreparably disfigured by telescope construction. Exceptions to legal protections have become normalized; the ongoing harm of industrial development is tolerated within a body of laws that, for over a century of capitalist liberal democracy under U.S. military occupation, treats astronomy as worth the collateral damage to the environment and Kānaka Maoli. As a result, large-scale development in a rare and fragile ecosystem and culturally significant place like Mauna a Wākea has become nearly impossible to prohibit. My analysis of this history suggests the State's legal conception of conservation is less about the principles of sustainability than maintaining authority to govern by supporting big science: just as it has with big business. In this chapter I survey the political history of Hawaiʻi as a U.S. imperial possession, with the Mauna Kea Observatories as accomplice and evidence, to explore how this relationship stems from a list of legal abuses that continues to compromise natural environments and alienate Kānaka ʻŌiwi from storied, sacred places.

Take for example, Hawaiʻi Revised Statutes 183, which was passed by Act 187 in 1961, just two years after Hawaiʻi was declared the fiftieth state of the union. This law created the State's four land use districts: Urban, Rural, Agricultural, and Conservation. In 1964, "the State Land Use Commission established the boundaries of the Conservation District that encompassed Mauna Kea," and these lands were to be placed under the "direct purview of the state Board of Land and Natural Resources."[1] The summit of Maunakea would be assigned to a new classification within the Conservation District called the "resource subzone." One of five subzones—including protective, limited, general, and special—the resource subzone accommodated a specific land use already in practice: astronomy. Though it is said to be "the most restrictive" of the five land use classifications, the resource subzone allows "commercial forestry" and "mining and extraction" in addition to telescope development. Exactly how such land use is "restrictive" or aligned with any practical notion of conservation is unclear to many, but the accommodation enables the state to treat the proposed Thirty Meter Telescope project as "consistent with the purpose of the conservation district." This contradiction between the "purpose" and principles of conservation was reconciled over the next three decades. HRS 183 provides that the purpose of the Conservation District is "to conserve, protect and preserve the important natural resources of the State through appropriate management and use to promote their long-term sustainability and the public health, safety and welfare."[2] However, HRS 183C, which created the subzone classifications and explicitly names "astronomy facilities" as a permissible land use within the Conservation District, only became law through Act 270 in 1994—that is, thirty-two years after the creation of the Conservation District. HRS 183C, which purported to "provide greater detail of DLNR's duties and powers in regulation of the Conservation District," in practice, functioned to retroactively create a means by which telescopes could be determined "consistent" with conservation. In other words, while Act 270 passed three decades after the first telescope was built, rather than conserving the integrity of lands meant to be protected, this law rationalizes an otherwise inconsistent land use after the fact.

Just as tourism has become hegemonic in Hawai'i, so too has its neoliberal conditions of possibility. In contrast to classical liberalism, which sought degrees of autonomy for market economies, neoliberalism seeks the infiltration of market philosophies into every aspect of society. Rather than promoting those philosophies, neoliberalism creates a "social reality that it suggests already exists."[3] Robert Fletcher's adaptation of Foucault's "governmentality" is instructive when considering how 'āina was transformed into "land" and commodity and "resource" within a state conservation policy that reproduces competing environmental strategies (or "environmentalities") that clash over appropriate land and natural resource management strategy. Neoliberal governmentality refers to ways in which biopower[4] operates as an exercise of authority not over the internal state of subjects but rather "the external structures within which they act."[5] Concerned less with employing disciplinary techniques to shape behavior, neoliberal governmentality involves hegemonic interventions in everyday life through incentive structures that determine degrees of agency to produce specified outcomes that privilege or enfranchise some but not others. Profoundly interventionist, the neoliberal state incentivizes subjects to behave as rational actors seeking individual self-interest and profit through enterprise and competition as a way of everyday life. In this way, neoliberalism not only refers to market rationality as the model of social life, but as a governing rationality it has become the raison d'être of settler environmentalism. Under these conditions, laws are written and interpreted in ways to reconcile the state's ideals of conservation with its contradictory practices of exploitation. With regard to the state government's land use and resource management practices, one consequence for Kānaka Maoli is what Lauren Berlant calls a "slow death," which is "the physical wearing out of a population and the deterioration of people in that population that is very nearly a defining condition of their experience and historical existence."[6] According to Fletcher, within the "zone of ordinariness" that neoliberal environmentality produces, "life building and the attrition of human life are indistinguishable." In the context of Maunakea and other sites of struggle in Hawai'i, it becomes difficult to distinguish "modes of incoherence, distractedness, and habituation from deliberate and deliberative activity." For this reason, environmental policy that allows astronomy expansion may be understood as a function of biopolitical structures that condition the social and cultural life of Kānaka Maoli according to the interventionist habits and extractive logics of settler capitalism, sociality, and statecraft.

In this chapter I argue that the history of Hawai'i as a settler colony of the United States conditions the terms of land use just as it has the very possibility of observatories at Maunakea in the first place.[7] In this context, the imposition of settler legal structures may be understood as both a condition and function of U.S. military occupation, particularly in how it normalizes and exploits scientific language, communities, and practices to undermine Indigenous valuations of place and space. To that end, the chapter examines legal categories and processes against analysis of the incommensurability of Kanaka 'Ōiwi relations to 'āina and settler dominion over land. This analysis and a timeline provide context for later discussion of the stakes for the settler state and the Mauna Movement in decisions on framing TMT politics. Before turning to a survey of the patchwork system of policy by which land became available for development, I should begin with some background on popular uses of Maunakea and its value to supporters of astronomy expansion.

Timeline of Maunakea Telescopes and Settler Valuations

Maunakea is a dormant volcano in the northern region of Hawai'i Island: in the ahupua'a[8] of Humu'ula and Ka'ohe in the moku of Hilo and Hāmākua, respectively.[9] The observatories sit mainly on a "summit plateau" in Ka'ohe where the ahupua'a meets Humu'ula to the east and southeast. As the tallest mountain in all of Oceania, Maunakea receives snowfall almost every year and is the only tropical alpine desert in the world. Below the summit is Keanakāko'i, the largest stone adze quarry in the Pacific, which dates to at least the thirteenth century. Also near the summit sits Lake Waiau, a body of water at such an unusual elevation that it continues to stump scientists as to how it formed and why it does not drain.[10] The summit is also one of only two locations inhabited by the rare wēkiu bug, currently "a candidate for listing under the Endangered Species Act."[11] From sea level, the mountain reaches to 13,796 feet (4,205 meters) in elevation. Measured from ocean floor to summit peak, at 33,474 feet (9,750 meters),[12] Maunakea is the tallest mountain on Earth.

Since 1968, the University of Hawai'i (UH) has held a sixty-five-year lease to three large areas on Maunakea's summit for astronomy purposes. Initially, leased lands consisted of all those above 9,200 feet but today include everything above 11,500 feet. The largest of the so-called UH Management Areas is the "Mauna Kea Science Reserve" (MKSR; also, the "Mauna Kea Observatory"), in which telescope development has currently been limited to a 525-acre parcel called the "Astronomy Precinct." UH also manages the "Mauna Kea Access Road"[13] that connects the Astronomy Precinct to the 19.3-acre Hale Pōhaku at 9,300 feet. For use of 11,288 acres,[14] the University of Hawai'i pays a nominal $1 per year to the State of Hawai'i in rent.

At 9,300 feet, the Institute for Astronomy's Mid-Level Facilities include the Onizuka Center for International Astronomy, the Visitor Information Station, and a gift shop called the Maunakea First Light Bookstore. Tour groups and amateur stargazers observe from the visitor center on clear nights, and most days tourists ascend to photograph the sunrises and sunsets while others play, sled, and snowboard when there is snow. Originally built as a construction laborer camp and equipment staging site,[15] the living quarters at Hale Pōhaku are "reminiscent of a moderate-sized alpine hotel," where astronomers and technicians stay for longer periods to avoid having to acclimatize each day before resuming work and dealing with the summit's extreme elevation.[16]

The State of Hawai'i's Department of Land and Natural Resources (DLNR) is tasked with enforcing conservation rules for the protection of specific areas on the mountain. In exchange for its lease, the university is responsible for the management of the Mauna Kea Science Reserve. According to the university's 1980 Master Plan, 95 percent of the MKSR was designated a Natural/Cultural Preserve Area in recognition of the need to protect the "natural and cultural resources" of the mountain.[17] The entire summit used to be known as the "Mauna Kea Ice Age Natural Reserve," but this area designation was reduced in the 1990s to exclude the Mauna Kea Observatories and distinguish the management responsibilities of UH from the State of Hawai'i. The entire MKSR falls within the State Conservation District.

For over fifty years UH has subleased portions of the summit to institutions responsible for the construction and maintenance of the nine optical/infrared telescopes,[18] the three submillimeter observatories, and the radio antenna array, which consists of eight 20 ft. (6 m.) dishes.[19] These instruments are owned and operated by a variety of national and scientific institutions, sometimes comprising international partnerships or government-funded ministries of science and research councils, nonprofit organizations, associations, coalitions, and interuniversity research institutes and centers. These entities sublet the lands on which their observatories sit from the University of Hawai'i. Most comprise multiple scientific and educational institutions that combine resources to fund the manufacture of telescope parts and the construction of the telescopes, domes, and adjacent facilities. What are referred to as the mountain's "cultural," "historic," "biological," and "environmental resources" have been points of controversy since around the late 1980s, especially as more construction has invited more scrutiny from environmental and Native Hawaiian rights advocates. Concerns include the mountain's ecological integrity, namely the condition of endemic plant species and insect and animal populations and habitat, as well as "cultural properties" related to Hawaiian "spiritual and religious practices." Grassroots activists have called on the university to better manage public and commercial activities—particularly as visitors and tour companies commonly litter, overcrowd the summit, and mistreat cultural sites and sensitive natural areas. Early demands for decommissioning older telescopes have increased since the direct action in 2015. Since the summer of 2024, Caltech has decommissioned its Submillimeter Observatory and UH Hilo decommissioned its Hōkū Keʻa Observatory.[20] Although many tons of steel, iron, concrete, plastics, chemicals, waste, debris, and other materials were removed, it is doubtful these two sites have been fully restored to their earlier condition. However, there is no doubt that the initiative to decommission and remove these observatories was the result of the sustained community direct actions of 2015 and 2019 and the decades of organizing that preceded them. The sixty-five-year lease expires in 2033 and, as the TMT depends on continued access, its renewal has been the subject of legal proceedings and much debate.

The community that supports astronomy expansion is just as diverse as the opposition, and many are also Kānaka ʻŌiwi, a seeming contradiction I explore in chapter 7. A common habit is to rehearse the summit's physical attributes as justification for another telescope. The rhetoric suggests these qualities outrank the environmental or cultural concerns of TMT opponents. People repeat the common list: Maunakea has atmospheric, geographic, topographical, climatic, and geological features "found no place else on Earth." Maunakea possesses a combination of low precipitation, low mean temperature, atmospheric stability, frequent clear nights, and high altitude.[21] Since Maunakea is a shield volcano in one of the most remote places in the world, airstreams have thousands of miles of undisturbed travel before reaching Hawaiʻi's shores, creating "smooth laminar flows,"[22] which greatly reduces atmospheric turbulence and light distortions. Capturing views of the northern sky that telescopes on summits south of the equator cannot, Maunakea is simply the best place on Earth to do ground-based observations.

Such practices suggest a very narrow understanding of what constitutes the exceptional, as if the Mauna's physical attributes render self-evident the urgency and mandate to build the TMT. A politics of delineation, the ritual disciplines the very terms of value to privilege the seemingly more objective relations of Western scientific practice and also favored within legal discourse. So long as the prevailing conservation models restrict the summit's value to a logic of technoscientific instrumentalism, alternative epistemes about Mauna a Wākea can be dismissed as unscientific, inferior, and political. This is the substance of the mythical global hierarchy of peoples and knowledges. In other words, while empirical knowledge is assumed inherently superior, repetition of the summit's measurable qualities restricts what other relations can be imagined.

Yet, these recitations serve to capture a very specific public imagination, one groomed through Hollywood sci-fi television and film and nearly a century of "space age" pop culture. As popular support for the project has come to depend on these shared imaginaries, TMT promotions and justifications tend to invoke frontier adventure, otherworldly discovery, and technological innovation using common tropes that normalized European colonization and westward expansion across Turtle Island throughout the nineteenth century. In such ways, capturing imaginations is paramount to not only shoring up support for another "world-class" telescope but also paying for it. The TMT relies on public and private funding channeled through federal agencies like the National Science Foundation, state universities, and scientific institutions within the five partner countries, and philanthropic donors like the Gordon & Betty Moore Foundation. And so the ideological certainty of empiricism instills not only investor confidence but a more ephemeral assurance about Western scientific knowledge and praxis that comforts a society on whose approval the TMT depends. This is why the project is also presented as an existential imperative. Astronomers are not merely recording celestial patterns but are also searching for answers to the world's oldest question: Where do we come from? As such imaginaries inform how Hawai'i and Hawaiians will be managed, they also provide insight on how astronomers have become "stewards" of Mauna a Wākea and Kānaka 'Ōiwi obstructions to progress: a self-serving mythology that has rendered 'āina available for settlement for over a century.

Whose Lands?

Hawai'i's legal status as an independent nation-state has been one of the most distorted aspects of its historiography. In 1843, Hawai'i's independence was recognized through dozens of treaties with countries around the world, including the U.S., Great Britain, and France.[23] Most U.S. citizens do not know this, do not believe it, or are indifferent to the fact, if they were ever exposed to Hawai'i's history at all. While neither private nor public education in the U.S. teach this history, several details are relevant to my analysis of the controversy over the TMT because they inform conventional beliefs about Hawai'i as the fiftieth state of the union and popular framings of Maunakea politics. Indeed, not only has Hawai'i's legal status been excluded from conventional historiography, the omission itself conditions modern Hawai'i as a capitalist settler state and U.S. imperial possession. To understand how astronomers became stewards of Maunakea and Kānaka 'Ōiwi and our allies became obstacles to progress, the history matters.

Kō Hawai'i Pae 'Āina, the Hawaiian kingdom,[24] emerged as a democratic nation-state in a time when "democracy" was only a nascent idea in most countries.[25] Hawai'i had established a declaration of rights by 1839 and extended to maka'āinana a place in the political process through its first constitution in 1840. It developed a bicameral legislative system in which all citizens could vote to elect members to the House of Representatives. A constitutional convention was held every twelve years, legislative enactments were passed on every even year, and the compilation of legislative laws with judicial decisions refined and defined the constitution.[26] Of its most significant achievements, the kingdom, by midcentury, became one of the first countries to transition to constitutional governance without bloodshed.

On January 16, 1893, a conspiring group of white businessmen—some kingdom citizens, others of foreign citizenship—colluded with the U.S. foreign minister, John L. Stevens, with the assistance of U.S. naval troops stationed at Honolulu Harbor, in arresting government officials, military forces, and the head of state, Queen Lili'uokalani, under the auspices of protecting "American lives and property."[27] A convenient if outlandish ploy to relive frontier dispossession, the stunt was denounced by President Grover Cleveland and members of Congress who, within several months, commissioned James H. Blount to lead an investigation of the events leading up to the invasion by U.S. troops, which found the aggressions toward a friendly country had led to U.S. violations of domestic and international laws.[28] Upon reading the Blount Report, President Cleveland famously and accurately named the unprovoked actions of the United States naval forces against the country of Hawai'i an "act of war."[29]

The conspirators initially sought annexation, but their efforts were thwarted when then-president Cleveland pulled the treaty back from Congress. This first attempt at annexation forced the conspirators to pursue new tactics to shield themselves from persecution for sedition should the United States abide by its own laws and restore Hawai'i's sovereign government.

From 1893 to 1898, while the U.S. Congress was split over how to proceed, Hawai'i citizens organized, launched a civil war, and staged petition drives, among myriad other acts of resistance—but justice never arrived. Some U.S. legislators with imperial ambitions saw Hawai'i as a prize, while others preferred a posture of nonintervention; many also exploited racist fears, arguing against annexation to avoid the "mainland" being flooded with nonwhite immigrants. As a conflicted Congress would neither restore Hawai'i's government nor annex the islands to admit Hawai'i as a state, during these five years the first and second treaty attempts would mark the beginning of a prolonged U.S. occupation of an independent state.

Amidst the uncertainty and indecision, the conspirators quickly refashioned themselves as the so-called Republic of Hawaii and seized power through acquiring the country's small armory and other armaments, but the U.S. military never left. President Cleveland's second term would end in 1897, enabling a hawkish William McKinley to disregard the U.S. constitution and treaty laws with Hawai'i's government. With the change of administrations and imperial designs on a new geopolitical possession in the middle of the Pacific, the U.S. set out to justify the occupation. A second attempt at legal annexation failed when a movement of aloha 'āina (patriots),[30] loyal to their country, organized a campaign of mass protests and petitions signed by tens of thousands, all of which effectively prevented Congress from ratifying an 1897 treaty of annexation.[31] Yet, as the U.S. waged war on Spain to acquire the Philippines, Congress devised justification through a rhetoric of military necessity. Passing a legislative act as self-authorizing theater, the "Newlands Resolution" was a domestic law with no legal effect outside of U.S. jurisdictional borders but was nevertheless held up as if it possessed the legal authority of a treaty.[32] That it does not possess this authority has never been directly addressed by the U.S. government. Over a century and a quarter later, the Newlands Resolution is cited by apologists and the ill-informed, including authors of conventional historiography and the official legal record. An example of the lasting effects of the annexation mythology is President Bill Clinton's 1993 so-called Apology Resolution, which ultimately served as an opportunity to further distort the record by acknowledging "the role of the United States" in "the overthrow of the kingdom of Hawaii" (not the "invasion" and subsequent "occupation" of an independent state) and apologizing to "Native Hawaiians" (instead of Hawai'i "citizens").[33] In 1899, Congress invented a new category and would call Hawai'i its "territory," discursively rationalizing its occupation. As a consequence of the historical amnesia and prevailing ignorance about the legal status of the Hawaiian state, the prospect of justice and liberation has lingered in constant states of deferral.

Authors of the established narrative have ignored, omitted, and misrepresented this legal history by refusing to learn the Hawaiian language or to cite the vast archive of Kanaka 'Ōiwi voices, effectively excusing and concealing the persistence of U.S. imperial occupation today. This archive, however—comprising hundreds of thousands of pages of newspapers, letters, and a variety of monographs composed in the native language throughout the nineteenth century—illustrates the extent to which Kō Hawai'i Pae 'Āina was a thriving democracy. It also attests to the sacred pilina 'āina, relations to land, that Kānaka 'Ōiwi have as well as the dynamic nature of Indigenous political thought and praxis. Yet, because of systematic erasure, most Americans know nothing of how the U.S. "acquired" the islands, let alone how the land on which telescopes were built became available in the first place.

The Mauna Kea Observatories were built on lands that, at one time or another, have been designated "ceded lands," "public lands," "trust lands," and "Conservation District lands" among others. Prior to the start of U.S. occupation in 1898, private owners shared control of lands across the islands with the kingdom's royal families and elected government.[34] Historically referred to as "Crown and Government Lands,"[35] since 1900 they have become known as "ceded lands," suggesting they were conveyed to the U.S. by some legal mechanism. Because they were not, it is more accurate to call them "seized lands." While all Hawai'i citizens were affected by the U.S. invasion, the steady alienation of Kānaka 'Ōiwi from their ancestral lands over more than twelve decades of U.S. occupation, and the reconfiguration of social relations to lands that this alienation imposed, has distinct implications for Hawai'i's Indigenous people.

A portion of these so-called ceded lands became part of the Hawaiian Home Lands (HHL) in 1920 through the passage of the Hawaiian Homes Commission Act, which ostensibly set them aside for the "rehabilitation of native Hawaiians"—the lowercase *n* indicating the required minimum 50 percent blood quantum to qualify for homestead eligibility. Portions of

Mauna a Wākea are also a part of the HHL land base. Coming under control of the newly styled "Territory of Hawaii" in 1900, the Crown and Government Lands were never adequately catalogued and, as a consequence of the imposition of foreign governance, hundreds of thousands of acres were illegally transferred to the U.S. military and private interests capitalizing on a nascent tourist economy and incessant growth throughout the twentieth century. Hawai'i lands essentially became the spoils of imperial invasion and military occupation, transferred under U.S. hegemony to the so-called Republic of Hawaii, then to the "Territory of Hawaii," and finally the "State of Hawaii."[36] When Congress passed the Hawaii Admissions Act in 1959, most of the ceded lands became public lands of the State of Hawai'i.

Public lands have since become a lucrative and indispensable source of revenue for the State, but according to the Statehood Act and Hawai'i State constitution, portions of the ceded lands were to be "held in trust" for the "benefit of native Hawaiians" and, through constitutional amendments in 1978, for the betterment of "Native Hawaiians." Note, the capital N signals a new category of "Native Hawaiian" and another phase in the racialization of Kānaka 'Ōiwi. The new category not only further distorts the legal identity of an ethnically diverse Hawaiian kingdom citizenry, as opposed to an ethnic national citizenry, but it also undermines Kanaka indigeneity in the era of the United Nations Declaration on the Rights of Indigenous Peoples by obstructing Kanaka 'Ōiwi self-determination.[37] More disconcerting, however, is that the state presupposes its own jurisdiction in that the discursive enables the material—that is, in the narrative of "holding" expropriated lands as a "Public Land Trust"—through retroactive and self-referential iteration of a legally impossible land conveyance. While the "betterment of native Hawaiians" may appear altruistic or reconciliatory, it is condescending and self-serving because the purpose of reclassifying Hawai'i as "territory" then "state" was ultimately about concealing a military occupation and violations of international law. In other words, the rhetoric of settler law creates a social reality that it pretends simply to name through a practice of recursive citation. Accordingly, a logic of Native elimination reduced eligibility for HHL allotments, such that Kānaka 'Ōiwi determined to be below the arbitrary and pernicious 50 percent blood quantum threshold might *legally disappear,* or at least be absorbed into an increasingly multicultural settler society invested in becoming or being American in Hawai'i and a logic of possession that defers

Kanaka ʻŌiwi liberation and self-determination, which I discuss in the next chapter.[38]

At the State constitutional convention held in 1978, the Office of Hawaiian Affairs (OHA) was created to serve Kānaka ʻŌiwi who are institutionally racialized as "less than half Hawaiian." The State agency continues to provide "Native Hawaiians" a variety of economic and other services but is limited in its capacity to challenge State policy regarding land use and resource management. Moreover, the State's record of failure regarding its trust obligations to either category of Hawaiian ("native" or "Native") has led to systemic abuses, including the mismanagement of public lands and constant delinquency in payments to OHA owed for State use of the Crown and Government Lands of the Hawaiian kingdom.

For over a century, the U.S. government, an indifferent settler public, the capitalist class, Hawaiʻi State government, and conventional historiography have coconspired a sustained disavowal of an accurate account of this history. However, things appear to be changing. For example, the now common phrase "U.S. occupation" was nonexistent in Hawaiʻi until the critical historical interventions of Hawaiian scholars beginning in the 1990s, and especially following the work of Keanu Sai.[39] What previously was described as "the overthrow of the Hawaiian Monarchy"[40] has been revised as "the U.S. invasion of the Hawaiian kingdom in 1893." Instead of reference to "the Territory of Hawaii," scholars now describe Hawaiʻi as an independent state under prolonged military occupation by the United States. The language matters because the official narrative is purposefully confusing, opaque, and incorrect. That opacity functions as a discursive contribution to the broader strategy of legitimizing an otherwise impossible U.S. jurisdiction in Hawaiʻi, which implicates Maunakea as well. This complex and contradictory assemblage of legal categories and land designations structures the disqualification of Kānaka ʻŌiwi who seek protection of lands, waters, and sacred places like Maunakea. As a distinctly neoliberal environmentality, the marriage of settler capitalism and scientific industry has allowed this legal history to be exploited for over a century of development across the islands. It also facilitates the continued normalization of industrial development in the name of science through legislative policy and judicial decisions. For some it means progress, adventure, and discovery, while for those with a critique of power, it is implicated in a pattern of decisions that leave Hawaiians for dead. Next, I briefly survey the emergence of the Mauna Kea Observatories to analyze how their neoliberal rationality conditions a settler legal system unable to account for Kanaka indigeneity and 'Ōiwi relationality to 'āina and each other.

Making the Mauna Kea Observatories

Beginning with a single 12.5-in. telescope and dome used to test the "seeing" potential of the site in June of 1964, and increasing each decade since, bigger and more expensive and technologically advanced telescopes have proliferated on the summit of Maunakea. The idea for early telescope development on the mountain is credited to Mitsuo Akiyama, an executive secretary of the Hawai'i Island Chamber of Commerce who contacted American and Japanese universities and research organizations in hope of developing Maunakea into an astronomical site, predicting that it may help the local economy following the devastation of a 1960 tsunami in Hilo. Planetary scientist Gerard Kuiper, an astronomer originally from the Netherlands who helped set up the University of Arizona's Lunar and Planetary laboratory, was the only one to respond to Akiyama.[41] By this time, it was becoming apparent that isolated high-elevation sites offered the best conditions for clear observations. Kuiper had spent time in the early 1960s scouting such locations and initially considered Haleakalā,[42] but because of frequent nighttime cloud cover, and noticing that Maunakea was more consistently clear, he eventually became interested in Hawai'i Island. Over half a mile higher than Haleakalā, Mauna Kea was very clear but extremely difficult to access. Kuiper's first site tests convinced him it was a superior location. In April of 1964, a small group of Hawai'i Island County employees,[43] several of their friends, Kuiper, and his assistant[44] began constructing a small telescope and housing structure, using "water from a lake near the summit, Lake Waiau . . . to make cement," for its foundations. Kuiper and his team received modest National Aeronautics and Space Administration (NASA) funds for supplies and equipment, plus $42,000 in State funds gifted from Hawai'i's first State governor, John A. Burns, for a six-mile gravel road to the summit and other construction costs. This first site-testing telescope was completed within three months. The initial observation tests made with the rather small, 0.3-m. (12.5-in.), telescope located atop Pu'u Poli'ahu, convinced Kuiper of just how exceptional Maunakea is for nighttime seeing.[45] It would not be difficult to convince others of the fact.

Over the next few years, Kuiper, representing the University of Arizona, began making plans to secure NASA funding and State approval for a 60-in. telescope. However, the University of Hawaiʻi, led by Haleakalā Observatory director and founding director of the Institute for Astronomy (IfA), John Jeffries, proposed a plan that was selected over Kuiper's proposal, obtaining the NASA funding for their own 88-in. (2.24-m.) telescope, which still stands on the summit today. The winning proposal for the second telescope at Maunakea was said to have been the outcome of "dirty politics."[46] As Barry Parker notes, once NASA selected the proposal for the UH 88-in. telescope and the State of Hawaiʻi made its $2.5 million contribution, "Kuiper couldn't believe it; he was furious. After all he had put into the project, it was a serious blow, and he was bitter about it for years, telling friends and strangers alike that he had discovered Mauna Kea and it had been stolen from him."[47] The idea that Maunakea was "discovered" or "stolen" from an astronomer in Arizona is ironic but also speaks to the prevailing sense of entitlement with which astronomers at this time claimed Maunakea as theirs. That entitlement is also revealed in the rapid growth of the observatory over the next decade.

Jeffries's telescope was completed in 1967. Dedicated and opened in 1970, it was the first fully computer-automated (and eighth-largest) telescope in the world. Kuiper's original 12.5-in. telescope was soon replaced by a University of Hawaiʻi-Hilo 0.9-m. telescope. Ironically, Kuiper initially had to convince the astronomy community that Mauna Kea was superior in atmospheric stability and seeing, while over the next few years attitudes would change dramatically. Soon, other countries became interested in building their own telescopes atop Maunakea, and the University of Hawaiʻi and the State of Hawaiʻi would oblige.

Ground was broken in 1974 for a $30 million, 3.6-m. telescope called Canada-France-Hawaii. During this time, infrastructure at Hale Pōhaku[48] was developed and IfA found its home in Hilo. Jeffries and the IfA defeated the University of Arizona for another contract to build its 3-m. NASA Infrared Telescope. Great Britain started their own 3.8-m. Infrared Telescope (UKIT) in 1975 on a shoestring budget of $5 million. All three telescopes were dedicated in 1979, while a deal was being negotiated between the Netherlands and Great Britain to build a $9 million, 15-m. telescope, the James Clerk Maxwell Telescope, which inspired the California Institute of

Technology (Caltech) and National Science Foundation to build its 10.4-m. Caltech Submillimeter Observatory. By 1987, eight large telescopes dotting the skyline along Maunakea's summit could now be seen all the way from Hilo.

Throughout the 1990s development continued. Started in 1986 and finished in 1993, the Very Long Baseline Array, a radio-telescope antennae system spanning ten sites around the world, made Maunakea home to one of its 25-m. dishes. Also in 1993, Caltech and the University of California's W. M. Keck Observatory (Keck I) "saw first light," followed three years later by its "twin," Keck II.[49] Japan completed the 8.3 m. Subaru Telescope in 1999. That same year saw the dedication of the Gemini Northern Telescope, a partnership between the United States, United Kingdom, Canada, Argentina, Australia, Brazil, and Chile. Then, the Smithsonian Astrophysical Observatory, in partnership with Taiwan, completed its Submillimeter Array in 2002, which comprises eight 6-m. dishes across the north end of the summit plateau. Although the Submillimeter Array consists of eight dishes, the university counts these mobile telescopes as a single "observatory," reducing the official count recognized by the Board of Land and Natural Resources from twenty-one to thirteen.

There were no legal restrictions placed on development or regulation of the permitting processes for new telescope projects during the first decade of Maunakea astronomy. Although the Conservation District had existed since 1961, its purpose was vague. Moreover, as outlined in the beginning of the chapter, the political designation of lands the district would encompass was determined in almost an ad hoc manner and not until 1978, when explicit rules were codified and new divisions created through a "subzone" system.[50] The first four telescopes, thus, were constructed under questionable circumstances as DLNR permits were issued retroactively; that is, after Hawai'i Revised Statutes Chapter 183 were amended to allow "astronomy facilities" in 1994. As previously mentioned, this suggests Maunakea was designated a "resource subzone" within the Conservation District *because* there were already telescopes there.

In 1968, when the original lease allowed for only *a single telescope,* there was no clearly defined permitting process, impartial environmental study, comprehensive management plan, or transparent public consultation system in place. The State of Hawai'i simply made things up as they went. The master planning process began only in the late 1970s, "when the community expressed alarm at the growing number of telescopes on the summit."[51] According to a State legislative audit conducted in 1998,

> In 1974, three telescopes were already in operation, and three others were being planned. Concerns were raised by local groups, including hunters and conservationists, who formed a loose coalition to challenge the increasing development of the summit. These concerns led to efforts to better control and plan and designate Mauna Kea's use for recreational and scientific purposes and the university proceeded with its own research and development plans.[52]

By 1976 the discourse had shifted, and environmental organizations, advisory committees, and other community groups now called for limiting the number of observatories *to six*. The public was no longer in favor of unchecked industrial development, but opponents showed good faith, which the university exploited.

I address the university's management failures directly in chapter 6, but suffice to say here the development of Mauna a Wākea into a world-class observatory was possible only because of a model of environmental state policy that diminished the capacity of communities to stop most forms of development in the context of U.S. occupation. Likewise, through a pattern of interventionist governance that undermines the ecological integrity of Maunakea and the competence of Hawaiians to maintain healthy relations with it, the State showed its willingness to compromise its obligations to Native rights holders in favoring the interests of big science.

The Cost and Benefits of Astronomy

It is in this context that economic and scientific imperatives have become entangled. The distinction between the production of "universal knowledge" through astronomical observation and the production of State revenue through "diversifying markets" is hazier than ever. Since 1968, the State of Hawai'i has leased the summit lands to the University of Hawai'i for $1 per year, which UH then subleases for another $1 per year to each of the observatories that build, maintain, and operate their individual telescopes and supporting facilities. These observatories—financed and operated by a range of entities based in the United States as well as France, Canada, Britain,

India, and Japan—pay for the construction and maintenance using revenue from renting out "viewing time" to individual researchers and teams of astronomers representing universities, governments, agencies, and institutions from around the world. Big science on Maunakea is a costly enterprise, if not a lucrative business. In 2011, *The Honolulu Weekly* reported that "in the past, the W.M. Keck Observatory on Mauna Kea rented out viewing time at $1 per second, which adds up to $30,000 per night,"[53] but according to the *Seattle Times,* in 2012 "one night's use of a Keck telescope is valued at $50,000."[54] The *Honolulu Star-Advertiser* reported in 2009 that Yale University paid the California Institute of Technology $12 million for an annual fifteen nights of observing time on the Keck telescopes over the course of ten years, which totals $80,000 per night.[55] While the university does not charge rent, UH instead receives some 10 to 20 percent of viewing time from each of the observatories for its own educational and research purposes; this is in exchange for providing the land by being awarded State permits on behalf of the telescope programs and spending its own millions in legal fees to circumvent community opposition and environmental policy through litigation.[56]

It is still unclear why the university has not collected more revenue from the subletters or why the State has not required more than the nominal $1 annual rent from the university. I asked Office of Mauna Kea Management (OMKM) director, Stephanie Nagata, why sublease agreements afford the university only "viewing time" on the telescopes in exchange for acquiring necessary State permits rather than what the Mauna Kea Hui call "fair market rent." This was of particular interest to TMT opponents because the University of Hawaiʻi spent millions of dollars to fight the legal challenges to State permits from 2010 to 2018. Since the university receives the majority of its funds from State allowances and student tuition, in a sense, State dollars were spent to defeat State environmental laws. Nagata indicated that the telescope owners do not charge for viewing time because the goal is not profit but rather the pursuit of astronomy. She told me that because price tags for telescope and facilities construction as well as electric energy and regular maintenance run in the millions, the grants and partner contributions go exclusively toward expenses and nothing else. The arrangement that the University Board of Regents has with the State Board of Land and Natural Resources requires only a nominal monetary transfer as a symbol of the lease agreement between "State agencies." Nagata says it is in the State's interests to support astronomy as a way to "diversify the economy . . . [because] unlike tourism, it is something the State can control."[57] Despite narratives about the noble ambitions of knowledge production and scientific discovery, Maunakea astronomy, for the State, is about maintaining a market- and investment-friendly posture, which it cultivates through policies that reproduce a probusiness environment.

In a single year during the first TMT contested case hearing, the university spent $1.1 million on legal fees to secure the permit in a fight against challenges brought by the Mauna Kea Hui.[58] As the university is a State institution funded mostly by tax dollars and sought an exception to DLNR's Conservation District use policy through the legal process, the State was essentially spending millions of tax dollars to defeat its own laws in the name of scientific industrial development on conservation lands.[59] The university's spending on private legal help in the contested case process doubled during that year, actually marking a four-year spike in expenditures for outside legal counsel. The amount exceeded what was paid by most other state agencies combined over the same period. Between May 2010 and March of 2011, UH spent $2.23 million, roughly $203,000 per month, while over the next forty-four months, the university spent only $3.8 million, or approximately $86,000 per month.[60] This spending hike was likely related to the legal challenges brought against the TMT permit. Interestingly, in the corresponding period of the spending increase in attorney expenses, the university's operating budget was $1.1 billion, of which 60 percent, or $670 million, was funded by the public through the general excise tax and personal income tax.[61] Essentially, taxpayers were financing UH efforts to circumvent state laws meant to protect the environment. A year earlier, from 2009 to 2010, the university was busy increasing student admissions while laying off 150 faculty and instructors and cutting the pay of most professors by 6.7 percent. These measures were a peculiar remedy to a $155 million budget shortfall the school faced after the effects of the 2008 banking system collapse. This data suggests the university and the State have substantial commitments to the economic and symbolic promise of big science on Maunakea, which would be severely undermined if transparency around such financial decisions became a priority—and so it has not.

In the push for the TMT, neoliberal rationality structures the states of exception by which environmental policy advances the private interests of a foreign corporate capitalist enterprise. Accordingly, market ideologies and principles of conservation are viewed not as incongruous but as "compatible." Within the State's environmental governmentality, most venues available to kia'i for making their own interventions are always overdetermined by these logics of extraction and exploitation.

The Farce and Tragedy of Contesting the TMT

Big science on Maunakea is a game of hyperbole. Each program justifies its existence through incantations of power, promise, and prestige; each telescope was once the biggest, fastest, and first in one aspiration or another. Astronomers say that to understand the evolution of the universe and the origins of all humankind, we must study the oldest, most distant light. The infinite expanse of space is rivaled only by astronomers' ambitions to know more, but the current telescopes are becoming obsolete. Just as funding construction depends on inspiring popular imaginations to garner support, so does winning permits to build them. Justifications for an undertaking as big as the TMT not only require a cost-benefit analysis but also a rhetoric of scale and monumentalism, emphasizing the TMT's feats and future contributions to anticipate and overcome legal challenges. To achieve the necessary moral advantage, discursive strategies to capture imaginations invoke the myth of hierarchies of knowledge and people by framing the project as a triumph of rationality over superstition. To this end, the State instrumentalizes scientific and legal objectivity to invent rationale and new categories of legitimacy.

If built, the Thirty Meter Telescope would be astronomers' latest monument to Western scientific achievement, taking eight acres of undeveloped land on the northern plateau of Maunakea. As of 2025, construction would run upwards of $4 billion, require excavation of 64,000 cubic yards of earth, burrow 20 feet below ground, and stand 18 stories tall.[62] With a primary mirror at 30 meters (98 feet) in diameter comprising 492 individual segments and nearly four times the size of the "twin Kecks," the TMT promises to be "the most technically advanced telescope in the world with observational powers many times greater than any available today."[63] Currently, however, a 39.3-m. "Extremely Large Telescope" (ELT), billed as "the world's biggest eye on the sky," is already under construction in the Atacama Desert of Chile.[64]

The astronomy community's vision to build the "next generation of large telescopes" on Maunakea surfaced around the late 1990s. It entered design stage in the early 2000s and steadily raised billions in public and private funds. The first permit approved for the project was issued to the University of Hawai'i at Hilo on behalf of the TMT International Observatory, LLC (TIO) by the Board of Land and Natural Resources (BLNR) on February 25, 2011. On April 12, 2013, that permit was upheld following a contested case hearing (CCH) in which the Mauna Kea Hui first organized with fierce aloha 'āina and grit.

Otherwise ordinary folks with regular day jobs, the Mauna Kea Hui comprises six "petitioners"—including Kealoha Pisciotta representing an organization of cultural practitioners called Mauna Kea Anaina Hou and Marti Townsend representing a nonprofit NGO called KAHEA: The Hawaiian-Environmental Alliance; Paul K. Neves, Clarence Kūkauakahi Ching, and Deborah J. Ward, each as "individuals"; and E. Kalani Flores, B. Pua Case, and their two children as the Flores-Case 'Ohana. In a time before arrests, the group displayed great courage by engaging in a space as hostile as settler courts and, although none are lawyers, each had to become proficient in State law.[65]

A contested case hearing is a "quasi-judicial administrative process governed by state law"[66] in which citizens are given an opportunity to intervene in State agency decisions that affect their rights. In this case, members of the public were allowed to petition the university's permit application by giving testimony and submitting evidence against the proposed project, while the applicant UH Hilo argued in the TMT's defense; all of which was overseen by an appointed hearings officer who acts like a judge to give final recommendations to BLNR.

By all accounts, both the 2011 and 2017 hearings were grueling. Transcripts reveal the myriad ways the Mauna Kea Hui, and Kānaka 'Ōiwi in particular, are routinely gaslit and misrepresented even within legal structures meant to serve them. The testimonies and knowledge of the university's "expert" witnesses were treated and cited as rational, objective, and scientific. Yet, while the hui and their witnesses were outwardly shown respect, their values and practices were treated as inauthentic, their concerns as politically biased, and thus their opposition as disingenuous. Alternative knowledges that did not affirm the neoliberal, capitalist interests of the settler state were humored, but treated as irrelevant. After weeks of testimony, the Land Board granted the first TMT permit in 2011, and the hui appealed to the State Supreme Court. They argued that BLNR had violated Conservation District rules, which require that a contested case be completed prior to issuance of a permit. In its defense, the State agency attempted to recast that permit as "provisional" and "conditional." Only after four years did the court finally hear the case, reversing the decision and revoking the permit in December 2015. The hui's many hours of labor called for celebration, but the victory was bittersweet as the decision to rescind the permit was not a result of the court acknowledging how the project would violate conservation policy but because the permit was granted *prior* to holding a contested case. In making a "procedural error," BLNR had "put the cart before the horse."[67]

Immediately after the high court rescinded the permit, the University of Hawai'i and DLNR prepared for a second contested case in 2017. After forty-four days of oral arguments and the hearing officer's recommendation, BLNR issued a new permit. Brought to the Supreme Court again on appeal, BLNR's permit was upheld in a 4–1 ruling in late 2018.

One of the most severe outcomes of this 2018 decision is that it established what Justice Michael D. Wilson described in his minority opinion as the "degradation principle."[68] The threat of this legal precedence is that it anticipates and rationalizes the future likelihood of environmental degradation using a classificatory system that establishes new criteria by which a "resource" (like Mauna a Wākea) may be denied eligibility for legal protection. The logic follows that despite "impacts" found to already exist have been determined "substantial, adverse, and significant," the prospect of future damage would not add to these impacts when weighed against the entirety of prior damage and the TIO's "mitigation measures."[69]

To achieve this rationale, UH and BLNR meticulously and discursively reassigned the meanings of key terms to reconfigure the criteria for eligibility for legal protection. For example, lawyers diminished the meaning of "substantial," "existing," and "impacts" by delineating new qualifying categories of "cumulative" and "incremental." The strategy also opened space for resignifications: "damage" and "degradation" were replaced by "impacts" to perform a conceptual rather than material reduction of harm. Despite the fact that two legislative audits had already found the previous four decades of industrial astronomy to be responsible for "substantial, adverse, and significant impacts,"[70] the court embraced the argument that the TMT would not add to these impacts because those previous impacts were "cumulative," and the TMT would add only "incremental" impacts, thereby not amounting to a significant increase. By inventing, assigning, and contrasting two new categories, the university, BLNR, and now the Supreme

Court would align to perform a legal trick: that is, *incremental* damage the TMT is likely to cause would be tolerated because it would be "mitigated" and would not *significantly* add to the *cumulative* damage already done over the previous four decades of industrial development on the summit.[71] In other words, the mountain is already damaged, so more damage cannot increase the overall damage in any way that requires further intervention.

The effect of the ruling reveals its tautology: it created a framework through which an assessment of prior damage as insignificant to provide a mechanism by which justification of future damage could be rationalized. Wilson argued the degradation principle serves

> to cast off cultural or environmental protection by establishing that prior degradation of the resource . . . extinguishes the legal protections afforded to natural resources in the conservation district. The degradation principle ignores the unequivocal mandate contained in the Hawai'i Administrative Rules . . . prohibiting a . . . CDUP [permit] for a land use that would cause a substantial adverse impact to existing natural resources . . . Using the fact that the resource has already suffered a substantial adverse impact, the BLNR concludes that further land uses could not be the cause of substantial adverse impact.[72]

The implications of this decision on future generations seeking protection of the environment are far-reaching. Justice Wilson adds that application of the degradation principle

> creates a threshold condition of damage—substantial adverse impact— that, once met, renders the resource available for future degradation. In so doing, the degradation principle presumes there is no natural resource value left to protect. The actions of prior and present generations extinguish the chance for future generations to protect the environmental and cultural heritage that once enjoyed legal protection.[73]

The decision and degradation principle indicates a glaring disregard for any commonsense understanding of the very concept of conservation and has the potential to undermine all future attempts to use State law to protect all of Hawai'i's conservation lands.

The ruling also points to something fundamental in how the scientific settler state values dominion over land as resource and possession, while Kānaka 'Ōiwi and settler aloha 'āina value Hawai'i as kinship relation. Differing views embody differing ideological commitments. That difference can be exposed in narratives of settler law that attempt to account for the natural, the sacred, and the human. It was precisely this gap in understanding and incommensurability of valuations of Mauna a Wākea that the personhood of a woman lizard/guardian spirit of the summit's Lake Waiau known as Moʻoinanea was challenged at the start of legal proceedings. Her presence, if not her physical form, emerged in the first contested case as a foil to settler state law and its discursive tactics of self-authorization.

Moʻoinanea and the Terms of Legitimacy

At the 2011 hearing, the Flores-Case ʻOhana requested Moʻoinanea—a moʻo wahine and a kupua[74]—be given standing to participate in the hearing. The sacred figure appeared to the family's youngest child who observed the moʻo wahine at Manaua, a "rain rock" and spiritual site in Waimea for which their ʻohana (family) cares. In her written testimony, Pua Case tells the story:

> During one visit to Manaua, Kapulei informed me that Moʻoinanea from Mauna a Wākea had come to visit Manaua and was sitting on a lower level of the rock. She described her to me completely including the style and design on her kīkepa.[75] As we left, she paused asking me to wait. She listened and stated that Moʻoinanea was asking if I could try one more time. When I asked her what she meant, she asked, "If I could try to stop the telescope from being built, but that if I could not, it was okay." She was requesting something of me, but also as if reading my mind, was giving me a way out at the same time. This is the one of the primary reasons our family was prompted to proceed forward in this contested case hearing, because of that request [sic].[76]

Pua Case, Kalani Flores, and daughters were granted standing, but Moʻoinanea was not. Though now something of a footnote in the longer struggle for Mauna a Wākea, the episode over the deity's legal standing exposed how settler law is incapable of accounting for Kanaka indigeneity. This failure poses a threat to the settler state as its own performance of legitimacy depends on a capacity to operationalize law in order to contain Kanaka indigeneity and delegitimize unwanted interventions. In this prehearing contest, there was a preoccupation with the question of embodiment that rendered unintelligible to the hearings officer and the law, the ontorelationality of Kānaka ʻŌiwi, which thus signaled the limits of settler legal discourse to account for its own difference. While law's authority is conditioned by its capacity to determine truths, Moʻoinanea revealed how Kanaka indigeneity exceeds the knowledge systems and presumed objectivity of the State and law. It also exposed a rupture in settler colonial hegemony.

In the prehearing, the Flores-Case ʻOhana argued on behalf of Moʻoinanea that she should be allowed to participate because she "has a substantial interest in this matter, resides on the summit of Mauna a Wākea, and can demonstrate that she and others will be directly and immediately affected by the requested action" of receiving a permit.[77] Two months later, the university stated its objection "to the inclusion of Moʻoinanea as a party to the contested case proceedings on the grounds that, because the petition asserts Moʻoinanea is not a human being, Moʻoinanea does not qualify as a 'person' and so does not have standing in these proceedings under Haw. Admin. R. § 13-1-32."[78] Hearings Officer Paul Aoki accepted the university's assessment that because "Moʻoinanea is a spirit, not a person, . . . [she] does not meet the requirements of Haw. Admin. R § 13-1-31 and 13-1-2 to be admitted as a party." Aoki wrote:

> After considering the issue, including the submission of the new written testimony from the Flores-Case ʻŌhana, the BLNR voted unanimously to adopt the Hearings Officer's recommendation to deny the petition submitted on behalf of Moʻoinanea.[79]

The discussion was rich with irony as Moʻoinanea's subjectivity was effectively produced in the law's disavowal of that subjectivity. For the BLNR to decide on whether to grant standing to someone considered "not a person" and "not a human being," but as *someone* nevertheless—as *someone* to be referenced, named, and invoked but ultimately rendered illegible within the "quasi-judicial" purview of the state—reveals a fundamental failure of settler law: ambiguity and contingency. Moʻoinanea emerged as an absent other, to be seen and unseen, extant and extinct, not unlike that which the state demands of Kānaka ʻŌiwi more generally, whose presence is welcome insofar as our conscription, appropriation, and disqualification affords the scientific settler state its requisite degrees of legitimacy and financial security—and thus cultural authority. Through a series of confused rhetorical blunders, Aoki groped for reason and rationale, in a debate that both substantiated and disavowed Moʻoinanea, exposing both the limits and function of settler colonial law as it used any ambiguity to reproduce its own authority and claim to reason.

In May 2011, Moʻoinanea was ultimately denied "the request . . . for waiver of the filing fee because no demonstration of financial hardship had been made. The Chairperson advised that failure to submit the filing fee might result in dismissal of the petition."[80] In that meeting, Kalani Flores offered a second request "for a waiver of the filing fee for the Moʻoinanea petition, asserting that Moʻoinanea 'is not employed' and does not receive any revenues generated by activities on Mauna Kea." In June, the Land Board sought an opinion of Moʻoinanea's standing by DLNR's Office of Conservation and Coastal Lands (OCCL) and, after its review, the OCCL presented its recommendation to deny standing to Moʻoinanea "for lack of standing and for failure to pay the filing fee."[81]

A brief media spectacle followed—further accentuating the limits of law's power to contain Kanaka indigeneity—when Moʻoinanea's subjecthood was affirmed in a *Hawaii Tribune-Herald* headline: "Official Says Spirit Can't Testify."[82] Staff writer Peter Sur reported that "Flores also argued that Moʻoinanea is part human, has a genealogy, can manifest herself as a person or a moʻo—a giant reptile—and cannot be seen by some because she 'resonates at a different vibration.'" Sur reported on UH Hilo attorney Tim Lui-Kwan's objection in the contested case hearing, in which he struggled to find the appropriate language to argue that a spiritual being could not also be a legal person because she is not a "living organism." The comedy of this scene was not lost on *Honolulu Magazine,* whose "Sour Poi Awards . . . Celebrating the best of the worst of 2011—the strange, the stupid, and the scandalous," featured a cartoon illustration of Lui-Kwan condemning a floating lizard apparition with a baffled judge observing from his pulpit. The petitioners' "spirited defense" of Moʻoinanea would nevertheless prove unconvincing to Aoki.[83]

This exercise allowed the Flores-Case ʻOhana to resist the State's claim to hegemony through a fundamental difference around which Kanaka indigeneity is substantiated. The contest over Moʻoinanea reveals how Hawaiʻi's settler society remains haunted by the specter of the Native whose prior existence, occupancy, meanings, and epistemes challenge the self-evidence of settler state law. ʻŌiwi valuations of land as ʻāina—that is, as embodied kin, ancestor, source of life, and more-than-human relation—cannot be contained within the logics of the State. For this reason, settler law remains vexed by its inability to fully absorb Hawaiians whose alterity, indigeneity, and distinct ways of knowing disrupt settler claims to legal and scientific objectivity. The impossibility of enveloping Kanaka indigeneity eventually leads to fissures in the hegemonic order, exposing contradictions of settler governance from legal determinations of land and peoples to the states of exception that justify abuses of power—as well as the myriad categories invented to normalize a capitalist social order to appear inevitable. However, the fact that indigeneity cannot easily be contained indicates there are cracks to be pried open and ruptures to be exposed to unsettle settler colonial hegemony. This chapter has argued that the struggle for Mauna a Wākea is part of the broader struggle over the ancestral lands of Kānaka ʻŌiwi. This can be seen in the legal venues and rhetoric of the settler state, where Moʻoinanea's personhood is paradoxically disavowed and affirmed, much the same as Kanaka subjectivity within settler colonialism under U.S. military occupation. It is also reflected in the paradoxes of Hawaiʻi's liberal multiculturalism, to which I turn in the next chapter.

3

MULTICULTURAL SETTLER COLONIALISM

The Gift of Maunakea

In 2014, Hawai'i State Governor Neil Abercrombie commented on the proposed Thirty Meter Telescope project in his State of the State address. Repeating the popular refrain that Maunakea is "the best place on the planet to observe the universe" as it "provides an unparalleled opportunity to advance our knowledge," he added a belief that "Mauna Kea is Hawai'i's gift to the world."[1] Two years prior in a monthly online news update, former UH President M. R. C. Greenwood expressed the university's commitment to the TMT, also describing Maunakea as a gift:

> The university is keenly aware of its obligation to be a responsible and thoughtful caretaker of the land that has been entrusted to our care on Mauna Kea. The mountain is a gift to all the people of Hawai'i, and we recognize our responsibility and kuleana to it. We deeply appreciate all of the work that has been done by the community to ensure that the TMT is done in the right way for the benefit of the people of Hawai'i.[2]

The gift metaphor affirms the State's twin ideological commitments to capitalism and U.S. empire vis-à-vis liberal multiculturalism. If Maunakea belongs to everyone, Kānaka 'Ōiwi have no distinct claim, be it religious or cultural. In this way, these speech acts obscure not only the capitalist economic and national security interests that condition the TMT's possibility but also how settler multiculturalism is the form colonialism takes in Hawai'i's contemporary moment. While presenting generosity and care "for all the people of Hawai'i," the gesture presumes a reality that many Kānaka 'Ōiwi contest, and by virtue of the myriad efforts to protect the Hawai'i's lands, waters, and Native life from ongoing colonial processes, the rhetoric of the gift simultaneously invokes and disavows Kanaka subjectivity. While narrative practices like these recast Hawai'i as an unproblematic settler possession, the gifting of Maunakea functions also to authorize a multicultural hegemony to which Indigenous subjectivity is an imminent threat. Beyond recognition of the State and university's responsibility to the land, these gestures signal a settler self-affirmation amid Native Hawaiian unrest about how those lands are used and frustration about how their dissent and desires go ignored. I flag this because the rhetoric is indicative of ways liberal settler entitlement, multicultural benevolence, and possessive legal authority over Hawai'i and Hawaiians enmesh and become normalized through recursive self-authorizing narratives. However, that recursivity is predicated on the systemic enforcement of a single universal reality that binds the settler state and industrial astronomy at Maunakea to one another, both requiring and reproducing the continued alienation of Kānaka 'Ōiwi from the land. In this chapter, I discuss the rehearsal of such universalizing habits and how they function to remake an otherwise impossible system of control over Maunakea just as they do Hawai'i and Hawaiians more broadly. My concern is that while such liberal multicultural discourses conjure and solidify settler belonging, white possession, and State legitimacy, they also signal a recurring disqualification of Kanaka subjectivity.

At first take, the idea of gifting Maunakea "to the world" and to "all Hawai'i's people" might appear harmless enough, but as an example of the multicultural form colonialism in Hawai'i takes, the gesture reveals how containing indigeneity becomes a priority of the settler state to satisfy its commitments to capital. Through disavowals and affirmations of specific expressions of Hawaiian-ness, the act of gifting becomes an exercise of power that hinges on containing a Kanaka indigeneity that is concerned with collective liberation. With a vibrant culture centering environmental and social justice in Hawai'i—as well as, in one form or another, Hawaiian independence—the very existence of Indigenous alterity unsettles, especially because it provokes settler society to take accountability for the socioeconomic and political privilege it enjoys at the expense of Native Hawaiians.

As such, the rhetoric and ideology of liberal democracy in Hawai'i—which the gift metaphor embodies—should be understood as a distraction intended to, as Tuck and Yang put it, "relieve the settler of feelings of guilt or responsibility."[3] Within the prevailing hegemonic order of Hawai'i's liberal multicultural society and capitalist economy, Indigenous claims to space, place, and rights are cast as excessive and viewed as clashing with the seemingly more inclusive civil rights to which "all Hawai'i's people" are entitled. In this way, the work of liberal multiculturalism under settler racial capitalism is that it invites everyone to participate, but participation is selective and confined to its structures of domination. Indigenous alterity, and thus discourse on colonialism, is a problem. Abercrombie and Greenwood's passing comments are effective because in their assumption of settler possession and authority over Maunakea (and Hawai'i) is also an erasure and inherent trace of an opposing claim: that Maunakea may be well cared for and stewarded by Kānaka 'Ōiwi if not for the U.S. military, whose tacit threat of violence it poses underpins contemporary society's hegemony in Hawai'i. Therefore, the attraction of this sort of rhetoric is in its productive capacity to absolve the settler of responsibility. As such, the compulsion to neutralize the potential threat of Native alterity is no accident, for there can be no contest to big science on the Mauna if the TMT is to be realized.

It is in this context that we might think of Kanaka indigeneity as one of the greatest obstacles to industrial astronomy, as it is to U.S. imperial control over Hawai'i. The gift is anything but innocent. Who gives and who receives reflects as much as it reproduces: a preferred set of meanings to be assigned to Maunakea, Hawai'i, and Hawaiians. While Kānaka 'Ōiwi and Native-led resistance to the TMT challenge the imposed myth of a single reality and global hierarchy of knowledges, containment of difference becomes a priority of the state.

In chapter 2, I analyzed ways in which neoliberal environmental policy under settler colonialism not only contributes to the alienation of Kānaka 'Ōiwi from 'āina but also reproduces settler authority, both of which condition the ongoing degradation of Mauna a Wākea. In building on the theme, chapter 3 offers a discourse analysis of ways in which Hawai'i's multiculturalism sustains settler innocence and authority, disavows U.S. military occupation, and underwrites the legal, social, and political disqualification of Kanaka 'Ōiwi subjectivity, thereby diminishing our capacity to protect our ancestral places. To this end, I look at the seemingly banal narrative practices of liberal recognition and multicultural inclusion that extend to settlers a sense of absolution from feelings of guilt for histories of participation in settler colonial occupation. Unpacking the ideological functions of these processes helps to explain how liberal expectations that astronomy and culture "co-exist" are not only misleading but also productive in remaking settler privilege and Kanaka ʻŌiwi subjugation.

From Elimination to Recognition

Before proceeding, I should elaborate on what I mean by "settler colonialism." The category is both a historical formation of power and an analytic concept. It describes the continuation of relations structured in domination where military invasion and colonization cannot be said to have ended and power is maintained through systems of control over land, resources, and the Native people who are subjugated through these systems.

Under conditions of settler colonialism, as Patrick Wolfe theorizes, "invasion is a structure . . . (not) an event."[4] While colonizers come to stay, the settler structure's "dominant feature . . . (is) replacement," and its "primary object . . . is the land itself."[5] Settler colonialism is constituted in the systematic deracination of Indigenous peoples from their ancestral lands to make way for settlement, and the process is ongoing. Eve Tuck and K. Wayne Yang add that settler colonialism is a complex formation of hegemonic power and "different from other forms of colonialism in that settlers come with the intention of making a new home on the land, a homemaking that insists on settler sovereignty over all things in their new domain."[6] Settler colonialism is neither temporally confined to a historical moment of conquest nor racially exclusive to nefarious Anglo settlers. As a constellation of systems, beliefs, practices, and cultural forms, settler colonialism persists at the level of hegemony. This means it is not in all instances a matter of power *over* peoples but frequently more about the degree of agency people have to realize an alternative. Through a variety of assemblages wherein social norms, cultural institutions, and ideologies cohere in nonnecessary combinations that implicate everyone living on lands from which Native people have been largely or entirely displaced, settler hegemony targets Native alterity by imposing structures Native people have little choice but to participate in for their survival.[7] As a source of capital and generational wealth, land becomes settler colonialism's "primary motive," its "specific, irreducible element"—its raison d'être.[8] Yet, because Native people refuse to give up their ancestral territories willingly, and settlers wish to reconcile colonial guilt with a desire to belong on expropriated lands, contemporary settler society remains bound to logics of Native elimination and possession.

From Anglo-settler squatting to genocidal conquest, policies of removal, and assimilation, across North America, nineteenth-century militarized frontier violence would give way to twentieth-century strategies of abstracted violence through ostensible acts of reconciliation, recognition, and inclusion. Specifically, efforts were made to reconcile nationalist ideals of liberal democracy with the material reality of continued displacement, oppression, and disavowal. So, as Glen Coulthard explains, shifting geopolitical relations and economic imperatives eventually

> forced colonial power to modify itself from a structure that was once primarily reinforced by policies, techniques, and ideologies explicitly oriented around the genocidal exclusion/assimilation double, to one that is now reproduced through a seemingly more conciliatory set of discourses and institutional practices that emphasize our *recognition* and *accommodation*. Regardless of this modification, however, the relationship between Indigenous peoples and the state has remained *colonial* to its foundation.[9]

The remedy to exclusion might appear to be inclusion. After all, the experience of so many Indigenous peoples has been defined by dispossession and removal from land as well as social and political marginalization. Wouldn't more rights be some consolation? However, as legal recognition is extended to Indigenous peoples, this model of inclusion is a sort of pacifying gesture that conceals the continuance of colonial violence through disavowal and disqualification of Native subjectivity. Liberal models of recognition provide a symbolic form of reconciliation between Native and settler that interpellates, or hails, the Native subject as a potential beneficiary of citizenship and rights under laws of the settler state.[10] In other words, the purpose of inclusion is to reproduce the colonial project under settler state authority. Fundamentally, liberal inclusion cannot account for indigeneity and Indigenous alterity as the project exists to rationalize legacies of foundational violence. Consent was never acquired without the tacit threat of continued violence, but that can be manufactured. When confronted by perpetual conquest and the fact that settlers never intended to leave, accepting the gift of recognition becomes a means of survival for many Native people, but at a cost. Indeed, the effects of assimilation are intergenerational, and the reality today is that even many Indigenous people affirm their interpellation by answering when "hailed" by the state. This is in part because Native subjectivity is constituted in hegemonic relationality to which even acts of survival through participation may serve as consent enough for the state to maintain disciplinary order.

For many Kānaka ʻŌiwi, the imperative to survive subjection under settler capitalism and U.S. imperialism has come at the expense of taking up collective struggle. Over the past thirty years, a central political question Hawaiians have faced is whether to remain "wards of the state" or accept official U.S. federal recognition, a precarious path to defending hard-won social programs, or "Native Hawaiian rights," which nevertheless are always "subject to the plenary power of the United States."[11] Coulthard describes such a politics of liberal state recognition as not "a source of freedom and dignity for the colonized, but rather . . . the field of power through which colonial relations are produced and maintained."[12] While both exclusion and inclusion have the capacity to subjugate, it is especially through liberal modes of inclusion that Kanaka indigeneity has become a priority of the state. As settler colonialism administers the logics of Native elimination, Native subjectivity is the central target. Disappearing Nativeness, if not all actual Native Hawaiians, becomes essential to securing a hegemony of unrestricted settler realities, from legal jurisdiction over lands, to social legitimacy and belonging to be prioritized over indigeneity. Indeed, not only is containing Nativeness within colonial hegemony more sustainable than actually eliminating Native people, but absorption of Native difference through recognition schemes has long provided ideological cover. Settler legitimacy depends on institutions and actions that embody the liberal virtues of equality, freedom, and individual rights through property, while its racialized logics systematically leave Black and Brown people for dead.

Put to work through administrative systems that instrumentalize liberal recognition and inclusion to control difference, settler hegemony recodes structural oppression as natural, or at least without alternative. They may operate through systemic and institutional forms as mundane bureaucracy, but the effects of legal recognition are long term and no less lethal to Native communities. One irony of Indigenous peoples accepting the gift of legal recognition is how the forms of violence that such demands for recognition historically sought to transcend are inexorably entwined with those models of inclusion.[13] In other words, refusing the gift of recognition poses a stronger chance for Indigenous people to practice, if not maintain, the substance of their alterity so many are concerned with remembering and revitalizing. Because the underlying logic of Native elimination itself continues to structure domination as liberal recognition, these systems are often difficult to spot. It is precisely because of their banality, their everydayness, that they are easily missed.

Under the hegemony of settler capitalism and U.S. occupation, liberal recognition also makes the Native subject into a sort of "gift," particulary when Indigenous alterity is treated as a market commodity—a symbolic resource for settler profit. This is one effect of the condescending notion that Kānaka 'Ōiwi are "Hawai'i's host culture," which is now ubiquitous across tourist (and astronomy) industry PR rhetoric. While Native people are conscripted into service of the settler state and our culture appropriated to sell vacations and property to foreigners, Native subjectivity is a constant battlefield on which contests over meanings to be ascribed to land and indigeneity are staged. Although settler amnesia does not disappear Indigenous claims to sovereignty, Kanaka indigeneity remains as much a site of struggle as Maunakea. Indeed, as Sherene Razack argues, "The definition of a successful settler project is when the Indigenous population has been reduced to a 'manageable remnant.'"[14] If only remnants remain, and if the current hegemony makes us forget who we are as Kānaka, what good is the gift of inclusion? No longer about explicit and physical extermination of Hawaiian people, the goal of this settler management is to eliminate self-determined Nativeness. This occurs discursively through legal, scientific, and political discourse, but the effect has material consequences, the least of which are houselessness and off-island migration. In other words, the extractive and possessive logics of settler colonialism target the terms of Kanaka legitimacy to alienate us from our land. Managing Indigenous alterity and subjectivity becomes a primary function of the state, which mines indigeneity to control Hawai'i's lands and waters, to conjure paths to settler innocence, and to reproduce the conditions of settler futurity in Hawai'i.

In contrast to theories based on logics of elimination, Maile Arvin focuses instead on the logics of possession, arguing it expresses "more precisely the permanent partial state of the Indigenous subject being inhabited (being known and produced) by a settler society."[15] This intervention opens space to account for a persistent settler nativism by which white settlers in Hawaiʻi first wrote "themselves into Polynesian pasts and futures."[16] According to Arvin, "Settler colonialism in Hawaʻi . . . is fueled by a logic of possession through whiteness," whereby Hawaiʻi and Hawaiians "become exotic, feminized possessions of whiteness—possessions that never have the power to claim the property of whiteness for themselves."[17] These ideas took shape in the late nineteenth- and early twentieth-century through pseudoscientific rationality mapped onto Hawaiʻi that posited Hawaiians as possessing a unique capacity for assimilation, presumably through genetic proximity to whiteness. Arvin explains how "possession, rather than elimination, articulates more fully the ways in which settler colonial practices of elimination and replacement are continuously deferred,"[18] adding how she sees "possession as expressing more precisely the permanent partial state of the Indigenous subject being inhabited (being known and produced) by a settler society."[19] This certainly occurred within conventional white historiography but also continues in Hawaiʻi's multicultural narrative, which treats colonization as a past completed and Natives as fully assimilated to the point there no longer are any *real Hawaiians* to speak of. While such narratives have sought to make settlers Indigenous, they may also be interrupted through sustained critical analysis of the structural reality that colonization persists through logics of possession and practices of replacement, whereby alternative realities are absorbed and managed. The remedy is not inclusion or recognition, but a critique and collective action.

Settler Colonialism in Hawaiʻi

Haunani-Kay Trask introduced an early analysis of settler colonialism in Hawaiʻi in the 1990s to explain why liberal conceptions of equality and civil rights will always fail Kānaka ʻŌiwi. She argued that because power is not structured according to a Black-and-white racial binary, but horizontally among predominantly nonwhite ethnic groups differently situated in relation to white supremacy, U.S. empire, and settler capitalism, any analysis of Hawai'i's contemporary condition will simply be inadequate in the absence of questions of Indigenous sovereignty and self-determination. She argued that Hawai'i requires a different analytic lens to confront the historical roots of the contemporary subjugation Kānaka 'Ōiwi endure. Simply put, understanding colonization in Hawai'i requires an analysis that recognizes "the color of violence" is not only a matter of white dominance over "black," "brown," "red," and "yellow," but "of settlers over natives and slaves . . . There is not just one binary opposition, but many oppositions."[20] Trask explains, "In settler societies the issue of civil rights is primarily an issue about how to protect settlers from each other and from the state. Injustices done against Native people—for example, genocide, land dispossession, language extinction, family disintegration, cultural exploitation—are not part of this intra-settler discussion, and therefore not within the parameters of civil rights."[21] A focus on civil rights is just insufficient for a colonial context.

Hawai'i's unique status as an ethnically, racially, and culturally diverse place has become an asset. As settler colonialism in Hawai'i operates through liberal ideologies, the instrumentalization of inclusion has functioned to diminish the political capacity of Hawaiians to assert and act on historically situated claims to land and self-governance. Though not absolute, the liberal settler state's general success in managing these claims has for generations been an economic asset to those settler communities who found greater opportunities in aligning with white capitalist heteropatriarchy under U.S. imperialism than with Native Hawaiians.

The idea that no single ethnicity holds a numerical majority in Hawai'i has also allowed a multicultural mythology about settlers and Natives to circulate, providing an indispensable cover for the role that settlers have and continue to play in the many forms of continued displacement, dispossession, and disqualification that Kānaka 'Ōiwi experience. And while liberal multiculturalism has allowed settlers to obscure their culpability in facilitating U.S. hegemony in Hawai'i, past and present, it has also enabled settlers to reproduce the power and privilege they have been afforded as shares in the spoils of empire, won through demonstrations of allegiance to the United States.[22] Though not without exception, this general historical alignment signals a settler investment in the American project and abandonment of Kānaka 'Ōiwi. While tourism depends on the façade of social accord and racial harmony, the obfuscation of subsequent social hierarchies has also become a primary function of the state, its legal systems, politics, and economic imperatives.

As such, Trask describes the "cultures and habits of life" in everyday Hawai'i as structured in a logic of "extermination," where the "ordered realities of confinement, degradation, ill health, and early death" continue to afflict Kānaka 'Ōiwi.[23] The "everydayness" of colonization is key. It is through a ritualized management and containment of Kanaka subjectivities within settler racial capitalism, performed across ideological state apparatuses through administrative and doctrinal forms that systemic and institutionalized subjugation for Native Hawaiians results in what Ruth Wilson Gilmore calls "group-differentiated vulnerability to premature death."[24] As a slow, ongoing subjugation through attrition, Trask describes the everyday, mundane, ubiquitous, and effectively ruthless oppression as a paradoxically "peaceful violence."[25] Often hidden in plain sight, banal systemic violence is normalized as it permeates every aspect of social life for Kānaka 'Ōiwi, who are distinctly targeted for our land. Understanding the nuances of settler violence within liberal multicultural modalities requires a relational analysis of how white hegemony in the United States has shaped the "cultural hierarchy" that persists in Hawai'i. Trask explains that

> the color of violence, then, is the color of white over Black, white over brown, white over red, white over yellow. It is violence of north over south, of continents over archipelagoes, of settlers over natives and slaves. Shaping this color scheme are the labyrinths of class and gender, of geography and industry, of metropolises and peripheries, of sexual definitions and confinements.[26]

Trask begins by recognizing how the United States was "created out of the bloody extermination of Native peoples, the enslavement of forcibly transported peoples, and the continuing oppression of dark-skinned peoples,"[27] but also how they persist through interlocking oppressions where indigeneity, class, gender, and race combine in various configurations. While liberal models of inclusion result in forms of subjection of other minoritized people of color as well, within Hawai'i's settler multiculturalism it has generally been other marginalized people of color, that is, non-Native Hawaiian people, who have avoided being subjugated within the structural processes that consolidate difference under rubrics of liberal freedom, equality, and civil rights; these non-Natives' broad political commitments have generally functioned to uphold rather than resist U.S. structures of domination. Trask's critique of the "normalcy of white dominance," however, does not substitute race for indigeneity or racism for colonization but instead articulates how subjugation under the broader category of "white culture" informs Hawai'i's racial/colonial hierarchy. Unlike in the United States where often many racialized groups seek to transform the nation-state, calibrating it toward a better realization of "American" ideals, the stakes for Kānaka 'Ōiwi are about our uninterrupted claims to ancestral places, lands and waters, and Indigenous sovereignty, as much as to independence as a nation-state, which I discuss in the next chapter.[28] In other words, there is no equivalent to be found in other social justice movements for what Indigenous self-determination, sovereignty, and decolonization demand. It is about the land and the terms of indigeneity to it. This speaks to the appeal of the hashtag #LandBack, as Eve Tuck and K. Wayne Yang argue, "decolonization is not a metaphor."[29] Decolonization is necessarily unsettling because it is about giving land back—it is not a matter of reform or reparation. While for many ethnic minorities or otherwise marginalized, minoritized, and subjugated groups within a given liberal democratic polity, civil rights may be an objective, but many Kānaka 'Ōiwi do not wish simply to be more fully integrated within the political landscape of the settler colonial state, regardless of its racial and ethnic diversity or the ostensible "gifts" of liberal democracy and legal recognition.

The question of Kanaka 'Ōiwi self-determination, decolonization, and military deoccupation of Hawai'i begins with interrogation of the very premise of the state itself and its claim to legitimacy. This is not to suggest other social movements in Hawai'i that seek justice are not also interrogating the fundamental premises of the U.S. project, but it is a call to strengthen the exercise of solidarity to also account for decolonization in conversation and collective action alongside Kānaka 'Ōiwi. Indifference toward the contemporary Hawaiian movement is a mark of colonization's structural violence. Social justice and decolonization should be understood as not mutually exclusive but rather mutually dependent, particularly when both focus their transgressive energies toward white heteropatriarchal settler capitalist imperial hegemony, which requires an all-hands-on-deck approach. In other words, an analytic of settler colonialism is less concerned with individual identities than centering Native communities while building collective action for collective liberation. In this way, the Indigenous-led Protect Maunakea Movement also has demonstrated its potential to unsettle the U.S. occupation of Hawai'i, the history of which implicates settlers of color whose solidarity is therefore imperative to decolonization, as well as liberatory futures for everyone in Hawai'i, not just Kānaka 'Ōiwi.

Asian Settler Colonialism

Over the last thirty years, critical scholarship on U.S. imperialism, race, and colonialism in Hawai'i has examined historical narratives about the collective experience of Asian communities and the relations of power that shape hegemony in the islands. Scholars have analyzed how the rise in the socioeconomic and political status of Asian people in Hawai'i today may be attributed to a collective resilience in the face of racial subjugation under white settler capitalism. However, that prosperity and political power has also come at the expense of robust analysis of the role that Asian communities have played in the story of Hawai'i's colonization, particularly since the U.S. "territorial" occupation began in the late nineteenth century and the well-being of Kānaka 'Ōiwi has since dramatically declined.[30] Discourses on "local" politics and "local" identity have emerged in ways that often gloss relations between Hawaiians and non-Hawaiians under these conditions. Forged through popular histories of the struggle and perseverance of late nineteenth- and early twentieth-century migrant workers predominantly from east and southeast Asian countries who, against the odds, triumphed over racial discrimination and labor exploitation to achieve the dignity and rights of U.S. citizenship, "local" subjectivity often functions to obscure histories' asymmetrical access to political and economic power, as well as the stakes of these politics for Kānaka 'Ōiwi. As such, the category "local" discursively reduces the substance and significance of Native alterity, as Kānaka 'Ōiwi are not simply another minority group that seeks full participation within the liberal state but one that holds a claim to state sovereignty. While "local" has value in distinguishing these communities from tourists and foreigners, as well as the historic working class from elite and ruling class, it has also been shown to first and foremost serve the interests of non-Hawaiians. Though certainly not every individual benefitted from the U.S. invasion and occupation of Hawai'i, local Asian settler communities have become politically and economically empowered under U.S.

colonial power. In many historic examples, these groups have facilitated expropriation of Native lands, less as an explicit program of colonizing as such than by virtue of simply holding offices in local territorial and state government and starting businesses where success under imperial racial capitalism often led to colonizing strategies and practices to which Kānaka 'Ōiwi were subjected.[31] Historical discourses celebrating the achievements of Asian immigrants who confronted white supremacy have also frequently nevertheless functioned to obscure histories of Indigenous struggle. As such, the analytic of Asian settler colonialism has value not in that it targets any specific ethnic group for vilification, but rather in how it redirects attention away from ephemeral identity formations or individual intentions and toward relations of power that result in collective privilege, as well as the systemic consequences of liberal multiculturalism for Kānaka 'Ōiwi. To this end, Asian settler colonialism as an analytic operates as a potential mode for building solidarity and creates an opportunity for confronting the paradoxes of histories among groups differently situated within settler capitalism and U.S. imperialism: by centering the experiences of Kānaka 'Ōiwi and the legal and political history of Hawai'i.

According to Bianca Isaki, "Asian Americanness" emerged in Hawai'i as "a debt accrued by reciting history as a particular identity-narrative."[32] She describes Asian settler colonialism as "the future of past practices of land theft and political control through which descendants of transnational contract laborers moved into middle class American-ness. Not having arrived as settler-conquerors, Asian settlers emerge as colonial agents over multiple generations."[33] Within the conventional story of immigration and democracy in Hawai'i, the upward class mobility afforded to descendants of transnational contract labor becomes entangled with identity formations built around narratives of perseverance and resilience. These narratives fit more neatly within U.S. liberal ideologies of freedom and individual responsibility than they do the anti-imperial and decolonial ideologies common among many Kānaka 'Ōiwi, particularly as white settler histories have cast Hawaiians as losers in the story of empire. As Asian settler subjectivity transformed from subjection under colonial plantation capitalism to "shareholder of colonial systems re-formed by economic globalization," the convergence of capital and liberal multiculturalism during Hawai'i's territorial-era began to structure new "entry-points for Asian settlers to access power in an American-Hawai'i."[34] Discourse that recasts this transition of oppression to enfranchisement as simply a triumph of liberal inclusion over racial dis-crimination, while ignoring imperialism and occupation, signals a degree of agency within U.S. hegemony that settlers in Hawai'i enjoy, yet is un-available to Native Hawaiians, particularly those who remember and advo-cate for our claim to independence from foreign rule.

Dean Saranillio describes the constellation of discourses, memories, and social practices telling a convenient past as "a master narrative" that reifies "anti-Asian oppression on the sugar plantations and valiant military service during World War II" to the point these struggles become an "alibi for continued acts of Native dispossession and marginalization."[35] For exam-ple, Saranillio explains, the mythology of statehood, viewed as "an antiracist, civil rights victory," becomes "a tale about a long struggle to oppose haole racist exclusion of Hawai'i's nonwhite communities" at the same time it is "an expression of self-determination that was democratically and defini-tively settled."[36] In this way, the conventional story about Hawai'i's statehood simultaneously invokes a sense of victimhood and valor as it manufactures a form of settler nativism. As Hawai'i statehood in 1959 extended shares in U.S. democracy through liberal multicultural citizenship, it also repro-duced white supremacist power and privilege. While Asian people found reprieve from plantation oppression and opportunity through access to democratic participation, the cost of making Hawai'i into a multicultural "melting pot" was, for Kānaka 'Ōiwi, the deferral of human rights to self-determination. Given this, Candace Fujikane argues that the point of Asian settler colonial critique is to advance "a methodological and epistemological shift away from predominant accounts of Hawai'i as a democratic, 'multi-cultural,' or 'multiracial' state by showing . . . instead the historical and political conditions of a white- and Asian-dominated U.S. settler colony."[37] This framing has been actively suppressed by Hawai'i's political system and its cash-cow tourism economy.

Multiculturalism as a Move to Innocence

For generations now, Hawai'i has been packaged and sold to the world as a commodity for touristic consumption. The Hawai'i Tourism Authority promotes Hawai'i as a vacation getaway, a playground, and an "escape" to a tropical holiday destination for "families, foodies, culture & history aficio-nados, nature lovers . . . romance seekers, outdoor adventurers, shoppers, and health & wellness enthusiasts."[38] The industry thrives on myths about Hawaiʻi's multiculturalism, selling ethnic diversity as much as its "exotic beauty." The market for film tourism has transformed Hawaiʻi into "Hollywood's backlot"[39] where North Shore beaches and Honolulu city streets stand in for Southeast Asia, and a community of hungry Asian actors play extras in blockbuster summer hits. Wedding tourism offers Hawaiʻi to couples looking to say their vows on a "white sandy beach" or in a "charming Victorian chapel."[40] The university hosts students and a system of academic tourism, while the Hawaiʻi Convention Center hosts event tourism to hundreds of thousands annually. Fantasies of a paradisiacal retreat inform how outsiders have come to see the islands for over a century now, and the State of Hawaiʻi has led the way, pitching a guaranteed experience of leisure with top-rated hospitality, "dramatic scenery," "epic beauty," and exotic charms with a "rich history" and culture.[41] Marketing strategies emphasize Hawaiʻi's multiculturalism to convince potential "visitors" that this destination is also fun and safe for the whole family, which begs the question: For whom is Hawaiʻi *not* safe? The veneer of multicultural and postracial amity has proven indispensable to tourism and for concealing any cracks appearing in Hawaiʻi's social hegemony. The myth of multiculturalism in Hawaiʻi emerged out of partial truths that I flag here to emphasize how its ideological function is to normalize the disavowal of Hawaiians as having legitimate claims to Maunakea (or Hawaiʻi), while enabling non-Hawaiians to assume the role of stewards and caretakers, if not Natives.

The celebration of multiculturalism in Hawaiʻi misidentifies ethnic diversity as a sign of postracial social harmony. The mythology, as Jonathan Okamura explains, can be traced to early twentieth-century anthropological and sociological research and eventually popular media discourse in which "glowing descriptions of race and ethnic relations in Hawaiʻi" were composed and circulated to create an image of Hawaiʻi as a "multicultural paradise."[42] This characterization is not only false, but it also obscures the socioeconomic inequalities that persist among ethnic groups. Despite the reality of socioeconomic stratification, the mythology has popularized a distorted view of Hawaiʻi as "a model of racial harmony" where a more "tolerant and peaceful coexistence" results in "harmonious" racial and ethnic relations. One problem with these early narratives is that claims were based on observations of rather trivial aspects of a perceived shared "local" culture and identity, which cited anecdotal evidence like Hawaiʻi's relatively high rates of intermarriage, varied ethnic customs, fusion of cultural foods, and so on, rather than on the empirical data that might otherwise reflect employment, educational attainment, housing ownership, and other socio-economic disparities. In sum, the myth of multicultural Hawaiʻi advanced the political and economic interests of the state and settler society striving for full citizenship within U.S. democracy. According to Okamura, the illusion of social harmony and amity prevents an adequate diagnosis of the socioeconomic realities that continue to define the lived experience of ethnic groups in Hawaiʻi.

The celebration of multicultural diversity in Hawaiʻi is what Eve Tuck and K. Wayne Yang describe as a "settler move to innocence." They argue there is a long history of non-Indigenous peoples groping for ways to assuage feelings of colonial guilt and endeavoring to reconcile settler "complicity, and rescue settler futurity."[43] Many non-Indigenous communities are satisfied with simply preserving their own civil rights over creating "more meaningful potential alliances" with Indigenous peoples, tribes, and nations who are struggling for sovereignty and self-determination. Tuck and Yang explain that while "the hard, unsettling work of decolonization" asks something very specific of all of us living on Native lands, moves to innocence "ultimately represent settler fantasies of easier paths to reconciliation."[44] In other words, rather than giving land, or much of anything at all, settler society and the state produce narratives and make gestures that perform reconciliation as a route to absolution but that ultimately uphold hierarchical structures of settler dominance and Native subjugation.

Instead of producing its proclaimed utopic vision of modern cultural, racial, and ethnic diversity, the work of multiculturalism in Hawaiʻi is to absorb the Native subject through logics of possession and liberal models of inclusion. Sherene Razack describes the superficial emphasis on cultural diversity as the "multicultural spiral" where a shallow understanding of cultural differences makes "power relations invisible and keeps dominant cultural norms in place."[45] Therefore, liberal multiculturalism—through celebrations of diversity and inclusion, cultural sensitivity, and mutual recognition—functions to make settlers into "innocent subjects . . . standing outside hierarchical social relations, who are not accountable for the past or implicated in the present."[46] It evacuates from conventional understandings and popular education the political and the historical, which settler colonial analysis requires. Restoring politics and history to mainstream knowledge about Hawaiʻi is not difficult, but it is unsettling, which is the point. In the search for reprieve from settler guilt, narrations of injury grope for absolution. The emphasis on multiculturalism diverts critical attention away from confronting how we are all implicated in systems of violence and focuses instead on settler victimhood and entitlement. A critique of power and history opens space to render legible how settler victimhood operates and activates multicultural ideologies.

From "Identity Creation" to Subject Formations

I need to pause for a moment here to discuss an intervention that inadvertently risks reproducing a discursive erasure of the claim to independence that Kānaka ʻŌiwi maintain. Even social justice–oriented interventions in multicultural discourse can sometimes miss the importance of settler colonial critique and indigeneity as an analytic, particularly as reform of liberal democracy and civil rights cannot account for the stakes of liberation for many Indigenous peoples. I notice a discursive example in Okamura's analysis of the "ways by which ethnic inequality and hierarchy are perpetuated in Hawaiʻi," which seems to treat settler colonization only superficially, and thereby leaves U.S. occupation unexamined. While he emphasizes identity formation as the preferred response among ethnic groups who perform cultural identity for political leverage, my concern is the implied critique of Kanaka indigeneity, as such an approach suggests articulations of Kanaka alterity are political and may thereby imply that they are performative or unsubstantiated. However, rather than identities and their "creation," which I argue risk being read as contrived and false, even deceptive, I emphasize subjectivities. The reason is that subjectivities may be articulated to form unities of distinct elements under changing conditions that are "not necessary, determined, absolute . . . (or) essential for all time" but that may be rearticulated in a variety of ways as relations shift.[47] Subject formations are complex, contradictory, and never fully coherent, as they inflect structural impositions as well as interventions in them.

On one hand, Okamura is sympathetic and supportive of the Hawaiian movement. He explains, Native "Hawaiians are not merely residents of a state but a native people with a distinct culture, history, religion, language, and ancestral ties to Hawai'i"[48] who "have become racialized and viewed not as a native people but as a racial minority."[49] Critical of the "constant legal and political challenges to Native Hawaiian rights and entitlements following" a key anti-Native court ruling known as *Rice v. Cayetano* in 2000—challenges that "demonstrate the superficiality and invalidity of the Hawai'i multicultural model in representing ethnic relations in the state"[50]— he also recognizes, "it must be understood that their political movements are not concerned with a nostalgic return to a romanticized past but instead are very much focused on gaining greater power and control over their collective lives and lands in the present and immediate future."[51]

On the other hand, however, because his focus is on "identity construction,"[52] Okamura treats Kānaka 'Ōiwi as another "ethnic minority,"[53] despite modest efforts to suggest they are not, in order to analyze how "disadvantaged groups"[54] in Hawai'i all share similar tactics to improve their conditions. For example, while explicating how social barriers historically constructed around ethnic identities continue to inform socio-economic inequalities among various ethnic groups, he writes, "Some groups, particularly those that are politically or economically disadvantaged such as Native Hawaiians, create and articulate distinct identities for themselves in order to advance their political or economic interests."[55] He continues:

> Native Hawaiians especially employ aspects of their traditional culture—such as language, rituals, values, and myths—to express their unique identity as kanaka maoli [*sic*] that distinguishes them from all other ethnic groups in Hawai'i. At the same time, they create a structural boundary with other island groups by emphasizing Hawaiian descent or ancestry as the primary criterion for being considered Native Hawaiian. The Native Hawaiian case underscores how identity signifies cultural and social difference, if not uniqueness, as the principal basis for advancing their claims and entitlements to land and other resources in Hawai'i.[56]

The implication here is that "Native Hawaiian" is an identity that Kānaka 'Ōiwi create to exclude others. As a critique of that posits this identity formation as simply a means to an end, it also suggests Native Hawaiian identity comes at the expense of building solidarity with "other island groups." Yet, those "ends" remain undeveloped, so there is no evidence given to defend the critique or its premise that Kanaka 'Ōiwi claims to land and entitlements are identity based. It presumes Kānaka ʻŌiwi emphasize "descent . . . [and] ancestry"[57] *in order* to distinguish themselves—to be "considered Native Hawaiian"—for the sake of reinforcing claims. The logic of the argument not only suggests Kānaka ʻŌiwi have shaped identity claims, they may have invented them, the implication being that the structures of control to which we are subject and collectively struggle against—from blood quantum policy to an Office of Hawaiian Affairs that may be governed and elected by non-Hawaiians—are about cultural and social difference rather than the terms of legitimacy by which alienation from land persists.

While Okamura deconstructs multiculturalism with consideration for disadvantaged ethnic groups, my difficulty is with how this focus on identity formation presumes *the reason* Kānaka ʻŌiwi assert difference is to advance claims and entitlements to land and other resources. If the claim here is that socioeconomic disadvantage gives rise to Kanaka articulations of group differentiation—that Hawaiians articulate indigeneity *because* of their disproportionately low socioeconomic status, educational attainment, health outcomes, and political capacity *or* to overcome them—the logic ends with Kānaka ʻŌiwi seizing an opportunity. While possibly, partially the case, the discussion fails to account for the ways subjectivities emerge, shift, transform, and endure, or to substantively engage power. I submit that it is the other way around: it is because other ethnic groups differently situated within settler society under the authority of U.S. imperial power disregard the ongoing structural reality that colonization continues that Kanaka alterity is misunderstood and misrepresented. The equivocation provides a redemptive function to the discourse of multiculturalism that I find troubling. In other words, while socioeconomic depression is not irrelevant, leaving out of the conversation the ongoing structural processes of colonization as a context for the ideological formations through which Kānaka ʻŌiwi articulate and compose Indigenous alterity, I would argue that the frame obscures more than it reveals, making an emphasis on identity problematic.

If Hawaiians are mistaken as opportunists, even if only discursively, who perform indigeneity as mere political strategy, then Kanaka articulations of socioeconomic and political difference are dubious at best, unfounded and inauthentic at worst.

Instead of identity formation, I would argue our analyses might benefit from examining subjectivities that emerge through a range of complex and contradictory articulations. This model abandons the irresolvable trap of an in/authenticity binary by opening space to assess how social relations structured in institutions of dominance within settler colonial contexts produce, foreclose, and sustain various subjectivities. This puts the focus on a settler society structured in dominance rather than a search for legitimacy of those subjugated to power. Subject formations, rather than identity formations, create such a space because they map power at the moment of signification. Indeed, subjectivities are forged and foreclosed in relation to ideological state apparatuses, like courts, agencies, legislature, the media, among others. Structured in dominance, they inform power relations in which some articulations are authorized and deemed legitimate, while others are suspect and targeted. The principal basis for advancing Indigenous claims is settler colonialism, not political, tactical, or dubious identity claims.

Stuart Hall's theory of articulation[58] accounts for the complexity and contingency that I am advocating for. The slippage between the meaning of "articulation" as *enunciation* or *utterance* and the meaning of "articulation" as *enjoined parts* provides the import of this insight. In the articulation of Kanaka indigeneity by which Mauna a Wākea is conceived as an ancestor, the question of that claim's legitimacy matters less than the conditions of possibility for this ideological articulation to become suspect, trivialized, or forsaken as illegitimate—Indigenous subjugation under U.S. imperial power. Power begins in language as the signification of ideology. Hall argues, "The moment of power is not in ideology or culture as an instance. The moment of power is in the historically situated invention of ideology in practices of signification."[59] This is the moment of epistemic closure, when "truth" or "authenticity" is assigned or disavowed, the imposition of one set of meanings over others. In our example, it is the moment at which Native Hawaiians are said to be creating identities for political ends. Articulation draws our attention away from any presumed reality and toward language, as power lies at the locus of enunciation, where ideology coheres around a particular project.

So, when Kānaka ʻŌiwi say our genealogical relationality to land offers a better explanation of our world, indeed, this is neither true nor false, neither a political strategy nor a universal reality, but it is an articulated ideology comprising combinations that are nonnecessary, absolute, or fixed. They reflect a society structured in dominance. As such, they are not random, they are logical. The ideology is not the problem, so much as its articulation is a threat for the intervention it makes within state apparatuses vying for hegemony. The point is to understand the terms by which articulations form and function to avoid the trappings (and violence) of an imposed, or a universal, inevitable, and sanctioned reality, such as those enforced by imperial science and settler law under foreign military occupation. Rather than focus on the legitimacy of Kanaka identities, even if only done inadvertently or discursively, if we examine their loci of enunciation within relations of colonial power that subject Natives and settlers differently, shifting subjectivities are not surprising. Where identity connotes permanence, subjectivity turns to structural relations of power. A focus on how subjectivities are forged and foreclosed through articulated ideologies therefore emphasizes contingency in the ways that subjugated groups differently confront power to open space for a nonessentialist cultural identity politics. In my view, this allows for a path to solidarity where identity succumbs to the sort of horizontal competitions on which colonialism and imperialism thrive. Hall's theory of articulation describes how meaning for any subject is always shifting, as he explains:

> A theory of articulation is both a way of understanding how ideological elements come, under certain conditions, to cohere together within a discourse, and a way of asking how they do or do not become articulated, at specific conjunctures, to certain political subjects . . . (put an)other way: the theory of articulation asks how an ideology discovers its subject rather than how the subject thinks the necessary and inevitable thoughts which belong to it; it enables us to think how an ideology empowers people, enabling them to begin to make some sense or intelligibility of their historical situation, without reducing those forms of intelligibility to their socio-economic or class location or social position.[60]

Instead of asking which and to what extent Hawaiian cultural and political thought and praxis are invented, why not ask: *What are the conditions of possibility for articulations of* Kanaka *indigeneity to be rendered illegitimate and to what end?* The difference is methodological and may lead to better analyses and lines of solidarity.

Regarding the question of power and discourse, Kānaka ʻŌiwi do not emphasize racial or ethnic difference *in order* to "advance their political and economic interests."[61] Instead, it is because Kanaka indigeneity is rendered illegible within the ideological state apparatuses formed under conditions of settler occupation that articulations of Kanaka alterity are disavowed. It is that Kanaka subjectivities are structured under such conditions that Kanaka ʻŌiwi political thought and praxis are rendered suspect in the first place. Moreover, questioning Kanaka articulations of culture to collective political action, particularly according to metrics of legitimacy imposed under conditions of settler colonialism, does more to reproduce settler innocence and settler nativism than reveal any truth about Hawaiian identity. Indeed, blood quantum policies, the politics of federal recognition, and even the very premise and promise of Native "rights" and "entitlements"— each held out as gifts for which eligibility hinges on performances of authenticity as vetted by non-Hawaiians—ultimately function to normalize the status quo of settler hierarchy structured in relations of dominance under U.S. imperialism.

While the examination of ethnic group differentiation as a response to socioeconomic inequalities is crucial, in my view, if this practice consolidates Indigenous peoples into "disadvantaged groups" or "ethnic minorities," it is not adequately tending to the sorts of power imposed on Kānaka ʻŌiwi and to which our collective actions are directed. At worst, they affirm epistemic closure and reproduce settler logics of possession. In the case of Hawaiʻi, the disavowal of Kanaka indigeneity operates discursively. It ignores the reason self-determination matters at all and sidesteps the question of decolonization entirely. The discursive consolidation of indigeneity into ethnicity (or race) is therefore problematic as it creates possible routes to settler nonimplication in ongoing colonial formations, whereby dominant groups, comfortable arguing from positions of injury and victimization, will employ the intellectual labor and rhetoric of social justice and potentially allied scholars as a path to settler absolution.

When defending our ancestral places and sacred sites like Mauna a Wākea through culturally informed direct action or articulating better worlds, we are not optimizing or capitalizing on our indigeneity but articulating a politics of decolonization, shaping subjectivities within and despite oppressive institutions and hegemonic orders. While articulations shift over time and in response to a variety of evolving factors, they are not reducible to political strategy. Rather, it is because articulations of Kanaka indigeneity are treated with suspicion as a condition of liberal multiculturalism that Kanaka subjectivities emerge, move, unsettle, languish, collapse, and so on. Given this, a focus on identity at the expense of a robust critique of colonialism risks a discursive foreclosure that is paradoxically resonant with liberal multiculturalism itself. In this way, as I have argued, liberal multiculturalism operationalizes settler colonial domination discursively and materially.

This is not to say that settler colonialism structures everything either, or that analysis of identity formations and strategic essentialism is irrelevant. Instead, my point is that an analysis of ethnicity and identity formation without a sustained nuanced analysis of settler colonialism's subjectivization of Indigenous alterity will be inadequate, particularly if we wish to account for what is at stake in movements for Indigenous self-determination and sovereignty. The stakes for Kānaka ʻŌiwi in the struggle for Mauna a Wākea and solidarity could hardly be greater.

The Multiculturalism of ʻImiloa Astronomy Center

After more than fifty years of astronomy development on Maunakea, there is now a well-documented history of management failures that calls into question the University of Hawaiʻi's stewardship and the state Board of Land and Natural Resources' oversight of permitting the observatories.[62] In response, over the last two decades of TMT planning, the university has sought to demonstrate its commitment to reform, touting a newfound promise of accountability to not only the astronomy community but to the broader public and especially to Native Hawaiians. While this renewal has led to "consultations," polls, and public meetings where "community engagement," "cultural sensitivity," and "public participation" are held up as evidence of due diligence and respect "for all perspectives," without a capacity to engage the political and therefore the popular call for a moratorium on new telescope development, they are largely performative.[63] In chapter 6, I will examine in detail how such a rhetoric of accountability within legal discourse, environmental reports, and management planning documents suggests the move toward reform models market efficiency. Here, however, I look at an example of bridge building that promotes a vision of Kanaka indigeneity in which the TMT is framed as inevitable, universally beneficial, and unproblematic. In describing communities with an interest in Maunakea as "stakeholders," the ʻImiloa Astronomy Center in Hilo has instrumentalized a liberal model of inclusion, offering multicultural programming meant to appeal to "all sides" under the auspices of achieving compromise across difference. I argue that discourses calling for coexistence on the Mauna through celebrations of Hawaiian culture, language, and a selective "ancient" history but that also avoids critical analysis of the substance driving Kanaka struggles for freedom and decolonization, let alone the decommissioning of all Maunakea observatories, serve ultimately to reify the mythology of multicultural harmony, which invents a position of noncomplicity and therefore a path to redemption for the scientific settler state.

Opened in Hilo in 2006, 'Imiloa was intended to serve as "a gathering place that advances the integration of science and Indigenous culture" and bring "together members of the Hawaiian and astronomy communities to share a common vision for the future."[64] The 'Imiloa Astronomy Center is a University of Hawai'i-funded community outreach and educational organization that provides support to UH Hilo and the Office of Maunakea Management through a range of services and offers "Hawaiian language and culture based enrichment programs that focus on local science research, cultural advancement and environmental stewardship."[65] In 2013, I interviewed several staff at the center to understand the role of multiculturalism in the center's programming, rhetoric, and public-facing image. While its embrace of Hawaiian language and culture is exceptional and admirable, its evacuation of critique and politics suggests this celebration of language and culture comes at the cost of critical engagement with the stakes of the Mauna Movement and the collective action to protect Maunakea.

On any given day you might find grade schoolers on a field trip enjoying the planetarium or a handsome "local" audience attending an evening lecture, art exhibit, book reading, musical performance, or other special event. Conceived in the mid-1990s, the original vision of the center was "to showcase the connections between the rich traditions of Hawaiian culture and the groundbreaking astronomical research conducted at the summit of Maunakea." In our interview, 'Imiloa Astronomy Center Director Ka'iulani Kimura explained the center was built to be "a conduit between the community and the university in order to present the work of the astronomy community on the summit to the public and to bring the concerns of the public to the university."[66]

As the center routinely includes programming and events promoting the Thirty Meter Telescope that invoke or employ Hawaiian language, values, and culture, ʻImiloa is also a site of ambivalence. On one hand, it represents the often thankless though necessary work of building bridges across political and ideological divides through art, science, and culture. Yet, as opportunities to engage the politics of astronomy, environmental degradation, or Indigenous politics are intentionally foreclosed in the space of the center and its events, I argue Kanaka subjectivity and epistemologies are contained in ways conducive to liberal multiculturalism and the TMT.

ʻImiloaʼs mission is to present "Hawaiian and scientific beliefs, theories and practices related to Maunakea, the stars, and the world around us," describing its work as

an integral part of the University of Hawaiʻi at Hilo, and therefore committed to improving the quality of life of the people of Hawaiʻi Island and state. Through strategic partnerships with programs of the University, Hawaiʻi-based observatories, local businesses and schools, we create opportunities that strengthen career awareness and workforce development, and contribute to our community sustainability.[67]

ʻImiloaʼs website also uses Hawaiian language and concepts to illustrate its "mission, vision & values":

KAIWIKUAMOʻO ʻIMILOA: Core Values

ʻImiloa means to seek far and is the Hawaiian word both explore and explorer [sic]. Through a Hawaiʻi lens, we explore our place in the genealogy of the universe and continually seek, learn, and adapt to our ever-evolving environment that inspires discovery and innovation through three core values.

1. Kamaʻāina—We honor our relationship to land, sea and sky and share this connection through personal and *enlightened hospitality.*
2. Naʻauao—We steward our collective knowledge and wisdom as provisional resources that illuminate our community today and tomorrow.
3. Hanakahi—We work together, drawing upon individual strengths and talents to harness our collective synergy and advance the mission of ʻImiloa.[68]

There is some irony that "kamaʻāina," "naʻauao," and "Hanakahi" are not translated but instead are assigned to these statements. For example, *kamaʻāina* is the word for "acquainted" and "familiar," as one born in a specific place might be.[69] It is also the term given to a "Native-born" person, though it does not necessarily denote indigeneity. Translated also as "host" and considering this entry includes an intent to share "enlightened hospitality," the rhetoric is invoking tourist marketing strategies. *Naʻauao* may translate to "knowledge," "wisdom," or "science," and that this term is linked to "stewardship" indicates the center's role in bolstering the university's claim to Maunakea through its pursuit of universal knowledge by way of giant telescopes atop Maunakea. Finally, *Hanakahi* "was used in poetry to designate the Hilo district" and is so named for "an ancient chief."[70] That this third entry is assigned the namesake of a chief known as "a symbol of profound peace" begs the question: Where does ʻImiloa stand in relationship to the Mauna Kea Movement? I read this and other rhetoric throughout ʻImiloa's discursive strategies as evidence of what is perhaps its primary mission: to sanitize the University of Hawaiʻi's actions in defeating community opposition to telescope expansion and normalize the Maunakea observatory through use of purposefully vague and universalizing language common to tourism PR discourses—but nuanced enough to deflect criticism for it.

Review of the university's expenditures in litigation to secure the TMT permits, the project's price tag of $2.6 billion, and the big science this telescope now embodies suggests the "collective synergy" has more to do with settler public relations than accurately representing Kānaka ʻŌiwi or the historical context by which this "collective" formed. Moreover, in light of the university's efforts to circumvent State conservation policy and Native Hawaiian rights, as discussed in chapter 2, the list of core values also raises questions of the extent to which the appropriation of ʻŌiwi culture and the enlistment of Native Hawaiians betrays such narrations of collectivity. For example, ʻImiloa's commitment to exploring "*our* place in *the genealogy* of the universe" and "*our* relationship to land" is ultimately an appropriation of Kanaka ʻŌiwi rhetorical strategies frequently used to articulate key values located in the cosmogonic genealogy of the Kumulipo. Here, Native epistemological concepts are transposed onto an Anglo-settler (i.e., Western/European-derived) practice of astronomy (in its contemporary industrialized form) to suggest the telescopes atop Maunakea were built with "genealogies" and "relations to land" in mind. The marriage of Kanaka ʻŌiwi values and this observatory may be defended through rhetorical gestures and ideological inventions but not physical reality. As this attempt to discursively infuse "things Hawaiian" with industrial astronomy and its expansion on Maunakea levels difference, it does so through presupposition of a universal human subject with a shared "genealogy" rooted in a post–Scientific Revolution/post-Enlightenment imperialist "explorer" tradition. The move undermines the distinct historical and continued violence of political subjugation that Kānaka 'Ōiwi experience under conditions of settler capitalism and U.S. military occupation. It is not only condescending but so forced that it reveals its intentions.

In a phone interview with 'Imiloa director Ka'iu Kimura, I asked how she views the center's relationship with the Institute for Astronomy. She explains that, growing up, she experienced pressure to either "go after science" or "divorce yourself . . . from the cultural values of where you come from because they are in conflict. I didn't personally want to see that be an issue anymore for the future generations coming up."[71] She was personally "on the fence" about the TMT until about 2001 when a very close uncle made the compelling argument that the TMT

> is going to be a resource for our community and if it ain't people from our own community participating and getting on board now, then pohō [*out of luck*] . . . We gotta get our own people involved in these conversations that people are having [that] you know the science community are having.[72]

Kimura explained that when the center was first created, even friends, family, and colleagues felt it was meant only to smooth over differences while ignoring "underlying issues"—and that the university just wanted to present a better image of itself. On "the flip side," she adds,

> sharing with the community that doesn't necessarily have regular access and engagement with the university and with the astronomy community, our job is to share with them what's going on. I grew up in Waimea all my life and I never knew what was going on in those observatories. I feel like our job is to share with the community what's going on in those observatories. Not necessarily to form or persuade any opinion, but just to put it out and to say this is what it is and have conversation around that.[73]

Kimura also received skepticism from those supporting the TMT. She described how some scientists distrusted the idea of a science center with a focus on culture, use of Hawaiian language in its exhibits, and the inclusion of concepts from the Kumulipo. They felt a science center should be strictly about science, and many couldn't understand why a seat at the table should matter to the community. In this sense, the fight was for inclusion and participation.

She also described how "the whole problem" before the university produced its Comprehensive Master Plan "was that our own local people weren't involved, and they weren't able to engage with the university . . . [who] were building out the summit."[74] So, under her leadership, ʻImiloa invited, "the chairman of the board and the president of Caltech University to come and meet with various community stakeholders, in particular those with adverse opinions towards astronomy development on Mauna Kea."[75] She felt the center's role should be "to create a new space for dialogue to happen around issues with Maunakea. I felt it was our kuleana to really live that and to have hard conversations between people on the issue." Focused on "community engagement," she described the center's commitment "to show both sides of the issue and to stay out of the politics and the political history of the debates" has paid off and that the university has heard the community's concerns "loud and clear." The evidence, Kimura explains, is in the new management plan.

> I think [the TMT leadership] . . . heard [the community saying], "have your plans for decommissioning ready. Why don't you remove *your own* telescope," because Caltech has another telescope up there, which they have committed to deconstructing and restoring. They also heard [the demand] to invest locally on the Big Island—education opportunity-wise. All those things the TMT came out with . . . it didn't come from their own . . . it came from them listening over and over to a lot of stakeholder groups on the Big Island. And I'm happy to see they've responded to that.[76]

While a case could be made that ʻImiloa's focus on "bringing communities together" and "getting local people involved" is commendable, there are several assumptions on which the center's mission is premised that trouble me. First, while it may "stay out of the debate" by avoiding engaging in it explicitly, the suggestion that the center might somehow operate outside of politics is itself political—by the simple fact that the contest for Maunakea is constituted in power. Abdication of a position while presuming to facilitate dialogue sets parameters around what is sayable, and thus *is political*. Second, consultation is not synonymous with consent. Despite earnest declarations that the university has truly heard the people, simply gathering information, recording perspectives, and giving a "seat at the table" does not necessarily lead to accountability. Indeed, because pulling the TMT was never an option, collecting data from public hearings, written testimonies, and focus groups amounts to preparation for contesting potential counterarguments. If terminating the project is never a real possibility, then "consultation" appears more to be about recontextualizing voices of dissent to perform due process, than evidence of accountability.[77] Moreover, now that we may reflect on the mass arrests of 2015 and 2019 and the threats of physical violence at the hands of militarized state police under orders of the state governor, the university's consultations should now be seen for what they are: the cost of doing business. Finally, while I appreciate the desire to make astronomy on Maunakea inclusive of Hawaiʻi's local communities, insofar as its vision of inclusion is fashioned on the liberal multicultural model of recognition outlined above, it functions as another effort to manage Kanaka dissent, further neglecting substantive engagement with the realities of settler colonization under U.S. occupation. Given this, the "seat at the table" idea mirrors the "gift" metaphor of liberal democracy. More about appearances than substance, participation for some may be an achievement, but it is also a convenient alibi for upholding the hegemonic status quo. What opportunities for solidarity with the Hawaiian movement are lost when the celebration of culture comes at the expense of analysis of power?

Coexistence as Containment

Returning to the performative rhetoric of "coexistence," now ubiquitous among advocates of the TMT, the seemingly conciliatory offering functions as a gesture toward compromise, that evacuates history while depoliticizing social relations through invoking a sense of liberal "benevolence." Presenting much like the gift-giving of Maunakea, "coexistence" manipulates hospitality to feign generosity and peace making. The past is the past, goes its logic, suggesting we should all just "move on." This move gaslights the opposition, as appeals to "co-exist" assume a moral high ground that anticipates opposition to the TMT only to trivialize the movement's principled objectives. While it proposes we all *get past the past,* "coexistence" recon-stitutes the performative appeal to make support for the TMT a virtuous position, while any opposition is reduced to unreasonable obstruction. Like-wise, while the "seat at the table" and the "gift" metaphors favor power, the ambiguity of this participation and generosity leaves the fate of Maunakea to those already empowered to construct, to permit, to arrest, and so on. Disavowing history and accountability, aligned with liberal multicultural-ism, "coexistence" levels difference, implying everyone is equally invested and impacted by the project, and no single group stands to lose more than any another. If Hawaiians oppose the "gift" of recognition or reject the appeal to "co-exist," we are painted as ingrates. As such, those who refuse the gift of "coexistence" are cast off as unreasonable. In this rhetorical game, demands for a moratorium now become excessive and Kanaka ʻŌiwi spir-itual relationality expressed through aloha ʻāina becomes irrational.[78] In these ways, "coexistence" appears to be an invitation to find common ground, but it is deeply invested in the possessive settler logics of Native replace-ment and, therefore, the management of Kanaka indigeneity.

Insofar as settler subjecthood coheres around the disavowal of Native alterity, containment is not only a priority of the settler state but its raison d'être. The settler state and settler society become obsessed with disavow-ing the prior claims to life, land, and ea in which Kanaka ʻŌiwi movements are grounded, recasting them as impossible, excessive, obsolete, unjust, or outmoded. Therefore, within such settler rationality, the Native subject becomes an empty vessel, a site of disqualification and disavowal where the "manageable remnant" of indigeneity is neutralized, and the settler "inherits" what remains: the land now emptied of Native people and Native claims. In this context, Kānaka ʻŌiwi are struggling for control over our very image. Interpellated by the state as "n/Native Hawaiians" and made into artifacts, scapegoats, militants, hosts, and consultants, the state condemns, discredits, and abandons, but also fetishizes to possess the Native subject, for its tourism economy especially cannot do without. We are an authen-ticating resource for settler affirmation and self-authorization, but actual Hawaiian people are a threat. Therefore, Kanaka ʻŌiwi subjectivity, as much as the land itself, is at stake in the contest for Mauna a Wākea and this explains the violence visited upon the kiaʻi in 2015 and 2019.

To some, it may be surprising that Kānaka ʻŌiwi are often willing to consult, accepting the gifts of liberalism, soliciting coexistence, and relishing a seat at the table. However, just as white supremacy functions most effectively through hegemonic consent of the subjugated, so too is settler colonization willing to accommodate all participants. Anyone can join in the multicultural mythology because its superficiality is the point. However, not everyone shares equally in the spoils of empire and capitalism, and this cannot be gleaned through a superficial approach. As argued in this chapter, settler colonialism seeks to eliminate discursively, if not actually, by managing Kanaka alterity and indigeneity through logics of possession and practices of disavowal that normalize settler replacement on the land—all lands. As such, Hawaiʻi's settler society constantly vacillates between desire and contempt for Kānaka ʻŌiwi, indicating how the Native subject is always a source of colonial anxiety and ambivalence.

Colonial ambivalence describes the contradictory reality of settler desire, the "continual fluctuation between wanting one thing and its opposite," the "simultaneous attraction toward and repulsion from an object, person or action."[79] Robert Young describes this ambivalence as the paradox that arises when "the periphery—the borderline, the marginal, the unclassifiable, the doubtful—has become the equivocal, indefinite, indeterminate ambivalence that characterizes the centre."[80] In Hawaiʻi, this ambivalence is expressed through the systemic, institutionalized management of Kanaka subjectivities, becoming not only a path to innocence but also to fully realized settler subjecthood. Against the malleable and desired Native subject, a settler sense of absolution, redemption, and selfhood, indeed, belonging becomes possible. The process is paradoxical. As Hawaiians are both necessary to settler subjectivity and necessarily a threat to its coherence, we are the spectral reminder of a colonial present. In this way, the consequence of colonial ambivalence is also a mark of its own impossibility: elimination deferred is also the possibility of its undoing.

In conclusion, this chapter has argued that liberal multiculturalism operationalizes settler colonialism in Hawaiʻi through discursive as much as physical and material practices—that is, through logics of possession and practices of replacement, containment, and management of Native bodies and Native alterity. Liberal democracy seeks to neutralize radical alterity—and in Hawaiʻi, Indigenous claims to life, land, and ea—by containing and managing Kanaka indigeneity through ideas, practices, and institutions meant to level difference and control prior knowledges and ways of being. But a liberal model of recognition and inclusion is also put to work for settler hegemony and to reproduce settler innocence as well as settler belonging. Agency can be attributed to settlers for whom investment in the American project offers a path to absolution from complicity in the ongoing structures of displacement and disavowal. The myths of Hawaiʻi as a multicultural paradise facilitate not only rampant tourist capitalism but the industrial astronomy now represented by the Thirty Meter Telescope. The point of this exposition of liberal multicultural settler colonialism has been an effort to emphasize the importance of a sustained colonial critique to make sense of how the TMT appears to be a gift to Hawaiʻi and the world. Without a politics and a critique of settler colonization, the ongoing hegemonic formations of power embodied in the debate over telescope development on Mauna a Wākea will remain obscured, illegible, and irresolvable.

4

A CONTINUUM OF STRUGGLE

So, when we (the "PKO gang") all got together, that's what
we talked about. We said there were two differences: one was
(1) struggle, resistance, absolute necessity, and (2) culture.

—TERRILEE NĀPUA KEKOʻOLANI-RAYMOND

Where Was the Opposition to Telescopes in the Beginning?

There is a common line of argument used by TMT supporters who wish to
discredit the kiaʻi for their activism against the project. It suggests community opposition today has come too late to be taken seriously. If Maunakea is so special, they ask, *where were these so-called land defenders in
the first decades of development? How could Hawaiians have let ten observatories be built on the summit if it is as precious and fragile as they say?
If this place truly is sacred, why did they not speak up until now?* The challenge posits the absence of spectacle—in such forms as direct action like
civil disobedience, roadblocks, and mass marches—as an absence of opposition altogether, suggesting it indicates a form of consent. Therefore, any
such activism today can be dismissed as arbitrary, capricious, and unjus-
tified. Framed as a desperate attempt to foil progress, the latecomer argument implies that the Maunakea Movement is contrived. As an invention
of straggler opportunists bent on obstructing progress-as-science out of
petty resentment, collective action against the project that centers culture
is seen as inauthentic or fraudulent. If protesting Hawaiians are not *real*
Hawaiians, then they have no *real* grievance. TMT opposition is dismissed
as merely a political tactic to achieve unrelated objectives. As such, kiaʻi are
painted as disingenuous, which suggests Kānaka ʻŌiwi are responsible for
any injury we attribute to the TMT. Such frames trivialize the movement
and vilify Hawaiians. If Hawaiians don't really know what injury is—if we
don't really know what we're doing in our opposition—no responsibility

can be assigned for the oppression Hawaiians claim to experience. Ultimately, asking why there were no early protests to telescope development is not innocent. A ruse that invokes a sentiment of disavowal, it presupposes settler innocence by virtue of its framing, and simultaneously incites suspicion of Maunakea activism. "Where was the opposition to telescopes in the beginning?" is not an innocent question. It depoliticizes and dehistoricizes legacies of Kanaka ʻŌiwi political thought and praxis.

Contemporary activism that centers culture and spiritual protocols has also been spun as an attack on astronomers. "Land defenders," or kiaʻi, are dismissed as "angry Hawaiians." The attack is not only on scientists but on science and rational thought, modernity, and democracy as well. Treated within legal and scientific discourses as having no legitimate claim to the Mauna, those who protest are painted as antiscience and irrational. As these discourses attempt an inversion of actual power relations—to imply that settlers are now marginalized by Kānaka ʻŌiwi—TMT advocates may assume a position of victimhood. This affords reason to cry foul and thereby pathologize collective action: *angry Natives who hate science are attacking astronomy.*

While it is tempting to counter such a charge with examples to the contrary, this does not necessarily tend to the larger question of what is at stake for Kānaka ʻŌiwi in the struggle for Maunakea, which concerns how Hawaiians, in protest and collective action with allies, are recast as unreasonable, irrational, antimodern, and subhuman. This has broader implications for Kanaka claims against settler colonialism under U.S. imperialism, which conditions the TMT's possibility and continued deferral of Kanaka self-determination and the deoccupation of Hawaiʻi. The goal of this chapter is to compose a different conception of humanity by centering Kanaka struggle as articulated by Kānaka ʻŌiwi, and to locate the TMT in a long history of displacement, alienation, and subjugation of Kānaka ʻŌiwi. This opens space to counter these claims but also to restore Kanaka humanity. To this end, this chapter briefly surveys the Hawaiian Renaissance to draw the throughline from nineteenth-century resistance to U.S. annexation and the contemporary Hawaiian movement and its latest iteration at Mauna a Wākea. Next, the chapter will perform the politics I am advocating for by presenting a portion of a transcript from an interview I conducted with Terrilee Nāpua Kekoʻolani-Raymond, a Kanaka ʻŌiwi political organizer and longtime peace activist with Nuclear Free and Independent Pacific; Hawaiʻi Peace and Justice; and Women's Voices, Women Speak. Aunty Terri's ʻike (knowledge) illustrates the broader analysis and contextualization that I argue is necessary to understand the struggle for Mauna a Wākea. Engaging questions about the TMT by drawing connections to earlier movements, Aunty Terri's experience reveals layers of analysis about the context in which the contemporary Mauna Movement acquires meaning for so many. In other words, it exists in a continuum of struggle. To understand the broader story of Kanaka ʻŌiwi struggle for life, land, and ea, is to understand the politics of Mauna a Wākea. While I conclude the chapter with comments on the larger stakes for Kānaka ʻŌiwi who compose ourselves back into humanity on our own terms, I begin by confronting the latecomer criticism directly. At the risk of reifying its premise—by taking it seriously enough to deconstruct by engaging it at all—I challenge the latecomer discourse enroute to our moʻolelo, or stories of Kanaka struggle, which I argue render the Mauna Movement legible on our terms. In these moʻolelo, we find validation of today's resistance, for it is a link in a chain of struggles beginning with the U.S. invasion of our country.

"Not a Peep of Dissent" in a Continuum of Struggle

In 2001, the *LA Times* published an article suggesting there was no opposition to astronomy on Maunakea in the early years, arguing, "When the first telescopes rose from the mountain . . . there was not a peep of dissent from Hawaiians."[1] While this is a popular refrain among TMT supporters—the idea that Hawaiians did not care much about the Maunakea observatory until only recently—it is also no accident that such myths proliferate. Much like the conventional historiography about Hawaiʻi itself, written mainly in English by white men invested in a U.S.-controlled Hawaiʻi, ignorance and indifference to the struggle of Kānaka ʻŌiwi has also proliferated.

Nevertheless, there has always been consistent opposition to U.S. empire in Hawaiʻi and the Pacific, and to understand the timing and shape of Kanaka ʻŌiwi political thought and praxis around the issue of Maunakea and the TMT, one must understand how Kānaka ʻŌiwi articulated struggle throughout the period we are said to have sat idle and done nothing to protect the Mauna, or the cultural forms that breathe life into the lāhui (the nation, the people). If one cares to look, stories of resistance on every island abound, despite efforts to suppress them through colonial education, Christian moralizing, and U.S. nationalist indoctrination. The reason stories of resistance remain is that under U.S. settler occupation, Kānaka ʻŌiwi have always lived precarious lives, and among the ways change has been achieved is through organized grassroots political action and social movements grounded in struggle as much as ceremony and celebration of cultural knowledge. Indeed, the political is a part of the Hawaiian Renaissance that is sometimes overshadowed by cultural practice. Yet, particularly in this context of cultural appropriation and exploitation of all things Hawaiian in the name of corporate capitalism and its tourist economy, it is the articulation of politics to ancestral knowledges in the various forms of dissent that has consistently nurtured the resolve, purpose, and kuleana of Kānaka ʻŌiwi and the Hawaiian movement. The embrace of culture has always been foundational in expressions of resistance, as they provide assurance that this is what our ancestors would do. In other words, Kānaka ʻŌiwi have always voiced our dissent, but some have been unwilling to listen. When we do listen, we find there was indeed "not a peep," but rather waves of dissent. The purpose of this chapter is to focus our attention to these voices and thereby compose another conception of humanity and to recognize that Kanaka struggle is grounded in ceremony and reciprocity as the basis of political expression today.

Learning from the perspectives of Kānaka ʻŌiwi, we find that a line can be drawn connecting late nineteenth-century resistance to U.S. annexation all the way to the mid-twentieth-century rise of the Hawaiian sovereignty movement and extending to the struggle for Maunakea today. The direct actions and uprisings at Hale Pōhaku in 2015 and Puʻuhuluhulu in 2019 were not without precedence. They reveal how struggle, for many, is not an aberration but a constant.

Still, it would be a mistake to conflate the timing of the Maunakea movement with tacit consent or indifference to construction of the observatories. As mentioned in the beginning of this chapter, although the timing of direct action against telescope construction has been used to argue that Hawaiians were "pro-development" or more complaisant back then compared to now, the truth is that many—both Kānaka *and* non-Hawaiians— have always opposed telescopes in some capacity. Yet, in the beginning they registered their disapproval through formal venues, the press, and state processes: submitting oral testimonies and written statements, showing up to town hall and other public meetings, participating in management planning, attending hearings, and later, going to litigation with the State. The reason direct action, protest, and mass demonstrations were not pursued before 2014 is because these other options had been exhausted by that time, and there were other struggles in myriad other parts of the islands that took attention away from the Mauna. Likewise, the State disregarded the dissent that was voiced but also appropriated these voices as explained in previous chapters—through neoliberal environmental policy and liberal multicultural strategies meant to manage Kānaka ʻŌiwi and our capacity to organize collective action to intervene in development projects.

By most accounts, Hawaiians were always part of the early responses to construction on Maunakea, but no movement was organized as such in those first two decades of construction. When I asked my interview respondents why, many explained that the other issues Hawaiians had to confront elsewhere across the islands were simply too time and energy consuming. Governance failures during Hawaiʻi's territorial years would lead to the Hawaiian Renaissance following statehood in 1959, marking the 1960s and '70s as a period of cultural and political awakening for Hawaiians, just as it was for other Black, Brown, and Indigenous communities across Turtle Island and Oceania. A series of dedications for newly constructed telescopes atop Maunakea through the 1970s would, by 1980, be described as a "flurry" of development that local communities addressed by calling for limits on the number of telescopes on the summit.[2] Condemnations increased throughout the 1970s and led to vocal public dissent through the 1980s, legal challenges in the 1990s, and explicit community action beginning in the 2000s. As discussed in chapter 2 (and explored further in chapter 6), that momentum compelled the Hawaiʻi Legislature to conduct an official audit of the University of Hawaiʻi's management in 1998 and again in 2005, which documented gross management failures, lease violations, and environmental degradation.[3] A series of legal challenges by the Sierra Club and members of the community brought a significant victory in 2005, when developers seeking to expand the Keck Observatory to include numerous "outrigger" telescopes failed to realize the project. It took close to two decades, but those who accepted the kuleana (responsibility) to fight the legal battles would learn that the legal process alone would not stop the TMT. At the time of this writing, the TMT is stalled because both fronts were pursued: direct action civil disobedience *and* the tedious, thankless, and exhausting legal struggle.

At least by 1974, local people were registering their dissent about the rapid development of telescopes at Maunakea through letters to the editors of local newspapers,[4] oral and written testimonies at public hearings,[5] and letters to the Department of Land and Natural Resources and the Governor's Office.[6] At the early hearings on the various telescope subleases, members of the public voiced concerns that the telescopes would compromise their cultural practices and family connections to the mountain.[7] They expressed concern that astronomy was becoming too big and growing out of control. Through the 1990s, there were also dozens of scientific studies and cultural assessments reporting on the impacts of development to summit species like the wēkiu bug and the silver sword; below-summit forest plants, birds, insects, and other animals; and archeological resources like historic cultural sites and traditional practices associated with them.[8]

A better accounting of historical events is also necessary. For example, to those not living on Hawaiʻi Island, activities on the summit of Maunakea were relatively out of sight and out of mind—until they weren't. However, for Hawaiʻi Island residents, by contrast, the appearance of big white domes was initially perceived as a nuisance, inspiring the popular call to "pop da pimples," which referred to the common desire to see the telescopes removed. And for many Kānaka ʻŌiwi living and working on the mountain's lowlands—from Kohala to Hāmākua and Hilo—bearing witness in silence caused enduring trauma. Oral histories recorded by Kepā and Onaona Maly show that many residents, particularly kūpuna, experienced great emotional distress, sadness, and depression because of that industrial development.[9] Such testimonies and records also function as evidence of dissent. Old-timers are often hesitant to speak up let alone participate in hearings, litigation, or protest activism. Also, it was only during the global shifts in power following WWII and through the era of international decolonization—and after the gains of the U.S. civil rights movement, the women's and gay rights movements, antiwar protests against the U.S. war in Vietnam, and student movements through the 1960s—that it became relatively safe for Kānaka ʻŌiwi to organize and challenge the structures of racial discrimination brought with U.S. imperialism and settler colonialism. It is an abdication of historicism and of responsibility to objectivity when journalists, TMT marketers and investors, State and university officials, historians, and other interlocutors ignore Kanaka 'Ōiwi expressions of dissent, dissatisfaction, and resistance as they have throughout the past century.

That said, other reasons *a more organized* movement did not arise in the first twenty years are more practical: Kānaka 'Ōiwi were simply overwhelmed fighting battles on so many other fronts. No activist or historian I spoke with in my research described a quiet period of the Hawaiian movement in which lands, waters, people, or rights were *not* under threat. Nobody spoke about an absence of dissent in general. Attention was elsewhere. In fact, as I recall one interlocutor phrasing it, "Kānaka 'Ōiwi are the hardest working activists I know. There is always a sacred site somewhere under threat and we do not sit idle watching."[10] In Hawai'i, there is always one form of development or another to which Kānaka 'Ōiwi must commit energies to protect in the long term.

During the period of the Keck Observatory planning, review process, and construction in the 1990s, Kānaka 'Ōiwi expressed opposition out of concern for burial sites and iwi kupuna (ancestral remains) known to exist on the summit. However, cultural protocols prohibit disclosure of the location of human remains anywhere because it is an Indigenous value that Kānaka 'Ōiwi uphold to never allow bones or burial objects to be found or disinterred. This inherently leads to conflict between settler development and Indigenous value systems, protocols, and expectations of settler society. Iwi found on the summit, the highest point in the islands, would most certainly belong to the highest-ranking ali'i. So, unearthing them would not only be perceived as an egregious violation of ethics and social relations but would also represent the greatest form of disrespect to that kupuna's descendants and to all Kānaka. Moreover, the fact that burials found and removed, as well as other historic and sacred sites, have been assessed as worthy of protection or otherwise, *not* by Indigenous cultural experts but instead by non-Hawaiian contract archeologists hired by the State, only adds insult.[11] Many also experience pain in the knowledge that countless piko and 'iewe—the afterbirth of newborn infants buried in hidden locations—have been exposed to sunlight because of decades of telescope construction on the Mauna. Discourse around the sacred increased during this time because tolerance and patience had run thin by the 1990s.

Non-Hawaiians were also outraged by the rapid growth of astronomy and the university's management failures. For example, according to environmental activist and former Sierra Club chair, Nelson Ho, the public had reason to be concerned about the health of the summit lands. When he visited Maunakea in the early 1990s, he was surprised to observe wind-strewn rubbish from the construction sites littering the slopes below the summit. In our interview, Ho told me of an experiment he conducted to raise public awareness of the problem of pollution caused by construction.[12] He and a colleague traveled to the summit, set a bearing, and ventured a mile out in a straight line, collecting all the rubbish in their path. So much debris was being discarded that Ho had filled several forty-gallon trash bags. These amounted to scientific samples that demonstrated the urgent need for formal regulation of construction and operation of the observatories. Discarded trash left by thousands of tourists who visit every week was also found near Hale Pōhaku. Recording every bit collected, they found McDonald's containers, food wrappers, and tourist maps; the further from the summit they traveled, the more "industrial waste" they found. Ho also explained how, contrary to the university's claims, fifty-five-gallon drums of hydrocarbon fuel and 4x8-in. sheets of pulverized insulation were clearly not rubbish brought by tourists or recreational visitors. He said the Hawai'i County mayor refused to handle the issue of industrial waste, so he eventually held a press conference in which he brandished a backpack full of trash with scraps bearing the names of the various telescopes.[13] Efforts like this reflect the shared valuation of 'āina among many non-Hawaiians and Kānaka 'Ōiwi.

Public opinion throughout the 1980s demanded better accountability, eventually resulting in the 1998 legislative audit of the University of Hawai'i and the State Department of Land and Natural Resources (see chapter 6). The auditor's report alerted the public to the summit's condition and systemic management failures over the previous three decades.

Attempts to address community concerns were tepid, at best, but eventually resulted in the first management plans. In 1974, Governor George Ariyoshi was compelled to act but only after his office became flooded with letters from the public to intervene in unregulated astronomy expansion. A *Hawai'i Tribune-Herald* special edition from 1980 entitled "Mauna Kea (Past, Present and Future)" featured a memorandum penned by Ariyoshi that year, which advised the BLNR chairman, Sunao Kido, to promptly draft a master plan.[14] It read in part:

I am concerned that social pressures for more intensive uses of Mauna Kea for scientific, recreational and other purposes pose a threat to the priceless qualities of that mountain . . .

To assure that full consideration is given to all aspects of permitted, controlled and prohibited uses, you are hereby directed to develop and promulgate, as expeditiously as possible, a Master Plan for all of Mauna Kea above the Saddle Road.

Finally, the promulgation of the Master Plan should include its adoption by the Board of Land and Natural Resources following public hearings, and should provide for both the enforcement of the Plan and procedures for its amendment.[15]

Ariyoshi's intervention fell short of demanding a moratorium on new development, but his call for better management would add pressure to the State Board of Land and Natural Resources. While it was neither prompt nor comprehensive, the first "Mauna Kea Plan" was created in 1977 and would soon be replaced by the "Mauna Kea Complex Development Plan" in 1982.[16] In 1981, the governor "designated certain sections of Mauna Kea to be the Mauna Kea Ice Age Natural Reserve Area," which delegated control of specific areas to the Natural Area Reserves System Commission, an administrative entity within the State Board of Land and Natural Resources.[17] A management structure was produced reluctantly and only after half a dozen telescopes were already built or under construction atop the summit. And far from evidence of complacency or tacit consent to development of the Maunakea observatory, the pressure applied to Ariyoshi and its outcome represents an early example of opposition, without which it is likely no management structure would exist at all.

By 1999, a year after the legislative audit found the university's management of the summit "inadequate to ensure the protection of natural resources,"[18] and the same year a new telescope with the two largest white domes went up on a now permanently leveled puʻu (cinder cone, hill), Hawaiians began to proclaim, "Enough is enough!" That year, the university held three public hearings in three Hawaiʻi Island districts to gather community input on the Mauna Kea Complex Development Plan. Residents—again, both Kānaka and non-Hawaiian—offered testimonies, demanded explanations for what was presented as a "need" to build more telescopes, and expressed their outrage over the university's poor management record and the Land Board's seeming inability to oversee management. While a time limit of three minutes was imposed on everyone giving oral testimony, finally, large numbers began to organize in opposition to astronomy expansion. University of Hawai'i-Hilo professor Manulani Aluli Meyer articulated a common sentiment:

> But we will fight this. We will do so in our spiritual acts, in our prayers, because of the nature of what has gone wrong in the past, and that is a misrepresentation, a misunderstanding of the needs of culture and the development of our people and the people of Hawai'i beyond the science.
>
> We are asking for simply a moratorium so that we can work together. And working together for science, for culture, for harmony, this will not need to be a major misunderstanding. It doesn't need to be. But currently I have watched this for years.[19]

Then-telescope operator for the James Clerk Maxwell Telescope and cultural practitioner Kealoha Pisciotta echoed the call for a moratorium:

> I really want to talk about the fact that at the last public hearing, the consensus was overwhelming: 'a'ole, no. The Hawaiian people said no, we've had enough. Enough is enough. We've given already, we've shared and we want it to stop now because we don't want any more . . .[20]

Hilo resident Moses Kealamakia, who "was born and raised in the shadow of Mauna Kea in Waimea," also demanded a halt to expansion, arguing the university and astronomers have taken enough already:

> By the end of the 1970s, more structures were on the summit. Now, the people were silent, but they tolerated the structures . . . By the 1990s . . . the summit was littered with massive structures. Pu'u Poli'ahu was bulldozed . . . the telescopes became larger and larger and there are more of them . . . My feelings are there should be a moratorium on any further construction.[21]

While dissent may not have taken the form of roadblocks and encampments, there has always been opposition to telescopes on Mauna a Wākea since the first decades of development. Indeed, protecting land and waters is as fundamental to Kanaka indigeneity as anything, and the story of struggle in Hawai'i is one of continuity.

Kū'ē Petitions and Permission to Resist

As previously mentioned, the latecomer narrative has precedence, as it follows a pattern among conventional histories about Hawai'i and Hawaiians. Stories of Kanaka 'Ōiwi resistance are frequently trivialized, distorted, or erased altogether. And if this specific experience is absent from the official record, today's protests appear arbitrary and unfounded. The foreclosure of Kanaka futurities begins with discursive erasures, which in turn, raise the stakes in confronting both historical and contemporary narrative practices.

For over a century of U.S. occupation, generations of Hawaiians have received a colonial education that teaches us that our land and country were lost to the United States because our ancestors, social and political systems, and cultural knowledges were simply inferior to those of the West. *We lost*, goes the narrative. *Be grateful the U.S. protects Hawai'i from the Chinese*, some argue. The hegemonic narrative suggests Hawaiians did not have the intellectual capacity or political will to stop annexation, rendering U.S. occupation inevitable and universally beneficial. Since the 1980s, Kanaka scholars have identified how these so-called histories are actually "the West's view of itself (read) through the degradation of (our) . . . past."[22] Their lasting effects signal what Haunani-Kay Trask calls an "intellectual colonialism," where the struggle runs deeper than soil to infect our ability to imagine, let alone to research or write alternatives.[23]

Conventional accounts of Hawai'i's history have omitted Native voices in an effort to erase any record of resistance to produce a futurity in which Natives do the heavy lifting for U.S. empire by reproducing cultural hegemony ourselves. To this end, historiography, as Noenoe Silva explains, "is one of the most powerful discourses that justifies the continued occupation of Hawai'i by the United States today."[24] Sadly, even many Hawaiians do not know that our ancestors opposed and successfully defeated *legal* annexation to the United States, and they did so twice—in 1894 and 1898. Until the 1990s, when scholars began interrogating the colonial racism of settler historiography, many Americans assumed Hawaiians simply did not oppose annexation, "in part because mainstream historians have studiously avoided the wealth of material written in Hawaiian."[25] Ron Williams explains that "95% of today's histories on Hawai'i have been based on only 6% of the newspaper archive, the English language newspaper archive."[26] That disregard for and inability to read primary source material composed in the Hawaiian language has obviously produced biased narratives but also a sprawling mythology presented as "history." On the detrimental myth of nonresistance, Silva argues,

> The consent or opposition of the citizenry of Hawaiʻi was insignificant [to conventional histories] . . . which aimed to present the annexation as a triumph of American political values, and thus as a good thing for Hawaiʻi. In order to create such a narrative, however, it was necessary for [historians] to overlook and to smooth over, as much as possible, the opposition of the Kanaka ʻŌiwi and their demands for a democratic decision-making process.[27]

The outcome is a void in public and private K-12 education and postsecondary curricula, to say nothing of the miseducation that defines a U.S. educational system in service of capitalism and empire.

Just one example is Gavan Daws's popular history *Shoal of Time*. In discussing prestatehood Hawaiʻi, Daws cites only the English-language archive to affirm his conclusion that Native Hawaiian efforts to stop annexation were "frivolous" and "worse than anyone thought it could be."[28] Describing the unjust but inevitable annexation, Daws writes:

> This was the ultimate dispossession. The Hawaiians had lost much of their reason for living long ago, when the kapu were abolished; since then a good many of them had lost their lives through disease; the survivors lost their land; they lost their leaders, because many of the chiefs withdrew from politics in favor of nostalgic self-indulgence; and now at last they lost their independence. Their resistance to all this was feeble. It was almost as if they believed what the white man said about them, that they had only half learned the lessons of civilization. Every so often a firebrand . . . would call them to arms, but the response was always a sorry one. They chose to operate within the conventions laid down by white men, and by doing so they put themselves at a disadvantage. They listened to political harangues and composed chants to fit the political occasion; they drew up petitions, and they read the stirring editorials in the Hawaiian language newspapers; but beyond that they did not go. And so they became Americans.[29]

Feigning sympathy only to paint resistance as hopeless, Daws does not analyze annexation and its causes so much as provide justification for it. His reference to "lessons of civilization" invokes a racialized moral economy that presupposes Native inferiority. As such, Kānaka ʻŌiwi have agency only insofar as we are responsible for our own colonization. The crux of this and other such "histories" is that our ancestors did not resist and had it coming. The myth of nonresistance leaves many puzzled, stunting the imagination, and thus foreclosing future decolonial possibilities. If history suggests we acquiesced to U.S. political and territorial control and that our ancestors gave up our country without a fight, then U.S. occupation can be reimagined as "admission" and "statehood," while foreign rule is recast as "progress."

The kiaʻi fighting to protect Mauna a Wākea today have a nineteenth-century analog in the movement that produced the Kūʻē petitions (briefly introduced in chapter 2), which instructs another historicism that opens space to imagine and build decolonial futures. Silva's rediscovery of the nearly forgotten antiannexation petitions in the nineties, long buried in the U.S. National Archives and Records Administration, reveals that Kānaka ʻŌiwi fought aggressively to stop annexation. This rediscovery debunks the mainstream narrative of ineffective, complaisant, ignorant, and grateful Hawaiians.[30]

Two Native organizations, Hui Kālaiʻāina and Hui Aloha ʻĀina, which formed in response to the Bayonet Constitution and the overthrow of the kingdom government and Queen, contrary to Daws's narrative, do not provide lessons of civilization but rather lessons of resistance to U.S. imperialism. In 1887, Mōʻī of the Hawaiian kingdom, David Kāwika Laʻamea Kalākaua, was forced at gunpoint to sign the Bayonet Constitution by the same white sugar planters who later orchestrated the 1893 U.S. invasion. The details are beyond the scope of this chapter, but suffice it to say this constitution severely diminished the civil rights of Kanaka ʻŌiwi citizens and expanded voting rights to white noncitizens. As a result, Hui Kālaiʻāina organized mass meetings, letters to government officials, statements published in the newspapers, and other measures to respond to the injustice. In 1892, Kalākaua's sister and successor, Queen Liliʻuokalani, responded to the cries of her people who, disenfranchised under the Bayonet Constitution, demanded that she promulgate a legitimate and equitable constitution. However, following the laws of her government, Liliʻu shelved the constitution with knowledge that repairing the damage of Bayonet could be done through the legislative process. However, the U.S. military–backed overthrow of Liliʻuokalani and her cabinet prevented that outcome. So, in response, mass protests were organized and petition drives initiated by the two hui.

From 1893 to 1898, Hui Kālaiʻāina and Hui Aloha ʻĀina, Queen Lili-ʻuokalani, and others attempted to persuade Congress, the newly elected President William McKinley, and Americans in general to abide by their proclaimed ideals of justice, liberty, and freedom and to remove U.S. troops from the Hawaiian kingdom, but to no avail. Details of the historical moment are readily available elsewhere, but germane to my point here is that the efforts of Hui Kālaiʻāina and Hui Aloha ʻĀina culminated in mass petition drives in 1897. These drives eventually rallied almost every Kanaka on all islands to sign their names to a document calling on Congress and McKinley to acknowledge the kingdom's resounding rejection of annex-ation and to pull the treaty. Known as the Kūʻē petitions, on which over thirty-eight thousand signatures were inscribed, the campaign effectively blocked legal annexation of the Hawaiian kingdom to the United States, as Congress was unable secure the required number of votes to ratify the treaty. In other words, organized Kanaka-led protest and political action stopped ratification of the legal measure by which the U.S. could assert jurisdiction over Hawaiʻi. Hence, the islands are under illegal occupation today.

The defeat of the proposed treaty of annexation forced the U.S. to circumvent its own constitutional laws for the purpose of rationalizing military occupation, which it did according to instrumentalist U.S. impe-rial logic as they were at war with Spain in the Philippines. While the U.S. military has remained in Hawaiʻi since 1893, the fact that no treaty of annex-ation was ratified because of the Kūʻē petitions as the expression of Native resistance provides an empowering legacy of struggle to which kiaʻi today look for inspiration. This legacy even functions as a form of permission to those who may be reluctant to join community protests. If our ancestors would rise in collective action to challenge abuses of power, why shouldn't we? In this way, the Hawaiian movement today is an extension of the work of Hui Kālaiʻāina and Hui Aloha ʻĀina.

I would argue that every single kiaʻi who ascended the Mauna and joined the struggle in 2015 and 2019 is not only aware of the Kūʻē peti-tions but can also wax poetic on the significance of defeating annexation and the absence of a formal treaty.[31] Indeed, most Native Hawaiians today are eloquent in articulating precisely how the struggle to stop the TMT is about far more than just another telescope, recalling this political history as a link in the story of Maunakea and the Hawaiian sovereignty movement. In sum, not only are scholars unsettling the conventional history and mythology of Native nonresistance to U.S. rule, but other communities—Indigenous and non-Hawaiian alike—are asserting and demanding an accurate historical narrative in explaining the conflict.

As Silva argues, the petitions "affirmed for (Hawaiians today) that their kūpuna had not stood by idly, apathetically, while their nation was taken from them. Instead, contrary to every history book on the shelf, they learned that their ancestors had . . . taken up the honorable field of struggle."[32] That commitment to defend our country, built upon an ethical positionality and practice of struggle, continues to shape Kanaka 'Ōiwi politics today and the grassroots activist organizing that led to the civil disobedience direct actions at Mauna a Wākea in 2015 and 2019. The continuity of Kanaka struggle against injustice and resistance to U.S. cultural hegemony may also be observed in the Hawaiian Renaissance of the late 1960s and through the early 1980s, especially as it culminated in the Kahoʻolawe and Kalama Valley land struggles through the mid- to late 1970s. However, most histories of this period fail to adequately account for power relations, and without a politics of struggle, grassroots community activism appears illogical and irrational. My intervention begins with a brief description of the Hawaiian Renaissance and some of the failures inherent in articulations of its significance. Then we will turn to an activist's account of her life and struggles as an organizer and land defender.

Hawaiian Renaissance and Failures of Imagination

After statehood, many began to examine the poor socioeconomic status of Native Hawaiians who were suffering after five decades of U.S. occupation. This generation began to ask, *What happened to Hawai'i and our people?* Kānaka were disproportionately unemployed, undereducated, and underrepresented in government and intergenerational wealth; yet they were subjected to racial discrimination in schools, in the workplace, and in settler state policy. By midcentury, Hawaiians were being displaced by tourism and suburban development, facing appalling health conditions and dying on waitlists for Hawaiian Homelands allotments. Assimilationist policies failed to deliver, while traditional knowledge *went underground*. Hawai'i became inundated with foreign capital investment, industrial growth, and increasing militarization. Yet, our kūpuna endured obstacles to basic economic security, desecration of sacred places, loss of our language, oscillating appropriation and stigmatization of our culture, and myriad other hardships. However, as conventional narratives about the Hawaiian Renaissance focused narrowly on aspects of Hawaiian culture that are not always overtly political, often failing to recognize the scale and significance of organized Indigenous-led resistance and the impact it had on Kanaka indigeneity, they also reify democratic liberalism and settler multiculturalism, thereby ignoring colonialism and empire. In this section I juxtapose this version of the Renaissance with a significant episode of the Hawaiian movement grounded in community struggle and land defense.

In 1979, George Kanahele described "the Hawaiian Renaissance" as a period of dramatic change.[33] Buoyed by the "spirit of defiance and rebelliousness" and America's countercultural influence on Hawai'i, Kanahele celebrated how "a once rich culture threatened with extinction has been able to survive and now appears to be thriving in spite of the odds against it." A decade of cultural revival, unapologetically "all native, made in Hawaii, by, for and of Hawaiians," now contested the touristic "haolefication" of Hawaiian culture, music, and hula. The explosion of interest in Native traditions led to new foundations, institutions, and organizations that served and educated communities in history and genealogy; visual, literary, and performance arts; and sports like surfing and outrigger canoe paddling. Kanahele applauds the revitalization of the Hawaiian language through immersion schools, the increase of Hawaiian enrollment in colleges and universities, and the creation of Hawaiian studies programs. Praising the seafaring accomplishments of the Hōkūle'a, Kanahele describes its voyage to Tahiti as "one of the most singular achievements to happen during the Hawaiian Renaissance."[34]

Reflecting on why such a movement did not emerge sooner, Kanahele describes earlier attempts as merely voices

in the wilderness that could not be heard above the din of oaths of allegiance to America. For the 1930s and '40s was a period of red-white-and-blue Americanization. Everyone tried to be good Americans which meant that you best submerge any feelings of being non- or un-American. The word "ethnicity" was unheard of. Being different, i.e., being Hawaiian or Japanese or Chinese and so on was not the in-thing to do [sic].[35]

Kanahele describes how, before the Renaissance, it was passé to act, speak, or *be* Hawaiian, but he stops short of theorizing Kanaka resistance or the myth of nonresistance. Instead, Kanahele cautions against an over-indulgent Hawaiian movement: "What we must carefully guard against . . . is resorting to methods that in the end are self-defeating, such as the reverse racism which some young Hawaiians manifest today."[36] There seems to be an implicit criticism of grassroots community activism and, perhaps, the civil disobedience strategies of the 1970s like those at Kahoʻolawe and Kalama Valley. Kanahele also appears to attribute the loss of culture, language, land, and power, to Native Hawaiians, particularly those who simply "tried to be good Americans." A critique of settler multicultural liberalism let alone U.S. occupation is nowhere on his radar. Histories like this sometimes appear more interested in securing shares in the "American Dream" than interrogating the violence on which it is premised. Reproducing the rhetoric of multicultural liberalism, Kanahele writes:

> Finally, there is a paradox about the Renaissance we need to understand. It is that the Renaissance does not only belong to Hawaiians. It belongs to non-ethnic Hawaiians, too . . . The plain fact is that historically non-Hawaiians have always played a large role in preserving and perpetuating Hawaiian culture and ideals . . . non-ethnic Hawaiians . . . who for one reason or another have come to identify themselves culturally, psychologically and spiritually with Hawaiianness. In the process, of course, some have become more Hawaiian than the Hawaiians, to the chagrin of the natives.

Kanahele's argument that Hawaiians are selfish with our culture appears strangely indifferent to the legacy of touristic exploitation and the rest but also oddly sympathetic to U.S. cultural hegemony, striking a conciliatory tone that extends settler innocence by throwing Hawaiians under the bus. Why not instead interrogate power? His implied critique, in my view, is misdirected.

The "political power that Hawaiians" hope to "one day enjoy," according to Kanahele, is a model of reconciliation but not resurgence, which, as argued in chapter 3, is a failure of imagination. Liberal democratic participation is not the same as decolonization. Assimilation, what Kanahele calls "Americanization," certainly calls for intervention, but the main obstacle for Kānaka ʻŌiwi, in the 1970s and today, is not a matter of equality, access, or inclusion but disqualification as legitimate and intelligent subjects under hegemonic formations since U.S. occupation began. Indeed, the myriad problems Kānaka ʻŌiwi endure are rooted in settler land grabs, disavowals of our history, and continued alienation from our ancestral places; not petty jealousies.

Moreover, not every Hawaiian wants more America or to be American. One example was my first kumu hula and beloved friend, Aunty Cecilia Akim, who once explained to me how, in 1959, she chose not to participate in what was ultimately a flawed referendum for statehood or to remain a territory. Echoing Haunani-Kay Trask, Aunty Ceci explained, "I am not American! I have never been American! I am Hawaiian and I didn't vote for statehood or for the Territory because the vote was already fixed!"[37] Akim, like so many other Hawaiians, understood the false choice was no choice at all, as independence was never an option. But unlike Kanahele, who suggests many Hawaiians felt it was best to "submerge any feelings of being non- or un-American," Akim and other kūʻē artists, activists, educators, and cultural practitioners understand that our problem is not a lack of access or inclusion, but self-determination. While settler colonialism welcomes our participation in U.S. cultural hegemony and our own structured oppression, it also offers empty promises on behalf of U.S. empire. Only with a critique of power and a politics of struggle can this become legible.

To this end, let me turn to my interview with Terri Kekoʻolani-Raymond. Our conversation was over four hours long, and while I include only a portion of the transcript here, it is an important account of this period and the contemporary Hawaiian movement. It is significant because the Mauna Kea Movement today becomes coherent only when it is contextualized within the broader legacy of Native Hawaiian struggle against militarism and empire, as militarism and empire condition the possibility of settler racial capitalism and U.S. cultural hegemony. The following is an excerpt from my interview with Aunty Terri, who offers an incisive analysis of this era.

Terrilee Nāpua Kekoʻolani-Raymond: A Life in Struggle and Resistance

In Spring 2014, Aunty Terri and I met at Koa Pancake House in Kaimukī for a morning of conversation about local politics and our activist community. There, she offered recollections about her family and childhood;

however, for the second part of the interview, we relocated to her office at the Quaker Meeting House in Mānoa to discuss her life as an organizer. I asked how she became an activist and how activism has shaped her manaʻo on being Kanaka ʻŌiwi. We also talked about the recent developments around the TMT and discourse on Mauna a Wākea, particularly in the larger context of struggle and resistance to U.S. empire in the Pacific.

It was a sunny midday in Mānoa. Open windows allowed trade winds to keep us cool as they rustled papers around her office. On the recording, birds are singing up a storm, a lawn mower roams in the distance, and Aunty Terri's hands can be heard tapping on the table, her index finger tracing circles as she develops a thought. She is in her element in this space where we are surrounded by keepsakes and makana gifted to her over years of travel and organizing. On the walls are framed pictures and artwork documenting the Hawaiian sovereignty movement, with flags, banners, and signs from protests past and present and telling stories of struggle.

Our conversation was recorded at a point when there were no mass marches, roadblocks, or encampments; and there had been very few organized acts of solidarity with the Maunakea Hui who were fighting the legal battle within the State bureaucracy. Grassroots political actions were limited to small sign-waving demonstrations and occasional rallies, mostly in Honolulu and Hilo. Even social media discourse and print and television news coverage of the opposition to the TMT was scarce, and most served the university and TMT interests by misrepresenting the hui and their supporters in ways that would suggest they opposed science rather than another telescope, or simply needed to learn exactly how the TMT would benefit everyone, including Kānaka ʻŌiwi, and then they would understand. In October of 2013, however, a community mural project at the University of Hawaiʻi at Mānoa, organized by artist and then grad student Haley Kailiʻehu, supported the Maunakea Hui by staging a provocative visual protest and public conversation, which exposed the university's neoliberal commitments to big science, as well as its contempt for activists.[38] The first direct action on the Mauna itself would not take place until October 7, 2014—months after our interview—when Kānaka and allies ascended the summit and disrupted a livestreamed groundbreaking ceremony that ended with a scathing condemnation by a young kiaʻi named Joshua Lanakila Mangauil—who chided the audience of TMT investors, executives, administrators, astronomers, and invited guests for "slither(ing) in like . . . snakes to . . . desecrate our sacred lands!" Mangauil asks, "Where are *your* sacred temples!?" Then he sent everyone home in humiliation for endorsing the charade.[39] After the groundbreaking spectacle, a proliferation of discourse about the TMT and the struggle finally began to emerge.

In this interview, Aunty Terri seems to anticipate a lot of what followed, though she had no intention of predicting any of it. Speaking to what it will take to stop the TMT, her analysis of the limits of official State processes and the sanctioned legal paths that are available for community input was incisive and insightful, as these forums were not designed to prohibit a project like the TMT but, instead, to validate it. Having lived a life as a community organizer and speaking truth to power as an unapologetic aloha ʻāina, Aunty Terri provides valuable context. My takeaway is that Kanaka ʻŌiwi political thought and action exist in a continuum of struggle. To understand the politics of the TMT, we must understand how Kanaka responses to the U.S. occupation of Hawaiʻi and the ethos of Kanaka ʻŌiwi resistance center on cultural forms and are thus rooted in ʻike kupuna, or ancestral knowledge—what Leanne Betasamosake Simpson describes as "the intellectual and theoretical home of resurgence."[40]

We began with Protect Kahoʻolawe ʻOhana (PKO) and the fight against over forty years of U.S. Naval bombing that permanently disfigured and polluted the sacred island. PKO compelled the Hawaiian Renaissance into a more substantive social movement for life, land, and ea. Aunty Terri described the influence of George Helm, the charismatic movement leader who died mysteriously when he and Kimo Mitchell, in 1977, went missing under suspicious circumstances while attempting to reach the island during a military exercise.[41] Their disappearance at sea pushed the Hawaiian Renaissance in a new direction, giving birth to a broad-based, decentralized "Hawaiian Sovereignty Movement," and demonstrating the importance of prioritizing culture, language, and ceremony for Native-led grassroots organized resistance. Aunty Terri explains how Helm's death changed everything:

TNK: George Helm and I were good friends from high school days, he went to St. Louis, I went to Sacred Hearts.[42] Kumu Lake[43] had a boys and girls club, we were in the same club. *They* did singing, and then *we* did hula.

So, I knew George before he got involved [in activism]. We used to have political debates, political discussions all the time. So he was really pressing me hard, like "who are you as a Kanaka—a Hawaiian person? I know you as an activist, but who are you *as a Kanaka*?" And how do we go back to our Kānaka and how do we talk to them . . . about the things that need to be changed. 'Cause a lot of the Kānaka at the time, especially the elders, were . . . "Don't rock the boat." You know? "Go with the flow." Some of the Christian kūpuna were like, "Don't get back into the [Hawaiian] religion. It's evil, it's 'diablo,' yeah?" And so we really were in struggle about all that kine a stuff.

And then I started hanging with the Kahuna Sam Lono[44] and spending a lot of time with him, 'cause he was piercing through this Christianity stuff. And so people like George, Emmett,[45] all the guys who were beginning to say we're gonna go to Kahoʻolawe, we're gonna do this. They started to hang with people like Kupuna Sam Lono, Aunty Emma DeFries,[46] and they were saying "it's OK [TK laughs]. It's OK, you can believe in your gods, it's alright." And this is who they are.

And so they were kinda *bridging*, helping us to bridge. And so I started hanging out with those guys and then that's when I came to terms with . . . "I have to understand myself as a Kanaka" . . . then I decided to go to Kahoʻolawe to help to stop the bombing.

ICS: What year?

TNK: I think it was '78.

ICS: After George had disappeared?

TNK: Yes, I went *because* he disappeared. I was already working with them [but] we were doing work in Mākua. We actually did a demonstration in Mākua, in support of the guys who were on the island. And so, we . . . I can't remember the years, but it was after '75, when all this was happening. Between 1975 and 1978.

[*Pause*]

ICS: What was the language used at this time? Were they talking about the "Renaissance" then? Were they talking of this thing called "the Renaissance?" I ask because it seems some would paint a rosy picture of that era by focusing only on the cultural aspects of the Hawaiian Renaissance. Were they emphasizing the "cultural" more than the "political, or . . . ?"

TNK: It was both.

[*Pause*]

Let me give you an example: about the . . . it was something we discussed when we had the ceremony of the state, of the military—the Navy leaving Kahoʻolawe. There was a really big gathering on the island. And that's when we actually had the chance, because of the good thinking of the organizers, they brought everybody. They didn't just keep it to their gang, the PKO gang. They opened up the ceremony to everybody who had ever gotten arrested or had played a major role in supporting the PKO effort, right?

So, when we all got together, that's what we talked about. We said there were two differences: [*she points to two fingers*] one was struggle, resistance, absolute necessity . . . and [the other was] culture. So, the ones rising up were the Hōkūleʻa guys.[47] And some of them didn't want to be associated with the struggle. Yet, they had to. If they wanted to do the "Real McCoy" trek of voyaging they had to go to where the voyaging was taught, and it was taught on Kahoʻolawe, it was one of the places that it was taught, but *a major place* that it was taught—that voyaging was taught. That's what Mau[48] talks about. And there was this thing, this this this . . . ahu . . . a thing [a sacred stone atop Puʻu o Moaʻula] on [the summit of] Kahoʻolawe, and Mau said, "This is actually a place where you have a stone canoe. And this is where the navigators learned to navigate." The military was bombing it. They were using it for a target [practice] and yet it was the very thing that used to do . . . to read the stars. That's how hewa [*wrong*] all of this shit is, right?

So, Hōkūleʻa guys saying "that's not our battle, we're into culture." Right? And yet, the contradiction is that the very thing that we're trying to say was so important to our people was actually a target to be destroyed by this country called "America!" Ha ha ha [*laughs aloud*]! So how could you not [be political]?

To answer your question, I think there was a lot more activism. *It was OK.* Israel Kamakawiwoʻole,[49] there doing political songs. "Hawaiʻi '78" comes out. It's OK to say. It's OK to say you're for struggle, it's OK to say stand up and rise with the people.

Now, in '78, right? After all of the landings take place, and PKO starts, coming to . . . to where it's at, right? People from the Democratic Party were starting to come to the meetings of the PKO and beginning to listen to who the . . . and observing who the leaders were and kind of cherry picking some of them to be part of a group, a working group, that would actually work on a constitutional convention initiative . . . building an office for strictly Hawaiians, and that was the budding of the OHA [Office of Hawaiian Affairs]. So, Aunty Frenchy,[50] Walter Ritte,[51] Francis Kahani, there were a lot of the leaders that kinda moved over to, into that working group who started forging ahead with the creation of that entity. But that entity in the 1978 . . . was for strictly Native Hawaiians—After *Rice*[52] it started to change. Then it changed, yeah? And so that is the . . . some of the stuff historically that a lot of people don't really understand. That it was *Hawaiian,* strictly, right? And it [OHA] was meant *to stop the bleeding.*

It was really meant to stop a lot of the stuff that had been going on for a long time.

So a lot of the activists and activism started going into that realm and then you had, of course, always a tension, how do you keep the activism and the grassroots on that level, meaningful and alive, right? Because the whole idea is not to be stagnant. Not to be . . . down in your lulls and say, "Everything is OK." *It's not!* But always to keep on making change . . . and to go through struggle to get there.

[*Pause*]

And then a lot of that energy was actually, purposefully shifted to working within the system, legislating change, getting a part of the state, actually going back to some of the ali'i trust[53] and challenging them, and questioning them, "What are you doing? How are you managing the land so it is actually set aside for our people." Big, big exposé on the Bishop Estate . . . and how the lands were being used for the personal profit of some of the trustees. All of those things were being attacked.

[*Pause*]

ICS: Why then, at this time? Why weren't people asking those questions about corruption or land, ten years before Kaho'olawe? Is it because of Americanization or . . .

TNK: That's all I can think of. Here's my take on this: for the culture—it went underground, yeah? So, it was contained in families. Right? And so families had traditional hula. And hula is stories. And some of it is . . . stories to teach lessons and stories of actual facts of what happened in a family, or in history, yeah? So it kind of became: *you had to know somebody who is going to teach you.* Hula was also commodified in a very bad way. It was exotic, women were exotic, it turned out to be something that was commodified and abused, right? but it never died.

And so during the Renaissance that's when some of the keepers of the hula, keepers of the culture, started feeling a little more comfortable . . . to come out. And it was really hard for them too because of the Christianity. But I think PKO had a lot to do with the crossing over. Uncle Sam Lono had a lot to do with the . . . challenging the system. I mean, he cursed the Bishop Estate Trustees for what they were doing [white-collar crimes]. They were kicking their own people off the land. So there was a lot of struggle going on.

I think it was a more, it was vibrant—that's the word I wanna use—it was very vibrant. And that's when you had, like I said, songs, y'know? Contemporary at that time, contemporary songs talking about social issues.

You have . . . [*inaudible*]. *It's OK to talk about things that are contemporary. That to me was the difference.*

And when we established ethnic studies [at the University of Hawai'i] it's like, "we're here. We're not leaving, we're part of the institution now."

Now let's get back to Maunakea.

[*Pause*]

ICS: So, a lot of people say there was no commentary or critique of Maunakea telescopes in the '70s. It's only now that Hawaiians are speaking up. What was your impression of what people thought or were saying about it back then?

TNK: . . . I think it was the '80s. You gotta remember there's a connection between the guys of Kaho'olawe and some of the ceremonies they're bringing up, and Kaho'olawe becomes like a beacon almost. It's where the Makahiki is restored. Right? Once you have Makahiki on Kaho'olawe, then you have Makahiki on Moloka'i . . . Big Island, and Keaukaha. And so the culture part of that, right? It's becoming a force. 'Cuz remember, on Kaho'olawe you were bringing out, and some of the kūpunas were saying, "It's OK, to talk about these things." And if we're gonna talk about these things, do it right. If we're gonna talk about us being Lanaka, then we're gonna talk about the Pacific Ocean and *all* of our relatives—the Māori, the Tahitians, the Ma'ohi . . . us as Maoli [Native, Indigenous] . . . then we're going to really look at who we are as a people through the Pacific, right? And I think that's where I'm gonna say where we come into another stage, and that's my background. The whole thing with Uncle Kekuni (Blaisdell),[54] the establishment of the Kōmike Tribunal[55] . . .

That is a very intentional assessment of the conditions of our people in their communities and their testimonies from them in the communities that they actually live in. Yeah, so that's where I think you might get some information about Maunakea . . . um, now to speak of . . .

[*Pause*]

So PKO is . . . it's really bringing out, and surfacing culture. Right. And that same kind of way that lands are growing and developing on the big island as well, it's kinda the backdrop for what eventually the Kanaka'ole, Pua Kanaka'ole them, and even Kealoha Pisciotta were putting out. If Kaho'olawe is sacred, all of the islands are sacred. What are the most outstanding sacred places, and how are we gonna talk about them?

And I think it's really, I would say, this is my own recollection, the Kanaka'oles had a lot to do with putting out the sacredness of Maunakea, Maunaloa, and that we as a people have beliefs and kuleana to protect these places. That to me is the difference.

In Kahoʻolawe, that wasn't present. It grew. It evolved. That consciousness evolved from struggle. Fighting for it and then allowing our people to develop their cultural roo . . . identity.

In Maunakea, I think it was kinda the opposite, in a way, where it was [about] identifying it as sacred. What is sacred? What does sacred mean to you? Define it. That being a place that is special, not only to us, but throughout the Pacific, it is the peak, throughout the Pacific. Right? And so it gives you a lens of us as a people throughout the Pacific having a common history and understanding of sacredness.

And . . . so I think that's where you have a lot of the line that you have today about, let the culture and that idea, *lead,* and then *frame* your fight from that position. Not the opposite.

And it brings you actually to a very common place with other Native peoples too. Whether you are Aborigine in the middle of Australia with your sacred places. Right? Like those mountains, the Red Mountains. Or if you're in Ecuador and you have the whole . . . it goes on and on, the Native people having sacredness separate from law and government.

Now does that mean that people, there are . . . does struggle factor in the fight for Maunakea? Absolutely. But it's how that struggle is constructed and framed that becomes a real question, and [I] think that's why there's a lot of discussion about how you do that.

[*Pause*]

ICS: I've met pro-TMT Hawaiians and anti-TMT locals, and what I find striking is the political issue is framed.

TNK: Right.

ICS: So, as an example, one particular Hawaiian who is prominent in the community explained to me he feels it's more important to have "a seat at the table," to have a say, otherwise they're just going to keep doing it no matter what [i.e., build telescopes]. So the best thing we can hope for is to get in, get some money for the community out of it, hold them accountable, make sure they're gonna satisfy our requirements to have a management plan, that they respect our wishes and not level anymore of the puʻu and put it where *we* want it so that it's not on the very top of the summit [since] we don't want it visible from all around the island, and so on. That the most we can do is give them pushback, but not stop the TMT, and if we don't take this "seat at the table," we don't have a say—they won't listen to us. Do you share that philosophy?

TNK: No, absolutely not. That's where I think that it, it almost comes really hard, harder for the people who say that they believe in their culture and the spirituality of the place. There's no negotiating to me, y'know? If you say there's already been enough that has been built up there . . . if you're saying that this is really one of the last places, space-wise, landscape-wise, right?, does it change it [the importance of that place]? No! You still have to protect that, the vastness, the space, the vista . . . that's your connection.

And the . . . and so, my leaning is, *that* should be respected [she's tapping harder on the table with her index finger, as if pointing to the Mauna]. When the people say that is a place that is important to us, and you keep on pushing us where you have to negotiate away and you have to adapt to the changes that we are going to make on you. Why? And I think we might be in a better place, I mean spiritually, more centered in order to say, "We don't want that." And we're going to tell you why. And we're willing to show and demonstrate to you how far we will go to protect that place. Basically that's how I feel. That's my feeling. It's gonna be a community of people, it's gonna have to be our people that's going to defend it.

And the reason why I come from this place, I have been doing work at Mōkapu[56] for so many years, since 1998. And I've seen how they talk you in circles, "Oh, we're only going to develop this. Oh, well you can have a little bit. You have . . . *have* a little kiosk, yeah? But we're gonna build this huge edifice in front of Puʻu Hawaiʻiloa."[57] Oh, we didn't level the puʻu, we just put this big monstrosity satellite in front of it, *that's all* . . . When what is the purpose of the puʻu and why is it sacred? Because of the vista, 360 degree vista . . . ocean. Land. Koʻolaus. Kualoa . . . that's the sacredness right there. And there's something about that place that gives us history and a sense of . . . who we are as a people. But *we* keep on getting compromised, and I would say that colonization also means that we compromise ourselves into believing that we can't have what we know we should be protecting.

And that's it brah. Ha ha ha ha! It took a lot of me to dig that out! Ha ha ha ha! Sorry! [*Our laughter almost turns to tears*]

[*Pause*]

TNK: But that's why I'm with the women's group too, and that's why we do genuine versus national security, there are some assumptions made . . . you don't have any right to clean water, clean land, a clean environment, a place in which there is no threat of violence. What do you think we are? Making this shit up? There have been two major world wars. People are supposed to learn from those things. Right? And really, what is our society if we don't try to strive for something . . . [*she pauses*] like that. You know? So that's it. And I hope I answered your question because, there is a real challenge I think with the proposed development of the telescope. Is a real real challenge. And I think it's just a matter of . . . of rolling up, among the Native Hawaiians, of rolling up your sleeves, and even though they say "no," go back. You gotta keep on going back. Go back to the people, their constituents. Don't walk away from a meeting at the university Board of Trustees, you gotta keep going back, talk to the board, talk to the people on campus, make them understand why that place is so significant, and why *we should* have a say of what happens to it.

[*Pause*]

ICS: Why *should* we have a say in what happens to it?

[*Pause*]

TNK: Because I think that's our, for our mamo, for our future. It's what . . . uh, one of Gwen Kim's children . . . Kalama,[58] she said . . . a lot of the places you guys grew up and saw are all concrete now. We don't have the same sense of orientation and feeling because it's gone. And so, I feel that's something, a voice we have to listen to, if it's gone, it's gone.

And I think it also speaks to what we value spiritually, I hate to say it, but it is our "church," that environment. The vastness. The connection. The sunrise. The pink and orange clouds beneath our feet, when you're on the top of Maunakea, you know? The understanding of who you are . . . relationship to your Māori brothers and sisters, calling out to them. The elements . . . All of that stuff is transforming spiritually, and it humbles you. Yeah? Why can't we have those places, um, preserved in place . . . for the future?

[*Pause*]

ICS: Doesn't science benefit humanity?

TNK: I think our people need to deal with that question.

ICS: I mean a lot of people argue astronomy is among the least harmful . . .

TNK: You know, Maunakea begs to differ. That's not true. . . . yeah. You're saying that that edifice, that structure, that technology is far more important than the belief system, the historical belief system, the system of a people that's been around longer than you. And in another way too, because we believe so much in recovering our 'ike, our knowledge as a people, you have a boat, without a engine [i.e., Hōkūle'a], sailing around the world, with sails, and doing a lot to tell people . . . that we're all connected.[59]

So, I don't know what to say. You have medicines in the forest. If you keep the forest a forest, the medicines grow and they can cure you. Versus a pharmaceutical that's so . . . worked over that, maybe it's not the best thing for you to take. Anyway, I mean, that traditional knowledge has to have, to me I think, we see value in traditional knowledge and it doesn't look like the industrial technological things that have come out of this kind of society. I'm not belittling it, I know it has . . . and that science is behind it, but where do we come to a crossroads, where do we draw lines? Limits?

And that's it. Is that OK?

Ha ha ha ha ha! [*She laughs aloud.*]

I'm really different, because I really think that analysis part is so important [tapping her index finger on the table] that we don't take things for granted when they say "law's this, and law's that." Law is made up by people; you can change it. And what have we learned? And as a woman, you know? I'm gonna tell you, this is what I see. And I don't want to be chained, and I'm not gonna be chained. And be told this is all you can hope to be, yeah? Like I would tell my younger women, "You could be a political strategist if you want to be" . . . "You don't have to be the cook and family maker." Ha ha! You make plans, and think through, and strategize making a family every single day. Right, so you apply the same into a sphere of community . . . or maybe a sphere of community beyond your borders, and maybe even to the world. And maybe even to the world. And then your audience and your connections become so much bigger and more enriching. Because then we begin to find what's our commonality. And what are the things we should leave alone. That's none of our business to touch. Yeah? That's another thing is, we don't have to be all mahaʻoi into everybody else's business too, sometimes, just gotta let it go. You know?

Or protocols, one thing I do, and I do it everywhere I go [*stands up and walks over to a shelf*] and I'll show you this picture, this picture is actually a good example. This is in Ecuador. It's . . . "No Bases" conference that was held in Ecuador. I went with my kīhei, yeah? And, when I went to this conference, I told the organizers—actually it was me, Kyle, and Ikaika[60]—I said, "It's really important that we ask the people, the first people here in Ecuador for permission to come into their country. Right?" And so some of the, then I found out, Oh, there's all kind of stuff happening here. They said, "Nah, nah, it's gonna take too much time! Oh, we can't find th—" I said, "No. We're not going in, to the conference unless we get a First Person to come to greet us so we can ask them for permission to come into their country and that we can give and exchange our gifts with them . . . period." Right? And so the organizer says, "Well, we can't do that in the conference." [We said] "Well, then *we'll do it outside*, before we come inside." Right? So, this is us outside [*shows me the picture*]. Ha ha ha! [*She laughs, as we look at the photo.*]

ICS: And everyone else agreed with you?

TNK: Yeah. Yeah. And so this is the shaman. And he came with a pū [conch shell blown like a horn], and his medicine, right? And he came with belts, embroidered belts, with the history of the people. Right? So, in that exchange we learned the history of the people, the culture, and we were given the blessings to talk. So, when he brought his pū, I'm going . . . oh my god—there's another one, they have the pū [like we Hawaiians do]—he did the four directions. I don't know why they do that. But all I know, that's what he did. And so all, everybody stood behind that. Right? So, that protocol, what I'm saying is that protocol alone brings a lot of 'ike, and a lot of relationship building. And I've, whenever I've gone in conferences in other countries. I always do this. I've done it in Australia, that's how I got my Aborigine friends. Ha ha ha ha ha!

[*Pause*]

ICS: So would you say this is solidarity work? Alliance building?

TNK: Yeah. Yep, in a Kanaka way.

ICS: And so to you, this is one significant aspect of protocol, and what it can do for you in building relationships.

TNK: But it's also a recognition of, and we talk about recognition all the time. It's recognizing, respect the people from the 'āina, yeah?

So, I think those are the things. Did I do this in the 1970s? No. I developed it along the way, to the point of feeling confident so it was hō'ike, it wasn't for show. But I was actually doing it for protocol, you know? I felt confident saying, 'O Terri Nāpua Keko'olani ko'u inoa . . . heahea wale . . . and, no Hawai'i mai au. [As if speaking to her hosts] I'm standing in front of you, your great beautiful mountains, your people, your animals, your rivers . . . I honor your people. May I ask, who are *you*? Right? Who *are* you? Right? "I come as a guest." And then they respond, "We are the so-and-so people. We come from these lands. Yeah? This is the background that we had . . . Oh, by the way," they go, this guy goes [*points to the picture*], "By the way, we know you. You people from Hawai'i. You've been here before," [*he said*] "Oh really?!" [*she responds*] Ha ha ha ha ha ha! [*she laughs boisterously*] . . . back in the old old old old old old days . . .

ICS: That's what he was referring to?

TNK: Yeah!

ICS: They had memory?

TNK: *They had memory!* You know? And so they go, "We here in Ecuador, we are the center of the world." And I said, "How can that be? We are?" Ha ha ha ha ha . . .

ICS: Ha ha ha!

TNK: And so we have a joke!

ICS: It draws connections.

TNK: Yeah, so it draws connections, like that.

And so it's the protocols you give to your kids too. Like . . . don't just go maha'oi into somebody's place. Learn how'da act before you you you go in. Because Americans, many times, act like that, they can go anywhere they like. They have a passport to anywhere. That's bullshit.

Anyway . . .

[*Pause*]

ICS: Can I ask you a few more questions or should we start wrapping it up?

TNK: Sure, go ahead [*as she walks over to put her photograph back on the shelf*].[61]

Aunty Terri's politics of struggle, analysis of militarism, and experience as an organizer draws important connections necessary to understand the ways in which forms of power interlock to maintain colonial domination over Hawai'i and Kānaka 'Ōiwi. From her mana'o, I learned that the struggle for Mauna a Wākea is inherently linked to the broader struggle for Hawai'i, and it is a struggle against U.S. occupation and settler cultural hegemony as much as it is about the TMT. In other words, they are not mutually exclusive. As such, the Hawaiian movement has many fronts to which Kānaka 'Ōiwi have committed and in a variety of ways. Moreover, we are not idle and have never been passive. We are strategic, with an awareness of the stakes for our future generations. While some work within the sanctioned venues of the settler state and federal government with the intention to "stop the bleeding," for Aunty Terri and many others, the lesson of the PKO era and the kū'ē wing of the Hawaiian Renaissance—and particularly the lessons gathered from her intellectual and activist genealogies—is that in the struggle to protect our sacred places, our ancestral homeland and our communities must be grounded in Kanaka worldviews and our own spiritual practices, Native language, and ancestral knowledges. These are the things around which Kanaka indigeneity coheres today as it always has, and that continuity was clear in the 2015 and 2019 direct actions at Mauna a Wākea.

Aunty Terri's work conveys the importance of recognizing *all our relations*—across Moananuiākea, Turtle Island, and beyond. This is done by learning and speaking our Native language and observing our cultural protocols that unsurprisingly are recognized by other Indigenous peoples throughout Oceania and the world over. In hindsight, I find these points especially remarkable as our Indigenous Oceanic 'ohana and representatives from other Native nations came to Pu'uhonua o Pu'uhuluhulu throughout the 2019 roadblock direct actions to show solidarity, gift makana, offer ho'okupu, and share mo'olelo with the kia'i. And these cousins who visited were welcomed using established protocols that are distinctly Kanaka—some new and some of old.

As Aunty Terri reflected on ways the cultural and political are intricately intertwined, and on the increased attention on Mauna a Wākea at that time, she almost foretells events to come:

> And I think we might be in a better place, I mean spiritually, more centered in order to say, "We don't want that." And we're going to tell you why. And we're willing to show and demonstrate to you how far we will go to protect that place. Basically, that's how I feel. That's my feeling. It's gonna be a community of people, it's gonna have to be our people that's going to defend it.

Indeed, as described briefly in the introduction, Kumu Pualani Kanaka'ole Kanahele's 'ohana and Hālau o Kekuhi conducted daily protocols through hula, pule, and ceremony with the discipline and frequency needed to uphold the kapu of the pu'uhonua as well as protect the kia'i. The rituals were not conjured for television cameras or Instagram, but instead to fulfill the kuleana of our lāhui, out of kinship obligations to 'āina and each other. That discipline, sacrifice, the protocol, and the kuleana underscore the continuity of struggle and cultural praxis for Kānaka 'Ōiwi as interwoven strands of a single aha (cord). The intersubjectivity of Kānaka and 'āina thus emerges not *in spite* of (or as mere *response* to) settler colonization and U.S. military occupation but independent of the oppression that Kanaka endure. In other words, it is no surprise Kānaka 'Ōiwi observe 'ike kupuna in struggle. It is as we have always done.

As the interview suggests, not only did it become *acceptable* to think, speak, and be Hawaiian, but *because* of Kaho'olawe and the land and water struggles since the Hawaiian Renaissance, Kānaka 'Ōiwi are able to find pride in expressing, performing, and cultivating indigeneity. In other words, Kanaka struggles for life, land and waters, the lāhui, and self-governance are not anomalous but instead reveal a pattern of responses to historical and ongoing injustices. Likewise, the Hawaiian consciousness that "evolved from struggle" that Aunty Terri describes is not an accident or aberration either but instead is a logical consequence of the nineteenth-century resistance against U.S. annexation that our kūpuna modeled for us. Not only does their activism give us permission to resist, but it teaches that resistance is our kuleana. Contextualizing Maunakea within this continuum of Indigenous struggle makes the violence of settler technoscience of the TMT legible.

Conclusion

In this chapter I have argued that the default settler contention against the Maunakea land defenders as too little or too late has a long and convoluted history that reaches to earlier myths of nonresistance to U.S. annexation. I have also argued that the struggle for Maunakea can only be understood if we examine the stories of earlier struggles for life, land, and ea, which have not always been easily accessible: itself a consequence of settler colonialism and white patriarchal historiography about Hawai'i and Hawaiians, which

Figure 23. Aunty Terrilee Nāpua Keko'olani-Raymond at Lā Ho'iho'i Ea, Thomas Square, July 30, 2023. Photograph by Kim Compoc.

is concerned more with self-affirmation than accuracy. That kiaʻi would block construction and devote their lives to defending not only Mauna a Wākea but also the myriad other wahi kapu and wahi pana across ka pae ʻāina o Hawaiʻi (the Hawaiian archipelago) indicates what is required of and what is at stake for Kānaka ʻŌiwi in this freedom struggle. This is a struggle to self-determine the future of Kanaka indigeneity and relationality to ʻāina. Given this, I contend we must look to our ʻike kupuna and ʻŌiwi educators, activists, artists, and aloha ʻāina who show us that our cultural knowledges are not only as scientific, expansive, rational, and legitimate as those of settler society; they are better suited to protect the fragile balance of life these places deserve. Attention to Indigenous voices on our terms opens space for us to compose a better conception of humanity and to recognize our own potential and value as aboriginal people of these islands. Now that I have discussed several accounts of our political and activist histories and some of the challenges that dismiss Kānaka ʻŌiwi and our knowledges as irrational through settler colonial frameworks, neoliberal environmentalities, and liberal multiculturalism, in the next chapter I turn to our Indigenous knowledge systems—particularly through examining several moʻolelo, mele, and moʻokūʻauhau—to explore why Mauna a Wākea is sacred to Hawaiians and worthy of protection in the face of arrests and state violence.

5

COMPOSING NATURE AND
ARTICULATING THE SACRED

Nature is not a thing, a domain, a realm, an ontological
territory . . . (but) is . . . a way of organizing the division between
appearances and reality, subjectivity and objectivity, history and
immutability.

—BRUNO LATOUR

All of our gathering practices and agricultural techniques, the
patterned mat of loʻi kalo, the breath passing in and out of the loko
iʻa, the Kū and Hina of picking plants are predicated on looking
ahead. This ensures that the land is productive into the future, that
the sea will still be abundant into the future, and that our people
will still thrive into the future. This is the future we are leading the
way to, the future we are going to live in, the future our ancestors
fought for, the future we still fight for. Come join us.

—BRYAN KAMAOLI KUWADA

In a *New York Times* editorial entitled "Seeking Stars, Finding Creationism," which appeared shortly after the first direct action on the summit
of Mauna a Wākea in October 2014, science writer George Johnson condemns the kiaʻi who disrupted the TMT groundbreaking ceremony by
invoking tropes of religious extremism and settler victimry. In the article,
Johnson claims astronomers are "still fending off charges of blasphemy . . .
[though, this time] not from the Vatican." Lamenting what appeared settled when the "old order was overturned, and dogma began to give way
to science," Johnson argues today's "religious fundamentalists" are newly
empowered Natives, now among the few "still waging skirmishes against
science" in a turn "back to the dark ages."[1]

This month a group of Native Hawaiians, playing drums and chanting, blocked the road to a construction site near the top of Mauna Kea and stopped the groundbreaking ceremony for the Thirty Meter Telescope . . . For them the mountain is a sacred place where the Sky Father and the Earth Mother coupled and gave birth to the Hawaiian people. They don't all mean that metaphorically. They consider the telescope . . . the latest insult to their gods . . . It can be difficult to tell how motivated such protests are by spiritual outrage and how much by politics. Opposition to the Mauna Kea observatories . . . has been going on for years . . . the new telescope is a pawn in a long, losing game.[2]

While Johnson suggests the "losing game" of Hawaiian subjection is tragic, if not inevitable, he also questions Native religious beliefs, passively challenging their authenticity, implying that stubborn self-indulgence is masquerading as cultural praxis. His point is that Hawaiians have lost the game of progress and should just get over it: they don't have what it takes to survive in the modern world, and their obsession with past grievances leads to mulish and irrational behavior. Johnson also suggests environmentalists have coaxed Hawaiians into a "marriage of convenience," to weaponize culture as a tactic, the risk of which threatens to "undermine the credibility of what may be perfectly sound scientific arguments about the effects of" the TMT on a "vulnerable mountain terrain."[3] In Johnson's view, Hawaiians are contradictory, duplicitous, naïve, inept, vengeful, and petty; but somehow, they cannot *also* be environmentalists. The possibility that he is misidentifying an Indigenous environmentalism for "spiritual outcry" and "politics" never occurs to him.[4]

In the piece, Johnson also conflates Native Hawaiians with "American Indian tribes" and argues that their fundamentalist beliefs have been "tolerated [by anthropologists and sociologists] out of a sense of guilt over past wrongdoings," and that "letting Indian creationism interfere with scientific research" is "logically . . . the same" as "Christian creationism interfering with public education." Finally, Johnson presumes to know Hawaiians better than they do themselves. Trivializing culturally informed activism as some irrational fear, jealousy, or self-indulgent obstinance, he continues, "The most radical among them refuse to bow to a science they don't consider their own. A few even share a disbelief in evolution, professing to take literally old myths in which the first people crawled out of a hole in the ground."[5] Ironically, Kānaka ʻŌiwi, like many other Indigenous peoples, believe in evolutionary theories closely resembling what Western science claims to have "discovered," and Johnson's rhetoric of scientific victimhood extends settler innocence in ways discussed in chapter 3. However, beyond the obvious anti-Native racism and ethnocentrism, what's most troubling about Johnson's critical posture is how it signals a failure of imagination that seems perfectly content with epistemic closure. Johnson's defense of industrial science ironically abandons scientific methodology, as he refuses to consider the possibility that Hawaiians possess knowledge forms and methods that are no less scientific than any other. Johnson's conception of progress seems to excuse unrestrained development and Native dispossession. His is an exclusive modernity, a space from which Indigenous peoples are naturally absent or one they will be expelled from if they should wander in.

Responding to Johnson's editorial, Bryan Kamaoli Kuwada published a piece on the blog *Ke Kaupu Hehiale* entitled, "We Live in the Future. Come Join Us," in April 2015.[6] In it, he unpacks Johnson's arguments first by tending to several contradictory tropes. On one hand, Kānaka ʻŌiwi are treated as if we are "unable to hack it in the modern world" and, in our activism, merely "slowing everyone down on the road to progress." Yet, on the other hand, we are also condemned for somehow daring to assert "ourselves as modern, innovative, future-looking native peoples," because that assertion contradicts "the image of living fossils that the rest of society" requires of us. Kuwada argues that when Kānaka ʻŌiwi *pay attention* to the past, it does not mean we are wallowing in it. To the "people who see themselves implicated in the injustices," he adds, what "makes them uncomfortable" is when we remember our histories—it "makes them tell us to stop showing it to them."[7] People who would share Johnson's view of Indigenous activism and industrial astronomy on Mauna a Wākea "want us to only be living in the past, so that their pain can end"—so they can worship another monument to Science and not feel guilty about it.[8] Finally, Kuwada offers a theory of *geological* and *genealogical* temporality, explaining how the kiaʻi fighting for Mauna a Wākea are "acting as kahu [caretakers] for our sacred places" and this work cannot be "measured in days, or weeks, or even years . . . [because it] spans generations and eras and epochs."[9] Looking to our genealogies—our moʻokūʻauhau—Kuwada speaks of connections:

Our genealogies are a backbone stretching to the very inception of these islands, and when we understand our genealogy, we know our origins, where we have been. We always have our ancestors at our back. That certainty gives us a wider possibility of movement, a more supple way to navigate through the world. Standing on our mountain of connections, our foundation of history and stories and love, we can see both where the path behind us has come from and where the path ahead leads. This connection assures us that when we move forward, we can never be lost because we always know how to get back home. The future is a realm we have inhabited for thousands of years . . . This is the future we are leading the way to, the future we are going to live in, the future our ancestors fought for, the future we still fight for.[10]

Recognizing this futurity is to understand *we have always been modern,* but this modernity is a continuum of relations, more rhizomatic than linear, a modernity more about connection than a narrow conception of "progress." In this chapter I examine this continuum of pilina (relations), which Kānaka 'Ōiwi articulate to the contemporary struggle for Mauna a Wākea and within the broader context of Native subjection on ancestral lands. The examples I engage are inflected as mele (songs, chants), mo'olelo (stories, histories, literature, ethnographies, etc.), and mo'okū'auhau (genealogical successions, genealogies): forms relevant to the myriad ways Kānaka 'Ōiwi sustain relationships with the natural world and the Mauna. Before engaging articulations of these sacred pilina, however, I will examine two concepts that, in my view, resonate with these conceptions of the natural and the sacred. I place them in conversation with articulations of Kanaka relationality to 'āina as provocations toward notions of truth and reality: this is a conversation unbothered by contingency and indeterminacy that might open space for deeper understanding of Kanaka relationality and what may only be approximated in the English language as the "sacred."

Composing Nature, Articulating Relations

Bruno Latour's playful attempt at "a compositionist manifesto"[11] stages an intervention in contemporary conceits that descend from three centuries of modernism, which has produced neither utopic futures nor its promised truths about our world. He argues, in one "gigantic, myopic, bloody, and sometimes comical blunder," the "modernist hero" has misunderstood "the flow of time" and alienated Man from Nature. The pair coconstituted in what he describes as "the great Bifurcation," Man's dominion over Nature is but one of its enduring legacies.[12] The Anglo-European seventeenth century being the "time of the great political, religious, legal, and epistemological invention of *matters of fact,*" the moderns imposed a vision of reality through fetishizing progress and innovating without precaution. Obsessed with a past to be escaped and Nature to be controlled, they conjured ancients against which modern superiority could be imagined and measured. Eventually, the introduction of an "absolute distinction between what is deaf and dumb and who is allowed to speak . . . [proved] a fabulously useful ploy" to impose an "ultimate reality, made of fully silent entities that were yet able, through the mysterious intervention of Science (capital S) to 'speak by themselves' (but without the mediation of science, small s, and scientists—also small s!)."[13] Latour distinguishes *futures* from *prospects,* arguing the Science of the moderns created our *future* but failed to contemplate our *prospects* for dealing with "things to come" like our current global environmental and climate crises. Too "busy fleeing their past in terror," they remain blinded by a refusal to *look ahead,* destroying futures they cannot see. Precisely because they travel forward without looking ahead, Latour argues, the moderns "have never been modern." Misidentifying alternative epistemes as "primitive" and Nature as a "resource," they disavow the rubble they make.

Several aspects of this compositionist method offer something to the conversation I wish to stage about Kanaka articulations of alterity and relationships to the natural world. Like Latour, I am less interested in "matters of fact" than "matters of concern"[14] and less concerned with unveiling a reality "behind the subjective fog of appearances"[15] than interrogating worlds taken for granted and realities imposed. In the case of Mauna a Wākea, a mark of the hierarchy of knowledges being imposed by settler colonial occupation and U.S. cultural hegemony consists of those encounters in everyday Hawaiʻi in which Kanaka ʻŌiwi knowledge, values, and relations to ancestral places are trivialized, fetishized, and even appropriated—only to be disavowed, bracketed, and marginalized by the real business of capital, science, or state imperatives. The compositionist asks: What possibilities emerge if that which is to be regarded through science is immanent, rather than transcendent? What if we were to analyze articulations of nature, not through methodologies that reproduce hierarchical knowledges dependent on "epistemological breaks" or utopic revelations of a real world beyond (frames derived by ethnocentric Anglo-American knowledge systems), but instead through the careful study of *worlds* "slowly composed."[16] What if we seek not some elusive truth by distinguishing "what is constructed and what is not constructed" but instead strive for a *better understanding* by recognizing the difference "between what is *well* or *badly* constructed, *well* or *badly* composed?"[17] That is what compositionism explores. In this chapter, I adopt such an approach, recognizing "there is no world of beyond" but only the worlds we compose.[18] The goal is not hierarchizing knowledge so much as understanding the Indigenous knowledge of Hawaiʻi, not as a means to an end—to rationalize industrial astronomy—but to understand *better*.

As discussed in previous chapters, Kanaka ʻŌiwi articulations of the natural, the sacred, and relations to ʻāina are routinely dismissed as invented for political gain and thereby recast as inauthentic and so on. In the contest over Mauna a Wākea, the implication is often that settler law and imperial science know Hawaiians better than Hawaiians know themselves. While many Kānaka ʻŌiwi will affirm U.S. liberalism by endeavoring to make Kanaka epistemes legible, the problem with the liberal multicultural settler capitalist state is its monopoly over the very terms of legibility. Those terms are designed to delegitimize Kānaka ʻŌiwi. As such, there is a risk of reifying U.S. cultural hegemony when we contend with discourses meant to trivialize Indigenous knowledges as invented or fraudulent by defending their legitimacy on those terms, that is, by furnishing evidence to the contrary or challenging them without questioning their premises. While providing more evidence of the value of Kanaka epistemes, more information and more examples risk more exploitation, appropriation, and misidentification because this may inadvertently reify the structures of disavowal; refusing them altogether is also a problematic alternative. Somewhere in this contradiction I want to recognize the consequences of explicating and of *not* engaging articulations of Kanaka epistemologies. The paradox is a mark of unfreedom and the work ahead. Indeed, the vision of world making to which this project is accountable *cannot not* engage Kanaka articulations of indigeneity, for that would leave the misrepresentations and disavowals uncontested. The stakes are too high to make this mistake. Moreover, this world making offers a *better* response—an intervention in liberal multicultural settler capitalist hegemony that is urgent and likely to protect lands, waters, and people. Therefore, I engage the epistemologies of Kanaka indigeneity to highlight ways in which the futurities envisioned within Kanaka sense worlds offer alternatives to the myopic, self-important, and violent conventions of history, law, and science that structure industrial astronomy on Mauna a Wākea, and capitalism and empire more broadly. If asked why I engage these articulations on their own terms—or why I might not treat Kanaka ideologies with the same scrutiny as settler colonial ideologies—my answer is that it is because I center my analysis on power. Kānaka 'Ōiwi have historically not enjoyed the autonomy and freedom, let alone means and capacity, to be heard on our own terms—to the extent we may protect our ancestral islands—yet the disqualification of our knowledges proliferates, as do ecological and social crises.

In chapter 3, I briefly introduced Stuart Hall's theory of articulation, emphasizing the slippage between meanings of "articulation" as *enunciation*, and as *hinge* or *connection*, which offers a productive space that moves beyond critique and toward intervention. As critique presupposes a reality to be exposed, a truth behind appearances, articulation locates power: not definitively in ideology or culture but instead in the moment of signification.[19] The shift in focus intervenes in the conventions of disavowal, because all knowledge and culture is ideological. For this reason, any criticism of Hawaiians for *using culture* as an *ideological* weapon is meaningless. But, how does an ideological discourse of, say, nature or the sacred become suspect, irrational, or inauthentic? This requires an intervention in relations of power. Articulation theory locates power in the significatory instance: when, for example, thought becomes unspeakable, and praxis is rendered fraudulent or criminal. Ideology and culture are not inherently political categories, but they may become political when articulated to a specific project in a particular context—toward stopping the TMT under conditions of settler capitalism, for example. Therefore, the critical question tends to the locus of enunciation where Hawaiian cultural ideology threatens the scientific settler state. This approach avoids reifying one particular ideology or another and instead tends to structured relations of dominance and subordination. In other words, it offers an analysis of power.

Hall's discussion of ideology is instructive:

> Thus, for me, the difference between one cultural formation and another cannot be conceptualized in terms of the distinction between ideology and science where the latter stands for "truth"; it cannot be thought in terms of mystification in the straightforward sense of "mystification versus enlightenment." It may be thought in terms of relative degrees of mystification or misunderstanding, but all culture is misunderstanding, in the sense that all culture imposes particular maps on everything. Everybody is not constantly mystified in the same way or to the same degree. *There are differences between a better and a worse explanation of something. But there is not truth versus mystification which we can write into the very a priori definition of ideology.*[20]

Like Latour and Hall, my engagement with Kanaka ʻŌiwi articulations of nature and the sacred is not meant to critique or debunk critiques of Kanaka epistemologies as obsolete or superstitious, modern or scientific. Instead, recognizing the neutrality of ideology, I ask: How do Hawaiians talk about and understand this relationship? Neither Latour nor Hall seeks to uncover (and thereby reify the notion of) a universal reality or truth. They seek neither transcendence nor *a world beyond.* Instead, the two theoretical interventions seek to create space for a better accounting of worlds carefully composed.

I am not interested in whether Kanaka ʻŌiwi relationality to ʻāina is true or authentic, constructed or imagined: instead, I am interested in how it is articulated and to what end. These articulations are neither necessary, fixed, or permanent, nor random, accidental, or arbitrary. The political is not intrinsic to any ideological thought or cultural praxis but is always contingent. It is when Kanaka ideologies of reciprocity and balance with nature become articulated to the politics of self-determination that Kanaka indigeneity undermines hegemony, becomes a threat to the state, and must therefore be subordinated—or defended. The ways that Hawaiians understand their relations to the natural world is political only insofar as settler capitalism and U.S. occupation have made them so.

As my analysis in this book is more concerned with conditions of possibility than epistemic closure—and understanding relationality rather than uncovering reality—the following examination of mele does not obsess over combinations of ideologies and social structures that render Native

Hawaiian identity or religion legitimate or authentic, superstitious, or rational. They do, however, offer insights into how those combinations by which Kanaka indigeneity and ontogenealogical relationality to ʻāina—as articulated to self-determination—might offer imaginaries less violent and in balance with other-than-human worlds, or "nature." After all, it is through such combinations that Mauna a Wākea becomes sacred, and the sacred pilina of Kānaka ʻŌiwi to the Mauna is renewed in the course of community-organized, direct-action land and water protection. Next, I turn to a common question asked when exploring the idea of Maunakea as a sacred place, one worth fighting against astronomy to protect: *How is it sacred?*

Mele and the Moʻokūʻauhau of Kauikeaouli

Looking at the knowledge traditions that connect people to place and moʻokūʻauhau, or genealogies, Mauna a Wākea appears as a kupuna (ancestor, elder), and therefore, kin. Most moʻokūʻauhau are relayed through two forms, mele (song) and oli (chant), although they were also preserved in the nineteenth- and twentieth-century Hawaiian language newspapers, some of which have subsequently been reproduced, translated, and analyzed by contemporary scholars. While the mountain is sacred because of this kinship relation, the language of "sacred" and "sanctity" fail to capture the meanings of this relationality. The English language can only ever poorly approximate what Kānaka ʻŌiwi sense, know, and feel. Likewise, Western religious connotations attached to such concepts as "religion" and "spirit" will only reinforce the hierarchies of knowledge that oppress. While my analysis too is insufficient, I introduce these constellations of meaning because they continue to give life to the movement for Mauna a Wākea, if for no other reason than because they compose nature and articulate relations *better*. Describing the significance of mele to Kanaka indigeneity, Leilani Basham explains:

> Mele, which are poetry, music, chants, and songs, have been a foundational part of the histories and lives of the Kānaka Maoli of Hawaiʻi. We have used mele to record and recount our histories and stories, as well as our ideas about the lives of our people and our land. Mele have been a vital part of our cultural belief systems and practices, our connection to our ʻāina, our land base, as well as our formal religious practices and our informal daily practices. Mele have also been vital to our political theories, ideas, and practices.[21]

Basham explains how pono—meaning "goodness," "uprightness," "correct," "virtuous," or "proper behavior"—was a foundational concept to Kanaka genealogical and land-based value systems long before the first foreigners arrived but also in the formation of a Hawaiian sense of self as a unified lāhui amidst the tectonic social, economic, and political shifts in the first decades after the arrival of Anglo-settlers. To this end, Basham analyzes mele lāhui, or "mele written in honour of the lāhui, the Hawaiian people and nation," showing how they offer a window into a Kanaka ʻŌiwi sense of the world that continues to inform contemporary political thought and praxis.[22] Mele can perform multiple functions at once, some depicting originary or emergence stories, or rehearsing the connections between people, places, and relations through use of mnemonic devices and layered meanings, all of which would serve a variety of pedagogic purposes. Mele inoa, for example, were composed in honor of a person or ancestor, such as a beloved mōʻī, exalting their name, place of birth, memorable deeds, or distinct leadership qualities. Often, mele inoa would reference the mōʻī's right to rule, always drawing connections between storied places and kūpuna. Some mele were written for wahi pana, or "historically and culturally-significant places," and others, mele aloha for example, were written simply to convey the great aloha and affection felt by a composer for a kupuna or valley, mountain range, region, sacred site, or island district.[23] Ubiquitous throughout, however, are these bonds between people and place that emerge through practices of nomenclature, metaphor, and kaona (hidden and multiple meanings).

In nineteenth- and early twentieth-century Hawaiian language newspapers, the common practice of recounting moʻokūʻauhau, or genealogies and genealogical successions, provided a highly specialized and cherished mode by which to explore pilina—or connections not only between people and place but also between past and present—and to contemplate familial or political relationships, ethical quandaries, and social matters of the day. Moʻokūʻauhau, therefore, might serve as a basis to challenge or defend the genealogical descent and qualification of a mōʻī and other aliʻi, to settle a dispute among members of a shared line, or to remind readers of enmities and alliances with relevance to contemporary issues. Before Hawaiʻi was modeled on the Anglo-European modern state, moʻokūʻauhau operated as a means by which one's legitimacy to rule was asserted. The practice of rehearsing moʻokūʻauhau reinforced cultural memory of collective

experiences and events, illustrating historical analogies and often emphasizing the qualities of a pono way of navigating changing times. Through
moʻokūʻauhau, people would express their aloha, dissent, and desires, and
it was through mele published in newspapers that readers were reminded
to take pride in their Kanaka ʻŌiwi sense of the world.

Such was the case of the mele hānau (birth chant) composed for the
newborn son of Kamehameha I, Kauikeaouli (1813–1854) entitled, "No
Kalani ʻKauikeaouli Kamehameha III," also known as "Hānau a Hua Ka
Lani"[24] and "Mele Hānau no Kauikeaouli."[25] This mele tells of Kauikeaouli's
chiefly descent from Papa and Wākea, but it does much more than justify
his royal lineage and right to rule. It begins, "O hānau a hua Kalani [sic],"[26]
the aliʻi (ruler), "Kalani gave birth," and, in seven verses, it describes how all
things, including the night, earth, clouds, sky, and the mountain of Mauna
a Wākea "belong to" or were "born to" Papa and Wākea. Drawing connections between the young mōʻī's birth and the elevated status of his genealogy, it foretells not only a troubled political reign ahead but also his destiny
as a great leader. For example, there are plays on Kauikeaouli's name ("place
in the dark sky") while several lines—"ʻO ke keiki pō lani keia a Kea i
hānau [sic]" ("This is the royal offspring of night borne by Kea") and "O
hānau ke ao, o hiki aʻe" ("The cloud was born, it rose and appeared")—
invoke imagery of an ambivalent night sky and future reign.[27]

First performed at the ceremonies during the birth of Kauikeaouli in
1813, at Keauhou, Kona, Hawaiʻi, the mele was printed around the time of
his birthday in the newspaper, *Ka Nupepa Kuokoa,* on March 24, 1866—
twelve years after his passing.[28] The mele affirms Kauikeaouli's sacred right
to ascendency as mōʻī of Ko Hawaiʻi Pae ʻĀina (Hawaiʻi, the nation-state)[29]
by way of his genealogy, which links him to the kuamoʻo kūpuna aliʻi,[30]
or progenitors of the chiefs and people, Papa and Wākea, the royal children
Hoʻohōkūkalani[31] and Hāloa, and Mauna a Wākea.[32] The mele also refers
to the near-death complication in the infant king's birth, which required
he be "prayed into life" by Kamaloʻihi, the high priest who revived the stillborn chief to consciousness.[33] The young aliʻi's precarious beginning would
be interpreted as prophecy of the obstacles to his reign and his achievements in overcoming them.

Sections in the mele hānau for Kauikeaouli also play with various elements of the name "Kauikeaouli," which describe natural phenomena—the
clouds, the "sky, light, day, daylight, and dawn"—but as Pukui explains, can

also "refer to the regaining of consciousness, and to achieving mental enlightenment," with which the societal shifts under his reign would forever be associated.[34] This "dawning" anticipates the emergence of a new sociopolitical order:

> So in this single nuclear element of Kau-i-ke-ao-uli's sacred name are clustered and concentrated the seeds of some of the major symbols and sweeping cosmological conceptions found in the language of this old noble poem.[35]

Referencing Joseph Poepoe's analysis, Silva adds, "The name aligns the ali'i with the heavens while maka'āinana are symbolically what is below, the land (the word "āina' forms part of the word 'maka'āinana')," which were the common people of society not of chiefly descent and who worked the land.[36] The mele hānau begins with Keōpūolani's long and difficult labor:

O ho'onā kū o ka malama,
O ka'ahē a ka 'īloli,
O ho'owiliwili e hānau Kalani.
'O ia ho'i, 'o Kalani, hānau Kalani.

This was a month of travail,
Of gasping labor,
a writhing to deliver the chief.
He is this chief, born of a chiefess.[37]

The mele continues with descriptions of Papa and Wākea's descendants—the fifth and final verse noting the birth of Maunakea. By linking Kauikeaouli to Wākea's namesake, Mauna a Kea, Kauikeaouli is associated with not only the mountain's physical beauty and prominence, which signifies the mō'ī's high rank, but also (and especially) with the genealogy of the Mauna as a child of Papa and Wākea and thus ancestor to Kauikeaouli as well.

The following segment from Pukui and Korn's translation of "No Kalani 'Kauikeaouli Kamehameha III'"[38] traces the mo'okū'auhau very briefly, locating the mountain as Papa and Wākea's hiapo, or firstborn "child." Ho'ohōkūkalani is the second-born, mother, and half-sister of Hāloa. Hāloa is the first ali'i (chief), born to Wākea and Ho'ohōkūkalani.[39] The mele establishes the birth order of the sacred sibling relationship, not through a family tree or bracket-style listing of names, marriages/partnerhips, and births but instead through imagery connecting people and place. The following verse introduces Papa, Wākea, Hoʻohōkūkalani, Hāloa, and Mauna a Wākea as the ancestors of Kauikeaouli:

O hānau ka mauna a Kea,
ʻŌpuʻu aʻe ka mauna a Kea.
ʻO Wākea ke kāne, ʻo Papa, ʻo Walinuʻu ka wahine.
Hānau Hoʻohoku he wahine,
Hānau Hāloa he aliʻi,
Hānau ka mauna, he keiki mauna nā Kea [*sic*] . . .

Born of Kea, was the mountain,
The mountain of Kea budded forth.
Wākea was the husband, Papa Walinuʻu was the wife.
Born was Hoʻohoku, a daughter,
Born was Hāloa, a chief,
Born was the mountain, a mountain-son of Kea . . .[40]

Many today understand Mauna a Wākea as an ancestor of the Hawaiian people and cite this among the numerous mele and moʻolelo as the basis of that knowledge, which in turn imparts an elevated status unto the Mauna as a place of ancestral bonds. Part of the claim that the mountain is family and something more than settler possession—a "resource" or "property"—comes from the idea of genealogical descent, whereby the Mauna is at once a wahi kapu,[41] a kupuna, and an elder sibling. In his groundbreaking manuscript, esteemed Kanaka ʻŌiwi educator, businessman, counselor, and scholar Davida Malo tells of variations on this moʻolelo, suggesting the idea of "birthing islands," while a common metaphor, was not ubiquitous.[42] Malo writes,

Ma ka moʻokūʻauhau o Wākea, ua ʻōlelo ʻia mai na Papa i hānau mai i kēia pae moku. ʻO kekahi lohe mai, ʻaʻole i hānau ʻia mai kēia pae moku; akā, i hana maoli ʻia e ko Wākea mau lima kēia pae moku.

In the genealogical account of Wākea, it is told that Papa gave birth to this archipelago [of Hawaiʻi]. Another thing that is heard is that these islands were not born, but were made by Wākea's hands.[43]

In contrast to the volcanic origin story of the islands according to Western geological and Earth sciences, the moʻolelo told by Kanaka ʻŌiwi scholars reveals Hawaiʻi Island is the first born to Papa and Wākea in the making of ka pae ʻāina o Hawaiʻi (the Hawaiian archipelago). While the moʻokūʻauhau of Papahānaumoku and Wākea is among the most prominent of the cosmogonic genealogies, its variations sometimes contradict one another.[44] For example, unlike "No Kalani ʻKauikeaouli Kamehameha III'," in the Kumulipo two island children—Hawaiʻi and Maui—are the first born to Papa and Wākea, followed next by a daughter Hoʻohōkūkalani,[45] who is the first human child. The next child born to Papa and Wākea is Hāloa, the firstborn chief, followed by Mauna a Wākea, the firstborn mountain. Kanaka ʻŌiwi archeologist Kekuewa Kikiloi explains that Wākea and Papa were not only "personified in the mythologies of earth and sky . . . [but] also thought to have been real people . . . [whose] story documents an important socio-political transformation in Hawaiian society when the sovereignty and control of the islands is taken by Wākea from the senior line of the Kumu-honua genealogy."[46] Kikiloi adds, "This places early Hawaiian society onto a trajectory towards the elaboration of religious practices and the rise in authority of a new type of chief, whose power is sustained and ordained through the religious system" that would become known as hoʻomanamana.[47] While some have treated these moʻolelo and socioreligious practices as retrograde superstition—and early moʻolelo of humans birthing islands or creating islands from their hands as naïve—the kūpuna who composed these mele, moʻokūʻauhau, and knowledge systems were not superstitious, naïve, or irrational. They were reverent toward the deeper meanings found within this body of knowledge passed down from their ancestors. Rendering ʻāina as family is significant also in that it has the potential to instill a deeper relationality between people and place—one that involves an ethical positionality and ecological sense of accountability—*as if life depends on it.* As Silva argues,

> One mustn't think our kupuna kahiko actually took the moʻolelo of Wākea and Papa literally, far from it. Rather, these are ingeniously crafted metaphors. They are carrying substantial symbolic weight and are also indicative of a way of being in the world and of conceiving the world and our place in it—we are part of a family that includes the sun, stars, ocean, and everything else in the world.[48]

What better futures might become possible if contemporary society were to adopt such a positionality that conceives of social responsibility to the natural world as fundamental and urgent? What if people today related to the living world as a kinship relation and a familial obligation constituted in the intimacies of genealogical descent? From this knowledge comes the concept of mālama ʻāina, which suggests that to care for the land is to care for oneself, each other, and future descendants just as the ancestors practiced and instructed.

The Moʻokūʻauhau of Papa and Wākea

While the moʻokūʻauhau of Papa and Wākea is among the most cited, the many variations of its telling have often contradicted one another. It seems haole historians have been more comfortable than Kanaka ʻŌiwi scholars in supplanting ambiguity with certainty, but in the variations a theme emerges with lessons for us scholars of Hawaiian culture, history, and politics today. For example, Noelani Arista describes how "an over reliance upon the publication of" Davida Malo's *Ka Moʻolelo Hawaiʻi* "in translation"[49] has undermined "the rich diversity of written and published materials produced by . . . Malo," the consequences of which have lasting implications on what constitutes authoritative knowledge about Hawaiian society, culture, and traditional practices. According to Langlas and Lyon, while it "is now the most widely used version of Malo's work . . . [there] are clearly problems with Emerson's translation . . . the most significant . . . [of which] is that only the translation is provided. Malo's Hawaiian text is not given, except for the mele and pule."[50] Worse, however, Emerson's "translation is written in a high-flown style very different from Malo's plain, even terse style. In too many places his translation is loose or inaccurate . . . [and] alters Malo's meaning by omitting something that Malo wrote or—worse yet—by inserting something not written by Malo."[51] In the work of contemporary scholars whose returns to nineteenth-century sources written in Hawaiian prioritize greater accuracy in their translation practices, the diversity of variations on the moʻokūʻauhau of Kānaka ʻŌiwi appears not to be a fault in Indigenous scholarship but instead the evidence that ambiguity is not as threatening to a Kanaka ʻŌiwi sense of ontological coherence as it has been to haole scholarship on Hawaiians and Hawaiian history, culture, and society. While acknowledging this variation, my retelling of the moʻokūʻauhau is to emphasize how our beloved nineteenth-century intellectuals allowed for multiple truths about the origins of Kānaka ʻŌiwi to coexist and that what matters most is a subsequent ethics of familial obligation and genealogical connection between people and place that these moʻolelo celebrate.

The koʻihonua[52] known as the Kumulipo is a cosmogonic genealogical mele that lists the emergence of all Kānaka ʻŌiwi and everything in the living world from the realm of the gods, or pō.[53] The moʻokūʻauhau of Papa and Wākea appears in the Kumulipo, which Malo explains introduces Laʻilaʻi as the "first person," a kuamoʻo kūpuna aliʻi, and the grandmother of Wākea, and whose grandparents and parents "were pō (manifestations of darkness) and with her human birth began."[54] With the akua called Kealiiwahilani, Laʻilaʻi had a son to be named Kahiko, or Kahikoluamea.[55] Kahiko and his wahine,[56] Kupulanakēhau, had two sons: Līhauʻula the elder, Wākea the younger.[57] Davida Malo explains,

> He wahine kā Wākea, ʻo Haumea kona inoa lā, wahine a Wākea, ma ka moʻokūʻauhau i kapa ʻia ʻo Palikū, he pali kona mau kūpuna a mau mākua. Iā ia, maopopo mai ke kanaka ʻana.

> Wākea had a wife named Haumea, who is Papa. Of that same Haumea, wife of Wākea, it is said in the genealogical tradition called Palikū, that her parents and grandparents were pali (cliffs). Beginning with her it is clear that there were humans [sic].[58]

According to the renowned nineteenth-century Kanaka ʻŌiwi scholar Samuel Mānaiakalani Kamakau, moʻolelo of Hawaiian origins were well kept, if often contradictory. In his account of the moʻokūʻauhau of Papa and Wākea, like Davida Malo, Kamakau also affirms that Kahiko was Wākea's father and Kupulanakēhau his mother.[59] However, in Mary Kawena Pukui's translation of Barrère's edited volume of his manuscript entitled *Ka Poʻe Kahiko: The People of Old,* Kamakau describes Hulihonua and his partner Keakahulilani as the "first man" and "first woman"—with twenty-eight generations preceding Wākea.[60] In Pukui's translation of Barrère's edited volume of Kamakau's *Tales and Traditions of the People of Old: Nā Moʻolelo a ka Poʻe Kahiko,* he explains in "the beginning of the world," Kumuhonua "reduced heaven and earth to fire," later remade them "by the breath of his mouth," and with his partner, Hālōiho, turned a gourd calabash into the earth, sky, clouds, sun, moon, planets, and stars.[61] The pair then "appointed Kū, Lono, Kāne, and Kanaloa as chief spirits, aliʻi ʻuhane,"[62] the first three of whom "made" the "first man," Welaahilanui, and from his body "tore" off a piece to create the first woman, 'Owē.[63] To them was born Kahikoluamea, or Kahiko, the father of Wākea. If according to Pukui's analysis of Kauikeaouli's birth chant, Ho'ohōkūkalani is the first human, while Malo has La'ila'i as the "first person," and Pukui and Barrére's Kamakau suggests the "first man" and "first woman" are Hulihonua and Keakahulilani; although the second of Pukui and Barrére's Kamakau locates Welaahilanui as the "first man," it seems nā po'e kahiko (the people of old) were not preoccupied with naming a single universal reality. Instead, it would appear they made space for variations on a theme, that is, the recalling of kūpuna i ka pō as a practice that signals the importance of genealogical relationality between people and place as a basis of Kanaka ontologies, ways of being, and what exists.

The Ko'ihonua of Kumulipo

Noenoe Silva discusses Wākea's genealogy by way of the Kumulipo in an analysis of early twentieth-century historian Joseph Poepoe whose accounts published in the newspaper *Ka Na'i Aupuni* from 1905–1906 provide a theory of Hawaiian origins in which human evolution is located within a genealogy that transitions from pō (night, period of darkness before humankind), to ao (time of light, and humans),[64] and to the mo'okū'auhau of Papa and Wākea.[65] According to Silva, Poepoe's understanding of the Kumulipo and the mo'okū'auhau of Papa and Wākea is that they were not only ingeniously crafted metaphors but models of *how* to read mo'okū'auhau in general. Poepoe was engaged in the preservation of ancient texts but also epistemological methods.

From Malo, to Kamakau, to Poepoe—and to early twentieth-century and other contemporary scholars including Mary Kawena Pukui, Rubellite Johnson, Lilikalā Kame'eleihiwa, Noenoe Silva, Pualani Kanaka'ole Kanahele, ku'ualoha ho'omanawanui, Noelani Arista, Marie Alohalani Brown, and Jamaica Heolimeleikalani Osorio—the sacredness of our island homeland comes from the memory of sacred intimacies among people and people to places. As mentioned earlier, one 'ōlelo no'eau, or poetical saying, reminds us that the people are connected to the land in he pilina wehena 'ole (an inseverable relationship) that is reaffirmed every time we care for the land as a sacred kuleana and familial obligation.[66] The mo'okū'auhau of Papa and Wākea is among the most influential accounts of Kanaka emergence, in part because of its contemporary articulation of genealogical relationality to contemporary expressions of aloha ʻāina activism. As Silva argues, most Kānaka in ancient times understood Papa and Wākea as ancestors and akua but also as metaphorical embodiments of the natural elements, or the "creative forces of nature."[67]

The procreative celebration of Papa and Wākea is recorded in mele koʻihonua, which Kamakau explains were "composed in the style, ʻano, of [naming] the most important of the children and the most important of the wives," wherein the kapu[68] mating of the royal pair, and their genealogies, is celebrated through the aesthetics of metaphor:

ʻO Wākea Kahikoluamea e a [sic],
ʻO Papa, Papa-nui-hānau-moku ka wahine;
Hānau Kahiki-kū, Kahiki-moe,
Hānau ke ʻāpapanuʻu,
Hānau ke ʻāpapalani,
Hānau Hawaiʻi, i ka moku makahiapo,
Ke keiki makahiapo a laua [sic] . . .

Wākea the son of Kahikoluamea,
Papa, Papa-nui-hānau-moku the wife;
Kahiki-kū and Kahiki-moe were born,[69]
The upper stratum was born,
The uppermost stratum was born,
Hawaiʻi was born, the first-born of the islands,
The first-born child of the two . . .[70]

This mele tells us that Hawaiʻi was the first of the island chain born to Papa and Wākea; it is the hiapo. For this reason, according to Pualani Kanakaʻole Kanahele and Edward L. H. Kanahele, the hiapo philosophy places us, Kānaka, in a direct relationship of responsibility to the first born—dependent on natural life cycles and connected through the sacred waters of Mauna a Wākea. While some think of the mountain as an inanimate entity, that Waiau, a body of water previously thought to never evaporate, naturally drained in the years between the 2015 and 2019 uprisings on the Mauna. This indicates not only that Mauna a Wākea is very much an animate entity but also that when Kānaka ʻŌiwi observe our kuleana, the hiapo responds. In a cultural assessment study written for the proposed Saddle Road realignment in 1997, Kanakaʻole Kanahele and Kanahele wrote that Kānaka ʻŌiwi recognized and practice[d] respect for hierarchy or hiapo for man and land alike. The mountain is sacred because it is the sacred child of Wākea. It is also the nourishment source for our land. The mountains and land were genealogically connected to [Kānaka] through the original ancestor[s], Wākea and Papa.[71]

Kanakaʻole Kanahele and Kanahele also connect the symbolic to the material, explaining "Wākea, Sky Father and Papa, Earth Mother. Between the two all things were born." According to Kameʻeleihiwa, the hiapo concept requires Hawaiians to treat the natural as sacred—to relate to nature with reverence as one would an elder but also as one should in relation to all that which gives life and nourishment. In this regard, the kuleana (responsibility, privilege) of all Kānaka ʻŌiwi is to care for Hawaiʻi as ʻohana—figuratively and materially—as a life-giving imperative.

A Unified Hawaiian Consciousness

The moʻolelo of Papa and Wākea also introduces us to another way of being—an indigeneity rooted in the land and the kuleana to care for it. Kekuewa Kikiloi explores the metaphor of "birthing" the Hawaiian Islands, suggesting it denotes a radical shift "in Hawaiian history when the sovereignty, as well as control over the islands, is lost by the descendants of the oppressive senior line of the Kumu-honua genealogy."[72] The social stratification among aliʻi (chiefs), kāhuna (priests), makaʻāinana (commoners), and kauwā (royal servants) is formed in this period of progressive social change, when "the island names are reconstituted and a new archipelago is 'birthed.'"[73] Although there are discrepancies among the moʻolelo of Kanaka origins, there is agreement that the connection of ʻŌiwi to place, to these islands, is not ambiguous, nor is the assertion of the contemporary relevance of that relationship to today's practices of resistance to displacement or desecration merely reactionary. Emphasizing the historicity of pilina between lāhui and ʻŌiwi, Kikiloi writes,

> The union of this couple (Papa and Wākea) results in not just the "birthing" of the archipelago but also the "birthing" of a unified Hawaiian consciousness—a common ancestral lineage that forges links between the genealogies of both land and people. Since that point on in our history, this archipelago and its people became inseparable, as the well-being of one becomes invariably connected to the well-being of the other.[74]

This unified Hawaiian consciousness underpins a continuum of rela-tionality. It is also a methodological instruction for contemporary kiaʻi ʻāina, as Maunakea today is defended as a family member and elder sibling. Within the reciprocity that this relationship provides, Kānaka ʻŌiwi are taught the sacred responsibilities, which might very well include collective direct action and civil disobedience. The unifying logic that informs the opposition to industrial astronomy today is rooted in these sacred pilina and the kuleana to aloha ʻāina.

Because all aspects of the natural environment are embodiments of the many akua, the moʻokuʻauhau also maps relations and kuleana. One of the most important lessons derived from the kapu mating of Papa and Wākea is the moʻolelo of Maunakea's sibling, Hāloa. It begins with the first two islands, Hawaiʻi and Maui, born to Papa, followed by Hoʻohōkūkalani, a daughter.[75] Kameʻeleihiwa's account of this moʻolelo and the Kumulipo describes Wākea as "seducing" Hoʻohōkūkalani, and to them a son—a pre-mature stillborn child named Hāloanaka (quivering long stalk)—was born.[76] From his buried remains grew a taro plant, the staple Indigenous first food: the kalo. Hoʻohōkūkalani and Wākea had a second son, also named Hāloa, who is considered the first aliʻi. Because kalo represents the historically and culturally important staple food on which society depended, its function in the moʻolelo is to express a link between the people and the land that grows the food. The lesson of kuleana to care for the land carried within this moʻolelo is embodied in the concept of aloha ʻāina, which persists today. Regarding this kuleana, Kameʻeleihiwa explains,

> In traditional Hawaiian society, as in the rest of Polynesia, it is the duty of younger siblings and junior lineages to love, honor, and serve their elders. This is the pattern that defines the Hawaiian relationship to the ʻĀina and the kalo that together feed Ka Lāhui Hawaiʻi. Thus, the "mod-ern" concepts of aloha ʻĀina, or love of the Land, and Mālama ʻĀina, or serving and caring for the Land, stem from the traditional model estab-lished at the time of Wākea.[77]

This reverence continues among Kānaka even today. The young are expected to respect elders because they become the land: people die, are buried, and from their decomposed remains become ʻāina. Therefore, sym-bolically and materially, ʻāina is an ancestor. Kanaka ʻŌiwi knowledge of this physical reality is interpreted by Kameʻeleihiwa as defining our obligations (or kuleana) to care for (or mālama) 'āina like we do our elders (our kūpuna). According to this system of reciprocity and valuation of land as family, because Hāloanaka is an elder to Kānaka 'Ōiwi today, so is kalo, one of his kino lau (*many bodies,* or bodily forms), also considered an elder. Today, the many lo'i kalo (taro patch) restoration and revitalization projects across the islands attest to the persistence of this value system of reciprocity and hiapo philosophy of mālama 'āina. And these commitments also inform contemporary resistance to U.S. cultural hegemony and settler colonial occupation. While many Kānaka 'Ōiwi maintain traditional food practices and spiritual relations reflected in these mo'olelo, *they* also animate contemporary land defense as a sacred pilina and kuleana. It is in such ways of sensing the natural world that Mauna a Wākea becomes sacred and worthy of protection.

These practices and relations cannot be reduced to the possessive and extractive logics of capitalism, colonialism, and empire. Nor are they evidence of irrational superstition or political maneuvering. Instead, these are evidence of a *better way* of doing and being, evidence of a continuum of resistance and relationality.

Birth Order and 'Ai Kapu

From the mele, *'O Wākea noho iā Papahānaumoku,* we learn the birth order of the islands and that Ho'ohōkūkalani was also a progenitor ancestor/akua and the daughter of and punalua[78] to Papa. The mele also conveys that Papa and Wākea eventually coupled to birth the remaining five islands. Emerson's translation is as follows:

'O Wākea noho iā Papahānaumoku,
Hānau 'o Hawai'i, he moku,
Hānau 'o Maui, he moku.
Ho'i hou 'o Wākea noho iā Ho'ohōkūkalani
Hānau 'o Moloka'i, he moku,
Hānau 'o Lāna'ikaula, he moku.
Lili'ōpū punalua 'o Papa iā Ho'ohōkūkalani.
Ho'i hou Papa noho iā Wākea.
Hānau 'o O'ahu, he moku,
Hānau 'o Kaua'i, he moku,
Hānau 'o Ni'ihau, he moku,
He 'ula a'o Kaho'olawe.

Wākea mated with Papahānaumoku
Born was Hawai'i, an island,
Born was Maui, an island.
Wākea returned and mated with Ho'ohōkūkalani
Born was Moloka'i, an island,
Born was Lāna'ikaula, an island.
Papa became jealous of Ho'ohōkūkalani.
Papa returned and mated with Wākea.
Born was O'ahu, an island,
Born was Kaua'i, an island,
Born was Ni'ihau, an island,
The red afterbirth was Kaho'olawe.[79]

Although Malo admits that it was unclear whether the 'ai kapu was established by Wākea or another, it was indeed an ancient kapu that lasted for more than six hundred years.[80] The 'ai kapu was a religious, political, and social system of the ruling ali'i in which spiritual symbolism established the basis of governance for centuries prior to the arrival of Westerners.[81] The Kapu System, as it is generally known, was structured around a fundamental separation between the ruling, priestly, and laboring classes, as well as all economic, social, and cultural life. An order with far-reaching implications, it also required the observance of gendered and spousal kapu, or restrictions that influenced many aspects of everyday life and collective social behavior, from eating and sleeping habits to kinship and social relations, including fishing, farming, manufacture, travel, ceremonial, and other social practices. The ultimate goal of the 'ai kapu, as Kame'eleihiwa argues, was to achieve pono, or balance, in every aspect of life with finite resources. The Kapu System manifested the values embedded within the teachings of mo'okū'auhau, mo'olelo, and mele in which land and resource management centered on human dependence on the natural environment.

Although the Kapu System was overturned in the early nineteenth century,[82] the kuleana it conveyed remains important to many Kānaka 'Ōiwi today, as witnessed in the Maunakea actions of 2015 and 2019. Marie Alohalani Brown describes how after the end of the Kapu System and the first American Protestant missionaries arrived in Hawai'i in 1820, Kānaka 'Ōiwi, and even Christian converts and many "others continued to practice Ho'omana Hawai'i," or "Hawaiian religion."[83] While this religion may have "gone underground" and stayed that way through much of the twentieth century, it never vanished. As such, today's observance of these sacred pilina and the kuleana to ʻāina exercised through and alongside acts of resistance continue to reveal alternative imaginaries for building better futures in the collective aspiration toward a model of pono that has a historical analog in the spiritual practices of our kūpuna i ka pō.[84]

While we live in different times and our struggles are manifold, complex, and sometimes contradictory, we continue to look to our moʻolelo for insights that may guide us toward futures less oppressive. This is no selfish desire for irretrievable pasts, nor a desperate turn toward "the dark ages." As Jamaica Heolimeleikalani Osorio explains, "Instead of being frozen in time and ink, moʻolelo move and shape-shift."[85] As such, they continue to offer contemporary readers possible alternatives that neither derive from nor reify colonial hegemony but strive toward pono. An example of such continuity and fluidity is in moʻolelo of the Mauna as a sacred piko.

The Piko

In Hawaiian, a piko is a "navel, navel string, (or) umbilical cord" and it may also be translated as "blood relations."[86] The human body is said to have two piko, or "summits," in addition to the navel, which include the "genitals . . . (and) crown of the head."[87] As another name for "summit," the refrain "ka piko kaulana o ka ʻāina" ("the famous piko of the land") was commonly used to celebrate Mauna a Wākea.[88] The Mauna is described as a piko also because it is an umbilical link between ʻāina and akua—the land below and our many gods/ancestors above. According to the symbolism of the piko, the umbilicus metaphor is reflected in the geography of the Mauna landscape. For example, Maunakea is a primary aquifer and source of fresh water that feeds the many rivers, streams, loʻi (irrigated terraces), māla (gardens), and communities below. Pua Kanakaʻole Kanahele explains that one "must look beyond the summit," when thinking of why the mountain is worthy of our aloha and mālama (care): "Mauna Kea *is* Hawaiʻi—there would be no Hawaiʻi had Mauna Kea not first risen. What occurs on the summit of Mauna Kea, filters down to, and has an impact on what is below."[89] This is both a figurative and material pilina. At this elevation, this is also the purest water—water from which mana (spiritual power) might be accessed at wahi pana (storied places) like Waiau.

An example was Queen Emma's 1881 visit to what some call "the piko of Wākea," the summit's body of water known as Lake Waiau. There, the widow of Mōʻī Alexander Liholiho, Kamehameha IV, Queen Emma, immersed herself in a symbolic act that affirmed her descent through the senior line of Papa and Wākea, as her journey was a spiritual pilgrimage to a source of ancestral mana. In this way, Emma's ascent was a political act that served as response to Mōʻī Kalākaua to whom she lost the 1874 election. A heated genealogical contest lasted for years after Kalākaua's victory as staunch Emma supporters claimed his lineage was not as prestigious as Emma's.[90] Kīhei and Māpuana de Silva explain,

> When Kalākaua embarked on his world tour in January 1881, Emma countered with this journey to the top of the world, to Mauna Kea. When Kalākaua sought recognition in foreign lands, Emma gained the approval of Wākea himself; she experienced firsthand the sacred piko at which father and mother, sky and land, conjoin.[91]

The piko of Wākea, the nourishing umbilicus of the Mauna, Waiau, in this instance, served as the Queen's symbolic and genealogical return to origins—affirming her connection to the akua, descent from the highest-ranking aliʻi kupuna, and therefore her legitimacy to serve as mōʻī. Although she was never to rule Ko Hawaiʻi Pae ʻĀina, it is no accident the story of this huakaʻi (journey) is remembered over a century later, particularly through numerous mele and hula commemorating the event. The Mauna was understood as a piko—as a way our kūpuna might commune with their kūpuna, which comprises a sacred pilina between people and place.

In another example, many families in areas around the lowland slopes of the Mauna historically practiced "a unique custom" of taking the piko of infants to Waiau, which established a "strong connection between the native families of Waimea and Mauna Kea" that persists to this day.[92] The practice consisted of carrying the piko (umbilicus) and ʻiewe (placenta) of a family's newborn children to the summit of Mauna a Wākea where the afterbirth could be hidden away in a cave, under a rock, or in Lake Waiau, thereby establishing the children as forever connected to the Mauna. In our interview, UH-Hilo professor of Hawaiian language and ethnographer Larry Kimura explained how, growing up in Waimea, it was just a practice he would hear about but didn't really pay much attention to. He said his mother kept an empty mayonnaise jar in which to collect the piko of the family's babies and, should someone in the family plan a trip to the summit, she would have them take the jar. The journey to the summit was always difficult, so it wasn't for everybody. Kimura's great-grandfather, William

Seymour Lindsey, was Queen Emma's guide on her two-day journey to the summit. He taught the trails to Kimura's granduncle, who kept the knowledge and would lead special visitors for many years after. Kimura said he was not certain the old timers really knew why such traditions as those for the piko were maintained, but when he asked his grandmother, she told him, "Every family has their own place. This is our family's sacred place" for depositing the piko where it would not be found.[93] His family always had a "piko rock" on the summit and a designated family member who could recall its location to confirm the piko and ʻiewe were always protected. It remains customary that piko and ʻiewe are buried in obscure places for if they were to be discovered, it is said that bad luck could befall the child, or worse. Kimura said that if there is a deeper reason for hiding the piko, the elders would generally not say; however, what is clear is how the pilina between the people and place forged on the summit is a sacred relation.[94]

This ʻike kupuna (ancestral knowledge) was affirmed by Pualani Kanakaʻole Kanahele who, in our 2012 interview, explained the building of telescopes on the Mauna has always been sacrilege because the very act diminishes "the elevated value of the mountain," reducing its status to "a very mundane category."[95] Kumu Pua challenged me to think beyond even human experience to ask: "What do you mean by sacred?"[96] After several conversations, I began to understand that answering this question was a kuleana I could not sidestep. The idea that the Mauna is sacred is a choice people make. It is not a transcendent, permanent, or universal truth but rather a preference that informs and is informed by the needs and desires of generations of Kānaka ʻŌiwi. Through careful study of the ways in which Mauna a Wākea is composed and articulated as something more than a resource for human consumption—more than a commodity to produce material wealth or a possession over which anyone has dominion—the value ascribed by Kānaka ʻŌiwi to the Mauna can only be described as sacred, however inadequate that term is. Similarly, this relation is neither invented nor pure, ancient nor modern. Not every Hawaiian will agree, but this valuation of the Mauna does persist as a constellation of sacred relations—as pilina—and the meanings found within the moʻolelo, mele, and moʻokūʻauhau affirm these places are worth defending as one would any sacred site.

Kumu Pua also explained how the Mauna is sacred by offering juxtapositions. On one hand, she describes "that which has been made by humans" and, on the other, "that which is made by nature, or that which will exist regardless of humans, human intervention, or consciousness."[97] For example, luakini are sacred, ki'i are sacred, and wahi pana are sacred, but not in the same way as Maunakea, which has nothing to do with human needs or desires. Instead, the Mauna is sacred because its value persists with or without us.[98] She also describes "a hierarchy of sacredness" among what is made by humans, but not among what is made by nature:

> The tops of the mountains have never belonged to man. In the mind of the intelligent Hawaiians, it's never belonged to man. The luakini—and the ki'is that they put on the luakini—are shaped by man. So, part of their knowledge of what is sacred, they help shape it, man helps shape it. The mountain doesn't have any of that. It's not touched by that. And so that's the different hierarchy in sacredness. So there's that sacredness that is totally natural, that totally belongs to the elements and our elemental deities. We have nothing to do with shaping it. And we have nothing to do with it being a benefit to us. But *it is beneficial* for us. We have nothing to do with the snow that falls up there and the water that it gathers. So, it's out of man's realm. That's the whole idea to me of the sacredness of Maunakea.[99]

Part of the desecration for Kumu Pua is in "exposing" the mountain to the everyday business of "man." Maunakea "belongs to the gods" and should not be defiled by or reduced to the needs of people. The anguish she and many others feel about the development of Maunakea is in knowing its natural state has been altered, and its sanctity continues to be violated: for much of its sanctity is preserved by allowing the Mauna to remain unaltered by human activity.

She also suggests the word "sacred" is "used so much that it doesn't really mean anything anymore."[100] She explained that many people simply cannot understand what it means to Hawaiians that natural phenomena—or a physical feature of the land—could be intimately understood as sacred for no other reason than because of their natural qualities that exist entirely outside of human influence. To illustrate this, Kanahele gave the example of the mountain's effects on the human body. Because the air is so thin, it is difficult to breathe; the body slows, thinking slows. People often experience stomach pains, or faint. Reactions can be severe, and some have died from altitude sickness. This, she says, is evidence that the mountain "doesn't belong to man . . . it's the land of Lono and Kāne."[101]

Here, she illustrated what it means to be in the realm of Lono and Kāne, and in explaining this she characterizes the mauna as a genealogical relation. The ahupuaʻa of Kaʻohe and Humuʻula share the summit of Maunakea, though Humuʻula reaches only nine thousand feet in elevation,[102] while Kaʻohe is a much larger ahupuaʻa that circles the top of Maunakea stretching from the northeast coast of Hāmākua to the top of Mauna Loa. Kaʻohe means "the bamboo," and is a reference to the bamboo plant's ability to capture water. The water caught from nodes of bamboo does not touch the ground and is thought to be among the purest for that reason. As such, the pure waters of the bamboo are considered sacred. The analogy suggests that because the mountain "feeds" people and "all living things" within the ahupuaʻa, "our erudite Hawaiians . . . [knowing] that water eventually makes its way down to our sea shore or to our springs or anywhere it exits . . . [also] had the idea or the conviction that Maunakea and the mountain systems, did exactly that: they captured the water in the nodes."[103] In other words, those observant Hawaiians who named Kaʻohe knew this mountain sustains life on the island. Without the natural water systems of Maunakea they "will cease to exist . . . and [while] it's a *direct* benefit to us, [it is also] *indirect* because it comes in a cycle."[104] As a life-giving cycle observed by the kūpuna, human dependence on it was honored in the very naming of the ahupuaʻa "Kaʻohe." Because the cycle itself is the work of "our elemental gods," we are being "godlike" when we go mauka (to the mountains), pick from the forest, give birth, and engage with natural cycles of life. Kanahele explains, "We are being godlike because we are actually continuing this cycle . . . So, to understand the mountain, you gotta understand all of that—that whole process."[105] This engagement with the natural, she explains, is part of the process called makawalu.

> It is logical, but is a godlike process because it allows life to flourish, to be maintained. So, they would name a place according to what that particular place is producing. And so they have an idea of what it's producing and so [it is known that] the top of the mountain is where the water for Wailuku River comes from and all of our little outlets that come down here, [are] also from the top of the mountains because they are all outlets from Wailuku, Waialama stream, Wailoa, etc.[106]

"So, it really is not just a symbolic desecration?" I asked. She adamantly replied, "No, it isn't." She reminded me that something becomes sacred symbolically because, originally, the symbolic "was the maoli, it was true, it was genuine, and so it becomes symbolic. And, so, the symbol doesn't last if there is no more truth to it."[107] I interpret this as an assertion of how the materiality of desecration affects our emotional and psychological states, our very well-being. The effects of these observatories impact not only the soil, the subsurface water and watershed, and other-than-human life forms on the Mauna but Kānaka ʻŌiwi on an intimate level. This damage can never be adequately measured by Western sciences and technologies, hence the conceptualization of the Mauna as *sacred*. This way of relating fulfills an intuitive need and impulse to *care for* life and that which gives life. To describe "environmental degradation" as "desecration" is true for Hawaiians (and brilliant) but also simply a way of expressing a recognition that our relationship with the Mauna, as with all the living world, can impact our material human condition. Any assessment of industrial development is inadequate without an accounting of the experience of Kānaka ʻŌiwi who internalize contemporary degradation as an assault on our very being.

When I interviewed Kumu Pua in 2012 and asked for her thoughts on what seemed to be growing into a larger movement (not yet a full-fledged "Mauna Movement"), she responded by questioning the assumption of a common understanding, asking what "we" might agree "protection" really *is*. She said, "I don't know what that *means. No building on Mauna Kea,* that's what I support. I think of all of the sacred places on all of the islands, Maunakea is at the top."[108] Addressing at once the symbolic, the ideological, and the material relationship Kānaka ʻŌiwi have to the Mauna, Kumu Pua challenges the prevailing settler relationship of *dominion over* land and the natural world. What would it mean to protect Mauna a Wākea from a place of care and familial relationality—as a commitment to pono? "Protection" is often the chosen framing of an environmentalist approach and is central to policies of the state, but "protection" is not a transparent term or unambiguous concept. It presupposes something very specific about human relations to land. With "protection," one imagines presiding over something rather than relating to it. Where is the space to consider one's obligation toward the natural world if we only conceive of land as something humans have control over? To think obligation is to consider what is pono. The idea that "nature" exists *out there* and outside of our naming practices and discourses fails to account for the import of language on how we understand the worlds we inhabit. The concepts of "nature," "the environment," and "resources" may be ubiquitous, but they are not self-evident, universal, or objective categories. Those very terms and their meanings are produced in and through discourse, not the other way around. And the dominant language is no more or less arbitrary than any composed by Kānaka ʻŌiwi. They have only become conventional because of relationships constituted in power. A key difference among these grammars, however, is that Kanaka relationality is about balance and reciprocity rather than control. And this is reflected in naming and narrative practices as much as by histories of collective human activities. As "protection" presupposes threat, the idea becomes meaningless within Kanaka ʻŌiwi thought worlds and lifeways.

In the summer of 2019, Kumu Pua would become one of the kūpuna to provide not only a cultural center and leadership for the kūlanakauhale at Puʻuhuluhulu but also a degree of traditional knowledge that would function as a kind of spiritual core for the movement; this provided momentum to the resistance as well as confidence that this movement is aligned with the desires, practices, and preferences of earlier kiaʻi ʻāina who also chose resistance over complaisance and to stand up rather than shut up. And through the generosity, discipline, and sacrifice of her hālau, Kumu Puaʻs leadership served also as a curriculum benefitting thousands who ascended the mauna throughout the nine-month demonstration. The very presence of the kūpuna in kūʻē, in everyday resistance, hosting visitors, comrades, families, and Indigenous tribes, and nations from around the world, functioned as a roadblock. It was not only a physical barrier—between the mauna and construction crews—that stopped the TMT. It was also the symbolic barrier—between regimes of meaning and relationality—that blocked the gaslighting, the manipulation, and misrepresentation of the TMT opposition. The Kū Kiaʻi Mauna Movement was about the land, yes. It was also about meanings ascribed to our relations. A sustained demonstration of ideological refusal, made at great risk of physical violence from state police, it was also an act that, for many young people, affirmed an otherwise difficult decision to participate in resistance through civil disobedience direct action. It is never easy to make that choice, but the courage and actions of the kūpuna affirmed for the next generation of kiaʻi that they were on the correct path and that their actions were pono. Indeed, the careful study of a tradition of ʻike kupuna articulated to kūʻē, assured kiaʻi they were neither alone, nor indulgent, nor excessive. As such, it was also a renewal of the communally shared commitment to struggle that has always been fundamental to ʻŌiwi conceptions of kuleana and pono, particularly in the face of U.S. military occupation and settler capitalism.

In the first days of the Puʻuhuluhulu encampment, led in no small part by the leadership of Kumu Pua, scores of kūpuna selflessly stopped construction crews from ascending the summit, over three dozen being arrested. Their acts of civil disobedience motivated the lāhui into action at Puʻuhuluhulu, as well as numerous other kūʻē that followed—from Waimānalo to Kahuku, Kapūkakī to Lāhainā, to Pōhakuloa and beyond. For nine months, the Kanahele family, Hālau o Kekuhi, and members of other hālau established and conducted daily protocols that ultimately functioned as an acknowledgment of the multitude of akua, ʻaumākua, and kūpuna who inhabit the Mauna. It also honored the sacred pilina between the piko and the lāhui in both symbolic and material ways. Hālau o Kekuhi would offer spiritual and cultural grounding to the collective, with political implications for the broader public perception of the blockade as well. It was festive, serious, intentional. The hālau not only gave of themselves and their labor, expertise, and knowledge but offered a representation of contemporary Kanaka ʻŌiwi cultural empowerment and self-determination through creative praxis with a spiritual core that descends through generations from kūpuna to moʻopuna. Images of these daily protocols were captured by local media and kiaʻi, posted to the social media accounts of thousands and viewed millions of times on a multitude of platforms spreading the message around the world. Each mele, oli, and hula told the story of our people, our sacred pilina to the Mauna, and this movement for freedom, ancestral places, and self-determination. Sharing the message of aloha ʻāina, they also functioned to recruit Kānaka ʻŌiwi who otherwise might have had reservations about participating in civil disobedience direct action. Puʻuhuluhulu nurtured the movement. The piko nurtures the lāhui. This is the sacred in relationality Kānaka ʻŌiwi have to our wahi kupuna.

Articulating Nature and Composing Relations

Mary Kawena Pukui's understanding of Kanaka relationality to the natural world also offers an important perspective on how Mauna a Wākea has become characterized as a sacred place. Writing in the 1950s about a relatively isolated community of "country Hawaiians" who lived in the southern district of Kaʻū on Hawaiʻi Island, Pukui theorized the concept of aloha ʻāina and the cultural traditions that were rapidly changing in urban areas.

> It is hard for the modern intellectually regid [sic] and extroverted mind to sense the subjective relationship of genuine Hawaiians to Nature, visible and invisible. But without in some degree *sensing the feeling* that underlies this quality of consciousness in those who live intimately in a condition of primary awareness and sensitivity on the plane of subjective identification with Nature, coupled with perceptions and concepts arising therefrom—without some comprehension of this quality of spontaneous *being-one-with-natural-phenomena which are persons, not things,* it is impossible for [the] foreigner . . . to understand a true country-Hawaiian's sense of dependence and obligation, his "values," his discrimination of the real, the good, the beautiful and the true, his feeling of organic and spiritual identification with the ʻaina [sic] (homeland) and ʻohana (kin).[109]

Many Kānaka ʻŌiwi today continue to relate to other-than-human worlds with an intimacy and relationality that is both genealogical and cosmological. And this sort of claim is not merely a political strategy to thwart progress, science, or good governance. Instead, I argue, this is an example of Kanaka articulations of intersubjectivity that are rooted in the lessons gleaned from moʻolelo and moʻokūʻauhau to make sense of one's environment and life therein. Kumu Pua describes moʻokūʻauhau as "the genealogical starting point of all things Hawaiian,"[110] and to understand ourselves and our world we must begin with the stories of who we are and where we come from. Symbolically and materially, the lives of the people and the land are woven together in a shared experience that travels across the generations through moʻolelo about these islands, our ancestors, foods, and families. We get to them by reciting our moʻokūʻauhau.

Kekuewa Kikiloi explains, "At the core of this profound connection is the deep and enduring sentiment of aloha ʻāina, or love for the land. Aloha ʻāina represents our most basic and fundamental expression of the Hawaiian experience."[111] Carrying this expression and experience into our contemporary moment will invariably shape the ways in which we construct, relate to, and protect ancestral places. This is neither blasphemy nor religious fundamentalism, antiscience nor irrational, but it is anticolonial.

Goodyear-Kaʻōpua elaborates on the familial aspect of aloha ʻāina with a materialist understanding when she argues, "Kānaka also recognize our connection to ʻāina as genealogical because we are composed of ʻāina; the organic material of which we are made literally comes from the earth and is constantly returning to it."[112] The aloha that Kānaka ʻŌiwi feel for ʻāina, particularly sacred places like Mauna a Wākea is certainly a symbolic affinity, but it is not a romantic or New Age sentiment. Instead, it is a rational comprehension of the material reality of our bodies as organic matter that is interdependent with our environments. This positionality accepts scientific explanations of our existence but not at the expense of our sacred pilina and collective kuleana to ancestral places.

For many Kānaka ʻŌiwi, nature is immanent, not transcendent. We understand that we are *composing* our realities, but we also recognize everyone else does as well, including scientists, governments, and capitalists. In this chapter, I have attempted to explicate how, although Kanaka ʻŌiwi compositions of nature and articulations of the sacred are no less constructed than any other, because they seek to achieve pono relations with the living world, they are *constructed better* than what we currently endure. Because our kūpuna are buried in these islands—the soil grows the food that nourishes our bodies—our obligations to the natural are conceived through familial relationality. While this may be difficult for the *modern, intellectually rigid* minds of some foreigners to understand, ʻāina is an integral and indispensable part of how we compose our humanity and articulate ourselves into being, and this reality comes with a kuleana to protect ancestral places.

Ty Kāwika Tengan's analysis of the term *ōiwi* captures such an ontological positionality as well, for it illustrates the rootedness of the people in the land. Although used in nineteenth-century discursive practices in Hawaiian language alongside other such referents for "aboriginal Hawaiians" as "kanaka," "kanaka Hawaii," "poe Hawaii," "kanaka maoli," "lahui Hawaii," and "lahui kanaka," etcetera, Tengan explains *ōiwi* "means ʻindigenous/native' and literally roots indigeneity in the iwi (bones) by identifying the people with the kulāiwi (ʻbone plain' or native land) where they bury the iwi of their ancestors, the same land that feeds their families and waits for their bones to be replanted by their descendants."[113] This articulation of Kanaka indigeneity to place is material and symbolic, for the iwi of our people eventually decompose to become the ʻāina itself. This orientation also acknowledges that under conditions of settler colonialism and U.S. occupation, Kanaka epistemologies are inherently political because they embody a prior reality that undermines power. While Kanaka indigeneity may function as a critique of power that animates our contemporary activism to protect sacred places, it is not defined by it. Instead, Kanaka indigeneity exists in a constellation of pilina that becomes legible only through humility, self-reflection, compassion, and a commitment to listen.

6

A FICTIVE KINSHIP

How did the University of Hawaiʻi become stewards of Mauna a Wākea and Kānaka ʻŌiwi obstacles to progress? In this chapter, I trace the emergence and normalization of this framing of the TMT controversy through a historical and discursive analysis of the project to show how the State of Hawaiʻi's commitments to neoliberal governance continue to shape its relationship to big science. To that end, I examine discursive practices within official State, UH, and TIO discourses in which the University of Hawaiʻi finds redemption, the TMT becomes defensible, and Kanaka subjectivity becomes disqualified within a legal system that remakes settlers into innocent victims and Native Hawaiians into dogmatic brutes.

A brief survey of the shifting narrative practices used to defend the university and the State, and over four decades of documented mismanagement of Mauna a Wākea, points to some of the ways in which the militarization and development of Hawaiʻi, combined with the State's dependence on an inherently unsustainable tourist economy, have conditioned a prevailing sense of entitlement and possession over Hawaiʻi that reimagines Indigenous lands as a settler inheritance. This paradox of settler victimry and entitlement coheres in popular discourse but especially within official management plans, environmental reports, court decisions, and other legal discourses. It is in this context of the State's failure to protect sites of ecological and cultural significance, coupled with the disavowal of its obligations to Kānaka ʻŌiwi, that a stalemate has resulted between the land defense movement at Mauna a Wākea (i.e., the Maunakea Movement) and the beneficiaries of imperial science and settler capitalism—a situation resonant with the broader politics of Hawaiʻi in which the ea (sovereignty, independence; life, breath) of our lāhui (nation, people) remains in a constant state of deferral. Analysis of the function and significance of these politics offers a path toward better understanding of the reasons Kānaka ʻŌiwi and non-Kanaka allies have resorted to collective direct action to protect the sacred.

Despite their promise of universal objectivity and claim to rational judgment, settler law and big science have failed Hawaiians; however, that failure is the point. As argued throughout this book, without a nuanced analysis of the politics of settler colonialism under U.S. occupation, the struggle for Mauna a Wākea makes little sense. It leads to condescension: *Why are Hawaiians so angry?* They ask, *What is wrong with astronomy and science? The telescope would allow us to understand the origins of our universe. How could anyone be opposed to that?* In the absence of a colonial critique, most answers reduce Native Hawaiians to ethnonationalist religious fundamentalists clinging onto retrograde beliefs, holding irrational grudges, and misdirecting resentment to protest anything at all. However, when conventional justifications for the TMT, belabored accounts of reform, and settler law and imperial science come under scrutiny, the ongoing disciplinary order of settler hegemony and U.S. military occupation become legible.

I argue that the idea of astronomer stewards and Native obstructionists is not an accident. It is part of a racial hierarchy that has been made and remade through legal and scientific discourses for over a century and a quarter. Not only does that frame instrumentalize difference and imagine impossible equivalences to sustain a prevailing social order structured in dominance, but as it invokes the time-tested and seemingly self-evident binary of modernity versus tradition (and science versus culture), it also reproduces the racial hierarchies that inform U.S. colonization across Turtle Island and imperialism around the world, rendering an independent Hawaiʻi unimaginable to many. As such, these frames signal an indulgence reserved for the beneficiaries of empire, capitalism, and patriarchy in Hawaiʻi, where Kanaka indigeneity is subjected to cultural appropriation and historical disavowal.

For corporate industrial astronomy to be refigured as stewardship at Maunakea, the State of Hawaiʻi had to reproduce the racial, cultural, and economic relations that have long-structured power relations across the U.S.

empire, for which legal and scientific ideologies have also proven effective in establishing the terms of authenticity and legitimacy where Black, Brown, and Native bodies may be targeted for subjugation. Likewise, the University of Hawaiʻi merely had to operate within the prevailing hierarchies imported by U.S. imperialism and global capitalism to preserve its monopoly on Maunakea. In this way, settler law and imperial science cohere around the TMT's monumentalism to rationalize ongoing subjugation. Insofar as the TMT's promise of triumphant modernism and existential discovery of the promise that transits empire in formation with the ideological imperatives of white heteropatriarchal settler capitalism, any intervention in industrial astronomy at Maunakea without a critique of colonial power will be inadequate. Such a view opens space for understanding the stakes of the Maunakea struggle for Kānaka ʻŌiwi, and the future of Kanaka indigeneity and relationality to ʻāina.

While demonstrations of a renewed sense of accountability to Native Hawaiians and commitment to protecting the lands and resources under State control might indicate a significant shift in tone, this chapter argues that such gestures are mostly performative. Rather than signaling a moral transformation, they indicate a desperate pursuit of redemption out of self-preservation. Because the maintenance of cultural, racial, and economic hierarchies in Hawaiʻi is about reproducing the state, capitalism, and empire, most efforts to reconcile competing interests in Maunakea betray their intended altruism. Accordingly, the rhetoric of sustainable stewardship, ethical management, and accountability to Hawaiians trumpeted by astronomers, administrators, politicians, and TMT supporters is more conciliatory than substantive. In other words, both the appropriation of things Hawaiian and the disavowal of Hawaiians have been instrumentalized discursively to redeem and reward power. As this chapter shows, the seeming transformation of the university has been mostly transactional, made reluctantly, and only to pacify dissent and perform legal compliance as a means to an end. Under such conditions, settler stewardship of sacred ancestral places like Mauna a Wākea has become normalized as an act of benevolence through which Native displacement masquerades as universal progress. I begin the chapter with a historical survey of the stakes and discussion of instrumentalized reform as the embodiment of a broader desire for settler absolution from colonial complicity.

The Keck Outrigger Defeat and a Reputation in Trouble

The idea of the University of Hawaiʻi as caretaker of Maunakea became a critical strategy as its renowned observatory became threatened by the Kanaka-led aloha ʻāina movement in the decade following the centennial commemoration of the U.S.-backed overthrow of the Hawaiian kingdom. However, stewardship was not always part of its vision for these lands. As outlined in chapter 2, the University of Hawaiʻi is tasked with managing summit resources, while the State of Hawaiʻi is responsible for overseeing the university's use and management of summit lands, which are part Conservation District land, part public land, and part Crown and Government Lands.[1] As the university has never been a management agency but rather is a State educational institution whose existence is indebted to the ongoing military occupation of Hawaiʻi, its vision and practice of management are entangled with the interests of empire and settler colonialism.

Since 1968, the university has continuously grown its astronomy franchise on the summit of Mauna a Wākea with a socioeconomic privilege and legal dispensation usually reserved for the military and the tourist industry. As four successive telescopes were built through the 1970s, there remained little public consultation, no clear management process, and only nominal governmental oversight. In the 1980s, State legislators and the Governor's Office began receiving complaints from communities who remembered the summit before the large white domes, increased tourist traffic, continually running generators, and wind-strewn debris and rubbish littering the landscape had become common. As development was consistent through the '90s, there were still no plans for cultural or critical habitat preservation, decommissioning of aging telescope facilities, or mechanisms for enforcement of lease responsibilities the University of Hawaiʻi had failed to uphold, let alone consequences for those failures.

In 1983, UH produced its first management plan, in which it initially responded to public pressure by agreeing to build only thirteen telescopes up to the year 2000.[2] This document was so narrow in scope that, beyond passing references, it addressed only the management of the Maunakea Observatory itself and not community concerns about the summit's natural, historic, or cultural properties. In 2000, the university next responded to a damning 1998 legislative audit by creating a "Mauna Kea Science Reserve Master Plan." However, this document proposed self-regulation through an agency of its own creation, the Office of Mauna Kea Management, over which the Board of Land and Natural Resources (BLNR)[3] would have no enforcement authority beyond decisions regarding the sixty-year Master Lease and future Conservation District Use Applications (CDUA).

Among Kānaka ʻŌiwi and other Hawaiʻi Island residents, there was increasing concern, not only about the growing number of telescopes but also the structure of governance that was more improvisational and opaque than long-term, strategic, or inclusive. Indeed, as governance of the Mauna was designed to justify big science and rationalize a commitment to unremitting growth of industrial astronomy, the University of Hawaiʻi eventually saw its public image deteriorating. To build more telescopes, the university had to better represent itself as a land manager and to appear not to exploit but "steward" Maunakea instead. By the 1990s, its monopoly on the use of land and management of resources at Maunakea would depend on improving its reputation.

While at this point, no project on Maunakea had yet been stopped due to public opinion, let alone organized community opposition, this would change in the first years of the new millennium. During this time, the movement to protect Mauna a Wākea had been confined to the sterilized spaces of legal discourse and sanctioned venues for community participation. The parameters of discourse were determined and controlled by the settler state, so watchdog communities making such interventions were forced to engage at times and in spaces designed to discourage oppositional perspectives and privilege the astronomy community and investors.

However, as with any structure, power is never without its fissures, and in the case of Maunakea astronomy, both Kanaka and non-Hawaiian communities would identify these vulnerabilities and disrupt the business-as-usual attitudes and pretenses of those pushing to expand telescope development. This began when the University of California (UC) and California Institute of Technology (Caltech)—two primary institutions behind the Keck Observatory and with the largest proprietary interests in the Thirty Meter Telescope—decided the Kecks were not enough. In 1999, UC and Caltech proposed the Keck Outrigger Telescopes Project. An extension of the recently completed Twin Keck Observatory—consisting of two separate large, white-domed facilities each housing individual telescopes that work in tandem[4]—the Outrigger Project would have led to construction of six new telescopes on the summit. With financial backing from NASA, an Environmental Assessment (EA) unsurprisingly found "no significant impacts" could be linked to the proposed new construction, despite forty years of astronomy on the Mauna and public outcry.[5] In 2002, the Office of Hawaiian Affairs (OHA) and community groups—who would come to be known colloquially as the Mauna Kea Hui—filed a lawsuit to challenge NASA's findings in this EA, arguing against the idea that astronomy had not significantly impacted the cultural and natural resources of the summit. Meanwhile, in 2003, UH's Institute for Astronomy (IfA) applied for a Conservation District Use Permit (CDUP) on behalf of UC and Caltech for the six new "outrigger" telescopes. However, before that permit was granted, a U.S. District Court judge ruled in favor of OHA and found that NASA's 1999 EA had failed to adequately address the "cumulative impacts" of industrial development up to that point. The court's decision forced NASA to prepare a full federal Environmental Impact Statement (EIS) for the Keck Outrigger Telescopes, which it announced in 2004 it would complete before fully funding the project.[6] However, after a lengthy contested case hearing, BLNR not only approved the university's CDUA and issued the permit for construction to begin, it also aligned with IfA's position that a comprehensive management plan was *unnecessary* and that, instead, a project-specific management plan—far more limited in scope—would suffice. That decision gave permission for the Keck Outrigger Telescope Project development to be begin without a comprehensive management plan in place, which community groups vehemently condemned. Up to this point, it might have seemed nothing could stop the project, as NASA funding appeared to be greenlit with *only a promise* to create a federal EIS, and the State had sided with the university in its approval of the permit. University of California and Caltech would continue promising grand discoveries by promoting Keck's potential to generate unrivaled knowledge about the universe and bring prestige to investor-institutions. It was a display of the potential power of off-island capitalist investment and big science under the protection of settler law and U.S. imperialism, necessary conditions for international scientific consortia—those wealthy institutional partnerships behind today's Extremely Large Telescopes (ELTs)—to entrench themselves at Maunakea. Things could hardly go wrong for the Keck community, until they did, as 2005–2006 marked a turning point when neoliberal environmentalism and industrial astronomy were confronted by organized community resistance through a protectionist politics grounded in Kanaka 'Ōiwi cultural philosophies and land-based value systems. Three major events coincided that benefitted the Mauna Kea Hui and land defenders in their ultimate victory.

First, community groups appealed to the State Third Circuit Court challenging BLNR's decision to issue the CDUP on the grounds that no federal EIS had yet been conducted for the Outrigger Project. By 2006, District Court Judge Glenn Hara would side with the Mauna Kea Hui, reverse the CDUP granted for the Keck Outriggers, and require a comprehensive management plan to be created before further development on Maunakea could begin.[7]

Second, the 1998 Legislative Audit was also being cited in these legal cases and circulating among the public. It found that forty years of astronomy activity had adversely impacted the resources of the summit and that the University of Hawai'i had failed to adequately meet its management responsibilities. The audit was an indictment not only of UH but also of the State of Hawai'i's resource management agency, the Department of Land and Natural Resources (DLNR), for its failure to hold UH accountable as the summit's master leaseholder. The auditor's executive summary stated the University of Hawai'i's management was "inadequate to ensure the protection of natural resources," controls were "late and weakly implemented," historic preservation was "neglected," and the "cultural value of Mauna Kea was largely unrecognized."[8] In their haste to build a premier astronomical observatory, UH did not think to remove old testing equipment constructed decades earlier or to clean up trash from construction sites until the public raised concerns. Likewise, DLNR failed to enforce "permit conditions, requirements, and regulations," the consequence of which is today's overdeveloped summit.[9]

Lastly, a now-completed Final Environmental Impact Statement (FEIS) found that "40 years of astronomy" on Maunakea had indeed caused "significant, substantial and adverse impacts . . . on the natural and cultural resources" of the summit,[10] adding that "foreseeable future activities" were likely to continue the trend.[11] The official shaming by the legislature would have become unsustainable for most institutions, but not UH. It was only after increasing public pressure by community groups and NASA's decision to withdraw its funding from the project in 2006 that UH's Institute for Astronomy withdrew its appeal of Hara's decision, and the project collapsed.

While these events led to a hard-won victory for Kānaka ʻŌiwi and accomplices, the University of California and California Institute of Technology had designs on its own ELT and would return with a new project and a new identity: the Thirty Meter Telescope International Observatory Corporation. In a sense, the struggle against telescope expansion since the opposition to the Keck Observatory has not ended but instead taken a new form; the mid-1990's wins were but links in a chain of refusals and acts of resistance to displacement and desecration.

To the activists I interviewed for this project, it has always been surprising that no Federal EIS had been conducted to determine the cumulative impacts of all of the observatories on the summit combined until the University of Hawaiʻi was compelled to do so in 2005 following vigorous community intervention, the incriminatory State audit, and as a precondition to build a fourteenth observatory: meaning six new telescopes. While this observatory was ultimately not built, it is no accident that astronomers and Hawaiʻi's governing class would see the Mauna as a limitless resource, for it is precisely such an extractive colonial logic that propels Hawaiʻi's tourist economy and death drive toward endless development, as it is with settler capitalism and U.S. military occupation more broadly. It is grotesque that abuse of Maunakea has become so normalized that such a relationship can be passed off as "management," but it is. The EIS and NASA's decision to pull out came *only after* community efforts and pressure had succeeded in raising public awareness about the desecration and degradation the Keck Outrigger Telescopes would cause. In other words, change occurred only because people organized.

However, this victory was quickly obscured by a new fervor centering on the Thirty Meter Telescope. Discourse surrounding the project speaks of scientific discovery, but its ideological foundation is the myth of a hierarchy of knowledges and peoples—a mythology based on stereotypes about Indigenous peoples as environmentalists and haole astronomers' forebears, and notions of Western science as universally beneficial and innocent, which extend to the University of Hawaiʻi a degree of redemption as reformed and newly accountable to Hawaiians. Sadly, the lesson drawn from the fall of the Outrigger Project was not that Kānaka ʻŌiwi and the aloha ʻāina movement were to be respected and Maunakea protected but that future projects required performing self-rehabilitation to quell public dissent. Such a task was not impossible but would take some imaginative rhetoric and legal discourse embedded within in a new management plan, a well-designed public relations campaign, and a new grammar of impact that would insulate the TMT from criticism.

Turning a New Leaf

As but one result of the U.S. imperial intervention in the domestic affairs of an independent Hawaiʻi in 1893, the University of Hawaiʻi and the State of Hawaiʻi have for over a century prospered from the spoils of military invasion and settler occupation. In response, generations of Kānaka ʻŌiwi have cultivated the seeds of resistance throughout the twentieth century. After several decades of Kanaka political action and what could today be called #LandBack movements—from Kahoʻolawe to Kalama Valley, and Waiāhole, Wao Kele o Puna, and Mākua to Hālawa Valley and beyond—a politically active and environmentally educated Hawaiʻi public grew increasingly critical of the destruction caused by astronomy, summit tourism, and industrial development on Maunakea. As mentioned earlier in the book, the first to enter litigation, prepare testimonies, participate in hearings, and organize communities against telescope expansion were all volunteers—local residents who had grown frustrated by years of unchecked desecration and degradation of lands controlled by the settler state under the auspices of "conservation." These were ordinary folks with no formal legal training or expertise. Confronting the university, the State, and other institutions, as well as telescope expansion advocates more generally, was an enormous undertaking that routinely subjected this group to false claims about their intentions and intelligence in attempts to discredit them and the movement to protect this sacred storied place. Self-taught out of necessity, these volunteers learned how to navigate the legal process and media landscape but without adequate resources.

By contrast, the university had teams of lawyers, with researchers and staffs, decades of experience, and the ability to bankroll protracted legal battles. However, the university had also underestimated these community volunteers' resolve and their aloha ʻāina. As conveyed by lawyers, conservation policy experts, and the activists I interviewed, this was a significant moment in which a cash-poor but tenacious and innovative group of volunteers—with genealogical, kinship, and spiritual obligations to the Mauna—fought tooth and nail to protect the summit against wealthy, connected, powerful, and ruthless institutions. The state and big science would align with an ideological commitment to settler capitalism and neoliberal policy around land and resources. Under the rubric of scientific discovery, this collaboration would optimize and reinforce an accommodating legal system, which in turn would borrow the scientific community's claim to objectivity, which aided in presenting decision-making through adjudication on matters of "conservation" rational while nevertheless providing the conditions necessary to begin development on an ELT at Maunakea.

Faced with losing its monopoly on authority over the summit in the wake of the Keck Outrigger defeat, the University of Hawai'i began work on the required comprehensive management plan. Again, that did not come out of an enlightened moral conscience, but of practical urgency to remove obstacles to building a new telescope. Indeed, it was the prospect of Hawai'i being home to the next *world's biggest telescope* and the prestige and money it could bring to the university and the State that fueled these efforts. Only by overhauling its management structure and composing a new, seemingly exhaustive guiding document could another project be realized, which was not only expected by the public, but legally required by the State Supreme Court. While the Keck Outrigger victory fortified the land defense movement, it was an educational experience for the University of Hawai'i, which now had a blueprint for securing a permit. "Accountability" became top priority, and optics were paramount. The task was to demonstrate both a mastery of technoscientific design as well as a commitment to better relations with Native Hawaiians and the broader public.

Repairing the university's reputation meant shifting the dominant discourse away from its management failures to a social reawakening. The University of Hawai'i was keen to document its efforts to observe due process and "do the TMT the right way," by scheduling "public consultations" (often amounting to promotional slide presentations) and gathering comments (though, from only a fraction of Hawai'i's residents). The university also leaned into rhetoric about the virtuous pursuits of astronomical research, such as TMT's potential for discovering "exoplanets" and "technological signatures" that could reveal intelligent life in the universe, which captured imaginations and public favor. However, rather than "turning over a new leaf" or merely supporting "one of the oldest of sciences" known to humanity,[12] in the course of its legal campaign to acquire a State permit, the university made arguments that would effectively undermine Hawai'i State conservation laws and Native Hawaiian traditional and customary rights; all for the sake of wealthy institutions across five countries with billions of dollars at their disposal. In essence, UH would posture environmentalism while undercutting its foundational principles. Eventually, however, the university's transformation would be exposed as simple rebranding.

Cultural Sensitivity, Inheritance, and the Ruse of Coexistence

In 2009, the University of Hawai'i completed its Comprehensive Management Plan (CMP) and in 2010 released the Final Environmental Impact Statement for the TMT.[13] To justify continued authority over the summit and to secure permits to build on conservation land, UH would have to produce these two documents. This demonstration of legal compliance was not only about convincing judges and State authorities that the university could properly manage Maunakea; more importantly, the public had to be convinced. With both documents, the university presented a vision of Maunakea's future in which management now appeared steeped in Hawaiian culture, and accountability to Native Hawaiians and respect for the environment were top priorities. In their content and arrangement, both documents present Hawaiian language and culture in uneasy juxtaposition with scientific and technical detail and planning information. Two terms would emerge as core principles: "cultural sensitivity" and "coexistence." Featured are sections eloquently written by cultural practitioners, presenting ideas and perspectives gathered from (often prior and unrelated) studies and staged alongside sections that discussed the science and technical specifications of the project.[14] Descriptions of the Mauna's environmental characteristics and Native cultural practices, social values, religious protocols, ceremonies, and various mo'olelo appear to signal the importance of the natural world and Maunakea to Kānaka 'Ōiwi. However, immediately following each of these sections, the narrative shifts to an explanation of how potential harmful impacts of the TMT would be mitigated: as in, less than they could be, or not as bad as previous impacts or impacts elsewhere. These turns reveal how each discussion of cultural sensitivity functions as a preface to the real order of business, that is science, technology, and project design. At first glance, the inclusion of information from a Hawaiian perspective is noteworthy and striking, but employing an analysis of colonialism, they reveal themselves to be strategies of cultural appropriation. The CMP and EIS might recognize culture but only insofar as they recenter, and thus privilege, astronomy.

An early example of this recentering that emerged as a theme in the CMP and EIS involved representing astronomers as heirs to Maunakea in what amounts to a settler inheritance fantasy. A range of multicultural rhetoric and discursive practices conjured a fictive relationship of familial descent from "ancient Hawaiians" to "modern astronomers," where investors, administrators, mathematicians, astrophysicists, architects, and engineers can envision themselves as following in the footsteps of kahuna (or priests) and kahu (or caretakers).[15] A move to innocence that Eve Tuck and K. Wayne Yang identify as a "settler adoption fantasy," it validates an ambiguous connection, then recodes it as descent, and provides the settler astronomer a claim to patrimony. With regard to this logic of possession, there is also an ideological replacement that this rhetoric performs, in which astronomers may "become without becoming" Kānaka ʻŌiwi.[16] The move levels difference and invokes the trope of Hawaiʻiʻs multiculturalism in a seemingly sympathetic gesture toward Hawaiians, only to excuse dispossession as inheritance.[17] This particular move to innocence provides the university and pro-TMT camp a sort of collective reprieve from feelings of colonial guilt by justifying the settler expropriation of Native lands as a thing of the past, or a violation for which nobody in the present is responsible.

Take, as another example, the imagined affinities summoned by former Keck Observatory director Fredrick Chaffee, who invoked inheritance and kinship to gloss over history and congratulate the observatory in an earlier Mauna Kea Master Plan Summary:

> After all, the ancient Hawaiians were among the first great astronomers, using the stars to guide them among the islands in the vast Pacific, centuries before anyone else had developed such skill. Long before Europeans and mainlanders, Hawaiian astronomers were studying the heavens with awe and wonder, the same feelings that draw modern astronomers to study the heavens. At this very deep level, I feel we are brothers and sisters.[18]

The imagined relationship between Kānaka 'Ōiwi and settler astronomers is not entirely arbitrary, as it is well-known that some early Hawaiians not only migrated from Kahiki (i.e., Marquesas and Tahiti) to Hawai'i but also navigated between those archipelagos, traveling back and forth across thousands of miles of open ocean. Indeed, one of the most celebrated achievements of the Hawaiian Renaissance was the construction and 1976 voyage of the *Hōkūle'a*, which sailed from Hawai'i to Tahiti and back, using only knowledge of the stars and elements, and entirely without use of Western navigational instruments. It was a feat that no one imagined could be accomplished until it was, only to then be appropriated in the service of conjuring a bond between Hawaiians and astronomers to justify continued land grabs.

Reminiscent of the "host culture" rhetoric common to "visitor industry" discourse that disingenuously implicates Hawaiians in poststatehood tourism, Chaffee's imagined kinship serves to further dislocate Kānaka 'Ōiwi through ancestors unable to speak for themselves. Hawaiians and astronomers are made into siblings, but the relation is hierarchical and counterintuitive for Kānaka 'Ōiwi insofar as the younger is somehow privileged above the elder. This is the "cultural sensitivity" that emerged after Keck.

The vision of possession as familial descent also hinges on a temporal hierarchy, or what Sandra Harding describes as the "modernity/tradition binary"—an existential contradiction in which primitive Natives and Western scientists occupy opposite ends of a linear conception of time, space, and evolution.[19] In this imaginary, "The specters of the feminine and the primitive" haunt scientific discourse. To maintain a position of rational modern subjectivity, the universal subject must distance himself[20] from anything that may be identified as traditional or premodern, which are categories assigned to women and Natives and reproduced through a hegemony of the white capitalist imperial heteropatriarchal order. Whereas Chaffee's statement appears to recognize Hawaiian technological and intellectual achievements, in this ideological frame Hawaiians are intrinsically outmoded and obsolete, forever confined to the past. By contrast, modern subjects—that is, the "Moderns"[21]—are the very opposite: technologically advanced, rational, forward thinking, and scientific. Notions of "progress" are conjured in this model of reality that also assumes time and human development follow a single universal trajectory with the West at its helm.

Indeed, in this vision of humanity, the "human" is also fashioned after the universal subject of modernity, or "Man." Hawaiians and other Indigenous peoples can only aspire to this humanity: desiring but never achieving fully human subjecthood.[22] As a redemptive vision of history and humanity, invocations of the tradition/modernity binary do less to honor Native Hawaiians or explain social relations than to rationalize the hierarchies of knowledge and being that privilege industrial astronomy at Maunakea.

Another example meant to convey this sense of cultural affinity between "ancient Hawaiians" and "modern astronomers" appears in the same 2000 UH Master Plan summary where a quote by Mōʻī David Laʻamea Kalākaua addresses a British expedition of astronomers dispatched to the Hawaiian kingdom to observe the 1874 transit of Venus. The Master Plan summary gives the impression that Kalākaua's support for the expedition indicates support for current Maunakea astronomy. In the document entitled, "Voices and Visions of Mauna Kea," the quote reads:

> It will afford me unfeigned satisfaction if my kingdom can add its quota toward the successful accomplishment of the most important astronomical observation of the present century and assist, however humbly, the enlightened nations of the earth in these costly enterprises.[23]

Appropriating a nineteenth-century quote to recast Kalākaua as a supporter of Maunakea astronomy today is misleading but also disingenuous. The British expedition was one of five that were sent to different locations around the world to observe Venus as it transits across Earth's view of the sun, the data from which would assist in developing a more precise measurement of the scale of our solar system. Published in the *Pacific Commercial Advertiser* in 1874, the Kalākaua quote is from a letter in which he welcomed the expedition, indicated genuine appreciation for their work, and offered the kingdom's logistical support. However, this context is entirely absent from the Master Plan. In other words, Kalākaua was supporting not the industrial development of Maunakea but, as he put it, the "costly enterprises to establish the basis of astronomical distances."[24] He was supporting four or five telescopes, none bigger than ten feet long and all temporarily positioned for a single event in Honolulu. No activity, let alone any permanent telescope, was ever proposed for Maunakea. So why omit any reference to the transit of Venus in the Master Plan? As Noenoe Silva has argued, "Colonial historiography . . . does not simply rationalize the past and suppress the knowledge of the oppressed,"[25] it obscures that knowledge using ellipses, transpositions, and recontextualizations to suit the preferred narrative of a hegemonic order. Revisions of history to draw connections between seemingly disparate events and ideas may not be inherently problematic, but when that narrative relies on a distortion of context used to suggest industrial development of a sacred place today would be supported by a historical figure—one unable to speak for himself—it is reckless and dangerous.

The vague notion of coexistence also proliferates TMT discourses, as discussed previously in the book. Invoked to suggest Hawaiians and astronomers should set aside their differences and share Maunakea, the ambiguity of this coexistence performs the requisite sympathy, humility, and seeming respect required of the university. As an ahistorical appeal that would depoliticize the TMT, as if all parties are equal—a relationship devoid of history and power—the demand to coexist functions as an implicit criticism of Hawaiians *who just can't get over the past or rise above their petty grievances.* The demand at once minimizes the stakes of the conflict over Maunakea and trivializes the struggle for its protection. More performative than substantive, the future vision of this entreaty always leads to the inevitable construction of the TMT. The *real* controversy is over *how,* not *whether* the TMT will be built. In other words, this demand for coexistence is ultimately about *the terms of existence,* and it is built neither upon collaboration nor consent but rather by an expectation that masquerades as negotiation and compromise. Any possibility of coexisting without the TMT is swiftly condemned as an irrational attack on science. Moreover, this frame presumes coexistence does not already occur on the Mauna, which is not true.

Perhaps more disconcerting, these juxtapositions present "religion" and "science" as discreet conceptual categories marked by hierarchical notions of progress, civilization, and reason that will always reproduce a conception of the Native that rationalizes ongoing settler and imperial violence. Tradition is never scientific, and science exists outside of culture—untainted and undistracted by culture's irrational subjective impulses. If Hawaiians practice culture, they cannot be scientific. In their religious fundamentalism, they cannot be rational. Implicit in these binary oppositions and the false plea to coexist, are over five centuries of European ethnocentrism. As science is associated with universal laws, empirical knowledge, rational thought, and objectivity, religion is associated with superstition, retrograde beliefs, and carnal and emotional indulgence. As such, science represents a triumph of modernity and humanity over primitive attachments. Enlightened by reason and science, astronomers have overcome the dogmatism of Native subjectivity, and thereby have achieved fully modern rational subjecthood. Indeed, none of this circulates at the level of conscious public discourse, but rather ideology, and it is everywhere present, if obscured, in the scientific, legal, and other discourses and pro-TMT rhetoric.

"Tradition" is also presented in such a way as to suggest a historical shift from cultural *specificity* to scientific *universality*. As primitivity gives way to modernity, Hawaiian knowledge is imagined as a link in an evolutionary chain that culminates in universal scientific knowledge about the origins of everything (and to which astronomers alone possess the omniscience to identify, name, and know). Hawaiian knowledge, discursively reduced to "tradition" and "culture," may be cataloged, even celebrated, but only insofar as it remains temporally relegated to a subordinate role and only to the extent it advances the interests of imperial science. In this way, Indigenous "culture" is presented as a predecessor to scientific "knowledge." As introduction to modernity, Hawaiian knowledge may be charming if antiquated, but never rational, modern, or universally relevant. Far from honoring Kānaka ʻŌiwi, our culture, and our histories, these discourses are dehumanizing.

Perhaps none of this should be surprising. After all, the CMP was never meant to center Kanaka ʻŌiwi or Indigenous scientific knowledge and praxis, and the Environmental Impact Statement was never meant to prohibit new telescopes. They were never meant to stop the TMT. Rather, both were designed to legitimize the university by recasting them as caretakers.

The Comprehensive Management Plan

The Comprehensive Management Plan (CMP) served as an extension of the 2000 Master Plan. Itself an update to the 1983 Mauna Kea Science Reserve Complex Development Plan, the 2000 plan was promoted as a "new paradigm" and "policy framework for the responsible stewardship and use of University-managed lands on Maunakea."[26] The CMP, however, had another objective as public scrutiny following the two audits brought negative attention to the university. This document was to serve as evidence that UH was now reformed. Over a thousand pages in length, the CMP consists of an executive summary, introduction and "cultural orientation," and background chapters on "management environment," "community engagement," "cultural and natural resources," "human environment," and "management component plans," as well as a ten-part appendix detailing "community outreach," four subplans—including various aspects of "cultural resource management," "natural resource management," "public access," "decommissioning objectives"—and another thirteen hundred pages of information about administrative processes, invasive species prevention and control, telescope operations, monitoring, maintenance, and other related topics. Through sheer volume, the CMP would demonstrate not only that every aspect of management of the summit resources had been accounted for, and due process observed, but also that the university had initiated a self-cleansing meant to indicate objectivity, contrition, and a newfound sense of responsibility to Native Hawaiians. Its attention to detail regarding environmental and social concerns almost mirrors the precision with which the CMP describes the TMT's technoscientific innovations.

However, its scope and attention to detail, and especially its performance of cultural competency and inclusiveness, would have to stand up to potential scrutiny from a range of interest groups including environmentalists, academics, scientists, activists, and Kānaka ʻŌiwi. Most importantly, the rhetoric of "cultural sensitivity" would establish the tone of the CMP as it captures the pretense of reform, though mainly nominal and absent any substantive change. While UH intended to display sympathy, humility, and respect, they ended up appropriating Hawaiian culture, language, and interlocutors.

For example, in its introduction, the CMP provides a section entitled "Cultural Anchor," which was meant to embody the university's new paradigm of self-reform. Its original source is from an earlier cultural study submitted as part of the Big Island's Saddle Road expansion project, which was authored by Edward L. H. Kanahele and Pualani Kanakaʻole Kanahele of the Edith Kanakaʻole Foundation in 1997.[27] In my interview with Kumu Pua, I asked about the insertion of this text into the body of the CMP. She told me she had no idea it was used for this purpose. In fact, the reason for the foundation's contribution to this study was to register into the official record a Native perspective on the sacred value of Maunakea in hopes of influencing the realignment project. This contribution to the earlier report, in my view, serves as an intervention, not an endorsement, of the growth and development the project represented. However, as the CMP was designed to ensure successful future permit applications for telescopes on conservation land, and to justify UH authority as land manager, without citation or indication of its original source and with key contextual markers removed, the addition of the Kanahele and Kanakaʻole Kanahele text into the CMP as a "Cultural Anchor," or preface, is misleading. As the authors' consent was never obtained, it also evacuates agency, which adds another layer of violence.

Another important point the university made in the CMP was a list of good deeds, seemingly to persuade skeptics that any potential adverse impacts of the TMT would be mitigated. These include, among other things, educating its telescope operators and the public about Hawaiian culture and the sacred value Kānaka attribute to Maunakea. In a section entitled "Cultural Orientation," the CMP explains the importance of Maunakea and education:

> It is clear that to many Hawaiians, Mauna Kea is more than a mountain; it is the embodiment of the Hawaiian people. As we embarked on the development of this CMP and gathered community input, it became apparent there is a general lack of understanding and appreciation of the cultural significance Mauna Kea holds for many Hawaiian people. It could simply be a lack of understanding and appreciation that leads to disrespect for the cultural and spiritual values associated with Mauna Kea, as well as to direct and indirect impacts to Mauna Kea's significant natural and cultural resources. It was therefore not only deemed appropriate, but necessary, to provide the users of this CMP with an orientation on the Hawaiian cultural significance of Mauna Kea.[28]

The notion that the CMP might identify and explain the nature of "disrespect for the cultural and spiritual values associated with Mauna Kea," when considering the university's record of management failures and its problematic citation practices in that very document suggests a sense of entitlement that contradicts the CMP's best efforts. While the idea that UH might defend Hawaiian cultural and spiritual values is central to its rebranding strategy, the gesture is more performative than substantive considering the CMP's purpose is to justify the university's authority on the Mauna as means to an end.

The Environmental Impact Statement

The Final Environmental Impact Statement (FEIS) for the TMT is also problematic. It documents views of the Mauna's sacredness from the perspectives of Kānaka 'Ōiwi and the variety of reasons many oppose the TMT. However, in doing so, it also reproduces the manifold justifications for the TMT expressed by the TIO[29] and others invested in the project. The FEIS was completed in 2010 "under the University of Hawai'i at Hilo's . . . direction or supervision" for Parsons Brinckerhoff by Cultural Surveys Hawai'i, Inc., and in compliance with Hawai'i Administrative Rules.[30] The document maps a wide range of community concerns about potential significant adverse impacts and the "mitigation measures" meant to resolve them as proposed by UH and the TIO. In this, however, is a tension related to how the document presents these diametrically opposed objectives. On one hand, the EIS surveys the Mauna's cultural and historical significance and community concerns about the TMT; yet, on the other hand, immediately following those sections and in every instance, the EIS then provides details that effectively serve as counterpoints to those values and concerns by illustrating the ways each individual impact will be mitigated and every concern resolved, or simply deemed inaccurate. These sections then conclude with descriptions of the many accommodations UH and TMT planners have promised accordingly. It is precisely in this methodology that I find the EIS problematic. The document discursively resolves the tension between damage and repair by recommending UH and TMT planners follow through with their promises (and in some instances, suggest they already have). The discursive resolution does not lead to a single recommendation to kill the project; instead, in its methodology and presentation, its effect is an implied recommendation to accommodate the TMT under certain conditions.

In many ways, the EIS is invaluable to kia'i as well. It includes documented oral histories, summaries of mo'olelo, and analysis of their significance, which illustrate how the Mauna has come to be viewed as a sacred place. It includes information outlining a variety of intellectual traditions, cultural practices, place names, and histories that tell of the value systems and relationships that Kānaka ʻŌiwi have maintained for generations. It also describes the "historic properties" and species habitats that comprise popular concerns about overdevelopment, as well as the various land designations and management structures of the Mauna. Volume 2 also includes over three hundred written statements and letters gathered during the Draft EIS comment period from federal, state, and county agencies, elected officials, boards and groups, businesses and organizations, and individual community members in support and opposition to the project. In its breadth of detail, the EIS is quite remarkable and seemingly more balanced than the CMP.

However, as the document's descriptions employ a rhetoric of certainty rather than contingency, it presumes the TMT's inevitability. For example, early in volume 1 after an opening preface that offers "Traditional knowledge" and information about Hawaiians' "cultural attachment," the document provides an executive summary that begins with a description of the University of Hawaiʻi's "proposed actions."[31] In this section, the authors outline what the proposing agency (UH) has promised in the CMP but presents this information as if the TMT has already been approved. For instance, it explains what "The TMT Observatory *will* consist of" and what "The Access Way, a permanent Project facility, *will* include."[32] After describing the "Project Purpose, Need, and Objectives" and "Existing Conditions at Project Locations," the narrative quotes a passage from the CMP in which authors' explain the significance of the piko metaphor to not only Hawaiians but also to the astronomical community, for whom "Mauna Kea is *the scientific umbilical cord* to the mysteries of the universe."[33] The EIS then reproduces the CMP's stated desire for "these two cultures [to] coexist in such a way that is mutually respectful and yet honors the unique cultural and natural resources of Mauna Kea."[34] Treating rhetoric as evidence by virtue of reproducing uncritically the University of Hawaiʻi's framing of "coexistence," such a gesture in the EIS instructs readers in a proper way to interpret the term and the document. As discussed previously, this particular use of "coexistence" is productive in that it ostensibly references while producing "two cultures." In that move, the EIS places them into ideological antagonism and then a hierarchy. In celebrating "coexistence," UH assumes the position of reason: they alone seek compromise. As such, UH aligns with scientific rationality, or the "culture" of rational science. Through implication, Kānaka ʻŌiwi are relegated to a position of irrational opposition.

Not coincidentally, however, what exactly this type of "coexistence" will look like remains ambiguous. As previously noted, any relevant discussion of how "coexistence" already conditions activity on the Mauna is unsurprisingly absent.

The executive summary reads:

> UH has been working to find ways for these two cultures to co-exist in such a way that is mutually respectful yet honors the unique cultural and natural resources of Mauna Kea. The most recent effort is the CMP recently approved by the BLNR and accepted by the UH (Board of Regents). The CMP provides for the stewardship of the land with a road map to conserve, protect, and preserve this unique and most special resource. The CMP is the culmination of years of work by OMKM (the Office of Mauna Kea Management) and UH Hilo in establishing the foundation for good management of UH's management areas.
>
> UH, UH Hilo, and TMT have gained an understanding of the cultural sensitivity of Mauna Kea through working with the community during the preparation of the CMP and this Final EIS. It is the intention of all those involved to be good stewards of the land and avoid miscommunication or unintentional disrespect between the Project and the community.[35]

Again, while the document is meant to consider the potential future impacts of the TMT on the Mauna, the EIS also reads as legitimation precisely because, as a seemingly exhaustive study, it seeks to have it both ways: it takes up the liberal concern with diversity and inclusion by incorporating Hawaiian voices and cultural information while recommending compromise in the form of "coexistence" without providing an adequate accounting of the structural conditions that have produced the social exclusions, environmental damage, and contradictory land use practices that prevail today and that impact Kānaka 'Ōiwi. Paired with a concluding set of recommendations that do not suggest terminating the TMT project or prohibiting future development, the EIS serves as a tool of redemption for UH, the TMT, and the TIO.

In another example, a quote by Kumu Pua Kanaka'ole Kanahele that comes from an interview she gave in 1999 to Kepā Maly was inserted into the EIS a decade later without drawing attention to its source and purpose, making what was actually a critique read as an endorsement.[36] In the quote, Kumu Pua discusses the importance of the piko to Kanaka 'Ōiwi families as it connects the child to the past, to the mama, and again to her mama, and "back, not only to the wā kahiko [ancient times], but all the way back to Kumu Lipo [sic]," the originary time, space, and energy from which Kānaka ʻŌiwi descend.[37] However, in the original text, immediately after she discusses the piko, Kumu Pua explains how Mauna a Wākea was historically used by Hawaiians for burial of iwi (human bones) and cremated remains, which, if included in the EIS, may have politicized the document because a central claim made by UH and the TIO is that no iwi exist where the TMT is proposed for construction. Moreover, also in the interview transcript from which this and several other passages were pulled, Kumu Pua articulates a case *for the removal of all telescopes*. She expresses her disdain for the fact that "something so trivial, and yet, in the minds of people" is treated as so important "because it cost a lot money, and it allows them to look out into space. And that kind of thing to us is so trivial. But the mountain itself, and the fact that it's way up there, is the most important [sic]."[38] Kumu Pua then addresses the critics of cultural practitioners who become vocal activists—challenging people who "want to throw it back in our face [and say to us], 'Well, you didn't say anything before.' . . . But we are saying it now." Kepā Maly asks Pua Kanakaʻole Kanahele about telescopes, and she declares the following in no uncertain terms:

KM: Yes, now is the time. So your manaʻo, flat out, about ka Mauna a Wākea, in regards to development of any kind, observatories or what in the summit region, would be?

PK: No, Nothing on the summit. They can go to other places in the world. They say this has to do with the economy, I don't see that economy filtering down. The economy is the biggest excuse. For the economy, we have given up all of our sacred places.[39]

This declaration of opposition is cut from the 2010 Final Environmental Impact Statement. If the EIS is meant to be a neutral assessment of the potential ways the natural, cultural, and historic properties of the Mauna could be undermined by the TMT, why excise this information? The edit suggests Kumu Pua's position is ambiguous or possibly in support of the TMT, which is misleading.

The state has been criticized for ignoring community dissent and concerns about overdevelopment and obstruction of traditional and customary Native Hawaiian rights. Because it does not explicitly recommend halting the TMT, yet frequently cites CMP research and rhetoric, one effect of the

FEIS is validation. It offers some space for Hawaiians and other residents to log complaints, but the document can only recommend doing the TMT "the best way." In this regard, the presence of Native voices allows the EIS to present as neutral—showing regard for both sides. However, presenting itself as objective, Native Hawaiians appear as foils to science and compromise.

Mitigation, Sustainability, and the Logic of Tolerance

One example of the violence that legal discourse has enabled appears in a discrepancy regarding how to characterize past and potential future impacts. The EIS acknowledges that "the past actions on Mauna Kea have resulted in substantial, significant, and adverse impacts to cultural, geological, and biological resources";[40] however, this is undercut when the university argues the "cumulative impacts" of previous development must be distinguished from "impacts associated with an individual project."[41] The distinction is teleological: it argues that an individual telescope will not significantly damage the mountain *any more* than what has already been done cumulatively, so no increase to the prior cumulative impact will occur in any substantial, significant, or adverse way should another be built. What it designates as "incremental" is discursively created only to be minimized when contrasted against "cumulative." In qualifying the impacts as "incremental," the probability of future damage the TMT will cause is rhetorically diminished to assuage concern and to justify a State permit. The EIS concludes, "In general, the Project will add a limited *increment* to the level of *cumulative* impact, but would not tip the balance of any specific cumulative impact from a less than significant level to a significant level."[42] No metric is given for what number of incremental impacts would tip this figurative scale, nor is the nature of this scale explained. Similarly, characterized as "impacts" instead of "damage" or "harm," the rhetoric invokes a logic of reduction instead of avoidance. Instead of avoiding harm, the goal is simply to reduce harm. Again, no construction has yet begun. So, to suggest possible future impacts can be assessed in advance is wishful thinking at best. The distinction between "incremental" and "cumulative" is arbitrary and self-serving but also functions as an effective instrument with which to resolve an otherwise persuasive critique *against* the project.

It would appear the goal is to push the discourse beyond the obvious reality: indeed, how could an eighteen-story, eight-acre industrial development project *not* result in additional substantial, significant, and adverse impacts to the mountain, let alone Kanaka ʻŌiwi cultural praxis?

This rationale and rhetoric were adopted by the State's Board of Land and Natural Resources when permits were issued for the TMT after two contested case hearings (in 2011 and 2017) and when the State Supreme Court affirmed both permits in 2018. While the EIS does not explicitly endorse the TMT, by repeating the university's preferred narratives, it reifies the logic of its arguments and thereby functions as an endorsement of the project. Readers of the EIS are left with the impression that the TMT and UH have anticipated every possible potential future harm the project may cause and resolved them in advance. For its approval of the CMP and the EIS, the State preserves legitimacy of its authority and affirms its commitment to neoliberal land management.

In the 2011 contested case hearing, the university cited expert witness testimonies to deny the potential of future adverse impacts by oscillating between recognition and denial and using rhetorical equivocations that helped the State justify its decision to permit the TMT. For example, UH attorneys argued that the TMT "would not have significant impacts on biological resources . . . because those species and habitats found in the TMT project site *would not be unique* to the project site but are also found elsewhere";[43] it "would not have any impact on burials";[44] it "would not have any substantial impact on any other historic properties" because *no known* such properties were identified by experts in the proposed site; it would not impact cultural practices because "no cultural practices *are known* to be associated with any specific historic property identified in or near the TMT project"; and the TMT would not obstruct view planes because no such view planes were used in a cultural practice legible to them.[45] Disavowing all possibility of future adverse impacts may not have been convincing to everyone, but these claims were eventually cited by a sympathetic DLNR when the Land Board decided to issue the TMT permit, and the Supreme Court ruled to affirm that decision.

The oscillation between recognition and denial of impacts, the categorical equivocation, the parsing of "substantial" vs. "significant," the indeterminacy of *what is known* to the university or otherwise, and the proposed measures to offset expected damage, suggest a deep ambivalence that haunts the university's claims to environmental stewardship and community responsiveness. These contortions also haunt the State's claim to conserve, govern, and arbitrate objectively. In its decision and order to uphold the TMT permit, the State Board of Land and Natural Resources accepted the university's *promise* of sustainability over any *actual evidence* in the historical record. In the decision, the Land Board reveals its underlying directive:

> The purpose of the conservation district rules is *not to prohibit land uses* . . . The TMT project provides for "appropriate management and use" that promotes the long-term sustainability of resources and the public health, safety, and welfare . . . By following the applicable provisions of the various relevant plans, sub-plans, and permit conditions, UHH [the University of Hawai'i-Hilo] and the TMT Corporation will conserve, protect, and preserve the important natural and cultural resources of the State, will promote their long-term sustainability, and will promote the health, safety, and welfare of the public.[46]

That the Land Board has no power to prohibit telescope development in the conservation district speaks to the neoliberalization of governance in Hawai'i. For example, take the university's proposed "mitigation measures," which were proposed in the CMP, promoted in the EIS, and persuasive to the State Supreme Court who ultimately approved the permit. The idea is that potential impacts could be offset through a list of commitments to future actions touted as mitigating damage. Among them include covering the TMT in a reflective surface to appear camouflaged against the sky, hanging Native Hawaiian art in the interior of its facilities, training astronomers and operators about the cultural history of Maunakea, hiring local construction companies wherever possible, and siting the project on the northern plateau instead of the summit. One of the most celebrated mitigation measures is the allocation of $1 million annually for grants, scholarships, and other educational programs "specific to Hawaiian culture," astronomy, math, and sciences, and "community outreach" in what it calls the "Community Benefits Package."[47] The funds are already being distributed by an entity called "The Hawaii Island New Knowledge Fund" (THINK) to applicants pursuing studies in STEM fields (i.e., science, technology, engineering, math). By funding STEM scholars and programs, however, the TMT is essentially investing in its own future. Just how these programs will mitigate damages to the Mauna and Kānaka 'Ōiwi is determined not by the communities impacted by them but by those responsible for them. In this way, potential adverse impacts are weighed against the project's expected future benefits to groups with a very narrow set of interests—a strategy that allows the State to legally determine that some future damage is tolerable enough to permit the project. In this way, the promised benefits of jobs, academic tourism, economic investment, and the prestige of technoscientific research and development proved to be a persuasive argument, indicating how the logic of mitigation was for the State another means to an end.

Some of my interview respondents celebrate the list of mitigation measures as long overdue and the $1 million a year as fair compensation. Others describe them as bribes. Resembling a pay-to-pollute model of neoliberal environmentalism, like cap-and-trade or carbon capture, the compensation approach to accountability hangs on a calculus of toleration, as impacts are considered tolerable if they do not surpass a threshold determined in law. According to its internal logic, some degree of damage may be deemed reasonable. However, what constitutes reasonable is arbitrary and based on the best possible compensation for enduring potential adverse impacts. In other words, substantial, significant, and adverse impacts are treated as acceptable if the price is right, which may be rationalized after the fact as "mitigation."

The idea of mitigation, like sustainability, is inherently contradictory. Facing criticism for their adverse environmental impacts, governments, corporations, militaries, businesses, and institutions like UH and projects like the TMT have adopted discourses of sustainability. Often, when one thinks of sustainability, they think of sustaining the health of the environment. Strangely, however, "sustainability" is as useful to the global response to our climate crisis as it is to polluters selling "sustainable development." In recent decades, "sustainability" has become ubiquitous among groups with vastly divergent interests. For example, environmental sustainability has now become a core value of both the military and conservationists. What is it about sustainability that makes the concept universally attractive to, say, both environmental organizations *and* corporate agribusinesses? I argue that like "mitigation" and "coexistence," the term "sustainability" is malleable. While it carries an ambiguously positive connotation that most people can support, its negative connotation frequently remains tacit.

Leerom Medovoi argues sustainability is so broadly adaptable because the term connotes ideas of "protection" as it connotes ideas of "tolerance";

the acceptance of a degree of damage, suffering, or injury. Tolerance accounts for an opposing force by *accepting* harm in small amounts, or to the verge of destruction. Medovoi writes, "Instead of suggesting the support of life . . . [this use of sustainability] signifies instead a suffering unto the edge of death."[48] This is because the etymology of "sustain" holds both positive and negative connotations. Consider the contradiction presented in chapter 2 in the gap between conservation principles and policy. While the conservation district is meant to designate lands to be protected, categories were invented to retroactively permit telescope development in the so-called resource subzone. That a rhetoric of "sustainable markets," "sustainable work forces," and "sustainable technologies" might appear alongside one that emphasizes "sustaining water" and cultural practices suggests an elasticity that is convenient to those tempting harm and destruction. The slippage between sustaining damage and sustaining life allows the TMT to present as an example of "sustainable development," even though industrial development clearly undermines the principle of environmental sustainability as the idea is generally invoked. Because of this slippage, the term holds a hidden capacity for broad and contradictory application.

During the contested case hearing, the Mauna Kea Hui was unconvinced by the language of stewardship and the tolerance model of sustainability promoted in the university's preoccupation with mitigating impacts through measures having little to do with stopping damage to the environment and Kānaka 'Ōiwi. The hui challenged the Land Board's decision and order to uphold the TMT permit, arguing:

> The law mandates the protection of sacred places, like Mauna a Wākea, and the practices that occur there, from inappropriate land uses. Everyone is responsible and accountable for their own actions that would adversely impact this sacred landscape. The true aspect of stewardship entrusted with the BLNR for our precious and public lands in the conservation district is to insure [sic] that these significant areas are acknowledged and preserved for present and future generations. *In essence, the development on the summit of Mauna a Wākea is a commercial enterprise under the guise of science, educational, and economic opportunities.*[49]

The university's assertion of increased cultural sensitivity, community responsiveness, accountability to Native Hawaiians, desire to coexist, and commitment to becoming better stewards of the Mauna was, to the petitioners and their many allies, without merit. Nevertheless, for the State, these claims proved enough to uphold the decision to permit the TMT.

Justifying construction of the TMT has not only meant representing the project, UH, the State, the TIO, and Western science as redeemable, but also *misrepresenting* Kānaka ʻŌiwi as inauthentic, unqualified, ineligible, and without claims to rights or land. This has been nowhere more effective and violent than within the exercise of settler law in permitting the TMT.

Legal Disavowal of Kanaka Indigeneity

The liberal model of inclusion through rights discourses around which the TMT has been deemed consistent with Hawaiʻi State law has functioned as an instrument of settler colonialism and its logic of Native elimination. In Hawaiʻi, the "traditional and customary rights" doctrine has become an organizing principle for the protection of Kanaka indigeneity and Native Hawaiian practices.[50] Traditional and customary rights are the grounds on which constitutional protections of various cultural practices and activities are determined. They have also become the terms of Kanaka subjection and legibility before the settler state—that is, the terms by which someone qualifies as authentic, or legitimately Native. The doctrine is structured such that both Native identity and protected practices now hinge on qualifying legal tests based on two historical dates. The earlier date, 1778, relates to Native identity, or criteria for someone to be recognized as Indigenous. The latter date, 1892, delimits the criteria for a practice to be recognized as eligible for State protection. I argue that it is through the reification of these arbitrary temporal markers that the settler state reproduces U.S. imperial control over Kānaka ʻŌiwi and our ancestral places. As a demonstration of the State's authority, it is an exercise of the power to affirm or disavow Native subjectivity. I begin with the politics of Native cultural rights, then turn to the politics of qualification, both of which have severe implications for Native subjectivity.

With origins in common law established in the kingdom era of Hawaiʻi and carried through the territorial period (1900–1959) and statehood (since 1959), land laws have always accounted for the rights of Kānaka ʻŌiwi. As Ulla Hasager explains, the "basis for establishing these rights in Hawaiʻi is proof of some version of 'customary and traditional' rights 'exercised for subsistence, cultural and religious purposes'" and they are "inseparable from many other rights, such as the right to religious freedom, burial rights, and historic preservations rights."[51] Since statehood, customary and traditional rights have generally been treated as merely the right of Native Hawaiians to access the privately owned lands of others in observance of recognized cultural practices. 'Umi Perkins explains, however, that in the nineteenth century, these rights were not simply about access to property owned by others. Rather, these were a guarantee of universal "vested rights" of all makaʻāinana[52] in *all lands* in the Hawaiian kingdom.[53] In other words, treatment of these rights as a gift of the settler state, and the misrepresentation of the state's dominion over lands, is not only a critical error but a distortion by design meant to foreclose the possibility of an accurate accounting of land laws and Native rights.

The traditional and customary rights doctrine today allows for the recognition of a cultural practice or activity to be protected under the State's constitution, providing the activity has been practiced for long periods, exercised without interruption in a specific area, and is generally accepted as "ancient" and "reasonable."[54] In 1995, the State Supreme Court ruling known as *Public Access Shoreline Hawaiʻi v. Hawaiʻi County Planning Commission (PASH)* determined reasonable application of this principle would pertain only to activities conducted on "undeveloped land" or "less than fully developed land."[55] The University of Hawaiʻi seized on the opportunity of this distinction by selecting the northern plateau for the TMT, having learned from the Keck Outrigger defeat that it would be difficult to obtain permits (and funding or popular support) for a project on the already developed summit. Because the proposed project site is considered undeveloped or less than fully developed land—though not insignificant or without historical-cultural value to Kānaka ʻŌiwi—UH argued traditional and customary rights were not applicable.

If someone seeks constitutional protection of traditional and customary rights for a cultural practice, the burden of proof that a project would obstruct this practice falls on the individual claiming the right to protection. In other words, someone who claims their rights are obstructed by a development project must defend their claim by proving that their practice is "authentic" in the eyes of the State and thereby satisfy a legal test to prove the practices being obstructed have merit as "traditional and customary." Specifically, the individual must furnish evidence that their cultural activity was "established in practice by November 25, 1892,"[56] was "associated with the ancient way of life," and continues as such to this day.[57] Because there is no comparable obligation placed on the developer to prove their proposed project *will not* obstruct the traditional and customary rights of Native Hawaiians, the law imposes a unique burden on Kānaka ʻŌiwi. It also locks what may qualify as a protected practice away in an invented category of "ancient way of life," which is not determined by Kānaka ʻŌiwi but arbitrarily imposed by the State. Put another way, the legal test forecloses self-determination and freezes the potential evolution and growth of Kanaka indigeneity through future emergent practices in a given location.

Similarly, a temporal logic of qualification and authenticity determines *who* qualifies as a legal subject to make a claim to constitutional rights protections in the first place. The authenticity of a claimant's identity as "native Hawaiian" is pursuant to the criteria established in the 1920 Hawaiian Homes Commission Act and codified at the 1978 State of Hawaiʻi Constitutional Convention. It reads:

> The State reaffirms and shall protect all rights, customarily and traditionally exercised for subsistence, cultural and religious purposes and possessed by ahupuaʻa tenants who are descendants of native Hawaiians who *inhabited the Hawaiian Islands prior to 1778,* subject to the right of the State to regulate such rights.[58]

The State affirmed the access and gathering rights of all Native Hawaiians in 1978, but the legal test was developed in subsequent case decisions. These rights would be leveraged in a move by UH attorneys to disqualify Kānaka ʻŌiwi petitioning the TMT permit. At the 2011 Contested Case Hearing, the 1998 *State v. Hanapi* decision (citing the 1995 *PASH* decision) was referenced by UH lawyers to outline the burden of proof the petitioners (i.e., the Mauna Kea Hui) were required to establish before even a claim to rights protections could be heard. According to *PASH* vis-à-vis *Hanapi*, whether one's cultural practice is entitled to constitutional rights protection as traditional and customary depends on three factors:

> First, he or she must qualify as a "native Hawaiian" within the guidelines set out in PASH . . . PASH acknowledged that the terms "native," "Hawaiian," or "native Hawaiian" are not defined in our statutes, or suggested in legislative history . . . PASH further declined to endorse a fifty percent blood quantum requirement as urged by the plaintiffs . . . Instead, PASH stated that "those persons who are ʻdescendants of native Hawaiians

who inhabited the island prior to 1778,' and who assert otherwise valid customary and traditional Hawaiian rights are entitled to [constitutional] protection, regardless of their blood quantum."

Second, once a defendant qualifies as a native Hawaiian, he or she must then establish that his or her claimed right is constitutionally protected as a customary or traditional native Hawaiian practice . . . The fact that the claimed right is not specifically enumerated in the Constitution or statutes, does not preclude further inquiry concerning other traditional and customary practices that have existed . . .

Finally, a defendant claiming his or her conduct is constitutionally protected must also prove that the exercise of the right occurred on undeveloped or "less than fully developed property."[59]

These legal tests were central to the university's legal strategy in both the 2011 and 2017 TMT contested case hearings as UH argued the petitioners had not adequately met the legal test for native Hawaiian identification:

With respect to the first *Hanapi* factor for establishing that conduct is constitutionally protected as a native Hawaiian right, although the Hearing Officer does not question that Petitioners Ching, Neves, Pisciotta, and

Figure 24. Illustration by Gary Robert Hoff; originally printed in *Hawaii Tribune-Herald,* February 17, 2013. Copyright Gary R. Hoff, 2013.

> Flores-Case ʻOhana are native Hawaiian, *Petitioners offered no testimony
> or other evidence to establish that they are descendants of native Hawaiians
> who inhabited the Hawaiian islands prior to 1778*. Therefore, Petitioners
> have not satisfied the first factor of the *Hanapi* analysis.[60]

Desperate to block the petitioners at every turn, the university's lawyers argued that Kanaka members of the Mauna Kea Hui had not adequately proven they are "native" because they had not furnished evidence
that their ancestors lived in Hawaiʻi prior to the 1778 arrival of British Naval
explorer Captain James Cook. As if the temporal criteria itself and its routine invocation are not violent enough, the appearance of this challenge at
the hearing enraged Kānaka ʻŌiwi and was the subject of public criticism
for weeks. The hearings officer ultimately rejected the university's challenge
to the petitioners' standing.[61] However, that an official State proceeding
functioned as a space for another state agency (i.e., UH) to challenge Indigenous land defenders by questioning their indigeneity demonstrates yet
another way in which settler law operationalizes Native disqualification and,
thus our continued alienation from ʻāina.

The Land Board, however, did accept two other claims that undermined
Kanaka indigeneity and self-determination. UH argued that the cultural
practices for which the petitioners sought rights protection was "contemporary," not "ancient," and thus was not traditional and customary as defined
by the legal test established in the Constitution and *Hanapi*:

> Petitioners have not offered evidence or testimony sufficient to establish
> that any of their practices with respect to Mauna Kea are entitled to con-
> stitutional protection. In particular, Petitioners have offered no proof that
> they are seeking protection for practices that were established by Hawaiian
> usage by November 25, 1892.[62]

Not only is it often difficult for many to locate evidence of a contemporary practice being established before 1892, but it is also a burden of proof
that settlers' rights are not contingent upon. The legal test not only asserts
the State's authority to determine what constitutes a legitimate Native cultural practice, it also precludes the possibility for Native Hawaiians to introduce and cultivate whatever cultural practice might emerge in the future.
This rights doctrine therefore has the effect of freezing Indigenous cultural
practice in time, while undermining Kanaka self-determination in decid-
ing for ourselves what constitutes legitimate cultural practice.

The year 1892 is significant because it was the year prior to the U.S. military invasion of Hawai'i that facilitated the overthrow of our country's head of state, Queen Lili'uokalani, and our democratically elected government. The idea is that a practice established after this date might be less authentic than one previously established, presumably because it would have been tainted by foreign influence. Ironically, while this signals a tacit recognition of the impacts that invasion and occupation have caused Hawaiians, the routine citation of this legal test never includes discussion of the violence that 1893 brought overall. In this way, the Native Hawaiian rights doctrine has often functioned as a tool of bureaucratic disenfranchisement through liberal recognition and inclusion.

As previously discussed, UH chose the northern plateau as a mitigation measure for the TMT's proposed site because, unlike the summit, it is undeveloped. However, according to the third *Hanapi* criterion, it is on "undeveloped" or "less than fully developed land" that constitutional protections for traditional and customary practices are applicable. So, UH had to offer a defense of their claim that these rights were not relevant with regard to this particular site. To do this, UH made two claims. First, they argued the northern plateau is in the resource subzone of the conservation district, which allows for astronomy.[63] Second, they argued the petitioners had not proven cultural practices were conducted at the proposed project site because they only described practices conducted on the summit. Additionally, UH cited the "expert witness" testimony of a non-Native contract archeologist who, following a review of prior reports, studies, plans, and related documents, found "no cultural practices are known to be associated with any specific historic property identified in or near the TMT project."[64] The rationale behind these two claims was crude and condescending, but it was also apparently convincing to the State.

University attorney Tim Lui-Kwan next argued that Hawaiians have no claim to obstruction of traditional and customary practices because, through their own admission, they could still conduct them *despite* the summit's condition as overdeveloped. Citing transcripts from previous testimony, he reasoned:

> In fact, some of the Petitioners even describe their ability to continue practicing cultural practices—you recall Pua Case when she described how she can continue her practice while looking at Mauna Kea with her

hands held above her eyes . . . Petitioner Paul Neves also described his continuing practices on Mauna Kea even with all the observatories in place and the mountain's summit developed.

Is a cultural practice *not* obstructed when one must cover their eyes to avoid the pain of seeing a giant telescope? While Native Hawaiian petitioners sought to add to the public record the fact of their resilience and resolve in the face of big science, UH chose to misinterpret them to suggest that, according to the petitioners' own words, they are still able to continue their cultural practices.

The Land Board eventually approved the permit, a decision that was later upheld on appeal by the State Supreme Court. Ultimately, the university had their interests prioritized over those of Kānaka ʻŌiwi. While the two authenticating dates for Native Hawaiian rights—1778 for aboriginal descent and 1892 for cultural practice—attempt to freeze indigeneity and restrict our future capacity to exercise self-determination on contested lands, the combined effects of these legal tests and liberal practices of inclusion reveal some of the ways in which the settler colonial logic of Native elimination has conditioned the TMT's possibility.

The rhetoric and discursive practices surveyed in this chapter reveal how a neoliberal approach to settler law under U.S. imperial occupation has provided the necessary conditions for another giant telescope to be built on Mauna a Wākea. Along the way, these discourses have also reinvented stewardship in such a way as to absolve the university of its long history of management failures and the State for its complicity in the settler colonial project. By conjuring "cultural sensitivity" and fictive kinships, UH and the pro-TMT community have also imagined a modernity expunged of fully realized, self-determining Kānaka ʻŌiwi. The narrative and legal practices by which the State and university self-authorize their monopoly over Maunakea have also facilitated a contemporary legal system of legitimation in which Kānaka ʻŌiwi qualify as "authentic" only insofar as we remain frozen in an irretrievable past and succumb to the expectation that we render our indigeneity legible to non-Hawaiians. Kanaka indigeneity is treated with suspicion as a method of disqualification of Native Hawaiians from legal subjectivity through liberal inclusion and rights discourse. It is through such legal management of Native subjectivity that the state and settler society produce their own legitimacy and absolution.

To build the Thirty Meter Telescope, the scientific settler state simultaneously commends and condemns Kānaka ʻŌiwi—a paradox that has proven useful to the university in performing legal compliance amidst land management failures and public criticism. As the rhetoric of "cultural sensitivity" toward Native Hawaiians with whom the university feigns a hope to "coexist" is deployed in ways that render UH and astronomers the ostensibly modern heirs to Maunakea and the summit's new caretakers, it also recasts Hawaiians as obstructions to progress who are legitimate only when "ancient." In finding redemption and absolution for settler institutions of colonialism, Kānaka ʻŌiwi appear as foils to the scientific production of universal knowledge and obstacles to modernity. The colonial ambivalence of settler desire and contempt for the Native subject through which the scientific settler state is reproduced relies on the appropriation of our culture. It also relies on the conscription of our people. As I will argue in the concluding chapter, it is only through a sustained critical analysis of these power dynamics and relations that we can make sense of the movement and its contradictions.

Debates surrounding the future of the TMT and Maunakea remain fixated on narratives that reproduce the tradition/modernity binary, which in turn repeats a vision of humanity and modernity from which Kānaka ʻŌiwi are exiled. While astronomy communities in Hawaiʻi wish to coexist, their desires are nevertheless entangled with a settler history and society that imagines fictive kinships and reconfigures dispossession as inheritance. If they wish to find common ground, it would be more productive to contemplate a solidarity that listens to Kānaka ʻŌiwi. They might then learn how the conscription of Hawaiians and appropriation of our culture, language, aesthetics, and epistemologies are symptoms of the continued violence of settler racial capitalism and U.S. imperialism in Hawaiʻi. Finally, the legal disqualification of Kanaka indigeneity and self-determination that operationalizes disenfranchisement and displacement, and on which the U.S. military occupation of Hawaiʻi depends, requires greater attention than what is currently wasted on pleas for "coexistence." In the final chapter, I examine the complex and contradictory reality of TMT support and opposition to argue that a nuanced critical analysis of power and colonialism opens space to understand why kiaʻi are choosing collective action over the legal systems of the settler state.

7

CONSTELLATIONS OF
RESISTANCE AND RESURGENCE

A Better Way of "Seeing"

I accept that some readers may find this book to be didactic because I have treated the TMT with a greater degree of scrutiny than I have Kānaka ʻŌiwi. As I explained in earlier chapters, this is no accident. With millions of dollars spent on attorneys, institutional promotional materials and programming, and law enforcement agencies across the islands—functioning as private security for the interests of the TMT—this project enjoys a degree of power and privilege that Hawaiians do not. A compliant corporate media and popular settler culture will represent the TMT as the epitome of scientific reason. It is pure, detached, and objective science, rational and invariably good. Conversely, Kānaka ʻŌiwi and our knowledges may be quaint, even marketable, but ultimately obsolete. Through repetition of binary oppositions that structure mythologies of hierarchized being and knowledge, TMT advocacy has every conventional advantage in the contest for Mauna a Wākea.

The scientific settler state has also more than adequately condemned the kiaʻi and the Mauna Movement for what it criticizes as excessive and radical identity politics. Denunciation of our community activism and gaslighting of our political expressions are ubiquitous. Indeed, the State's politics of respectability, which would shame Kānaka for our cries of injustice and strategies for social change—has become the air we breathe in settler Hawaiʻi under the hegemony of U.S. occupation. So, no. I have not treated the Maunakea Movement, the kiaʻi, or Kānaka ʻŌiwi with the same level of critique that I have the TMT and its justifications.

As the settler state controls the terms of discourse surrounding Maunakea vis-à-vis its ideological apparatuses, it also reifies a dualistic framing that serves to normalize Native subjection by writing us off as religious zealots. Indeed, the state's ideological apparatuses—from popular media, to conventional historiography (and especially the legal structures of self-legitimization) those bureaucratic administrative processes, the court proceedings and hearings, the procedural schedules, permitting policies, and systems of ostensibly rational governance—collectively serve to reproduce the prevailing social hierarchies of knowledge and being, which, particularly in the case of Maunakea astronomy, thereby reproduce a Native Hawaiian subject that has no legitimate grievance, no claims to injury, and no cause to complain, let alone challenge the TMT. In fact, to cry foul is *to feign* injury, the implication being that our opposition is disingenuous and thus our character deceitful and unprincipled. As described throughout the book, the cultural authority of the astronomy community at Maunakea stems primarily from its claim to rational thought and reason in *matters of science.* That claim is at once projected onto, borrowed and bolstered by, and modeled after the state's own monopolistic claim to rational thought and reason in *matters of law.* Insofar as science and law are in this way co-constituted in settler imperial power, the recursive loop of self-authorization maintains a status quo premised on the idea of a natural hierarchy of difference and being, and thus, the normalization of Native subjection—conditions that structure empire's possibility. For these reasons, I cannot treat Kānaka ʻŌiwi with an "equal" measure of scrutiny as I have the TMT; just as the Mauna Movement and the TMT can never be equals under social relations of power that are structured in dominance.

Kānaka ʻŌiwi are a displaced people, alienated from our ancestral lands by militarism, tourism, and rampant development. Our culture is fetishized and appropriated and our historical experience distorted by an unsustainable, insatiable social order that refuses to acknowledge its own conditions of possibility. As white settler colonial histories have functioned to conceal, excuse, and misrepresent the realities of Kanaka subjugation (and that of Indigenous peoples in all colonized lands), our contemporary condition remains equally distorted and often hidden away. Nevertheless, Kānaka ʻŌiwi are not a monolithic community. To miss this is to miss what is at stake in the struggle for Mauna a Wākea. I will return to this.

Up to this point in the book, I have argued that to understand the struggle for Mauna a Wākea, we must understand the larger struggle against the interlocking oppressions of U.S. cultural hegemony, imperial science, and settler capitalism in Hawaiʻi. However, while I have taken a stance against the TMT, I may be criticized for invoking binary oppositions myself, even if only discursively. I recognize this is a tension that runs throughout the book despite my best efforts. Indeed, the juxtaposition in my last few paragraphs is an example. Therefore, it is not enough to acknowledge that the relations and experiences of the Maunakea Movement or the TMT campaign are complex and contradictory. In this chapter I will illustrate what this means as I explicate *how* they are complex and contradictory through an analysis of power to speak to resistance and solidarity. Through five examples, I examine *what it takes* for Kānaka ʻŌiwi to embrace and advocate for development of the TMT on Mauna a Wākea, and *what it takes* for non-Kanaka allies to resist and be in solidarity with other kiaʻi. This, in my view, might offer a way of resisting the reductive dualisms that are premised on and thereby reproduce ideological hierarchies (e.g., science vs. religion, scientists vs. Hawaiians, etc.). Instead, and paradoxically through another juxtaposition, I will show that an approach to power and resistance that confronts their contradictions with nuance may better resist the binary-reifying pitfalls of conventional discourses that leave Kānaka ʻŌiwi subject to deletion. Discussing the complex and the contradictory character of narrative practices also presents a more capacious frame to better identify what is at stake in the struggle for Mauna a Wākea.

I think of this as a practice of inspecting structures of domination for their fissures. In them, we might peer into the other side of power and dominance. I hope to pry these fissures further open until the light of possibility and liberation shines through. Currently, it seems that only kiaʻi can detect this light on the other side of settler occupation and imperial power. But the futurities illuminated give us hope and the motivation to continue in our struggle for life, land, and ea; even in the face of millions of dollars spent to dismantle the Mauna Movement, and the cultural authority afforded the TMT and the state. This light represents truth, a beam of hope exposed when the structures of our oppression are ruptured, be it through direct action, sustained critique, or creative decolonial praxis in the courts or on the Mauna. The light of future liberation is why Kānaka ʻŌiwi and Kiaʻi Mauna fight as we do, contradictions and all. Indeed, just as the first light when day breaks first touches the summit of Mauna a Wākea, when our movement ruptures power, the first light to shine through the structures of our subjection exposes the violence of those telescopes and shines on our lāhui. A beam that points us toward ea, this light, in its daily return at dawn, is recursive, as it brightens our struggle and warms our relations to life and land.

A broader lens not only may render legible the connection between the TMT and the legacies of violence brought with settler colonialism but also how an anticolonial analysis can better account for the contradictions that make our lāhui so complex, and thus worth fighting for—whether one is Kanaka or not. In this book I have argued that without a sustained critical analysis of power, the controversy over Mauna a Wākea makes little sense. But to find deeper meaning amidst the cacophony of competing claims does not require fluency in Hawaiian language or a Ph.D. in astrophysics—it requires self-reflection, humility, and a commitment to proceed slowly. Only in this way, I argue, might we adequately account for power, knowledge, and resistance. Confronting contradiction does not mean all parts are equal. It does not mean we search for purity. It means we bring nuance to our interventions so hierarchies of difference and being become legible, as the struggle for Mauna a Wākea is about meaning and its making.

I do not claim to be an expert on Mauna a Wākea, Hawaiian history, or the Thirty Meter Telescope, but I have documented some of the perspectives of those who are. In writing this book, I have found that, while there are many "truths" about the value and importance of Maunakea, to focus one's attention on those whose perspectives come from an experience of oppression offers far better insight into how we got here. In my view, it is only through close attention to the words, actions, and knowledges of those for whom settler capitalism and imperial occupation do not benefit that we find meaning. I juxtapose several examples of competing truths about the Mauna to illustrate how a critique of power is key to understanding our struggle.

Early in my research, I found most puzzling the contradictions that not all Hawaiians oppose the TMT, and not every haole supports industrial astronomy in wahi kupuna (ancestral places). Similarly, not everybody finds Maunakea sacred or sacred in the same way, or big science defensible in every instance or at all costs. After my first handful of interviews, the paradox struck me as both fascinating and frustrating: a puzzle that I could not ignore. At that time, I wanted to know: How did astronomers become stewards of Maunakea and Kānaka ʻŌiwi obstructions to progress? I leave you now with a revised question: What are the cognitive adjustments one must perform to rationalize their advocacy for construction of another giant telescope on Mauna a Wākea?

The Dissonance

As discussed throughout the book and previously outlined, conventional frames about the TMT rely on assumptions about science that reproduce stereotypes about Kānaka ʻŌiwi even if only through discursive implication. They construct a humanity and a sense of modernity from which we are estranged. Because we value and practice our culture and language in how we express our resistance, we are said to be cultish, dogmatic, and unreasonable. In our failure to comprehend the TMT's *importance for all humankind*, not only are our knowledges denied but so is our humanity. This is what is at stake in our struggle. I have argued that a critique of power is crucial for making sense of our resistance. This became clear in my interviews with Kānaka ʻŌiwi who support and haole who oppose the TMT.

While my interlocutors repeated common ideologies that emphasize the TMT's scientific merits and universal benefits, I found their support to be void of any critique of power, or politics of imperialism, capitalism, social movements, or struggle. Instead, their positions of support for the TMT assumed the self-evidence of science and law. Are Kānaka ʻŌiwi not "scientific?" Does a permit to build, granted by law, make it moral— does it make it pono? My interview respondents employed a rationale that expresses a combination of self-preservation and resignation. What I mean by this is that my interlocutors expressed ideas about the need to find compromise, often for the most practical reasons, most of which seemed to imply a rationalization of a given status quo but with no intention to consider inspecting them directly, let alone with me in an interview. I wondered if there was concern about funding for programs or their own employment? Does one's professional status, reputation, or collegial relations rest in the balance? There was a strong sense of U.S. patriotism that rested precariously alongside a pride in one's Hawaiianness. There was also a sort of urgency to overcome what was perceived to be a victimhood complex that it was implied other (or, *political*) Hawaiians must overcome. Sometimes my respondents would rebuff through equivocation claims that the TMT would desecrate the Mauna: What is sacred, *really*? Isn't *all land* sacred to somebody? If we protect every piece of land, there would be no development. What would that mean for jobs? Some expressed a sort of toleration of desecration. What I mean here is that it seemed desecration would be tolerable so long as there is compensation, a specified set of limits, or participation in the decision-making process. There was always a deference to the state in this regard. There was also a naïve confidence in the State's policies and laws, if not a clear understanding of how they are informed by its ideological commitments. Doing "TMT the right way" meant securing a "seat at the table." There was an uncritical trust in the promise *to mitigate* harm rather than prevent it. The implicit acceptance was striking. A consequence of this pragmatism, resignation, and desire for compromise, to "coexist," is a gross depoliticization of history and an indifference to questions of power.

In the rest of the chapter, I juxtapose the rhetoric of TMT advocates and Kiaʻi Mauna in unexpected places, featuring interviews with three Kānaka who support the TMT and two non-Hawaiians who oppose it. They reveal ways in which the Movement for Mauna a Wākea—indeed, our lāhui—is complex, if contradictory. I will then argue that confronting this reality does not weaken the movement but rather signals a way out of the colonial trap of reductive binarisms that reify a world of hierarchized being. When we, in this way, critically engage relations of power that leave so many for dead, we also discover what makes the lāhui stronger, our claims more precise, and our visions of futurity more accountable to history.

Getting Past Colonialism: Interview with Paul Coleman

Before his untimely passing in 2018, Native Hawaiian UH Institute for Astronomy professor of astrophysics, Paul Coleman, gave me two interviews; the first was at the IfA campus in Mānoa in late 2012 and the second was during a day-long drive and tour of the Keck Observatory in early 2013, which I discuss in chapter 1. Dr. Coleman was a longtime advocate for Maunakea astronomy and a vocal supporter of the Thirty Meter Telescope project. A favorite instructor with frequently overenrolled courses, he was also a role model for other Native Hawaiians aspiring to become astronomers in a profession predominated by white men. Coleman explained that over the course of his career he endured racist microaggressions but also the frequent ridicule of other Hawaiians who saw him as a "sellout." For these and other reasons, Coleman's positionality was paradoxical as a member of two very opposing camps. This offered him a unique vantage point that allowed him to identify with the desires of astronomers to observe the universe, as well as scrutinize Kānaka who challenged telescope development.

My takeaway from our conversations is that Paul Coleman refused to be compelled to prove or defend his Hawaiian-ness *or* to be denied participation in his beloved field of scientific study. What remained elusive, however, was an analysis of power. Indeed, politics were all but absent. When I asked about Native Hawaiian claims to land and sovereignty, Coleman had little to say and would frequently return to the science and technological aspects of the observatory. When asked about the conventional historiography of Hawai'i, or U.S. imperialism in the Pacific more broadly, his responses suggested he viewed them as unrelated to Maunakea.

I found Paul Coleman to be someone who sought a balance between development and diplomacy and between professional goals and public accountability while acknowledging the importance of protecting this sacred place. Our views diverged on the question of what constitutes the sacred. Beginning with thoughts on excess and limits, he addressed a common argument that if Maunakea can be built, there is nothing to stop the State from developing on other sacred sites:

> But that is true anywhere. And this isn't development in the way most people talk about development. Most people talk about development as the condominium or the hotel or whatever. This [the TMT] doesn't add people to the square footage of the mountain . . . I think what . . . [the activists] are afraid of is that after the TMT goes up, there will have to be the giant hotel next to it to keep the world's wealthiest happy, y'know? I don't think that's the correct way to think about it. I think the correct way to think about it is that the only reason Maunakea is a prime site is because there is no development on it. You develop it more; you develop it right out of being a worthwhile place to do astronomy.[1]

While some would argue the summit is already overdeveloped and a protectionist (if not a Native Hawaiian) orientation is "the correct way to think about" the TMT, Coleman is arguing that not all development is identical. For him, though limits may be necessary, things could be worse.

But if the only standard for overdevelopment is the example of Waikīkī, not only does this lack imagination, it also trivializes the scale, impact, and distinction of *industrial* development. It also fails to adequately comprehend how kiaʻi understand desecration.

When addressing the opposition to the TMT, Coleman argues activists are just ill-informed. This is another common refrain among TMT advocates: if given an opportunity to study astronomy, mathematics, and physics, naysayers would eventually come around. But Coleman also suggests some are just inherently unreasonable:

> If you're too strict one way or another, then what it's going to tell me is that no matter how much I discuss with you, you're never going to change your mind. Then, I guess, we're just going to have to leave them behind.

Should only kiaʻi, or Kānaka ʻŌiwi, be expected to carry the burden of compromise? I asked for his opinion about arguments made by land defenders who suggest Maunakea development cannot be understood outside of the broader context of U.S. militarization of Hawaiʻi. He reasoned:

> What a lot of people don't realize is that science is really a very small part of the budget of any country. Look at the United States' budget. It's something like $.52 out of every dollar goes to military. Twenty something cents goes to health. Science is something like, nothing: point zero zero zero zero zero . . . pennies. It's that people like to think, "Awe those rich astronomers," or y'know, "that's a rich project." . . . it may be a billion-dollar project, but it's our *only* billion-dollar project . . . Now if you can prove that . . . [the TMT] had military applications, you could build it . . . because, of course, the military has all the money. And they have all the money everywhere.

His response suggests that billions spent on militarism is problematic not because of militarism, but because astronomers deserve a cut. Perhaps Coleman misunderstood my question, but he did not seem to consider the question of power, let alone the politics of settler colonialism or U.S. military occupation. Asked about the TM's price tag, Coleman suggested the Mauna Kea Hui takes the extreme position of seeking to prohibit "science" itself, and this represents a sort of irrational detachment from reality. Reducing the concern about potential impacts of the TMT to an unrealistic opposition to "learning things," he returns to military spending, but minus a critique of militarism:

> Is . . . [the TMT] worth the investment of money? So, my perspective has always been, no matter what, learning more about things is always better than not . . . you know, we say we're such a rich nation and all that. So, we should be able to keep doing science, but you need to be realistic, and you need to be part of the world and understand that many people in parts of the world are suffering. Are you taking away from possible things that can help them? Well, I feel that as long as there's a $50 billion-dollar budget that goes to military, I don't care because we can keep going if they're willing to.

Coleman also explained to me how difficult it is for a young Kanaka astronomer to return home to do science because the field is competitive, jobs in Hawai'i are limited, and research travel is expensive. His story is common and the argument for expanding opportunities to practice top tier science "at home" is compelling.

> When you're teaching your kids in the eighth grade about biology in New England and you're teaching them about weather systems somewhere else, and you're not teaching them about volcanology, and you're not teaching them about oceanography, and not teaching them about astronomy, then you are teaching your children to go away. Right? So what you need is a change in perspectives so that you start teaching your kids to fill the jobs that are gonna become available here. And there will be a couple thousand jobs, in and around astronomy—not necessarily astronomers, because—oh, yeah, there will be some of those—but most of the jobs, three-fourths of the jobs associated with this effort will be other things. So why can't every single one of those positions be filled by someone from here—and from the Hawaiian perspective, someone who is a Hawaiian kid, y'know? Why not?

Although his estimate of the number of permanent jobs the TMT will likely bring to Hawai'i may be inflated, his point about offering opportunities to bring Native Hawaiian scientists home is persuasive. At this point, I wished to avoid reifying the rescue narratives of economic security and jobs that dominate discourse on the TMT and to instead return to the question of power. I again asked how the TMT might be understood in the broader history of U.S. imperialism in the Pacific. His response suggests colonialism is a past event rather than ongoing structure:

> Unfortunately, there's this whole colonialism thing going on, and so, you have to, somehow, get past that. It's kind of easy for us [astronomers] to get past that because I don't feel like a colonial person . . . I feel like I'm one of the slaves! Ha-ha! But it's not like . . . it's not like I feel like I'm going to *dominate* anybody, y'know? "You are going to do this! . . . Here, I offer you a $100,000 a year job! You will take it!" Nah, but . . . I think from the astronomy perspective it's less of a big leap to get over that . . .

As the promise and potential benefits of the TMT are weighed against a suspect activist opposition, histories of colonialism are misunderstood and distorted, hierarchical social relations become normalized and ignored, and Native Hawaiian claims to land become suspect and violable. His argument also suggests an analysis of history and power might be distractions from the real business of science, cosmic discovery, and the production of universal knowledge:

> I think that in a sense, with astronomy— . . . not to make it anymore . . . self-important than it already is— . . . we're doing one of the best things that humans can do. We're just here to find answers. We're not killing anybody. We're not going to sell our things on the side. We're trying to advance our knowledge, maybe for the betterment of people, who knows, maybe just because they want to know, because it's curiosity.

Be it due to indifference or ignorance, by suggesting the telescopes are harmless, really only about "curiosity," and little more than an an effort to "find answers," the conventional defense of Maunakea astronomy leaves little space for a sustained, nuanced, and critical analysis of power.

Finally, Coleman characterized technoscientific industrial astronomy as aligned with traditional Kanaka sciences, equating the work of contemporary scientists with kahu, or "priests,"[2] of the days of old.

> Since Hawaiians have always been so intimately connected with astronomy, I think doing astronomy on one of the best mountains in the world for it and as guests of the host culture, that's, I think is a great thing. And I think it fits in with the Hawaiian perspective of kahuna and a normal person, the maka'āinana, because a kahuna is a guy who learned a lot of

science and his craft and he is an expert. And so you leave those things for the experts and the rest of us, normal mortals, we do the things that normal mortals do.

At times in our interview, Coleman seemed to recognize the grievances of the Protect Mauna Kea Movement and the elders and residents who knew a time before the telescopes. But in others, his suspicion of what he perceived as exaggerated performances of cultural identity suggests he shares a common misunderstanding about the objectives of land and water protectors as being inauthentic and the use of culture as a means to achieving short-sighted goals. Although he pointed out contradictions on both sides of the TMT controversy, his responses spoke to an assumption that industrial astronomy and big science produce real knowledge for the universal benefit of all humanity and that analysis of militarism, capitalism, or settler hegemony are irrelevant. As such, the opposition to the TMT is a misdirected vendetta, rather than a logical response to power and the subjugation of Kānaka ʻŌiwi. For that broader context to become legible, I would argue one must develop a politics of colonialism. Otherwise, such distortions can result in a colonial inversion in which the beneficiaries of U.S. occupation and settler hegemony are remade into victims, while the real objects of colonial oppression are recast as perpetrators of violence against scientists. Coleman's aversion to questions and consideration of power represent the ways in which liberal multicultural discourse about Hawaiʻi's contemporary condition serves to depoliticize the TMT. If the Maunakea Movement can be successfully trivialized and the kiaʻi made to appear irrational and irrelevant, very little else stands in the way of large-scale technoscientific development projects at Mauna a Wākea.

An Impossible World: Interview with Larry Kimura

In my interview with cultural researcher and UH-Hilo professor of Hawaiian language Larry Kimura, we discussed the local opposition to the TMT and the role religious and cultural practices have played in community efforts to protect sacred places since the Hawaiian Renaissance.[3] A beloved figure in the Hawaiian community, Dr. Kimura is celebrated for his work as a Hawaiian language preservationist, scholar, and educator at UH Hilo and for helping to establish the ʻAha Pūnana Leo Hawaiian Language Immersion

School. During the '70s and '80s, Kimura conducted hundreds of oral history interviews with native speakers, creating an archive of 'ike kupuna (ancestral knowledge) in 'Ōlelo Hawai'i that remains a vital resource for researchers today. As previously discussed, one connection Kimura has to the Mauna is through his great-grandfather who, as a paniolo in the area, led Queen Emma's famous 1881 expedition to the summit.[4]

At the time of our interview, Kimura was serving as Hawaiian cultural planner and interpreter for UH Hilo's 'Imiloa Astronomy Center[5] and for over a decade had volunteered on Kahu Kū Mauna (KKM), the advisory council comprising Kanaka 'Ōiwi Hawai'i Island residents, which was created to advise the Mauna Kea Management Board, the Office of Mauna Kea Management, and the UH Hilo Chancellor on cultural matters relating to the university's management areas, including the TMT.[6] During his tenure, the council came under public scrutiny for not taking a position against the project. While the council agreed with most Hawaiians that the summit was already overdeveloped, Kahu Kū Mauna endorsed the TMT so long as "mitigation measures" were implemented to reduce impacts, among which is the promise that the TIO[7] will pay $1 million annually to STEM education and projects.

Kimura is neither an activist nor a traditionalist. He does not adamantly defend Maunakea astronomy, but he also does not condemn astronomy expansion. And while his contributions to language revitalization are clear, his politics are not. Offering thoughts on the U.S. relationship to Hawaiians, his responses were vague and noncommittal. Most striking, however, is that while his views on Hawai'i social movements were uncritical of imperialism, capitalism, or big science, his critique of Hawaiians whom he sees as lacking authenticity or as romanticizing cultural traditions appeared developed.

We began with poststatehood activism and opposition to Maunakea astronomy through the 1970s. He explained that "this thing called astronomy wasn't something easily comprehended. I don't even know if it's . . . comprehended so much today." When I asked if he recalls *any* organized challenge to telescopes in those days, he said,

> No . . . and this is why astronomers ask us, as Hawaiians or local people, "where were Hawaiians back then? Why . . . only now [do you protest]?" That's a good question. And I think because Hawaiians were not really

Hawaiians yet . . . the Hawaiian Renaissance was in the beginning of '69. So, this is after the first telescopes were just going up . . . An awareness of what's happening to the indigenous people . . . the so-called Renaissance phase, was . . . ten years after statehood, [so this timing] makes sense because the push to become a state was very strong, from Hawaiians or whatever ethnic group you're talking about . . . So, once that was accomplished, then there was time to kind of look around and see what's happening.[8]

Kimura views the 1970s as a period of transition in which attention was divided and Indigenous political identity only nascent. Elders were skeptical of political activism because, during the territorial years, "being Hawaiian," as he put it, "was unfashionable." Acknowledging how the U.S. civil rights movement ignited a sense of cultural pride among Hawaiians, Kimura expressed skepticism about today's activists, whom he describes as "Hollywood Hawaiians." He implied some Hawaiians perform their politics through cultural practices that are not historically accurate and invoke the idea of "sacredness" without fully understanding what "sacred" means. "We have to define what *is sacred*," he reasoned. Frustrated about what he sees as a common misunderstanding that "*Hawaiian-ness*" means we must behave like stereotypes, he adds that

> now "Hawaiian" . . . has to be determined. *What is Hawaiian?* Wearing a malo, or wearing my jeans? That kind of extreme *evolvement* of what is the Hawaiian today, where we have left off . . . this point [of] departure from what was more solidly understood, more commonly, [or] more normally understood . . . as *Hawaiian* . . . it's a *growing* at the same time, and . . . kind of a nebulous place to be. Thank goodness we still have many [Hawaiian] things we can depend on. And we still have to depend on our solid foundations . . . whatever we have . . . left.[9]

Kimura believes the idea of "Hawaiian" should be based on more than an idealized past and that indigeneity is evolving. Next, he flags what he sees as a contradiction in the anti-TMT movement, particularly among those using culture to express political interests. Citing the ancient adze quarry at Maunakea, he challenges those who claim the TMT as an offense by referencing what he sees as opposition to modern technology:

> Of course, [our ancestors] . . . didn't go up there with bulldozers and dynamite because they didn't have those things, [but] if they had, would

they use . . . [them]? Well, I mean sitting there in the cold, freezing your ʻōkole off, and just using one hammer stone . . . trying to break this rock? If they had dynamite, you think [they] wouldn't use it? *I think that they would.* Humans are humans. So, what is this *Hawaiian thing?*[10]

This view seems to suggest early Hawaiians would also be keen to build telescopes on Maunakea if they had the means. In my view, this implies the Maunakea Movement is hypocritical. Though he may seem to claim Hawaiians are no less modern or tech oriented than astronomers, because his criticism suggests the TMT is just another modern tool like a drill or chisel ancient Hawaiians might have used for breaking rocks, its logic serves to trivialize the TMT opposition by pointing to a hypothetical contradiction: that today's kiaʻi do not understand their own ancestors also used modern tools. The charge re-creates a dichotomy of primitive versus modern subjectivity, and through recitation of the seeming contradiction, the TMT finds redemption. If the Maunakea Movement has forsaken modern technology by opposing the TMT, how does this not bolster charges that the kiaʻi are antiscience and, thus, irrational?

I asked Kimura whether Native Hawaiian participation in spaces like Kahu Kū Mauna might inadvertently serve to legitimize the misuse of sacred places. Doubtful of alternatives, he argued participation at least offers space to use State law to assert limited influence. Defending a "seat at the table," Kimura evokes a multicultural respectability politics and liberal desire for political inclusion. He argues, "I think that is the only way to move and to evolve as a Hawaiian. You can't just evolve [by] falling off into the sky," meaning, to be relevant, Native Hawaiians must engage with the state on the state's terms.

That's what these issues do, hopefully . . . [they return us] to our foundations. From there, try to see how we can become, without the real authority, to become a little bit more responsible in making decisions that can make some difference in some authoritative manner.[11]

In the absence of "real authority," Kimura is resigned to make the most of a bad situation. Next, he addresses what he calls "extremists" who "don't want any telescopes up there," arguing:

. . . we are saying the same thing, except . . . how do we do it? How do you get to that point? Because, if we kept yelling and yelling and going to court,

I mean the louder we yell the more we go to court, the more we . . . [need] funds to pay for lawyers. [This] is one way . . . [and] certainly people are trying to do that, however, if there are other ways . . . [to make change], why not? . . . Certainly, there are people . . . [using] other ways too. And we are not objecting to other ways. Because, as I said, Kahu Kū Mauna's objective is, first . . . no new telescopes should be on the very top . . . on the very summit . . . which is about a 500-acre precinct. Therefore, when this idea of a new telescope came up, [we said] "no, you just cannot." "Ok, well, then how about over here [referring to the northern plateau]?"[12]

Kahu Kū Mauna, despite being an entirely Native volunteer advisory group, would only challenge the TMT insofar as demand it is built away from the summit and that a cut of the revenue go to "the community." In other words, with only a limited voice and no way to stop the TMT, the "seat at the table" model of liberal inclusion is as good as it gets.

Concerning the Mauna Kea Hui's legal interventions, which preceded the first scenes of direct action civil disobedience on the Mauna by a decade, Kimura suggests Hawaiians are

more reactive than active, unfortunately. But that's better than *not* doing anything, I guess. So, it's OK. But we have to become a little more proactive, which I think is a different level of consciousness and being comfortable, feeling natural in it. A lot of reaction is to discomfort and not being a part of the bigger picture.[13]

This "bigger picture" seems to suggest that had TMT opponents sought to negotiate within the State and TMT before the project was approved, it might have yielded different results. This, however, also suggests the hui *did not* participate in the available legal discourse and venues (though they had) or that this participation was not proactive (though it was). While "reactive" connotes "reactionary," as in impulsive and late, it trivializes the rationale for opposition. As such, the kiaʻi are responsible for their own failure. However, as documented throughout this book, the TMT permits were not granted *because* the community was idle, slow, distracted, obliging, or ineffective, but *despite* their proactive attempts to intervene.

I asked Kimura about whether he saw any limits to participating in Kahu Kū Mauna or other state agencies, which appear to validate the TMT, particularly since KKM has no authority to make decisions about the Mauna. He defended the participatory model as a means to leverage, to move in a new direction for the mountain. And getting to that new direction is going to be [difficult] . . . but I think . . . Kahu Kū Mauna . . . can help. I'm not saying it will make a difference, but you have to have faith that it can make a difference and help to move it into a quote-unquote, "Hawaiian"—more of a "Hawaiian way" of managing what's there and what's not going to be there. What should be there and what's not going to be there—whether Hawaiians should be a part of astronomy, science or not . . . in Hawai'i on Maunakea, in a way that is positive or negative, *or not,* for the Hawaiian people . . . first . . . indigenous people and then [all the] people of Hawai'i. And if we can make a contribution in that way to the rest of the world, identify it [the TMT] as Hawaiian. This is good.[14]

While making it "more Hawaiian" is not a new idea, this "new direction" celebrates a kind of participation that aspires only to make the TMT less bad. While Kimura argues participation in the management process allows Hawaiians to "make a difference," he settles for an ambiguous "faith" that something positive will come of it instead of a political commitment toward self-determination. Kimura adds the following:

It is better to be trying to effect change for Hawaiian concerns by participating . . . People would say . . . we are just rubber-stamping and mainstreaming, *that's* the way we are participating. And I think that, in a way, is true—the mainstreaming part—only because there is so much controversy about it. So, the University, who is in this major role of authority here, is not making any major *movements,* we *cannot move* because of courts. Until that is cleared, it's hard to make major movements. So, ok, maybe that process has to be encountered. And then after that, hopefully, [it will be] more Hawaiian . . .[15]

Here, Kimura is arguing the criticism over such participation is only a result of the controversy surrounding the TMT and *not* the result of history. When the TMT receives final approval, he also argues, Hawaiians will "hopefully" make the TMT their own. To me, this seemed a strange aspiration but signals what I read as a sense of resignation to comply instead of resist—or critically analyze power. I asked what he expects Native Hawaiians to get from the TMT.

So, I am not taking up all of your time right now to list all of the so-called positive things that TMT is setting precedence for—in funding and paying and things like that–because you can get that, I hope, hopefully, well, from the legal documents or just straight from the mouths of other people. Now, what is TMT doing that other observatories *are not* doing for the populace of Hawai'i . . . the population of Hawai'i, the citizens of Hawai'i, not just, not just indigenous people, and you could do a list of those things, and so, anyway . . .[16]

I asked if he was confident the mitigation measures UH has proposed are adequate for protecting Maunakea.

I don't think it's adequate. I don't think anything is going to be a hundred percent perfect. So "adequate" to me sounds like it's almost perfect. But it's not, it's never enough. But it's a beginning. It's something. It's, I guess, very minutely, to me, moving in a certain direction that appears good. And that's about all, you know, at this point in time, that I can say. Because I don't know if I'm going to be around to see the real major changes. As I said, because of all this litigation, progress has been very slow in the area of Hawaiian—quote unquote—development. However, it is, I guess, potent for that. I think if more Hawaiian people can participate in it . . . I guess we're not supposed to be radical, we're not supposed to be normal, but I think *it is radical* to participate in a so-called, umm, I don't know what you want to use, a "colonized world" or "haole world" or whatever you call it . . . "not Hawaiian," or you know, "impossible" or whatever.[17]

The idea of participating in a process—which presents only impossible choices of which prohibiting further development is not one—seems less "radical" than conciliatory. If KKM and "consultation" can be used to suggest Native Hawaiians have given consent, what is this "seat at the table" if not a ruse? Considering the hollow rhetoric of "coexistence," I asked Kimura what he feels a mutually beneficial compromise between the TMT and kia'i might look like.

Well, I don't know what the word "compromise" can mean, but I guess it's in the dictionary; it's an English word. But participating is, in whatever fashion—whether you're going [to] do this extreme thing, "This is Mauna a Wākea. It's sacred! Get off of it! Get off of our mountain!" Or, we want to be, um, I guess . . . participating in a bigger picture, where you don't have the authority to tell them, "get off the mountain." You can *say it,* you can *scream it,* you can bulldoze it, or whatever it means, but that doesn't mean you have the ultimate say. So how do you get to that point? If you call it "compromise," well that's *your* opinion. But if you *participate*—in trying to be *less* reactionary, reactive—but, at the same time you are being reactive—but participating in a way that you can make differences that haven't been thought of before, then I think that's a bit more proactive.[18]

Skeptical of the term "compromise," as in the sense of *compromising one's values,* Kimura refused to address what practices of diplomacy exist that might not lead to the TMT. If KKM cannot protect the summit from further development, what is "participation" if not a euphemism for "consent?" I said, "In some ways, it sounds like you're resolved to accept a degree of participation because anything other than that is unrealistic, or unlikely to—" He interrupts and says,

It's almost like asking, "Well, what would *you* say would make it Hawaiian?" One answer would be, "remove everything completely" and that would make, not astronomy Hawaiian, but keep the Hawaiian-ness of Maunakea. But you know that's only one use of the mountain. We have Hawaiian homesteading going on, not on the summit, but on the slopes of Maunakea. We have forestry, just whatever, we have all kinds of concerns going on, on Maunakea. It's not just the summit. So, what's the Hawaiian-ness if you were to remove all the telescopes? What? I think the telescopes, in one positive way, kicks us in our 'ōkole *to make us be more Hawaiian.* So, you know Hawaiian homes, and forestry, and the watershed, and invasive species and everything else, and if Pele is to erupt on Maunakea, all of that is going to keep us Hawaiian, not just waaaaay back when the adze makers went up there . . . we're not like that anymore. We don't live in that world anymore. But we respect that. So how? You can take a horse to water, but *you can't* make it drink. So, you can tell the astronomers, "This is how you should believe, you don't believe this way, and I think you should believe in this way." But you can't make them believe as a Hawaiian. You can make them do certain things, yeah, pay so much money, do certain things . . . ? Build your road in a certain way or consider taking them off because they are too old—and who's paying for it because they set up a fund. Don't tax the citizens of Hawai'i for that—why should the University go to the Legislature to ask them to pay for that? These people should pay for these things. And if we're gonna consider renewing this lease . . . then it's an opportunity, look at it as an opportunity. We cannot get 100%, but let's look at the best we can get out of it.[19]

Kimura's pragmatism confronts the impossible with a simple response: because little else can be done, at least it forces us to be more "Hawaiian." I wonder, at what cost do we take this "opportunity"?

Another Level of Desecration: Interview with Chad Kālepa Baybayan

Chad Kālepa Baybayan was nineteen when he got involved with the Polynesian Voyaging Society, over the years serving as captain, navigator, and crewmember of the deep-sea voyaging canoes (or, waʻa) Hōkūleʻa, Hawaiʻiloa, and Hōkūalakaʻi on crossings to Tahiti, Nuku Hiva, Marquesas, Pitcairn, Mangareva, Rapanui, and Japan among others. Before his untimely passing in 2021, Mr. Baybayan had been navigator in residence at the ʻImiloa Astronomy Center since 2000[20] and a volunteer with Kahu Kū Mauna (KKM) since 2003. Recognized as an expert in wayfinding and carrier of cultural knowledge, Baybayan shared his expertise and experiences with audiences around the islands and the world.[21] As a vocal advocate of the Thirty Meter Telescope, Baybayan had also written editorials and given oral testimony and public talks on connections he saw between noninstrument ocean navigation and Maunakea astronomy. In our interview at his ʻImiloa office in 2013, he shared thoughts on those connections. He described how he interpreted early Hawaiian voyagers who, because they had traveled across the Pacific in search for new lands, were essentially predecessors of today's astronomers.

I found Baybayan intriguing because, like Coleman and Kimura, he was both a highly respected cultural practitioner and a very public champion of the TMT project. And like KKM, he believed that with the Comprehensive Management Plan, the summit ecosystems and Native cultural practices would be unharmed, and, with a cut of revenues, the TMT would benefit everyone. As he put it, "Gotta kick in money to the community. The TMT proposal set a bar, a useful baseline for future negotiations . . . it's a good plan."[22] He reasoned that while the "footprint should be limited, the observation of the telescope is too important to stop."[23] If there are "environmental protections, according to law," the project should be approved.[24] I began with a question about the Mauna Kea Hui's characterization of Maunakea as sacred. Baybayan repeated the idea that to charge the TMT with desecration is to oppose science:

All places are sacred. The whole island system is sacred. We just need to treat it with its due respect . . . astronomy follows that tradition of treating the summit with due respect. They understand and appreciate the opportunity to work on that mountain and I'd like to think they support the stewardship of that mountain . . . Given that there's going to be construction and there's no way of getting around it, then it's about doing it well. If you don't have an appreciation for science, then you will never understand why the TMT is necessary. It's an asset for specific kind of work.[25]

Resigned to accept the inevitability of the project, Baybayan took the position of conditional support based on the TMT's promise of mitigation measures.[26] Like KKM, he felt decommissioning older telescopes and siting the TMT on the "relatively benign" northern plateau was enough and that the best the council could do was to push for "best management practices."[27]

In a 2011 contested case testimony, Baybayan told the story of how, in the 1970s, Nainoa Thompson combined the lessons in Western astronomy he was taught by Will Kyselka—a geologist and former Bishop Museum planetarium manager—with the Carolinian navigating traditions taught to him by Mau Piailug—master navigator from the Micronesian island of Satawal and senior mentor of the early Hōkūleʻa crews.[28] While the ancient Hawaiian navigation techniques were nearly extinct, combining Western and Satawalese systems enabled Thompson to construct a new method of noninstrument navigation that, while an adopted hybrid form, is no less Hawaiian just because it is not "pure." In fact, it is this idea of cultural mixing that grounds Baybayan's openness to integrating the foreign with the Indigenous, which he argues is something Hawaiians have always done:

Today wayfinding exists as an example of restored practice that has emerged from the synergy of culture and astronomy, of indigenous knowledge and scientific paradigm, and the ability of different perspectives to work together and create a healthy, dynamic, and viable cultural practice [sic].[29]

There is an assumption here that culture and astronomy were mutually exclusive for Kānaka ʻŌiwi in earlier times, and that a "healthy, dynamic, and viable cultural practice" in the present or future for Hawaiian people *hinges on* large telescope development.[30] Part of the reason I wanted to interview Baybayan is because of an editorial he published in *West Hawaii Today* in which he suggests the TMT is not the highest form of desecration, but rather denying children access to this synergy *is*:

> As a Hawaiian, I recognize I am a descendant of some of the best naked-eye astronomers the world has known. It is culturally consistent to advocate for Hawaiian participation in a field of science that continues to enable that tradition and a field in which we ought to lead. I firmly believe the highest level of desecration rests in actions that remove the opportunity and choices from the kind of future our youth can own.[31]

How TMT opposition or dissolution of the project would deny the future of our youth access to participation in Western or Kanaka sciences remained unanswered here, but in my view the general claim is meant to elicit a sense of moral urgency, for which children are often a useful alibi. Asked whether he sees "Hawaiian sciences" being diminished, disavowed, or marginalized in the prevailing discourses around the TMT, Baybayan responds:

> Now . . . I believe there is science and there is 'ike. I think that they exist in two separate fields or domains. But I don't believe there is a "Hawaiian science." I just believe there is 'ike, because science has got its own set of protocols to follow and one thing that science cannot express is spirituality. So that is why I believe our knowledge *is just* 'ike. And to me science is just a label. I don't have to label what I know as "Hawaiian science." I just believe . . . let science belong to the scientists and let us guys, let us Hawaiians give our body of knowledge, let's just call it 'ike. And I'm happy, I'm really confident in the fact that our knowledge is valid and very strong. But I don't want to contextualize it by stealing a label and trying to adapt that label to what *we know*. Because, again, like I said, science cannot express spirituality. And our knowledge was very spiritual.[32]

While it is easy to say Hawaiian knowledge is just as "valid and strong" as any other, the world in which these terms and conversations are taking place does not recognize 'ike as a body of knowledge—or method of knowledge production—that is equal to science. As discussed in chapter 6, the now ubiquitous modernity/tradition binary, as with the binary of science versus religion, presupposes science has already won the ideological contest of scientific reality over religious superstition. While Baybayan appears to celebrate 'ike by suggesting "science cannot express spirituality," it is the framing through juxtaposition that matters here because the distinction of 'ike from science is based on both the modernity/tradition binary *and* the myth of a natural hierarchy of the world's knowledges and peoples.[33] While one might agree that 'ike is just as valid and strong, the suggestion that characterizing Hawaiian knowledge, or 'ike, as science is a sign of cultural insecurity, or *an act of theft*, is problematic. Indeed, the idea that Hawaiians are "stealing . . . the label" of science presupposes the idea that Hawaiian knowledge *cannot also be scientific*, which itself presumes Hawaiians are an unscientific people.[34] This aligns with the popular charge that kia'i are anti-science insofar as it concedes the terrain of science to a framing of astronomy in which science is constituted in the modernity/tradition binary and mythology of hierarchical being, which thereby relegates Native people to obsolescence as primitive and superstitious. The Native subject can only ever aspire to enter modernity, for which, it is implied, the tutelage of white settler society is key.

When I asked how he developed his views on science and the importance of the TMT, Baybayan described a dystopic image of humanity's collapse:

> I just think I have a long perspective on the whole topic of exploration. Quite frankly, I know that we won't as a human race [survive, and] . . . ultimately it comes down to . . . What's the big question we're trying to answer here [with Maunakea telescopes]? As a human race, and as the inhabitants of this planet—this planet is doomed to die. It's just a natural cycle of life. And that's scientific, because eventually the sun is going to keep on growing and it will become too hot to inhabit this island. I mean this island planet [Earth]. So, quite frankly, our future lies someplace among the stars—the future of humanity does. And that is like light years away of thinking. But we gotta go through . . . all these hurdles before we can actually think about where we're going to inhabit next. So . . . it's a long-term question, but we gotta keep on, we gotta take these baby steps to answer the inevitable question [which] is where are we going to live next? This conversation is going to take a long time to answer, but it needs to [be had].[35]

I read this response as signaling Baybayan's understanding of exoplanet research, which is a branch of astronomy whose mission is to search for planets orbiting other stars that may be conducive to harboring life. This field of research has sparked public imaginations that astronomers have used to justify calls for the continued funding of ambitious astronomical projects like the SETI Institute.[36] The field has also encouraged fantastical ideas that tend to characterize our planet's future destruction as inevitable. Citing the global environmental crises as evidence, the implication of an uninhabitable future Earth makes the search for exoplanets and, thus, the TMT appear necessary and urgent.

I asked about ordinary Hawaiians who are just trying to live and defend our lands, rights, and futures here on Earth. Is this a part of the conversation we should be having? He continues:

> Yeah, I ask the astronomers: "Why is it so important that we explore the universe? Why don't we work on solving the problems of humanity on this planet instead of trying to answer the question of the universe?" But I understand . . . that it's a long-term project and that we gonna have to understand the universe to give humanity any possibilities of survival. Now I don't know if I'm the only person that adheres to this philosophy . . . And it's not that I'm gloomy or doomed. It's just that I realize that that's the practicality of it . . . I mean, we come from a people who are the greatest oceanic explorers. Why did they explore? . . . Why did they look to the horizons and new lands? It was always about the hope for a better future for their community. So, I think of that approach when I support astronomy.[37]

The idea that the future survival of humans is dependent on our relocation to another planet may sound outlandish, but it has been a persuasive strategy to sway public opinion in favor of the TMT. And while the connection between a dystopian pop cultural vision of escape from a future apocalypse and the ocean voyaging achievements of early Hawaiians may seem tenuous to some, Baybayan was receptive. I expressed my skepticism that astronomers and Hawaiians share similar methods of exploration or ambitions to discover distant worlds, particularly considering the matter of scale and the technological requirements to build new giant telescopes. He responded:

> Our traditional knowledges absolutely did not require huge development projects to produce our knowledge. No, we just sat on the beach and observed the night's sky. They're just totally different domains of work that they do. I mean, oceanic voyaging was done on the ocean, so you can do that on the beach. There's no need to go to the mountain. Whereas to study the universe, you need crystal clear skies and Maunakea has those crystal-clear skies. So those are two different requirements. One thing that they have in common is that it doesn't have anything to do with the

technical aspects because they are just totally removed [but] . . . we share a common curiosity for the night's sky, a common use of the night's sky. And that's it. These people, they explore the universe for whatever reasons or rationale . . . And we use the night's sky in a certain way. That's as close as the unifying concept comes. It's the sky up above our head, but . . . our intentions are totally different. So, we have no singularities in the intent or the intentions of our work, but we do have a common thread and that's the night's sky.[38]

I asked if building an 18-story facility on 8 acres of undeveloped land despite the pleas of so many Kānaka complicates his decision, to which Baybayan responded, "It is what it is."[39] "Is it ethical?" I asked. "I could argue until we're blue in the face, but this is what it's going to take to do that kind of work. There's no way around it," he said.[40] Like Coleman and Kimura, Baybayan argued if early Hawaiians had these technologies, they would build their own TMT.

Now I looked at the history of Kamehameha. When he died, he had a telescope, a compass, [and] Western instruments that he acquired. I think he had a curiosity about science. Now you can speculate all you want, "If he was here today and so on." I would think that if they were faced with the question, they would be supportive. Because Kalākaua actively wanted to engage in this scientific curiosity. So, I think there is two sides of the argument . . . Those that would say, the ali'i would say "no," and those that the ali'i would say "yes . . ." But they were curious people.[41]

In his oral testimony at the 2011 TMT contested case hearing, Baybayan cites "resources" and Keanakāko'i—the famous basalt quarry where stone adzes were created prior to the introduction of Western materials—arguing construction of the TMT is no different from the activities of early Kānaka 'Ōiwi on the Mauna. He equivocates:

I believe that Mauna Kea adze quarry . . . the largest in the world, offers conclusive evidence that the ancients recognized the importance of Mauna Kea's rich resources and its ability to serve its community by producing the tools to sustain daily life. They ventured to Mauna Kea, reshaped the environment by quarrying rock and left behind evidence of their work, and took materials off the mountain to serve their communities. And they did this with the full consent and in the presence of their gods. Using the resources on Mauna Kea, I believe, such as the adze quarry, as

a tool to serve and benefit the community, as in the case of the practice
of astronomy, it's consistent with the example of this past land use. And I
would say consistent in the way Hawaiian trusts use their land asset to
the benefit of beneficiaries.[42]

To suggest the TMT would be celebrated by our aliʻi, or is comparable to the Western gadgets owned by Kamehameha, or that its construction is *not unlike* earlier uses of the Mauna where stones were quarried
to make tools, seemed more a confirmation of preexisting beliefs than an
analysis of history, particularly when considering the scale of expenditure,
labor, and resources. It also seemed the point was more about affect than
accuracy.

While Baybayan did answer some of my questions about his experience and thoughts on the Hawaiian Renaissance, Kahoʻolawe, and militarism in Hawaiʻi, it seemed that none of this was, to him, relevant to the TMT.
Baybayan described his disapproval of the U.S. bombing of Kahoʻolawe
and war in general, and the significance of Hōkūleʻa to the cultural resurgence since the 1970s. However, he did not view astronomy expansion
on Maunakea as being connected to the larger story of power in Hawaiʻi.
Landing on an economic rationale, he echoed Coleman and Kimura's sense
of resignation:

> I mean we need an economy, right? We need an economy, we need
> money to do things, to build things, to run programs, and where is that
> money gonna come from? I mean tourism is the number one industry in
> Hawaiʻi and as much as development has made impacts on the island
> landscape, I think it had to . . . otherwise you wouldn't have an economy
> to sustain these islands. With the population base being the numbers that
> it's at, I don't know how we can sustain ourselves. I mean, I think we are
> just getting by right now. We need income.[43]

In my view, Baybayan's comments reflect an acceptance of an idea
of inevitability that Kānaka ʻŌiwi have little control over what happens to
our lands and waters. The TMT is justified in his belief that nothing can be
done about, say, the effects of climate change or the possible future annihi-
lation of our planet. Considering such prospects, why toil over protecting
Maunakea? Why not "optimize" its "resources?"[44] *What is sacred anyway, and
says who?* Perspectives like this are invaluable to the TIO and the university, not only because they affirm the neoliberalism of settler state priorities

but also because they affirm the disavowal of Native grievances that reproduce the status quo. It's conciliatory but also, in my view, unimaginative. It avoids the real work of imagining differently, and the radical possibility of institutionalizing an Indigenous ethic and praxis of care, of the Mauna and all ʻāina, including the lāhui. While Baybayan celebrated the gifts of Western science, I wondered: Are exploration and "curiosity" about "the night's sky" enough of a "common thread" to justify the TMT? At what cost do we overlook the history and ongoing structures of power that condition the TMT?

The cognitive bias required to justify the TMT is notable here, but may also serve to normalize a hierarchical framing of knowledge and being that is constituted in the lofty and sweeping promises of industrial techno-science on Maunakea. In these visions of Western science and Kānaka ʻŌiwi, we are asked to concede more than our islands and lāhui can bear. We are asked to relinquish our sacred ʻāina for some ill-defined "greater good." In that concession, we affirm our subordination, but we also abdicate our kuleana to mālama, to care for the ʻāina and each other, including our future generations. It also excuses rather than questions power. Such a practice of compromise and accommodation not only risks forfeiting this kuleana to steward sacred places, but as a model of toleration and expediency that is untenable, it also puts our very self-determination at risk. The most important question to ask may not necessarily be, "How did astronomers become stewards of Maunakea and Kānaka ʻŌiwi obstructions to progress?" but "By what spiritual, mental, and emotional dissonance does one adopt an ideological position that redeems continued industrial development of a fragile and biodiverse ecosystem and the desecration of this unique wahi kupuna?" Interrogation of those moral acrobatics leads us to what is at stake in this struggle for Mauna a Wākea.

These Are Sacred Grounds: Interview with John and Ruth Ota

In our 2012 interview, John and Ruth Ota described how they came to support Kānaka ʻŌiwi and oppose the TMT.[45] I found it striking that their stance does not come from a naïve sympathy for Hawaiians or a sense of settler guilt but instead from a political commitment to solidarity. From this position of social and historical accountability, it is lived experience that informs both their critique of state militarism and their identification with the spiritual relationality Hawaiians articulate to their resistance. While neither Mr. or Mrs. Ota critique imperialism or capitalism directly, unlike Coleman, Kimura, and Baybayan, they do offer a sustained, nuanced, and critical analysis of power. And their descriptions were cogent, citing the abuse of Hawai'i's lands and waters in the preparation for U.S. wars; the mistreatment of Japanese Americans and U.S. war veterans since the Second World War; the fact that a majority of Maunakea telescopes are "foreign-owned" and their "universal benefit" is dubious; the possibility the TMT would be used for national defense applications; and the disrespect with which Hawaiians are treated by federal and state governments in their defense of sacred sites. Their counterhegemonic narrative practice embodies self-reflexivity and a settler politics of refusal. In other words, the Otas refuse the "gifts" of liberal multiculturalism, empire, and settler capitalism, opting instead to be in solidarity with the Native people of Hawai'i.

I interviewed Mr. and Mrs. Ota in September of 2012, just two years prior to the 2014 groundbreaking ceremony disruption and well before the two major direct action mass protests of 2015 and 2019. A retired couple in their seventies at the time of our interview, the Otas do not identify as activists, but nevertheless frequently attend and provide written and oral testimony at various public meetings, BLNR hearings, EIS exploratory meetings, contested case proceedings, and other events. As I began my research, Pua Case advised me to connect with the Otas because of their unique subject positions as non-Hawaiians in support of Kānaka 'Ōiwi. As Case put it, they represent the diversity of the communities who back the movement to protect Mauna a Wākea. That the Otas refuse the spoils of U.S. militarism and settler capitalism despite their status as middle-class retirees within Hawai'i's prevailing ethnic and racial hierarchy undermines charges against the Mauna Movement as comprising Hawaiian militants, religious fundamentalists, or cultish traditionalists. As John and Ruth Ota do not fit these stereotypes, they complicate conventional representations of the movement.

John Ota is a third-generation descendant of Japanese immigrants to Hawai'i and a retired Marine. The first Asian American Marine to become a U.S. officer in the Corps, Mr. Ota began by describing his credentials, which included circling the world "thirteen times" and "turning" former big city gang members "into Marines," surviving combat in two U.S. wars, and working as an aviation mechanic with "secret clearance" on planes that would transport atomic bombs for tests conducted in Nevada. His training and experiences led to a civilian career with Boeing until his second retirement in 2000. Much of the reason Mr. Ota opposes the TMT is based on his experience as a serviceman and his exposure to Agent Orange:

> I went to Korea and . . . Vietnam, fought in that combat over there and came back. And while I was there, I got sprayed with Agent Orange . . . At that time, I *didn't know* what Agent Orange *was*. Only after I retired did I find out what Agent Orange is and what it could do. But while I was in Vietnam, I felt that spray coming down on me. I knew I got sprayed with that stuff . . .
>
> This one friend of mine, he's Hawaiian, he came home [from the war] . . . and had baby with his wife . . . But what they determined was that when he . . . and . . . his wife [tried] to make that baby . . . [they learned he] was infected with dioxane. And so, the kid was born as an invalid from birth. So, the veterans administration . . . he filed a claim after he found out about what Agent Orange can do . . . and he got himself 100% disability, and the kid got 100% disability, and . . . his wife got . . . a percentage out of the whole thing. So, they were all being paid by the Department of Veteran's Affairs so much money per year for the rest of their life because it screwed up the whole family.[46]

Because he has followed the history of militarism on Hawaiʻi Island and has personally witnessed military pollution, Mr. Ota is also skeptical of governmental claims of good stewardship over the lands they control:

> Since 1942 when . . . they brought the two divisions of Marines and station them in Waimea, they used to go on the side of Maunakea and fire live explosives—try to practice for their invasions of other Pacific Islands. That place is loaded with ammunition . . . unexploded ammunitions, the whole bit, everything. And all of Waimea area is just full of it, all the way down Kawaihae . . . down to the beaches. And so is Hilo Harbor where they dumped a lot of ammunition off the ships right outside the harbor, and so is same way with down south in South Point . . .[47]

Living in Hilo after the war, Mr. Ota remained close with a Native Hawaiian friend who would tell him about the Hawaiian sovereignty movement. Ota began reading histories of Hawaiʻi, learning about nineteenth-century Hawaiian kingdom laws and society. He took particular interest in

ancient cultural practices too, from which he learned of the supreme desecration it was to expose the remains of one's ancestors:

> . . . looking at Maunakea, I grew up in this place and even as a kid I went
> up there many times and I know what it looked like. And I knew it was
> sacred grounds even from when I was young kid, because every time I go
> up there, I get chicken skin [taps the table] . . .
> [*Long pause*]
> I can't explain why. I *don't know why.* But it's like I'm stepping on
> somebody's grave or something. To me, that is what I feel like. And I
> know that mountain has got a lot of graves up there. They should be
> marked, yes, by Hawaiian standard where you stack stones and all that.
> But stacked stones is good temporarily . . .[48]

He next recounts an understanding of why so many graves were un-
marked, as to protect the bones from exposure to light. Describing what
he'd learned about the "days before Kamehameha took over all of this island"
and how each "tribe" had "boundaries" and

> medicine men, . . . that would take care of all the sacred stuff . . . within
> the tribe. And . . . it was actually forbidden for . . . anyone who took a
> dead body and buried [it] . . . they were forbidden to disclose where that
> body was buried. And the punishment was death. So, they never did dis-
> close where a lot of the bodies were buried. Consequently, a lot of the
> bodies could even be buried on Maunakea and they did find a lot of them
> up there, belonging to the tribes. Even with all the projects that's going
> on around up that mountain up there about telescopes and making sure
> the grounds are good and flat and all that, my real big concern is that all
> these burial grounds are going to be uncovered and they're going to be
> exposed.[49]

Because it is so rare to hear non-Hawaiians describe the importance
of protecting iwi kupuna (ancestral remains) and moepū (funerary possessions), let alone the meaning of those values from a Kanaka point of view,
it was refreshing to learn his perspective on these politics:

> Personally, in my own belief . . . the way I think, I don't think anybody has
> the right to disturb anybody's grave or burial grounds. That [Maunakea]
> is *a sacred ground* . . . [*wind blows, bits become inaudible*] . . . for the gov-
> ernment or nothing! . . . . [*inaudible*] . . . that's how I look at it. People that
> is buried there should not be able to be disturbed or moved. That's not

right . . . [*inaudible*] . . . That is why when they talk about burial grounds and all that, and they say, "well we found bones here" and all of a sudden they enclose it and they pick up all the bones, and remains and they rebury it somewhere else. [*He exhales, pauses*] Those bones are fine right there . . . they should leave 'em alone! That's not right.[50]

I ask Mr. Ota about the common argument that some will make about the importance of scientific discovery and the benefits of the TMT for all of humankind. He scoffs:

My view of the telescopes is they should not be there. The whole issue of putting man on the moon or Mars or wherever . . . the telescope and all that . . . thing is, using telescopes to peer into the sky . . . [they] say . . . "Hey I discovered a new planet." I said, "Is that new planet going to feed anybody on Earth? How is it going to benefit anybody except the military and the individual?" . . . [*inaudible*] . . . So [they say] . . . they discovered a new planet and my name goes down in history. All that crap. "Nobody can benefit from it except me." It's all bull crap. It don't mean nothin'. But the search for going out to another planet in my thinking is because they've run out of resources on Earth. All the countries run out of resources . . . So, now they gotta find some resources on another planet that they can use to create things with. Mankind has pillaged Earth for all its worth. There's no more replacements.[51]

John Ota is surprisingly sensitive to the subjection Kānaka 'Ōiwi cite in describing our oppression and spiritual and cultural values, as well as the environmental destruction caused in the name of economic development.

I turned to the reasons he gives testimony at public hearings, meetings, and the legal proceedings in which he is not even a direct participant. He described how obvious it is when the University of Hawai'i, the State, the federal government, or scientists gaslight the opposition:

They try to make it appear like it's good for educational purposes . . . their point is towards education. My point is, you can study as much as you want up in the sky what it is and what it can do and all that. *How is that gonna feed anybody on the ground?* . . . Where is the medium, of the balance, that can accommodate? Being an astronomer has nothing to do with feeding the people on the ground . . .

The EIS process . . . or whatever they call it anymore . . . It is a bunch of games that is being played by whoever is conducting it. They use the words and they get the people to testify to . . . and they say, "there is no significant impact" . . . or use words that are so far above to make it look like whatever's down there [*he pounds on table*] . . . that their activities doesn't really mean anything to the normal people. It won't disrupt their lives because there only "minimal impact" . . . and what they do is take about fifteen people [experts], maybe even twenty, and each explains about a certain area of an issue, and [they] group them all together and say "of all of these twenty, there's not minimal impact on it [the mountain]. We have evaluated it and now . . ." But *they* have evaluated it. *They* have evaluated it. Not the Hawaiians or community. So, *there's no truth in it!*[52]

Mr. Ota demonstrates his respect and solidarity with the Mauna Kea Movement by showing up and lending his voice:

I'm a strong believer of the rights of the Hawaiian people. And I believe the United States did wrong by the Hawaiian people and the kingdom. But by myself, there's not a lot that can be done. I go to these meetings to try and help them in whatever way I can.[53]

Ruth Ota also supports the rights of Kānaka 'Ōiwi. She was a young woman in 1979 when she moved to Hawai'i from Wisconsin. Shortly after befriending a Native Hawaiian woman who had moved to her working-class neighborhood in Madison and became close with her siblings, the pair traveled to Hawai'i Island and stayed with her friend's 'ohana.

I came here for a 10-day . . . visit and she just, and her father, just took me all over the place. And in doing so, told me a lot about the customs and Hawaiians . . . I learned a lot . . . I'd never met such wonderful people. I'd never seen such beauty. And I'd never felt spirit the way I felt it here . . . So, I went back, and I announced to my family I am moving and in three months' time I had sold my stuff and I was back to stay . . . I was single . . . had pretty much had a nasty divorce, I had a nasty marriage. I didn't care to date. I was just fine by myself . . .[54]

She took a job as a hostess at Ken's Pancake House and would often spend her weekends taking her two-wheel drive to Maunakea. A spiritual person, Mrs. Ota would park and meditate, enjoying the air, the mist, the sounds, the sun, and solitude. She described to me how, ever since she was a little girl, she had "precognitive dreams." I will admit, I almost thought this was going to be some hippie tale about becoming Native or something, but I was soon enthralled by her story of one particular visit to Lake Waiau in which she almost passed out from the hike back to her car and such physical exertion at this altitude. Only after a "chicken-skin" encounter alongside the road—the details of which I felt it improper to reproduce in writing—did her visions reveal their meaning. She eventually befriended Pua Case in 2010, and after some time together, Ota recounted her dreams and this particular encounter at Waiau. Case, whose family has a spiritual connection to one kupua on the Mauna, immediately affirmed her belief in the legitimacy of Ruth's experience because of her own. The two became close friends.

This and other stories tell me Mrs. Ota's opposition to the TMT and support of Kānaka ʻŌiwi is grounded in spirituality, *as well as* a politics of solidarity. As a non-Hawaiian, I find that Mrs. Ota's relationship to Kānaka ʻŌiwi, Mauna a Wākea, and spiritual praxis complicates conventional representations of the TMT opposition that impose a binary framing and pits Hawaiian vs. settler, religion vs. science, and tradition vs. modernity. Instead, Ruth Ota's solidarity centers on a critique of power and affirmation of Kanaka relationality to ʻāina. As a self-described "outsider," Mrs. Ota is an ally who shows gratitude for these teachings she's received on how to be a good visitor at Maunakea:

> What you want to know is, during those times, and this is why, I know what Pua and others profess, they will say, "This mountain is sacred." And it is. It is sacred. And in my goings up there, I had been taught that you don't desecrate. You don't spit your gum out. You don't urinate on the grass . . . *you respect things* . . . I was the guest. You just don't do anything. So, I would just *be* . . .
>
> There isn't anybody who can tell me this place isn't sacred . . . I think we have plenty [of telescopes] up there now. I don't think we need this big albatross they want to put up there. They are encroaching on Lake Waiau . . . but these are sacred grounds. And when I go to these meetings, and I hear what these people are saying and *not saying* and trying to stuff it down your throat—how wonderful this is and how it should be built; there is nothing spiritual about it. They just have closed ears. But of course, they have closed ears. Because *either you are spiritual or not*. It's not as if I go to church every Sunday. It's not that. It's what you take away from church on Sunday and what lives in here [*touches her chest*].[55]

Like Coleman, Kimura, and Baybayan, Mr. and Mrs. Ota's comments reveal how perspectives on Maunakea and the TMT are often complex and contradictory. In her opposition to the TMT, she resists reducing local people to a monolith and instead reveals how the lāhui is racially, ethnically, culturally, and politically diverse. This is a multiculturalism that resists possessing Kānaka ʻŌiwi or becoming Native. Mrs. Ota does not seek absolution from accountability or innocence from power relations that structure settler dominance, but instead models a brave commitment to solidarity. While many settlers are unaware or indifferent toward the contemporary condition of Kānaka ʻŌiwi, the Otas refuse the inheritance of settler power and the spoils of imperial conquest. I should be clear, the Ota family also lives in contradiction. Their advocacy for Kānaka ʻŌiwi does not mean they do not also participate in the cultural hegemony of liberal multiculturalism, neoliberal environmentalism, settler capitalism, or U.S. nationalism to some degree. However, our interview shows how John and Ruth Ota confront the contradictions and the tensions constitutive of settler U.S. hegemony through unapologetic and public displays of solidarity with Kānaka ʻŌiwi. Like so many kiaʻi, the Otas also strive to be pono.[56] It is practical and ideological, but it refuses to claim innocence or concede to power for the sake of expediency. In doing so, they demonstrate a critical self-reflection in their everyday lives, denouncing settler privilege through activism and building with and alongside of Kānaka ʻŌiwi: "And so my kuleana is to give them all the support I feel I can," says Mrs. Ota. This is a coexistence that is nonhierarchical, critical, self-reflective, and humble. These are old school Kanaka ʻŌiwi values. Grounded in support of Indigenous freedom, return of lands, self-determination, and ea, the Ota family also shows how the lāhui and the contemporary Hawaiian movement are not only for Kānaka ʻŌiwi, but instead are big enough for everyone.

The Recursive First Light of Aloha ʻĀina

While some might agree the basic principle of coexistence is not inherently problematic, exactly what form this coexistence might take matters greatly. On whose terms shall we coexist? According to what norms or worldviews will this "coexistence" occur? Will it be the sort of coexistence that reproduces the social distortions of liberal multiculturalism, the violent abandonment of settler capitalism, and the prolonged occupation of U.S. militarism that alienates Kānaka ʻŌiwi from our ʻāina? Will it foreclose the possibility of decolonization and mark us for deletion?

In this chapter I have juxtaposed the rhetorical and narrative practices of two general perspectives on the TMT across my interviews. The first is a position of advocacy for the TMT common within conventional state discourses and the astronomy community, which I argue avoids critical self-examination of the broader sociohistorical context of U.S. imperial and settler capitalist hegemony in Hawaiʻi. The second perspective reflects an analysis of power, and is shared among those who consider deeply the reasons that so many Kānaka ʻŌiwi have opposed the TMT and committed to civil disobedience direct action to protect the Mauna from astronomy expansion. This requires an attention, not an aversion, to history and politics. As an embodiment and practice of sustained, nuanced critical analysis of relations of power in Hawaiʻi, the commitment to understanding how Kanaka-led resistance provides a model of engagement that prioritizes solidarity, decolonization, and Indigenous knowledge as the basis of collective struggle deserves attention. As this approach to politics models a coexistence that seeks balance to achieve justice, rather than to reproduce hierarchy as compromise, it is also where I conclude.

Throughout the book I have analyzed some of the discursive practices by which settler institutions and big science have assumed the role of stewardship over Maunakea, while Kānaka ʻŌiwi have been cast as obstructions to science and progress. I have also argued that to understand the reasons for Kanaka ʻŌiwi articulations of the sacred to contemporary political resistance in defense of ancestral lands and waters, Kānaka ʻŌiwi must be heard—and *heard on our terms*. However, listening *alone* cannot account for all Kānaka ʻŌiwi, for we are not a monolith. Likewise, any treatment of Native Hawaiian politics that reproduces the reductive binarisms that made possible the Maunakea observatory in the first place will only lead us to another impasse and prove insufficient to dismantle the multicultural settler logics of possession through liberal inclusion. We open more opportunities to meaningful transformation when we resist the essentializing grammars of binarity and the condescension of reconciliation and recognition. Instead, when we embrace the radical diversity of our lāhui and capacious possibilities of ʻike kupuna when articulated to resistance, we advance with a mind to our past that informs our future.

However, while some Hawaiians support the TMT, and we confront the reality that our lāhui is complex and contradictory, as I have argued, it is only through a critique of power that we may render the violence of settler science and the TMT legible. To do this requires an analysis of power, hegemony, and resistance. Indeed, it is true that our ʻike kupuna, our ancestral knowledge, can be used to support industrial development and telescope expansion on the Mauna. However, when it informs our movements for ea, this ʻike also has the potential to strengthen our relations to ʻāina, ancestral places, the sacred, and to each other. As these constellations of resistance have the capacity to unsettle power, they also require that we refuse the gifts of settler racial capitalism and U.S. empire.

A practice of patient, compassionate, and self-reflexive critique and analysis is needed right now. This also includes the courage to think critically, expansively, and with nuance; to confront the contradictions of our lāhui as we continue our struggle for collective liberation. This, in my view, is pono (just, right). It has served our lāhui well since long before Puʻuhuluhulu, and I am confident it will lead our movements for life, land, and ea to pono futures. To this end, we must never relent in our commitment to liberation through care for our wahi kupuna as well as the deoccupation of all Kō Hawaiʻi Pae ʻĀina from all forms of militarism. In other words, we must critique, resist, and reclaim power through our aloha ʻāina.

I chose the title of this book because it revealed itself on that sunrise of the autumnal equinox we observed during the Polohiwa. When some people go to the Mauna, they look to the stars. So do we, but we also look to the horizon, our past, and to our ancestors. While an astronomer may refuse to look around—his gaze fixed on the stars, peering into space from his privilege in the shadows of anonymity, naming the universe and *our humanity* along the way—he often fails to see our lāhui: the very people on whose ʻāina and continued subjugation these giant telescopes depend. Ironic isn't it? How the TMT astronomers are all-seeing yet so blind at the same time—gazing into space and refusing to look at our people who surround their instruments of imperial power, saying "enough is enough." While their claim to Maunakea is totalizing, the knowledge of *our* universe is far from universal. Indeed, the settler technoscientific practice of looking at Maunakea reproduces the violence that conditions its possibility.

Conversely, our ʻike honors our kūpuna, our kuleana, and our ʻāina.[57] While some look to the stars and fetishize the white-domed structures that litter our sacred Mauna a Wākea, I see the returning first light of each day that gives life to all things. When we visit the Mauna, it is in ceremony and in struggle. And when our ceremonies inform our struggles, it is not because of the leverage it provides, but because it is how we have always related to place and space, to each other, and to our ea. This is the ʻike we honor by chanting at sunrise. And while astronomers describe *first light* as the inaugural moment a telescope first comes online, for Kānaka ʻŌiwi, the first light is that which shines first on our sacred Mauna. The light that first touches the red dirt of the summit as it emerges above the clouds and into the realm of Wākea, as it does every day, is a recurring first. In this way, our movements for life, land, and ea are also a recursive light that is gathered and greeted by our oli and is reflected in our struggle for Mauna a Wākea.

Indeed, Mauna a Wākea is part of a continuum of struggle whose genealogy stretches to the resistance of our kūpuna against two U.S. attempts to annex Hawaiʻi in 1893 and 1897—both of which were defeated by our ancestors' collective kūʻē. This struggle continues to compose Kānaka ʻŌiwi back into humanity. It gives life to our communities in times of trauma, grief, and mourning, constellating our rich history of struggle from Kalama to Kahoʻolawe, Mākua to Pōhakuloa, Kahuku to Waimānalo, Waiehu to Lāhainā, Naue to Kōloa, and many others.[58] Why does the lāhui lock arms to block bulldozers? The answers lie in these constellations of resistance to U.S. occupation and settler capitalism across Hawaiʻi, which can be observed through the fissures of power that structure our lives.

In this book I have explored some of the ways in which Kanaka indigeneity emerges through a genealogical relationality and ʻike kupuna that binds people to place, Kānaka to ʻāina. As told through our moʻolelo, mele, and moʻokūʻauhau, we understand these bonds are familial and ontological. While neither invented nor without contradiction, these connections animate the kuleana of so many Kānaka ʻŌiwi that it compels them to defend ancestral places even at risk of professional reprisal or personal injury. It is an unconditional, courageous, and unapologetic commitment to aloha ʻāina. As a mindful decision, it is also the reason Kānaka ʻŌiwi cannot stand by while our sacred places are desecrated in the name of some foreign, ostensibly "greater good." This aloha ʻāina also instills another commitment: that is, the responsibility to preserve the well-being of our lands and waters and our distinct Indigenous ways of being for the sake of future generations. In other words, our aloha 'āina continues to breathe life into our movements as a shared sacred pilina that links our lands and our people in familial relationality that gives meaning to our struggle. E kūpa'a mau i ke aloha 'āina.

NOTES

Introduction

Attributed to the kāula (prophet) Kapihe of Kona, Hawai'i, the mele in this epigraph is a wānana, or prophecy, composed during the reign of ali'i nui, Kalani'ōpu'u. Adapted from David Malo, *Hawaiian Antiquities (Mo'olelo Hawai'i)* (Honolulu: Bishop Museum Press, 1951), 115, the mele was routinely performed in protocol ceremonies at Pu'uhonua o Pu'uhuluhulu in recognition that it was a time of hulihia, or revolutionary change. Jonah La'akapu Lenchanko, *Kūkaniloko: A Hālau of Ākeaakamai of Kāne,* master's thesis (University of Hawai'i at Mānoa, 2015), 117.

1. Aloha 'āina may be translated as "love of the land," "love of one's country," and "patriot," but it has gained a variety of additional meanings and uses over the last fifty years of Kanaka 'Ōiwi activism. Idiomatically, some land and water protectors in the activist community, at least in Honolulu, with whom I have been close for decades, sometimes refer kia'i as "aloha 'āina." I discuss the concept in detail in chapters 4 and 5.

2. Kūpuna can be translated as "elders" (and "ancestors"). The thirty-nine kūpuna arrested on Maunakea include: Jim Albertini, Sharol Ku'ualoha Awai, Tomas Belsky, Roberta Bennett, Marie Alohalani Brown, Gene Kini Kaleilani Burke, Luana Busby-Neff, Richard Maele DeLeon, Alika Desha, Billy Freitas, Patricia Momi Greene, Desmon Haumea, Ho'oulualoha Flora Ho'okano, Deena Hurwitz, Keli'i "Skippy" Ioane, Mary Maxine Lani Kaha'ulelio, Ana Kaho'opi'i, Nohea Kalima, Kalikolehua Kanaele, Pualani Kanaka'ole Kanahele, Deborah Lee, Donna Keala Leong, Danny Li, Carmen Hulu Lindsey, Leilani Lindsey Kaapuni, Abel Lui, Liko Martin, Jimmy Naniole, Edleen Peleiholani, Renee Ku'uleinani Price, Hawley Reese, Ranette Puna Robinson, Loretta Ritte, Walter Ritte, Mililani B. Trask, Onaona Trask, John Keoni Turalde, and Noe Noe Wong-Wilson. See *Hawai'i State Foundation on Culture and the Arts,* "Report of the State Foundation on Culture and the Arts to the 2023 Legislature, S.C.R. 97, S.R. 87, H.R. 119 (2022)," December 29, 2022, 64–65; ku'ualoha ho'omanawanui, 2022, "He Pū'ao ke Kai, He Kai ka Pū'ao (Ocean as Womb, Womb as Ocean): Mana Wahine Aloha

'Āina Activism as Return, Revival, and Remembrance," *Amerasia Journal,* 48, no. 2: 107–23. https://doi.org/10.1080/00447471.2023.2241487; *Hawaii Tribune-Herald,* "DLNR Releases Names of Those Arrested on Maunakea," July 24, 2019, https://www.hawaiitribune-herald.com/2019/07/24/hawaii-news/dlnr-releases-names-of-those-arrested-on-maunakea/; Stand for Mauna a Wakea, "The day is finally here!" Facebook, July 4, 2022, https://www.facebook.com/standformauna awakea/.

3. An LRAD (long-range acoustic device) is "a speaker system and sound energy weapon developed in the early 2000s for use by the U.S. military" to cause pain in the human ear for crowd dispersal and suppression of civil disobedience protest and other demonstrations. Daphne Carr, "Understanding the LRAD, the 'Sound Cannon' Police Are Using at Protests, and How to Protect Yourself From It," *Pitchfork,* June 9, 2020, accessed January 5, 2023, https://pitchfork.com/the pitch/understanding-the-lrad-the-sound-cannon-police-are-using-at-protests-and-how-to-protect-yourself-from-it/.

4. "Kānaka Maoli" and "Kānaka Hawai'i" may be used interchangeably with "Kānaka 'Ōiwi," which is my preference when referring to the aboriginal people of the Hawaiian Islands throughout this book. I discuss this and the kaona (hidden, deeper meanings) of 'Ōiwi in chapter 5. I include a kahakō (or macron) when using the word as a noun, or it can be substituted with "people," and no kahakō when used as a descriptor or in the singular. While I mahalo my kumu and editors, particularly Noenoe Silva and Ākea Kahikina for advising me in my use of 'ōlelo Hawai'i, all mistakes are mine alone.

5. While it is reductive to call this a "wahine line," the phrase appears to be commonly used. However, there were nonbinary, transgender, genderqueer, and AFAB kia'i in addition to cis wāhine in both this and the June 24, 2015, direct actions that have been described as such.

6. Throughout the book I use "the state" with a lowercase "s" when referring conceptually and broadly to the settler capitalist state, the U.S. nation state, and the colonial state—which are not synonyms, but interlocking forms and practices that cohere in/as various ideological institutional apparatuses. Conversely, I use a capital "S" when referring specifically to the State of Hawai'i.

7. Kaleikoa Ka'eo pointed out this unprecedented aspect of the police operation in Mikey Inouye, "Like A Mighty Wave," YouTube, December 9, 2019, video, 15:19 mins. https://youtu.be/4J3ZCzHMMPQ?si=uAJ4P9F9vQSF0dhw. Regarding the TMT's price tag, a decade ago, when I was conducting interviews and beginning my research, it was said the TMT would cost $1.4 billion. As I write these words, various reports suggest it has increased to over $3 billion. The TIO would suggest delays caused by the protests are to blame. For more, see Dennis Overbye, "Good News and Bad News for Astronomers' Biggest Dream," *New York Times,* March 8, 2024, https://www.nytimes.com/2024/03/08/science/astronomy-extremely-large-telescope.html?searchResultPosition=1#; Richelle Boyd, "Henry Yang's Thirty Meter Telescope Meets New Managers and Long-time Protesters," *Santa Barbara Independent,* July 18, 2023, https://www.inde pendent.com/2023/07/18/henry-yangs-thirty-meter-telescope-meets-new

-managers-and-longtime-protesters/; Audrey McAvoy, "US Environmental Study Launched for Thirty Meter Telescope," *Phys.Org,* July 20, 2022, accessed July 21, 2023, https://phys.org/news/2022-07-environmental-meter-telescope.html#:~: text=The%20agency%20published%20a%20notice,%242.65%20billion%20 Thirty%20Meter%20Telescope.

8. K. Kamakaokaʻilima Long, in Mikey Inouye, "Like A Mighty Wave," YouTube, December 9, 2019, video, 15:19 mins. https://youtu.be/4J3ZCzHMMP Q?si=uAJ4P9F9vQSF0dhw.

9. Kiaʻi may be translated as "guard" or "caretaker," and has been adapted to signify Kanaka ʻŌiwi land defenders (also, "kiaʻi ʻāina"). I have heard both Native and non-Native activists suggest this term is nonspecific with regard to genealogy, although several of my interlocutors are adamant that only one who is Indigenous should be referred to as a "kiaʻi."

10. Throughout the book, I use "Mauna a Wākea" or "Mauna a Kea" in reference to the mountain that rises into the realm of "Sky Father," or Wākea, who is an ancestor-akua (god) and the Mauna's (mountain's) namesake, and may also be translated as "the expanse of the sky." As "Mauna a Wākea" signifies a constellation of meanings, it evokes Kanaka ontologies that are embraced by many in the Maunakea Movement. Though also spelled as "Mauna Kea," this spelling is often overdetermined by the simple descriptive translation as "white mountain." I have opted for "Maunakea" to align with common use among ʻōlelo Hawaiʻi scholars but make no evaluative claims about which is best, correct, or problematic. All choices are political.

11. See Liko Martin, "Hawaiʻi Loa, Kūlike Kākou," accessed January 25, 2023, https://www.likomartin.org/lyrics.

12. Ea may be translated as "breath," "life," and "sovereignty," signaling the expansive ways in which Kānaka ʻŌiwi relate to such ideas as freedom, autonomy, and social relations.

13. Leon Noʻeau Peralto, *Kokolo Mai ka Mole Uaua o ʻĪ: The Resilience & Resurgence of Aloha ʻĀina in Hāmākua Hikina, Hawaiʻi,* Ph.D. diss. (University of Hawaiʻi, 2018), 2. See also, Davianna P. McGregor, Nā Kuaʻāina: Living Hawaiian Culture (Honolulu: University of Hawaiʻi Press, 2007).

14. Indeed, these events invoked the imagery of "Kaulana Nā Pua," or "Famous are the Flowers," also known as "Mele ʻAi Pōhaku," or the "Stone-Eating Song," in which the lyrics opposing the 1893 invasion of our country and protesting the threat of annexation to the United States expressed the Royal Hawaiian Band members' refusal to sign an oath of loyalty to the treasonous conspirators who became enfranchised by the U.S. military occupation, even when their employment and livelihoods hung in the balance. For a fuller description of the kaona of this mele and its historical significance, see Kim Compoc, "Emergent Allies: Decolonizing Hawaiʻi From a Filipin@ Perspective," Ph.D. diss. (University of Hawaiʻi, 2017); Kevin Fellezs, "Nahenahe (Soft, Sweet, Melodious): Sounding Out Native Hawaiian Self-Determination," *Journal of the Society for American Music* 13, no. 4 (2019): 411–35.

15. Throughout the book, I mainly use "the Maunakea Movement" or simply "the Mauna Movement," particularly as I am often referencing events that

occurred prior to what would become popularly known as "the Kū Kiaʻi Mauna Movement" and "the Protect Mauna Kea Movement" following the collective actions of 2015.

16. For recent, essential texts on Mauna a Kea, Puʻuhonua o Puʻuhuluhulu, and Kanaka ʻŌiwi thought worlds more broadly, I recommend Noʻu Revilla and Bryan Kamaoli Kuwada, eds., *Biography: An Interdisciplinary Quarterly* 43, no. 3 (Honolulu: University of Hawaiʻi Press, 2020); *Everything Ancient Was Once New: Indigenous Persistence from Hawaiʻi to Kahiki* (Honolulu: University of Hawaiʻi Press, 2021); Candace Fujikane, *Mapping Abundance for a Planetary Future: Kanaka Maoli and Critical Settler Cartographies in Hawaiʻi* (Durham: Duke University Press, 2021); Jamaica Heolimeleikalani Osorio, *Remembering Our Intimacies: Moʻolelo, Aloha ʻĀina, and Ea* (Minneapolis: University of Minnesota Press, 2021).

17. "Mauna" can be translated as "mountain" and "mountainous region," and in the book I refer to "the Mauna" as many longtime kiaʻi do in reference to Maunakea.

18. Also known as the "Daniel K. Inouye Highway," it was named after the former Hawaiʻi State senator whose time in Congress was spent mainly brokering deals that would provide land to the U.S. military and constant revenue streams for the settler state.

19. With occasional exceptions, I use the "Oceania" instead of "Pacific" and "Turtle Island" instead of "North America" throughout the book.

20. With settler racial capitalism, I am adapting Quynh Nhu Le's "settler racial hegemonies," which Le argues "names the uneven incorporation of Indigenous and non-Native racialized communities' social, cultural, and political articulations into the imperatives of the settler state, thus reinscribing the territorial claims and telos of the settler nation." My use of the term is meant to signal how racial capitalism and settler colonialism in Hawaiʻi are co-constituted within U.S. imperial occupation and interlocking. See, Quynh Nhu Le, *Unsettled Solidarities: Asian and Indigenous Cross-Representations in the Américas* (Philadelphia: Temple University Press, 2019).

21. Sharon Holland and Tiz Giordano, "What Love Looks Like in Public," *Southern Cultures*, Sanctuary Issue 28, no. 2 (Summer 2022).

22. An "inseverable relationship." Mary Kawena Pukui, *ʻŌlelo Noʻeau: Hawaiian Proverbs & Poetical Sayings* (Honolulu: Bishop Museum Press, 1983).

23. ʻĀina may be translated as "land," but it also means so much more. While I theorize the concept in more detail throughout the book, I should note the term may also be translated by its constitutive parts as "that which feeds."

24. Jamaica Heolimeleikalani Osorio, *Remembering Our Intimacies: Moʻolelo, Aloha ʻĀina, and Ea* (Minneapolis: University of Minnesota Press, 2021)

25. Osorio, *Remembering Our Intimacies*, (2021).

26. This is why appropriations of aloha ʻāina by the University of Hawaiʻi and the State of Hawaiʻi—the two main proponents of the TMT—are so offensive to kiaʻi.

27. The ancestors in the realm of the gods (i.e., the deceased).

28. ʻIke kupuna may be translated as "ancestral knowledge." I also use ʻike Hawaiʻi elsewhere when referencing "Hawaiian knowledge," which I argue is both scientific and exceeds science as conceived in its European-derived ethnocentric and hegemonic sense.

29. Mary Kawena Pukui, ʻŌlelo Noʻeau: Hawaiian Proverbs & Poetical Sayings (Honolulu: Bishop Museum Press, 1983).

30. Contrary to pro-TMT accounts and the State's propaganda, the kiaʻi were only denying access to TMT construction crews. Access to all observatory personnel and State and County officials was never restricted. However, during this time, Kānaka ʻŌiwi would eventually be denied access beyond the State police checkpoint just mauka (up the mountain) from the kiaʻi, thereby violating State laws concerning Hawaiian Home Lands and judicial laws protecting Native hunting, gathering, and access rights for customary and traditional purposes.

31. Gina Starblanket, "Being Indigenous Feminists: Resurgences Against Contemporary Patriarchy," in Making Space for Indigenous Feminism, ed. Joyce Green (Halifax and Winnipeg: Fernwood Publishing, 2017), 33.

32. Glen Sean Coulthard, Red Skin, White Masks: Rejecting the Colonial Politics of Recognition (Minneapolis and London: University of Minnesota Press, 2014), 13.

33. Jodi A. Byrd, Alyosha Goldstein, Jodi Melamed, and Chandan Reddy, "Predatory Value: Economies of Dispossession and Disturbed Relationalities," in Social Text 36, no. 2 (135) (June 2018): 13.

34. Byrd et al., "Predatory Value," 14.

35. Byrd et al., "Predatory Value," 14.

36. Byrd et al., "Predatory Value," 14.

37. From July 14, 2019, through March 2020.

38. See, for example, the essays by Joy Enomoto and Māhealani Ahia, among many others, that were published in Noʻu Revilla and Bryan Kamaoli Kuwada, eds., Biography: An Interdisciplinary Quarterly 43, no. 3 (2020).

39. See Revilla and Kuwada, Biography.

40. Pua Case, "Ala Hulu Kūpuna," Mauna Kea Education and Awareness, https://www.mkea.info/kkulu-album-lyrics/2023/6/4/o-hnau-ka-mauna-a-kea.

41. Though never deployed, Ige had flown the troops to Hawaiʻi Island to stand by for orders, signaling his willingness to mobilize an even greater number of militarized police to quash dissent, all in the name of protecting the private interests of industrial astronomy and capital. The National Guard remained a threat and source of anxiety for several months.

42. See Revilla and Kuwada, Biography.

43. See Big Island Video News, "TMT Opponents Halt Groundbreaking Ceremony," YouTube, October 8, 2014, video, 20:59 mins., https://www.youtube.com/watch?v=SZ4Gt35hs-s.

44. Noelani Goodyear-Kaʻōpua, "Protectors of the Future, Not Protestors of the Past: Indigenous Pacific Activism and Mauna a Wākea," in South Atlantic Quarterly 116, no. 1 (January 2017): 190.

45. Goodyear-Kaʻōpua, "Protectors of the Future, Not Protestors of the Past," 190.

46. Jamaica Heolimeleikalani Osorio, *Remembering Our Intimacies: Moʻolelo, Aloha ʻĀina, and Ea* (Minneapolis: University of Minnesota Press, 2021) 160.

47. Haole is frequently used in reference to any white person but historically referred to any foreigner. See Mary Kawena Pukui and Samuel H. Elbert, *Hawaiian Language Dictionary*, rev. ed. (Honolulu: University of Hawaiʻi Press, 1986).

48. Though I use the single-word spelling, "Maunakea," members of the hui expressed in my interviews and our correspondences an understanding that the "correct spelling" is "Mauna Kea," arguing "if it was good enough for Queen Liliʻuokalani, it is good enough for us." And while UH Hilo, ʻImiloa Astronomy Center, and the TMT use the single-word spelling, Mauna Kea, Anaina Hou argues this was a politically subversive move to assert authority and undermine the Mauna Movement by appropriating ʻōlelo Hawaiʻi. Out of respect for their stance, I use the two-word spelling when referencing this group of longtime kiaʻi as "the Mauna Kea Hui." Kealoha Pisciotta, email message to author, September 13, 2012. After many conversations about this point with my interlocutors, however, including feedback from book reviewers, kiaʻi, and ʻōlelo Hawaiʻi readers, I understand *both are correct*. As discourse is fundamental to power and politics, spelling matters. Words matter. My use of "Maunakea" throughout the book is meant to align with the norms and preferences of a potential future ʻōlelo Hawaiʻi readership.

49. For a brilliant online collection on these and other Kānaka Maoli struggles, see University of Hawaiʻi at Mānoa Library, "Hawaiʻi – EA Hawaiian Activism Movements 1960–2010: ʻĀina," https://guides.library.manoa.hawaii.edu/c.php?g=1126349&p=8217306, accessed on April 16, 2025.

50. Qualities relayed from elders and celebrated in Leanne Betasamosake Simpson, *As We Have Always Done: Indigenous Freedom through Radical Resistance* (Minneapolis: University of Minnesota Press, 2017), 13.

1. In Ceremony

The first quote in this epigraph comes from a quote by Pualani Kanakaʻole Kanahele in my interview recorded on December 14, 2013.

1. Hōkūnohoaupuni may be translated as "ruling star." See Mary Kawena Pukui and Samuel H. Elbert, *Hawaiian Language Dictionary*, rev. ed. (Honolulu: University of Hawaiʻi Press, 1986), 76.

2. For a concise analysis of this hierarchy, see S. Shankar, "#WeStandWithMaunaKea, Anti-Colonialism, and the Limits of Academic Liberalism," January 23, 2019, accessed November 3, 2020, https://sshankar.net/tag/mauna-kea/.

3. Alexander Weheliye, *Habeas Viscus: Racializing Assemblages, Biopolitics, and Black Feminist Theories of the Human* (Durham, N.C.: Duke University Press, 2014).

4. As mentioned in the introduction and detailed later in this chapter, I use "Mauna a Wākea" throughout the book to refer to the mountain because this name acknowledges its rise into "the expanse of the sky," or the realm of "Sky Father"—that is, Wākea—who is an ancestor-akua and the Mauna's namesake. I prefer "Mauna a Wākea" as it signifies a constellation of meanings that evoke Kanaka ontologies and, as such, is counterhegemonic.

5. Peter Galison, "The Many Faces of Big Science," in *Big Science: The Growth of Large-Scale Research*, ed. Peter Galison and Bruce Hevly (Stanford, Calif.: Stanford University Press, 1992), 2. See also Michael Adas, *Machines as the Measure of Men: Science, Technology, and Ideologies of Western Dominance* (Ithaca, N.Y.: Cornell University Press, 1989).

6. See Elizabeth Fox Keller, "A Clash of Two Cultures," *Nature* 445, no. 8 (February 2007): 603; Michael Adas, *Machines as the Measure of Men: Science, Technology, and Ideologies of Western Dominance* (Ithaca and London: Cornell University Press, 1989).

7. Alexander Weheliye, *Habeas Viscus: Racializing Assemblages, Biopolitics, and Black Feminist Theories of the Human* (Durham, N.C.: Duke University Press 2014), 4.

8. Chanda Prescod-Weinstein, *The Disordered Cosmos: A Journey Into Dark Matter, Spacetime, & Dreams Deferred* (New York: Bold Type Books, 2021).

9. *Mauna Kea: Temple Under Siege*, directed by Joan Lander and Puhipau (Nāʻālehu, HI: Nā Maka o ka ʻĀina, 2005), ʻŌiwiTV, https://oiwi.tv/oiwitv/mauna -kea-temple-under-siege/.

10. Reed Flickinger, "A Measured Look at Gov. Abercrombie: Who Have We Got Here?" *West Hawaii Today*, April 1, 2012.

11. Among its many translations, pono refers to goodness, uprightness, morality, correct or proper procedure, excellence, true condition or nature, upright, virtuous, and fair. I tend to think of pono as indicating balance. See Mary Kawena Pukui and Samuel H. Elbert, *Hawaiian Language Dictionary*, rev. ed. (Honolulu: University of Hawaiʻi Press, 1986).

12. *Mauna Kea: Temple Under Siege*, directed by Joan Lander and Puhipau (Nāʻālehu, HI: Nā Maka o ka ʻĀina, 2005), ʻŌiwiTV, https://oiwi.tv/oiwitv/mauna -kea-temple-under-siege/.

13. The Hawaiian Home Lands or "homesteads" were created in the 1920 Hawaiian Homes Commission Act and are designated portions of the State of Hawaiʻi's public lands set aside by the U.S. government to be granted as allotments for eligible Kānaka ʻŌiwi according to a 50 percent blood quantum rule.

14. A kumu hula is a master instructor of Hawaiian chant, song, and dance and carrier of traditional Indigenous knowledge about places, plants, animals, ancestors, and others.

15. For information about these plants see *Wehewehe Wikiwiki*, https:// hilo.hawaii.edu/wehe/.

16. Aloha ʻāina can be translated as "love for the land," or love for one's country and homeland.

17. S. M. Kamakau, "*Instructions in Ancient Astronomy as Taught by Kanea-kahoowaha, One of the Counselors of Kamehameha I*," trans. from the *Nupepa Kuokoa*, August 5, 1865, for the Maile Wreath by W. D. Alexander, in Hawaiian Almanac and Annual for 1891 (Honolulu: Black & Auld, Printers, 1891), 142–43; Maud W. Makemson, "Hawaiian Astronomical Concepts II," in *American Anthropologist, New Series* 41, no. 4 (October–December, 1939); Rubellite K. Johnson, *The Kumulipo Mind: A Global Heritage in the Polynesian Creation Myth* (Honolulu: Rubellite K. Johnson, 2000); Michael E. Chauvin, *Useful and Conceptual Astronomy in Ancient Hawaii* (Honolulu: Mauna Kea Books, 2000); Martha Warren Beckwith, ed. and trans., *The Kumulipo: A Hawaiian Creation Chant* (Honolulu: University of Hawai'i Press, 1951).

18. This section is based on periodic informal interviews throughout the day with Coleman on June 6, 2013.

19. This was the first of two interviews I conducted with Dr. Coleman, my analysis of the second appears in chapter 7.

20. Paul Coleman, interview by author, May 8, 2013, Mānoa, digital recording.

21. Paul Coleman, interview.

22. This is paraphrased.

23. Jeff Corntassel, "Re-envisioning Resurgence: Indigenous Pathways to Decolonization and Sustainable Self-determination," in *Decolonization: Indigeneity, Education & Society* 1, no. 1 (2012): 86–101.

24. This translation was suggested by Noenoe Silva over Alexander's: "the way to the navel of Wākea." Noenoe Silva, personal communication; Kamakau, "*Instructions in Ancient Astronomy as Taught by Kaneakahoowaha*," 142–43.

25. Kamakau, "*Instructions in Ancient Astronomy as Taught by Kaneaka-hoowaha*," 142–43; Maud W. Makemson, "Hawaiian Astronomical Concepts II," in *American Anthropologist* 41, no. 4 (October–December, 1939), 589–96.

26. I elaborate on the meanings associated with the naming of Mauna a Wākea in chapter 5.

27. Katrina-Ann R. Kapā'anaokalāokeola Nākoa Oliveira, *Ancestral Places: Understanding Kanaka Geographies* (Corvalis: Oregon State University, 2014), 48–54.

28. Oliveira, *Ancestral Places*, 48.

29. Oliveira, *Ancestral Places*, 48.

30. Oliveira, *Ancestral Places*, 50–51, n. 24, 129. Pukui and Elbert, *Hawaiian Dictionary*, 170.

31. I elaborate on this ko'ihonua in chapter 5.

32. Nā Maka o ka 'Āina, *Temple Under Siege*.

33. Kaona also refers to a word's multiple or "hidden meanings." See Mary Kawena Pukui and Samuel H. Elbert, *Hawaiian Language Dictionary*, rev. ed. (Honolulu: University of Hawai'i Press, 1986), 130. Lilikalā Kame'eleihiwa translates kaona as "deeper meaning." Lilikalā Kame'eleihiwa, *Native Land and Foreign Desires: Pehea Lā E Pono Ai?* (Honolulu: Bishop Museum Press, 1992), 79. For a brilliant study of the concept of kaona, see Brandy Nālani McDougall, *Finding*

Meaning: Kaona and Contemporary Hawaiian Literature, (Tucson: University of Arizona Press, 2016).

34. Kīhei and Māpuana de Silva, "E Hoʻi ka Nani i Mānā," available at Kaʻiwakīloumoku: Pacific Indigenous Institute, https://kaiwakiloumoku.ksbe .edu/article/mele-e-hoi-ka-nani-i-mana (accessed on April 10, 2025); Puakea Nogelmeier, *He Lei no ʻEmalani: Chants for Queen Emma Kaleleonalani* (Honolulu: Bishop Museum Press and Queen Emma Foundation, 2001); Leon Noʻeau Peralto, "Portrait. Mauna a Wākea: Hānau ka Mauna, The Piko of Our Ea," in Noelani Goodyear-Kaʻōpua, Ikaika Hussey, and Erin Kahunawaikaʻala Wright, eds., *A Nation Rising: Hawaiian Movements for Life, Land, and Sovereignty* (Durham, N.C., and London: Duke University Press, 2014).

35. In traditional Hawaiian geographies, mokupuni (islands) are divided first into moku (larger districts) then into kalana (smaller districts), and finally into the subdistricts called ahupuaʻa. Ahupuaʻa may be divided further into areas called ʻili. See Oliveira, *Ancestral Places*. For analysis of traditional moku divisions and other ʻŌiwi geographies, see B. Kamanamaikalani Beamer, "Na wai ka mana? ʻŌiwi Agency and European Imperialism in the Hawaiian Kingdom" (Ph.D. diss., University of Hawaiʻi at Mānoa, 2008).

36. Kealoha Pisciotta, email message to author, September 13, 2012.

37. Citing oral comments recorded by Kepā Maly, given by panel participants Emma Kauhi, Leinaʻala Teves, Pua Kanahele, and Larry Kimura at UH Hilo on December 1, 1998, Maly explains, "Mauna Kea and Mauna Loa are both considered to be kupuna; the first born, and are held in high esteem." See Kepā Maly, *Mauna Kea Science Reserve and Hale Pōhaku Complex Development Plan Update: Oral History and Consultation Study, and Archival Literature Research: Ahupuaʻa of—Kaʻohe (Hāmākua District) and Humuʻula (Hilo District), Island of Hawaiʻi, A Report Prepared for Group 70 International*, appendix B, B-14 (Honolulu: Kumu Pono Associates, 1999).

38. E. Kalani Flores, TMT contested case hearing, oral testimony. See Board of Natural Resources, State of Hawaiʻi, *In Re Petitions requesting a Contested Case Hearing Re Conservation District Use Permit (CDUP) HA-3568 for the Thirty Meter Telescope at the Mauna Kea District, Island of Hawaiʻi, TML (3) 4-4-015:009*, DLNR No. HA-11–05, Vol. VI, September 26, 2011, 22.

39. Aunty Pualani Kanakaʻole Kanahele framed her understanding of the material mystery of the summit on the body in this way in our interview. December 14, 2013, Hilo, digital recording.

40. For a brilliant discussion on Oceanic mobilities of "Indigenous Moanan peoples," thoughtworlds, and tempospatial conceptions of indigeneity and social harmony marked by tā (time) and vā (space), see Tēvita O. Kaʻili, *Marking Indigeneity: The Tongan Art of Sociospatial Relations* (Tucson: University of Arizona Press, 2017).

41. Pukui and Elbert, *Hawaiian Dictionary*.

42. See Sam Low, *Hawaiki Rising: Hōkūleʻa, Nainoa Thompson, and the Hawaiian Renaissance* (Honolulu: University of Hawaiʻi Press, 2019); E. S. Craighill Handy and Mary Kawena Pukui, *The Polynesian Family System in Kaʻū*,

Hawai'i (Honolulu: Mutual Publishing, 1999); Moke Manu, *Hawaiian Fishing Traditions* (Honolulu: Noio/Kalamakū Press, 2006).

43. Brandy Nālani McDougall, *Finding Meaning: Kaona and Contemporary Hawaiian Literature* (Tucson: University of Arizona Press, 2016), 52–85.

44. McDougall, *Finding Meaning*, 83.

45. State of Hawai'i Department of Land and Natural Resources.

46. Kūkahau'ula was translated as "the pink tinted snow god," by Emma Ahu'ena Taylor (Ahu'ena), "a Hawaiian historian of royal lineage" who, in 1931 published an account that was cited by Kepā Maly and Onaona Maly that describes "the sacred nature of Poli'ahu" and "the various attributes of Waiau, Lilinoe, and Kūkahau'ula" (53). See Ahu'ena Taylor in *Paradise of the Pacific*, July 1931 as cited in Kepā Maly and Onaona Maly, *"Mauna Kea-Ka Piko Kaulana o ka 'Āina" (Mauna Kea-The Famous Summit of the Land): A Collection of Native Traditions, Historical Accounts, and Oral History Interviews for: Mauna Kea, the Lands of Ka'ohe, Humu'ula and the 'Āina Mauna on the Island of Hawai'i*, Prepared for the Office of Mauna Kea Management (Hilo: University of Hawaii-Hilo, 2005), 53; Fred Stone told me of a type of red algae that grows on the snow of Mauna Kea, which may also have been one of the sources for this name. Personal email, September 11, 2014.

47. Kepā Maly and Onaona Maly, *"Mauna Kea-Ka Piko Kaulana o ka 'Āina,"* vi.

48. Kepā Maly and Onaona Maly, *"Mauna Kea-Ka Piko Kaulana o ka 'Āina,"* 53.

49. Kepā Maly and Onaona Maly, *"Mauna Kea-Ka Piko Kaulana o ka 'Āina,"* vi.

50. "E Ala Ē" is an oli composed by the Edith Kanaka'ole Foundation.

51. When I refer to the protests at Hale Pōhaku, I am referring to the 2015 encampment and direct actions that occurred amidst the various facilities at 9,000 ft. and the crosswalk across from the Onizuka Visitor Center.

52. See Noenoe Silva, Aloha Betrayed: *Native Hawaiian Resistance to American Colonialism* (Durham, N.C.: Duke University Press, 2014).

53. Ea can be translated as life, breath, sovereignty, and independence.

54. Kristin Kahaloa in Michelle Latimer, dir. *Rise*, "Hawaiian Sovereignty," S1E6, *Viceland* (Vice Productions, 2017).

55. Interpellation is an Althusserian concept that refers to the experience of being addressed by "state apparatuses," or institutions, in ways that presuppose a particular identification of the one being "hailed," regardless of the accuracy of that identity. The moment of being "hailed" is the moment of interpellation. Althusser theorizes that ideologies become internalized when the call is answered. Kanaka have a rich history of refusing settler interpellation. See Louis Althusser, "Ideology and Ideological State Apparatuses (Notes toward an Investigation)," in *Lenin and Philosophy and Other Essays*, trans. B. Brewster (New York and London: Monthly Review Press, 1971), 127–86.

56. Pualani Case, interview by author, September 24, 2012, Waimea, digital recording.

57. Case, interview.

58. Case, interview.

2. Neoliberal Environmentalities and Monuments to Science

1. The Auditor of the Sate of Hawaiʻi, *Audit of the Management of Mauna Kea and the Mauna Kea Science Reserve: A Report to the Governor and the Legislature of the State of Hawaiʻi*, Report No. 98–6, February 1998.

2. Haw. Rev. Stat. Subsection 183C-1.

3. Robert Fletcher, "Neoliberal Environmentality: Towards a Poststructuralist Political Ecology of the Conservation Debate," in *Conservation and Society* 8, no. 3 (2010): 173.

4. I use biopower in reference to the capacity of a hegemonic bloc to let specific bodies live and others die, particularly through "the reproduction of life in ways that allow political crises to be cast as conditions of specific bodies and their competence at maintaining health or other conditions of social belonging." See Lauren Berlant, "Slow Death (Obesity, Sovereignty, Lateral Agency)," *Critical Inquiry* 33, no. 4 (Summer 2007): 765.

5. Fletcher, "Neoliberal Environmentality," 175.

6. Lauren Berlant, "Slow Death," 2007, 754.

7. While I adopt Haunani-Kay Trask's framing of Hawaiʻi as a settler colony of the United States, later in this chapter I acknowledge how this conceptualization is useful more as an analytic of sociopolitical and economic realities than of Hawaiʻi's legal status according to international law or the "official" record according to sanctioned U.S. histories.

8. "Land division usually extending from the uplands to the sea, so called because the boundary was marked by a heap (ahu) of stones surmounted by an image of a pig (puaʻa), or because a pig or other tribute was laid on the altar as tax to the chief." See Mary Kawena Pukui and Samuel H. Elbert, *Hawaiian Language Dictionary*, rev. ed. (Honolulu: University of Hawaiʻi Press, 1986), 9.

9. Mokuoloko can be translated as district or "interior island." See Kepā Maly, *Mauna Kea Science Reserve and Hale Pōhaku Complex Development Plan Update: Oral History and Consultation Study, and Archival Literature Research: Ahupuaʻa of—Kaʻohe (Hāmākua District) and Humuʻula (Hilo District), Island of Hawaiʻi (various TMK)* (Hilo: Kumu Pono Associates, 1999), 7.

10. Although commonly written as "Waiau," Hawaiian Language oral histories show the name of the lake was traditionally pronounced with the ʻokina, or glottal stop: "Waiʻau." See Maly, *Mauna Kea Science Reserve*, A-2.

11. Jesse A. Eiben and Daniel Rubinoff, "Wekiu Bug," accessed October 18, 2012, http://www.ctahr.hawaii.edu/rubinoffd/rubinoff_lab/projects/wekiu_bug/ wekiu%20bug.htm. I learned a great deal about the politics of university-funded research on Maunakea from horticulturalist Deborah Ward and Dr. Fred Stone. Ward is a former UH Department of Natural Resources and Environmental Management faculty member and longtime environmental educator. The late Dr. Stone was an entomologist who, along with Frank Howarth, first studied the wēkiu and the impacts of telescope construction on population and habitat.

According to Stone, when the university assumed strict control over wēkiu habitat monitoring, a 2005 NASA Keck Outrigger Project EIS was so severely edited that the research data and recommendations of these two prominent entomologists had arbitrarily been removed, indicating what was described as the university's "misrepresentation, deceit, and/or fraud." Since the university's devaluation of Stone and Howarth's findings, it remains questionable to this day whether the wēkiu will receive federal protections. Fred Stone and Deborah Ward, interview by author, June 8, 2013, ʻŌlaʻa, digital recording.

12. *Mauna Kea Comprehensive Management Plan, UH Management Areas,* January 2009, 3–1.

13. The Mauna Kea Access Road cuts through portions of the lands within the jurisdiction of the Department of Hawaiian Homelands, but for which DHHL has never received consultation or compensation. See the Royal Order of Kamehameha I, Moku O Mamalahoa-Heiau O Helu ʻElua and Mauna Kea Anaina Hou, *Mauna Kea–The Temple: Protecting the Sacred Resource, A Report Submitted to the Department of Land and Natural Resources. Used by permission of Mauna Kea Anaina Hou* (2001), 12.

14. In 1998, 2,033 acres were removed and placed under the Mauna Kea Ica Age Natural Area Reserve (NAR). The original lease granted the University 13,321 acres. See Pacific Consulting Services, Inc. *The Draft Environmental Assessment for the Mauna Kea Comprehensive Management Plan.* Prepared for University of Hawaiʻi, 2009, 1–1.

15. The Royal Order of Kamehameha I, et al., 12

16. Sierra Club member and longtime Hawaiʻi conservationist Nelson Ho jokingly described the dormitories as "Mauna Kea's Swiss chalet," noting a common critique of the incessant growth on the Mauna over the last four decades. Nelson Ho, interview by author, September 24, 2012, Hilo, digital recording.

17. University of Hawaiʻi at Hilo, *Final Environmental Impact Statement, Vol. 1: Thirty Meter Telescope Project, Island of Hawaiʻi* (May 8, 2010), 3–142.

18. The Keck Observatory is considered a single "observatory," although it consists of the two telescopes housed in the two largest domes on what was the highest peak of the summit (Puʻu Hauʻoki) before it was leveled and reduced in height during construction in the 1990s.

19. The Very Large Baseline Array (VLBA) is technically not an "observatory" but considered single antenna. See University of Hawaiʻi at Hilo, *Final Environmental Impact Statement,* 2–6.

20. Under the current management plan, UH commits "to no more than nine facilities on Maunakea" by 2033. See "Maunakea: 1st Telescope Decommissioning Complete," *University of Hawaiʻi at Mānoa News,* June 2, 2024; "Decommissioning of Caltech Submillimeter Observatory on Mauna Kea Complete," *Big Island Now,* July 2, 2024; Kay Thomas, "After 50 Years, A Telescope at the Top of Mauna Kea Will Be Removed," *Hawaii News Now,* June 28, 2025.

21. See, for example, the University of Hawaiʻi's closing arguments in the TMT contested case hearings: State of Hawaiʻi, Board of Natural Resources, Transcript of Closing Arguments, Prepared by McManus Court Reporters, *In Re*

Petitions requesting a Contested Case Hearing Re Conservation District Use Permit (CDUP) HA-3568 for the Thirty Meter Telescope at the Mauna Kea District, Island of Hawai'i, TML (3) 4-4-015:009, DLNR No. HA-11–05, Vol. VII, September 30, 2011, 20.

22. Paul Coleman, interview by author, May 8, 2013, Mānoa, digital recording.

23. For detailed scholarship on the legal status of Hawai'i and its many other implications today, see Sydney Lehua Iaukea, "E Pa'a 'Oukou: Holding And Remembering Hawaiian Understandings of Place and Politics," (Ph.D. diss., University of Hawai'i at Mānoa, 2008); B. Kamanamaikalani Beamer, "Na wai ka mana? 'Ōiwi Agency and European Imperialism in the Hawaiian Kingdom," (Ph.D. diss., University of Hawai'i at Mānoa, 2008); Stephen Kūhiō Vogeler, "'For Your Freedom and Ours': The Prolonged Occupations of Hawai'i and the Baltic States," (Ph.D. diss., University of Hawai'i at Mānoa, 2009); Peter Kalawai'a Moore, "He Hawai'i Kākou: Conflicts and Continuities of History, Culture and Identity in Hawai'i." (Ph.D. diss., University of Hawai'i at Mānoa, 2010); Donovan Preza, "The Empirical Writes Back: Re-Examining Hawaiian Dispossession Resulting from the Māhele of 1848," (MA thesis, University of Hawai'i at Mānoa, 2010); and William Daniel Kaipo Kauai, "The Color of Nationality: Continuities and Discontinuities of Citizenship in Hawai'i" (Ph.D. diss., University of Hawai'i at Mānoa, 2014).

24. In the nineteenth century, the nation-state of Hawai'i, what many today call "the Hawaiian kingdom," was known as Kō Hawai'i Pae 'Āina. In this and later chapters, I use capital letters, as this was the pronoun form. I also use the shortened "Hawai'i," in reference to the nation-state of Hawai'i.

25. See William Daniel Kaipo Kauai, "The Color of Nationality: Continuities and Discontinuities of Citizenship in Hawai'i" (Ph.D. diss., University of Hawai'i at Mānoa, 2014).

26. William Daniel Kaipo Kauai, interview by author, June 2022.

27. For more on the details of the Queen's intention to promulgate and eventual cancellation of a new constitution demanded by maka'āinana who had been politically disenfranchised by the 1887 Bayonet Constitution that was forced upon the previous King Kalākaua at gunpoint, see Jonathan Osorio, *Dismembering Lāhui: A History of the Hawaiian Nation to 1887* (Honolulu: University of Hawai'i Press, 2002).

28. See David Keanu Sai, "The American Occupation of the Hawaiian Kingdom: Beginning the Transition from Occupied to Restored State" (Ph.D. diss., University of Hawai'i at Mānoa, 2008); See also, David Keanu Sai, "A Slippery Path towards Hawaiian Indigeneity: An Analysis and Comparison between Hawaiian State Sovereignty and Hawaiian Indigeneity and Its Use and Practice in Hawai'i Today," *Law and Social Challenges* (University of San Francisco School of Law) 10 (Fall 2008): 68–133.

29. Haunani-Kay Trask, *From a Native Daughter: Colonialism & Sovereignty in Hawai'i* (Monroe, Maine: Common Courage Press, 1993).

30. As mentioned briefly in the introduction and chapter 1, *aloha 'āina* may be translated also as "love of the land and of one's country." Mary Kawena Pukui

and Samuel H. Elbert, *Hawaiian Language Dictionary,* rev. ed. (Honolulu: University of Hawai'i Press, 1986).

31. See Noenoe K. Silva, *Aloha Betrayed: Native Hawaiian Resistance to American Colonialism* (Durham, N.C.: Duke University Press, 2014).

32. Requiring in each house a mere two-thirds majority vote, passage of this congressional act exemplifies early efforts to rationalize imperial conquest through settler colonial law. See "Newlands Resolution," U.S. Congress, House, *Joint Resolution to Provide Annexing the Hawaiian Islands to the United States (1898),* HR 259, 55th Congress, 2nd session, July 7, 1898. Subsequent congressional acts including the so-called Organic Act of the Territory of Hawaii and the Hawaii Statehood, or Admission Act, cited House Joint Resolution 259 as "the joint resolution of annexation," thereby inventing new legal categories through passive and recursive citation of false legal events to conjure an otherwise impossible U.S. title over Hawaiian kingdom territories.

33. U.S. Congress, Senate Resolution 19, *A Joint Resolution to Acknowledge the 100th Anniversary of the January 17, 1893 Overthrow of the Kingdom of Hawaii, and to Offer an Apology to Native Hawaiians on Behalf of the United States for the Overthrow of the Kingdom of Hawaii,* Public Law 103–150, S.J. Res. 19, 103d Congress, November 23, 1993.

34. By law, Hawai'i's aboriginal tenants, the maka'āinana, held one-third "vested rights" in all lands in perpetuity, regardless of ownership. While the details of this legal provision of the 1848 Māhele are not the subject of this study and require greater attention, the groundbreaking scholarship of Donovan Preza examines this history. See Donovan C. Preza, "The Empirical Writes Back: Re-Examining Hawaiian Dispossession Resulting from the Māhele of 1848" (Ph.D. diss., University of Hawai'i, 2010).

35. See Jon M. Van Dyke, *Who Owns the Crown Lands of Hawai'i?* (Honolulu: University of Hawai'i Press, 2008); Beamer, "'Ōiwi Agency," (2008); Sai, "The American Occupation of the Hawaiian Kingdom," (2008).

36. One reader of this manuscript advised me to hold the State and university accountable for their practice of spelling words in 'ōlelo Hawai'i incorrectly. While I have added the 'okina to "Hawai'i," corrections did not appear in official spellings by either the State or University of Hawai'i until the 1990s. In this sentence I use their original spelling purposefully.

37. The distinction of "native" vs. "Native" signals the racializing colonial logic of elimination by which Kanaka 'Ōiwi eligibility for Hawaiian Home Lands allotments could be reduced through the arbitrary and pernicious invention of blood quantum. Those of "50% blood quantum" or greater (i.e., lowercase *n* "native Hawaiians") would ostensibly qualify for benefits under the Hawaiian Homes Commission Act of 1920, while those below that amount (i.e., capital *N*-"Native Hawaiians") would be ineligible. See J. Kēhaulani Kauanui, *Hawaiian Blood: Colonialism and the Politics of Sovereignty and Indigeneity* (Durham and London: Duke University Press, 2008).

38. Kauanui, *Hawaiian Blood.*

39. See endnote entry 27.

40. While some aspects of the aliʻi system were similar to European monarchies, they were not analogues, meaning Hawaiʻi was never an absolute monarchy. The mōʻī, including Kamehameha I, could never act alone but instead acted in consultation with a number of advisors, including what might be called a council—and many powerful aliʻi, which included powerful women and various kahuna—along with his closest advisors, who were high-ranking aliʻi. Also, starting with Kamehameha II and ending with Kamehameha V, every mōʻī had a Kuhina Nui without whose approval nothing got enacted into law or made policy. With two exceptions, all the Kuhina Nui were women. Noenoe K. Silva, personal communication, April 12, 2022.

41. Barry Parker, *Stairway to the Stars: The Story of the World's Largest Observatory* (New York and London: Plenum Press, 1994).

42. Haleakalā was home to the Haleakalā High Altitude Observatory site since 1961; its first solar telescope completed in 1962 and dedicated in 1964. See *UH Institute for Astronomy*, accessed January 6, 2021, https://about.ifa.hawaii .edu/facility/haleakala/.

43. Hawaiʻi Island Chamber of Commerce executive secretary and friend, Howard Ellis, head of a Mauna Loa weather station.

44. Alika Herring was also from the University of Arizona and would stay on the summit for several weeks performing the first tests from the telescope building the data to prove that Maunakea's atmospheric transparency made it a superior site. See Parker, *Stairway to the Stars*, 29.

45. Michael J. West, *The Gentle Rain of Starlight: The Story of Astronomy on Mauna Kea* (Waipahu, Hawaiʻi: Island Heritage Publishing), 2005.

46. A letter to Kuiper by assistant, Alika Herring, as quoted in Parker, *Stairway to the Stars*, 35–38.

47. Parker, *Stairway to the Stars*, 35.

48. Hale Pōhaku was named after the stone cabins that were built in the 1930s by the Civilian Conservation Corps working on a forest reserve boundary fence. See Leigh Fletcher, "Hale Pohaku, the Stone House," *Planetary Wanderings* (blog), Blogspot, February 7, 2013, accessed January 6, 2022, https://planetary weather.blogspot.com/2013/02/hale-pohaku-stone-house.html.

49. The proposed Keck Outrigger Telescopes project, which consisted of four smaller telescopes designed to act in unison and described as a single telescope, was effectively stopped in 2006 when NASA withdrew its funding. Although accounts of the project's demise are conflicting, without the opposition, there would today be four more Keck telescopes on the Mauna today.

50. Lea Hong, phone interview by author, March 12, 2014, digital recording. See also, State of Hawaiʻi, Department of Land and Natural Resources, Office of Conservation and Coastal Lands, https://dlnr.hawaii.gov/occl/coastal-lands -program/.

51. Sierra Club comments on the proposed TMT, *Draft Environmental Impact Statement,* July 7, 2009, 101.

52. The Auditor of the Sate of Hawaiʻi, *Audit of the Management of Mauna Kea and the Mauna Kea Science Reserve: A Report to the Governor and the Legislature of the State of Hawaiʻi,* Report No. 98–6, February 1998, 4.

53. See Tiffany Hervey, "Mauna Kea–Sacred Summit or Cash Cow? Controversy over the Thirty Meter Telescope," *Honolulu Weekly,* September 14, 2011, *KAHEA: The Hawaiian-Environmental Alliance,* http://kahea.org/press-room/press-clips/mauna-kea2013sacred-summit-or-cash-cow-controversy-over-the-thirty-meter-telescope.

54. Brian J. Cantwell, "Mauna Kea's Observatories: Big Science at the top of Hawaii," *Seattle Times,* September 14, 2012; See also, Association of Universities for Research in Astronomy (AURA), "Calculation of Time on Keck," National Optical Astronomical Observatory, accessed November 15, 2012, http://ast.noao.edu/system/tsip/more-info/time-calc-keck; I learned through my interviews with UH IfA representatives that the monies accrued through observation rents return to cover regular expenses to keep each telescope operational, though I have been unable to verify this.

55. *Honolulu Weekly,* September 14, 2011.

56. The amount of viewing time varies from sublease to sublease.

57. Stephanie Nagata, interview by author, June 13, 2013, Makiki, digital recording.

58. Rob Perez, "Legal Fees Spike at UH," *Honolulu Star-Advertiser,* June 12, 2011.

59. Nanea Kalani, "Civil Beat Shares University of Hawaii Salaries," *Honolulu Civil Beat,* September 1, 2010.

60. *Honolulu Star-Advertiser,* June 12, 2011.

61. *Honolulu Star-Advertiser,* June 12, 2011.

62. See "8 Acres? 18 Stories? TMT? A'ole," *KAHEA: The Hawaiian-Environmental Alliance* (blog), February 18, 2011, accessed April 6, 2012, http://kahea.org/blog/8-acre-18-story-development-in-mauna-kea-conservation-district-seeks-permit.

63. "Thirty Meter Telescope Hawai'i Environmental Impact Statement Process," *TMT,* accessed April 6, 2012, http://www.tmt-hawaiieis.org/#1.

64. "The European Extremely Large Telescope: The World's Biggest Eye on the Sky," *European Southern Observatory,* accessed October 2, 2012, http://www.eso.org/public/teles-instr/e-elt.html. The ELT is under construction atop Cerro Armazones. Its name was shortened from the "European Extremely Large Telescope" or "E-ELT" to "ELT" in 2017. In 2021, developers announced the TMT would be delayed two years "to heal (its) relationship with the community and to recover from the delays caused by the pandemic," noting also the challenge of new regulatory obstacles enacted as a result of the 2019 Pu'uhuluhulu actions. See Timothy Hurley, "Construction of Thirty Meter Telescope Delayed at Least 2 Years," *Honolulu Star-Advertiser,* October 11, 2021.

65. Participants in the many legal proceedings varied, but the bulk of my interview research was with these folks.

66. *KAHEA: The Hawaiian-Environmental Alliance* (blog), "What Is a Contested Case Hearing?" April 5, 2011, http://kahea.org/blog/what-is-a-contested-case-hearing.

67. Supreme Court of the State of Hawai'i, SCAP-14–0000873, "Appeal from the Circuit Court of the Third Circuit" (CAAP-13–0000873; CIV. No. 13-1-0349) December 2, 2015, 5–6.

68. Supreme Court of the State of Hawai'i, SCOT-17–0000777, SCOT-17–00000811, and SCOT-17–0000812, "Appeal from the Board of Land and Natural Resources (BLNR-CC-16–002 (Agency Appeal))," "Amended Dissenting Opinion by Wilson, J." November 30, 2018.

69. Identified in the TMT Environmental Impact Statement, the UH Comprehensive Management Plan, and the Conservation District Use Application, a list of "mitigation measures" was presented as "evidence" to argue the permit is compliant with state law.

70. The Auditor of the Sate of Hawai'i, *Audit of the Management of Mauna Kea and the Mauna Kea Science Reserve: A Report to the Governor and the Legislature of the State of Hawai'i,* Report No. 98–6, February 1998; See also, The Auditor, State of Hawai'i, *Follow-Up Audit of the Management of Mauna Kea and the Mauna Kea Science Reserve, A Report to the Governor and the Legislature of the State of Hawai'i,* Report No. 05–13, December 2005.

71. Supreme Court of the State of Hawai'i, SCOT-17–0000777, SCOT-17–00000811, and SCOT-17–0000812, "Appeal from the Board of Land and Natural Resources (BLNR-CC-16–002 (Agency Appeal))," "Opinion of the Court by McKenna, J., in which Pollack, J., Joins Except as to Part V.C.1," October 30, 2018.

72. Supreme Court of the State of Hawai'i, SCOT-17–0000777, SCOT-17–00000811, and SCOT-17–0000812, "Appeal from the Board of Land and Natural Resources (BLNR-CC-16–002 (Agency Appeal))," "Amended Dissenting Opinion by Wilson, J." November 30, 2018, 3.

73. Supreme Court of the State of Hawai'i, SCOT-17–0000777, SCOT-17–00000811, and SCOT-17–0000812, "Appeal from the Board of Land and Natural Resources (BLNR-CC-16–002 (Agency Appeal))," "Amended Dissenting Opinion by Wilson, J." November 30, 2018, 24.

74. Mo'o wahine may be translated as woman reptile/dragon and is a guardian spirit.

75. A kapa worn over a woman's shoulder and under the opposite arm, covering her torso.

76. B. Pualani Case, "Written Direct Testimony of B. Pualani Case," Petitioners' exhibit, G-02, WDT submitted to DLNR, (2011); document emailed to the author and used by permission of B. Pualani Case.

77. State of Hawai'i, Board of Land and Natural Resources, "Findings of Fact, Conclusions of Law, and Decision and Order; Certificate of Service," *In Re Petitions requesting a Contested Case Hearing Re Conservation District Use Permit (CDUP) HA-3568 for the Thirty Meter Telescope at the Mauna Kea District, Island of Hawai'i, TML (3) 4-4-015:009,* DLNR No. HA-11–05, Exhibit A-318, February 23, 2011.

78. As quoted in, State of Hawai'i, Board of Land and Natural Resources, Hearing Officer's Report, DLNR File No. HA-11–05, November 30, 2012, 8.

79. State of Hawai'i, Board of Land and Natural Resources, Hearing Officer's Report, DLNR File No. HA-11–05, November 30, 2012, 9.

80. State of Hawai'i, Board of Land and Natural Resources, Hearing Officer's Report, DLNR File No. HA-11–05, November 30, 2012, 6.

81. State of Hawai'i, Board of Land and Natural Resources, Hearing Officer's Report, DLNR File No. HA-11–05, November 30, 2012, 6.

82. "Official Says Spirit Can't Testify," *Hawaii Tribune-Herald,* June 20, 2011.

83. "A Spirited Defense," *Honolulu Magazine,* January 4, 2012, http://www.honolulumagazine.com/Honolulu-Magazine/January-2012/Sour-Poi-Awards-2012/index.php?cparticle=2&siarticle=1#.U6pd5I1dV_0.

3. Multicultural Settler Colonialism

1. Governor Neil Abercrombie, "State of the State Address," Hawai'i State Capitol, Honolulu, January 21, 2014, http://governor.hawaii.gov/blog/2014-state-of-the-state-address/.

2. "UH Update: Monthly Report from President M.R.C. Greenwood, UH System News," March 2011, *The University of Hawai'i System,* http://www.hawaii.edu/offices/op/reports/march2011.php?item=4.

3. Eve Tuck and K. Wayne Yang, "Decolonization Is Not a Metaphor" in *Decolonization: Indigeneity, Education & Society* 1, no. 1 (2012): 21.

4. Patrick Wolfe, "Settler Colonialism and the Elimination of the Native," in *Journal of Genocide Research,* 8, no. 4, (New York and London: Routledge, 2006), 390, 387–409.

5. Patrick Wolfe, *Settler Colonialism and the Transformation of Anthropology: The Politics and Poetics of an Ethnographic Event* (London and New York: Cassell, 1999), 163.

6. Tuck and Yang, "Decolonization Is Not a Metaphor," 5.

7. Wolfe, "Settler Colonialism and the Elimination of the Native," 390.

8. Wolfe, "Settler Colonialism and the Elimination of the Native," 387–409.

9. Glen Sean Coulthard, *Red Skin, White Masks: Rejecting the Colonial Politics of Recognition* (Minneapolis: University of Minnesota Press, 2014), 6.

10. Louis Althusser, "Ideology and Ideological State Apparatuses (Notes toward an Investigation)," in *Lenin and Philosophy and Other Essays,* trans. B. Brewster (New York and London: Monthly Review Press, 1971), 127–86.

11. For work on U.S. federal recognition in the context of Hawai'i, see Noelani Goodyear-Ka'ōpua, Ikaika Hussey, and Erin Kahunawaika'ala Wright, eds., *A Nation Rising: Hawaiian Movements for Life, Land, and Sovereignty* (Durham, N.C.: Duke University Press, 2014); J. Kēhaulani Kauanui, "Resisting the Akaka Bill," in Goodyear-Ka'ōpua et al., *A Nation Rising* (Durham, N.C.: Duke University Press, 2014), 312–30; Noelani Goodyear-Ka'ōpua, "'Now We Know': Resurgences of Hawaiian Independence," in *Politics, Groups, and Identities* 6, no. 3 (London and New York: Routledge, 2018), 453–65; David Uahikeaikalei'ohu Maile, "'A'ole Is Our Refusal," in Hōkūlani K. Aikau and Vernadette Vicuña

Gonzalez, eds., *Detours: A Decolonial Guide to Hawai'i* (Durham, N.C.: Duke University Press, 2019), 194–99.

12. Coulthard, *Red Skin, White Masks: Rejecting the Colonial Politics of Recognition,* 17.

13. Coulthard, *Red Skin, White Masks: Rejecting the Colonial Politics of Recognition,* 3.

14. Sherene H. Razack, *Dying from Improvement: Inquests and Inquiries into Indigenous Deaths in Custody* (Toronto: University of Toronto Press, 2015), 5.

15. Maile Arvin, *Possession Polynesians: The Science of Settler Colonial Whiteness in Hawai'i and Oceania* (Durham, N.C.: Duke University Press, 2019), 16.

16. Arvin, *Possession Polynesians,* 16.

17. Arvin, *Possession Polynesians,* 3.

18. Arvin, *Possession Polynesians,* 16.

19. Arvin, *Possession Polynesians,* 16.

20. Haunani-Kay Trask, "The Color of Violence" in *Social Justice* 31, no. 4 (98), Native Women and State Violence (2004), 9.

21. Haunani-Kay Trask, *From a Native Daughter: Colonialism & Sovereignty in Hawai'i* (Monroe, Maine: Common Courage Press, 1993), 31.

22. Dean Itsuji Saranillio, "Why Asian Settler Colonialism Matters: A Thought Piece on Critiques, Debates, and Indigenous Difference," in *Settler Colonial Studies,* 3, no. 3–4 (2013): 280–94.

23. Haunani-Kay Trask, "The Color of Violence," in *Social Justice* 31, no. 4 (98), Native Women and State Violence (2004), 10.

24. Ruth Wilson Gilmore, *Golden Gulag: Prisons, Surplus, Crisis, and Opposition in Globalizing California* (Berkeley: University of California Press, 2007), 28.

25. Trask, "Color of Violence," 9.

26. Trask, "Color of Violence," 9.

27. Trask, "Color of Violence," 9.

28. Trask, "Color of Violence," 9.

29. Tuck and Yang, "Decolonization Is Not a Metaphor," 1–40.

30. See Candace Fujikane and Jonathan Y. Okamura, eds., *Whose Vision? Asian Settler Colonialism in Hawai'i* (Los Angeles: Asian American Studies Center, 2000); Candace Fujikane and Jonathan Y. Okamura, eds., *Asian Settler Colonialism: From Local Governance to the Habits of Everyday Life in Hawai'i* (Honolulu: University of Hawai'i Press, 2008).

31. George Cooper and Gavan Daws, *Land and Power in Hawaii: The Democratic Years* (Honolulu: University of Hawai'i Press, 1990).

32. Bianca Isaki, "A Decolonial Archive: The Historical Space of Asian Settler Politics in a Time of Hawaiian Nationhood" (Ph.D. diss., University of Hawai'i at Mānoa, 2011), 8.

33. Isaki, "A Decolonial Archive," 3.

34. Isaki, "A Decolonial Archive," 8–9.

35. Dean Itsuji Saranillio, *Unsustainable Empire: Alternative Histories of Hawai'i Statehood* (Durham, N.C.: Duke University Press, 2018), 19.

36. Saranillio, *Unsustainable Empire,* 5.

37. Fujikane, "Introduction" in Fujikane and Okamura, *Asian Settler Colonialism*, 3–4.

38. See Hawai'i Tourism Authority, "Set-Jetting in Hawai'i: The Three Best Hawaiian Islands for Film Buffs," *The Hawaiian Islands* (2023), accessed August 19, 2019, https://www.gohawaii.com/.

39. Hawai'i State Tourism Authority, https://www.gohawaii.com/fr/blog-down-under/set-jetting-in-hawai%E2%80%98i-the-three-best-hawaiian-islands-for-film-buffs.

40. See "The Best Wedding Venues in Hawaii," *The Best Hawaii Wedding*, https://www.thebesthawaiiwedding.com.

41. *Hawai'i State Tourism Authority*, https://www.gohawaii.com/.

42. Jonathan Y. Okamura, "The Illusion of Paradise: Privileging Multiculturalism in Hawai'i," in *Making Majorities*, ed. D.C. Gladney (Stanford, Calif.: Stanford University Press, 1998).

43. Tuck and Yang, "Decolonization Is Not a Metaphor," 3.

44. Tuck and Yang, "Decolonization Is Not a Metaphor," 4.

45. Sherene H. Razack, *Looking White People in the Eye: Gender, Race, and Culture in Courtrooms and Classrooms* (Toronto: University of Toronto Press, 1999), 9.

46. Razack, *Looking White People in the Eye,* 10.

47. Lawrence Grossberg, ed., "On Postmodernism and Articulation: An Interview with Stuart Hall," in *Journal of Communication Inquiry* 10, no. 2 (Thousand Oaks: SAGE, 1986), 53.

48. Jonathan Y. Okamura, *Ethnic Inequality in Hawai'i* (Philadelphia: Temple University Press, 2008), 99.

49. Okamura, *Ethnic Inequality in Hawai'i*, 106.

50. Okamura, *Ethnic Inequality in Hawai'i*, 108.

51. Okamura, *Ethnic Inequality in Hawai'i*, 100.

52. Okamura, *Ethnic Inequality in Hawai'i*, 99.

53. Okamura, *Ethnic Inequality in Hawai'i*, 3.

54. Okamura, *Ethnic Inequality in Hawai'i*, 2.

55. Okamura, *Ethnic Inequality in Hawai'i*, 4–5.

56. Okamura, *Ethnic Inequality in Hawai'i*, 123.

57. Okamura, *Ethnic Inequality in Hawai'i*, 123.

58. Peter Osborne and Lynne Segal, "Interview: Stuart Hall: Culture and Power," in (Canterbury: Radical Philosophy Group, 1997), 24–41; Lawrence Grossberg, ed., "On Postmodernism and Articulation: An Interview with Stuart Hall," in *Journal of Communication Inquiry* 10, no. 2 (Thousand Oaks: SAGE, 1986), 45–60.

59. Osborne and Segal, "Culture and Power: Interview with Stuart Hall," 29.

60. Grossberg, "On Postmodernism and Articulation: An Interview with Stuart Hall," 53.

61. Okamura, *Ethnic Inequality in Hawai'i*, 92.

62. This was determined by the State auditor in 1998 and is the subject of chapter 6.

63. These phrases appear in promotional literature and pro-TMT advocacy that eventually came to proliferate within legal discourses and management plans as well. I unpack this language and their implications in chapter 6.

64. 'Imiloa, accessed April 6, 2022, http://www.imiloahawaii.org/.

65. 'Imiloa, accessed April 6, 2022, https://imiloahawaii.org/aboutimiloa.

66. Ka'iu Kimura, phone interview by author, June 17, 2013, digital recording.

67. See 'Imiloa, accessed May 12, 2013, http://www.imiloahawaii.org/.

68. See 'Imiloa, accessed May 12, 2013, http://www.imiloahawaii.org/.

69. Mary Kawena Pukui and Samuel H. Elbert, *Hawaiian Language Dictionary*. Rev. ed. (Honolulu: University of Hawai'i Press, 1986).

70. Mary Kawena Pukui, Samuel H. Elbert, and Esther T. Mookini, *Place Names of Hawai'i*, 2nd ed. (Honolulu: University of Hawai'i Press, 1976).

71. Kimura, interview.

72. Kimura, interview.

73. Kimura, interview.

74. Kimura, interview.

75. Kimura, interview.

76. Kimura, interview.

77. Kimura, interview.

78. I discuss the concept of aloha 'āina in chapters 4 and 5.

79. Robert J. C. Young, *Colonial Desire: Hybridity in Theory, Culture and Race* (London and New York: Routledge, 1995), 153.

80. Young, *Colonial Desire*, 153. See also Homi K. Bhabha, *The Location of Culture* (London and New York: Routledge, 1994); Franz Fanon, *Wretched of the Earth* (New York: Grove Press, 1965); and Franz Fanon, *Black Skin, White Masks* (New York: Grove Press, 1967).

4. A Continuum of Struggle

1. Usha Lee McFarling, "Science, Culture Clash Over Sacred Mountain," *Los Angeles Times*, March 18, 2001.

2. *Hawaii Tribune-Herald*, January 27, 1980, quoted in Kepā Maly and Onaona Maly, *"Mauna Kea-Ka Piko Kaulana o ka 'Āina"* (Mauna Kea-The Famous Summit of the Land): A Collection of Native Traditions, Historical Accounts, and Oral History Interviews for: Mauna Kea, the Lands of Ka'ohe, Humu'ula and the 'Āina Mauna on the Island of Hawai'i, Prepared for the Office of Mauna Kea Management (Hilo: University of Hawaii-Hilo, 2005), 632.

3. I discuss the 1998 and 2005 Legislative Audits of the University of Hawai'i and the Keck Outrigger opposition in chapter 6. See Auditor of the State of Hawai'i, *Audit of the Management of Mauna Kea and the Mauna Kea Science Reserve: A Report to the Governor and the Legislature of the State of Hawai'i*, Report No. 98-6, February 1998; Auditor of the State of Hawai'i, *Follow-Up Audit of the Management of Mauna Kea and the Mauna Kea Science Reserve: A Report to the Governor and the Legislature of the State of Hawai'i*, Report No. 05-13, December 2005.

4. This was conveyed to me by Nelson Ho, interview by author, September 24, 2012, Hilo, digital recording; Deborah Ward and Fred Stone, interview by author, June 8, 2013, 'Ōla'a, digital recording.

5. See Nā Maka o ka 'Āina, "Transcript of Public Meeting on the Mauna Kea Science Reserve Master Plan, held at University of Hawai'i–Hilo, May 27, 1999" (Nā'ālehu, Hawai'i: Nā Maka o ka 'Āina, 1999).

6. Lea Hong, phone interview by author, March 12, 2014, digital recording.

7. Hong, phone interview.

8. Many of them are included in the FEIS for the Outrigger Telescopes Project. National Aeronautics and Space Administration, *Final Environmental Impact Statement for the Outrigger Telescopes Project, Vol. 1, Mauna Kea Science Reserve, Island of Hawai'i*, NASA, Universe Division, Science Mission Directorate, Washington, DC (2005). For example, see Ross Cordy, "A Regional Synthesis of Hāmākua District Island of Hawai'i," Prepared by the Historic Preservation Division Department of Land and Natural Resources, Honolulu (1994); Pualani Kanaka'ole Kanahele and Edward L.H. Kanahele, "A Hawaiian Cultural Assessment of the Proposed Saddle Road Alignments," Project A-AD-6(1), Hilo, HI (1997); Charles Langlas, Thomas R. Wolforth, James Head, and Peter Jensen, *Archaeological Inventory Survey and Historic and Traditional Cultural Assessment for the Hawai'i Defense Access Road A-AD-6(1) and Saddle Road (SR 200) Project, Districts of South Kohala, Hāmākua, North Hilo, and South Hilo, Island of Hawai'i*, Paul H. Rosendahl, Ph.D., Inc., Hilo. Prepared for RUST Environmental and Infrastructure Inc., Phoenix, Arizona. On file, State Historic Preservation Division, Kapolei, (1997); Patrick C. McCoy, *The Mauna Kea Adz Quarry Project: A Summary of the 1975 Field Investigations,* Bishop Museum, Honolulu. On file, State Historic Preservation Division, Kapolei, (1977); Patrick C. McCoy, Archaeological Reconnaissance Survey, Report 2 in *Cultural Resources Reconnaissance of the Mauna Kea Summit Region*, by Holly McEldowney and Patrick C. McCoy, pp. 2.1–2.38, Bishop Museum Anthropology Department, Honolulu. Prepared for Group 70, Honolulu. On file, State Historic Preservation Division, Kapolei (1982); Holly McEldowney and Patrick C. McCoy, "Archaeology Reconnaissance Survey," in *Cultural Resources Reconnaissance of the Mauna Kea Summit Region*, Department of Anthropology, Bishop Museum (1982). F.G. Howarth and F.D. Stone, "An Assessment of the Arthropod Fauna and Aeolian Ecosystem Near the Summit of Mauna Kea, Hawaii," Unpublished consultants' report prepared for Group 70 (Honolulu Hawai'i, 1982).

9. Kepā Maly and Onaona Maly, *"Mauna Kea-Ka Piko Kaulana o ka 'Āina" (Mauna Kea-The Famous Summit of the Land): A Collection of Native Traditions, Historical Accounts, and Oral History Interviews for: Mauna Kea, the Lands of Ka'ohe, Humu'ula and the 'Āina Mauna on the Island of Hawai'i*, Prepared for the Office of Mauna Kea Management (Hilo: University of Hawaii-Hilo, 2005).

10. Personal communique with Noenoe K. Silva. For countless examples see, Noelani Goodyear-Ka'ōpua, Ikaika Hussey, and Erin Kahunawaika'ala Wright, eds., *A Nation Rising: Hawaiian Movements for Life, Land, and Sovereignty* (Durham, N.C.: Duke University Press, 2014).

11. See Kepā Maly, *Mauna Kea Science Reserve and Hale Pōhaku Complex Development Plan Update: Oral History and Consultation Study, and Archival Literature Research; Ahupuaʻa of—Kaʻohe (Hāmākua District) and Humuʻula (Hilo District), Island of Hawaiʻi (various TMK)*, Prepared for Group 70 Intl. (1999), particularly the interview with Sonny Alohalani Kaniho and Daniel Kaniho Sr. 150–182. According to the TMT EIS, there have only been two confirmed burial locations on the summit and four other likely burial spots. See University of Hawaiʻi at Hilo, *Final Environmental Impact Statement, Vol. 1: Thirty Meter Telescope Project, Island of Hawaiʻi* (May 8, 2010), P-2. However, although some accounts of burials appear to be speculation, the possibility of burials anywhere would be hard to determine and locations unknown because of cultural protocols, which strictly prohibit disclosure of such information.

12. Nelson Ho, interview by author, September 24, 2012, Hilo, digital recording.

13. Ho, interview.

14. *Hawaii Tribune-Herald*, January 27, 1980, quoted in Maly and Maly, "*Mauna Kea-Ka Piko Kaulana o ka ʻĀina*," (*Mauna Kea-The Famous Summit of the Land*) (2005), 631–637.

15. Ariyoshi to Kido, November 1, 1974, as quoted in *Hawaii Tribune-Herald*, January 27, 1980, quoted in Maly and Maly (2005).

16. Auditor, State of Hawaiʻi, *Audit of the Management of Mauna Kea and the Mauna Kea Science Reserve, A Report to the Governor and the Legislature of the State of Hawaiʻi, Report No. 98–6*, February 1998, 4.

17. Auditor, State of Hawaiʻi, *Audit of the Management of Mauna Kea and the Mauna Kea Science Reserve*, 6.

18. Auditor, State of Hawaiʻi, *Audit of the Management of Mauna Kea and the Mauna Kea Science Reserve*.

19. Nā Maka o ka ʻĀina, "Transcript of Public Meeting on the Mauna Kea Science Reserve Master Plan, held at University of Hawaiʻi–Hilo, May 27, 1999" (Nāʻālehu, Hawaiʻi: Nā Maka o ka ʻĀina, 1999), 17.

20. Nā Maka o ka ʻĀina, "Transcript," 17.

21. Nā Maka o ka ʻĀina, "Transcript," 54–55.

22. Haunani-Kay Trask, *From a Native Daughter: Colonialism & Sovereignty in Hawaiʻi* (Monroe: Common Courage Press, 1993), 153.

23. Trask, *From a Native Daughter*, 153.

24. Noenoe K. Silva, *Aloha Betrayed: Native Hawaiian Resistance to American Colonialism* (Durham: Duke University Press, 2004), 9.

25. Silva, *Aloha Betrayed*, 2.

26. Ron Williams, "Claiming Christianity: The Struggle Over God and Nation in Hawaiʻi, 1880–1900," (Ph.D. diss., University of Hawaiʻi-Mānoa, 2013).

27. Silva, *Aloha Betrayed*, 124.

28. Gavan Daws, *Shoal of Time: A History of the Hawaiian Islands* (Honolulu: University of Hawaiʻi Press, 1989), 294–95. The United States designated its colonial possession the "Territory of Hawaiʻi" in 1900, just following its war with

Spain in the Philippines and two years after "annexing" the islands to satisfy its logistical needs in the outset of that war.

29. Daws, *Shoal of Time*, 291. The ellipsis referenced Robert Wilcox whose unsuccessful counterinsurgency failed to restore the legitimate government and Queen Liliʻuokalani to power.

30. Silva, *Aloha Betrayed*.

31. Even popular songs commonly demand the U.S. to "show me the treaty." See "I Am Not American (featuring Kaʻikena Scanlan)," on Kāwika Aspili, *I Am Not American* (Single), Spoon Meat Entertainment, 2019.

32. Silva, *Aloha Betrayed*, 4.

33. George S. Kanahele, "The Hawaiian Renaissance," May 1979, Polynesian Voyaging Society Archives, The Kamehameha Schools Archives, http://kapalama.ksbe.edu/archives/pvsa/primary%202/Default.php.

34. Kanahele, "Hawaiian Renaissance."

35. Kanahele, "Hawaiian Renaissance."

36. George Huʻeu Sanford Kanahele, *Kū Kanaka–Stand Tall: A Search for Hawaiian Values* (Honolulu: University of Hawaiʻi Press, 1986), 27.

37. Cecilia Akim, interview by author, 1998, Punaluʻu, Oʻahu, cassette recording.

38. My interview with Kailiʻehu and other participants in this solidarity protest is discussed more fully in my dissertation. See Joseph A. Salazar, "Multicultural Settler Colonialism and Indigenous Struggle in Hawaiʻi: The Politics of Astronomy on Mauna a Wākea" (Ph.D. diss., University of Hawaiʻi at Mānoa, 2014).

39. The spectacle, thankfully preserved on YouTube, rallied hundreds of kiaʻi who, the following April, would join the next stage of mass demonstrations—replete with the storied roadblocks, encampments, and civil disobedience direct actions—that led to state arrests of dozens of kiaʻi but also to a stalled project. See David Corrigan, "TMT Opponents Halt Groundbreaking Ceremony," *Big Island Video News,* YouTube video, 20:58, October 7, 2014, https://youtu.be/SZ4Gt35hs-s.

40. This intellectual and theoretical home of Indigenous resurgence, Simpson argues, comes "from within Indigenous thought systems, intelligence systems that are continually generated in relationship to place." Leanne Betasamosake Simpson, *As We Have Always Done: Indigenous Freedom through Radical Resistance,* (Minneapolis: University of Minnesota Press, 2016), 16.

41. For more on their aloha ʻāina and the protest landings that ignited the Protect Kahoʻolawe Movement, see Rodney Morales, ed., *Hoʻihoʻi Hou: A Tribute to George Helm & Kimo Mitchell* (Honolulu: Bamboo Ridge Press, 1984).

42. Sibling Catholic schools in Kaimukī, Honolulu, Oʻahu.

43. Kumu John Keolamakaʻāinana Lake, the great kumu hula (hula teacher).

44. Samuel Hoopii Lono, a kahuna hoʻomana Hawaiʻi (or "priest" of traditional Hawaiian "religion").

45. Noa Emmett Aluli, a Molokaʻi physician, early Kahoʻolawe activist, and Protect Kahoʻolawe ʻOhana co-founder.

46. Aunty Emma Rosalind Hoopii Kanoa deFries, the late great educator, kahuna nui, kumu hula, composer, and antinuclear activist, was a practitioner of Hoʻomau Hawaiʻi (Hawaiian religion) and spiritual leader for the PKO.

47. The Hōkūleʻa was the first double-hulled, long-distance, open-ocean voyaging canoe to sail from Hawaiʻi to Tahiti; back in 1976 it navigated the seas without use of Western instruments, using only Polynesian star navigation methods, ancestral knowledges, and other traditional techniques.

48. Pius Mau Piailug was the master navigator of Satawal who taught the first Hōkūleʻa crew members the traditional navigation techniques that made the 1976 Hawaiʻi–Tahiti voyage possible.

49. Isreal Kaʻanoʻi Kamakawiwoʻole, also "Bruddah Iz" or just "IZ," the famous and beloved Niʻihau-born, Mākaha-based singer/songwriter who died at the age of thirty-eight.

50. Adelaide Keanuenueokalaninuiamamao "Frenchy" DeSoto, longtime Waiʻanae community leader, activist for the protection of the Mākua Valley, and original member of delegation that created the Office of Hawaiian Affairs, or OHA, during the 1978 State of Hawaiʻi Constitutional Convention.

51. Walter Ritte, a lifelong Molokaʻi-based political organizer and community leader who was also part of the original PKO family.

52. *Rice v. Cayetano*, also *Harold F. Rice vs Benjamin J. Cayetano*, 528 US 495 (2000), in Library of Congress, https://www.loc.gov/item/usrep528495/ (accessed September 13, 2013) was a targeted attack on Native Hawaiian-only Office of Hawaiian Affairs elections that invoked colorblind ideological rhetoric to challenge Hawaiian institutions for "racial preferences" and "special rights" within Hawaiʻi State and U.S. federal courts systems. It was one of the most damaging state Supreme Court decisions in history, with repercussions impacting Native Hawaiian rights, entitlements, and programs to this day.

53. The "aliʻi trust" refers broadly to the Native Hawaiian trusts of the royal families. Endowed from property and businesses in the nineteenth century, the aliʻi trusts were established for the benefit, health, and well-being of Kānaka Maoli today. They include such organizations as Kamehameha Schools/Bernice Pauahi Bishop Estate, Queen Liliʻuokalani Trust, King Lunalilo Trust and Lunalilo Home, and Queen's Hospital/Queen Emma Land Company.

54. Dr. Richard Kekuni Akana Blaisdell was a professor emeritus of medicine at the University of Hawaiʻi at Mānoa, a peace activist, and longtime educator/organizer who advocated for Hawaiian independence from the United States rather than federal recognition by the U.S.

55. The 1993 grassroots event People's International Tribunal coincided with series of events that observed the centennial anniversary of the U.S. invasion of the Hawaiian kingdom and "called upon the United States and the world to recognize the inherent sovereignty and self-determination of the Kanaka Maoli people and . . . their right to decolonization." See Kekuni Blaisdell, "I Hea Nā Kānaka Maoli? Whither the Hawaiian?" in *Hūlili: Multidisciplinary Research on Hawaiian Well-Being*, Vol. 2 (Honolulu: Kamehameha Schools, 2005).

56. Mōkapu is a peninsula on the northeast-facing coast of Oʻahu, adjacent to Kailua. Originally known as Mokukapu, or "sacred district," Mōkapu was a meeting place for Kamehameha I and his Oʻahu aliʻi, and today remains sacred to Kānaka ʻŌiwi for its significance to the continued observance of Makahiki ceremonies. Since 1941, the United States has operated its Marine Corps Base Hawaiʻi (MCBH) as a restricted area enjoyed solely by U.S. troops and their families. It is a thoroughly militarized site where patriotism, pollution, war games, and militourism intersect, while Kānaka ʻŌiwi wishing to conduct ceremony here must request permission through the military bureaucracy.

57. A cinder cone or hill on the peninsula that, as the highest point and, like Mauna a Wākea, is sacred.

58. Kalamaokaʻaina Niheu.

59. Polynesian Voyaging Society: Hōkūleʻa, "A Voyage for Earthy," accessed July 30, 2023, https://hokulea.com/.

60. See Kyle Kajihiro and Ikaika Hussey.

61. Terri Kekoʻolani-Raymond, interview by author, April 17, 2014, Kaimukī, digital recording.

5. Composing Nature and Articulating the Sacred

1. George Johnson, "Seeking Stars, Finding Creationism," *New York Times,* October 20, 2014.

2. Johnson, "Seeking Stars, Finding Creationism."

3. Johnson, "Seeking Stars, Finding Creationism."

4. Johnson, "Seeking Stars, Finding Creationism."

5. Johnson, "Seeking Stars, Finding Creationism."

6. Bryan Kamaoli Kuwada, "We Live in the Future. Come Join Us," *Ke Kaupu Hehiale,* April 3, 2015, accessed June 16, 2022, https://hehiale.com/2015/04/03/we-live-in-the-future-come-join-us/.

7. Kuwada, "We Live in the Future. Come Join Us."

8. Kuwada, "We Live in the Future. Come Join Us."

9. Kuwada, "We Live in the Future. Come Join Us."

10. Kuwada, "We Live in the Future. Come Join Us."

11. Bruno Latour, "An Attempt at a 'Compositionist' Manifesto," in *New Literary History* 41 (2010): 471–90.

12. Latour, "'Compositionist' Manifesto," 485–86.

13. Latour, "'Compositionist' Manifesto," 476.

14. Latour, "'Compositionist' Manifesto," 478.

15. Latour, "'Compositionist' Manifesto," 476.

16. Latour, "'Compositionist' Manifesto," 488.

17. Latour, "'Compositionist' Manifesto," 478.

18. Latour, "'Compositionist' Manifesto," 475.

19. Lawrence Grossberg, ed., "On Postmodernism and Articulation: An Interview with Stuart Hall," in *Journal of Communication Inquiry* 10, no. 2 (Newbury Park, CA: SAGE, 1986), 45–60; Peter Osborne and Lynne Segal, "Culture

and Power: Interview with Stuart Hall," in *Radical Philosophy 086* (November/December 1997), 24–41. https://www.radicalphilosophy.com/interview/stuart-hall-culture-and-power, accessed April 10, 2025.

20. Emphasis is mine. Osborne and Segal, "Culture and Power," 30.

21. Leilani Basham, "Mele Lāhui: The Importance of Pono in Hawaiian Poetry," in *Te Kaharoa* 1, no. 1 (2008): 152; See also Leilani Basham, "Ka Lāhui Hawaiʻi: He Moʻolelo, He ʻĀina, He Loina, a He Ea Kākou," in *Hūlili: Multidisciplinary Research on Hawaiian Well-Being* (Honolulu: Kamehameha Publishing, 2010).

22. Noelani Goodyear-Kaʻōpua, "'Now We Know': Resurgences of Hawaiian Independence," in *Politics, Groups, and Identities* 6, no. 3 (2018), 452–65 is but one recent example of scholars who make these connections.

23. Basham, "Mele Lāhui."

24. Noenoe Silva cites Joseph Poepoe's analysis of the mele under this title, and both inform my analysis here. See Noenoe K. Silva, *The Power of the Steel-Tipped Pen: Reconstructing Native Hawaiian Intellectual History* (Durham, N.C., and London: Duke University Press, 2017), 174–213. Shared and cited by permission of the author.

25. This title is found in Mary Kawena Pukui and Alfons L. Korn, trans. and eds., *The Echo of Our Song* (Honolulu: University of Hawaiʻi Press, 1973), 12–28.

26. Pukui and Korn, *The Echo of Our Song.*

27. Pukui and Korn, *The Echo of Our Song.*

28. See Silva, *Power of the Steel-Tipped Pen*; Lilikalā Kameʻeleihiwa, *Native Land, Foreign Desires: Pehea Lā Pono Ai? How Shall We Live in Harmony?* (Honolulu: Bishop Museum Press, 1992), 31; Kepā Maly and Onaona Maly, *"Mauna Kea-Ka Piko Kaulana o ka ʻĀina" (Mauna Kea-The Famous Summit of the Land): A Collection of Native Traditions, Historical Accounts, and Oral History Interviews for: Mauna Kea, the Lands of Kaʻohe, Humuʻula and the ʻĀina Mauna on the Island of Hawaiʻi*, Prepared for The Office of Mauna Kea Management (Hilo: University of Hawaii-Hilo, 2005), 8–9.

29. In the nineteenth century, the nation-state of Hawaiʻi, what many today call "the Hawaiian kingdom," was known as Ko Hawaiʻi Pae ʻĀina. I use capitals to signify the pronoun form, unlike in the case of "the Hawaiian archipelago," which translates to ka pae ʻāina o Hawaiʻi. Personal communication with Noenoe K. Silva; see also Ilima Long's explanation at Ilima Long, @ItsIlima, "'O ke ea o Ko Hawaii Pae Aina, oia ka noho Aupuni ana' is often translated as 'the ea of the Hawaiian archipelago. . . .'. But it's capitalized, referring to the official name of the sovereign independent territory of the Hawaiian Kingdom. 'Hawaiian archipelago' depoliticizes it." *Twitter*, July 7, 2021, 1:20 p.m., https://twitter.com/ItsIlima/status/1412838971797815298.

30. Kuamoʻo kūpuna aliʻi translates as the "royal ancestral backbone."

31. In Malo's *Moolelo Hawaii* (1992, 242), Emerson notes that Hoʻohōkūkalani "means to bestud the heavens with stars, the starry sky, the stars of heaven." Kikiloi translates the name as "the starring of the heaven," while Kameʻeleihiwa translates it as "to generate stars in the sky." See Kekuewa Kikiloi, "Rebirth of

an Archipelago: Sustaining a Hawaiian Cultural Identity for People and Home-land," in *Hūlili Journal* 6 (Honolulu: Kamehameha Publishing, 2010), 83; David Malo, *Hawaiian Antiquities: Moʻolelo Hawaiʻi*, Special Publication 2, 2nd ed., trans. Nathaniel B. Emerson (Honolulu: Bernice Pauahi Bishop Museum, 1997); Kameʻeleihiwa, *Native Land, Foreign Desires*, 23. Both Pukui and Korn, *The Echo of Our Song* and Langlas and Lyon, *The Moʻolelo of Hawaiʻi of Davida Malo: Hawaiian Text and Translation* use ʻokina and kahakō for some hua ʻōlelo Hawaiʻi they reproduce or transcribe, but not for "Hoʻohokukalani." I have chosen to use Kameʻeleihiwa and Kikiloi's spelling of Hoʻohōkūkalani.

32. Hāloa translates to "long breath," but may also be translated as "long taro stem or stalk," at once a poetic and literal reference to the moʻokūauhau aliʻi (royal genealogy) and the kalo plant. See Joseph Poepoe, *Kuokoa Home Rula* 7, no. 19, May 7, 1909.

33. Pukui and Korn, *The Echo of Our Song*, 13.

34. During Kauikeaouli's reign, Ko Hawaiʻi Pae ʻĀina underwent enormous change in a short period. As mentioned in chapter 2, Hawaiʻi established a dec-laration of rights in 1839 and, in 1840, secured international legal recognition of its independence as a nation-state modeled on governmental elements of other states at the time. Hawaiʻi's first constitution was also created in 1840. Its legisla-ture was a bicameral system through which all citizens could vote to elect mem-bers to the House of Representatives. A constitutional convention was held every twelve years, and legislative enactments were passed on every even year. The compilation of legislative laws along with judicial decisions refined and defined the constitution. While gender and class inequities required attention, Ko Hawaiʻi Pae ʻĀina was far more democratic than many other states and many European monarchies during the same era. Many envision what improvements could have been accomplished in Hawaiʻi had the United States not invaded in 1893 and maintained a military occupation that continues to this day.

35. Pukui and Korn, *The Echo of Our Song*, 14.

36. Silva, *The Power of the Steel-Tipped Pen*, 189.

37. Pukui and Korn, *The Echo of Our Song*, 14 and 20.

38. Pukui and Korn, *The Echo of Our Song*.

39. The concept of *firsts* plays an interesting role in the ancient worship practices conducted at heiau (literally "ensnaring time," or temples) where, as Kekuewa Kikiloi explains, "offerings and sacrifices were important religious invest-ments . . . (and) Ethno-historical records show that earlier Hawaiian ritual prac-tices typically included the offering (or ʻsacrifice') of first-born animals, first fruits of the earth, and first caught fish." See Kekuewa Scott T. Kikiloi, "Kūkulu Mana-mana: Ritual Power and Religious Expansion in Hawaiʻi: The Ethno-Historical and Archaeological Study of Mokumanamana and Nihoa Islands" (Ph.D. diss., University of Hawaiʻi, 2012), 82.

40. Pukui and Korn, *The Echo of Our Song*, 17 and 23.

41. A kapu is a prohibition or restriction, signifying something or some-place that is forbidden while also connoting sacredness. Wahi is a place, location, or site. See Pukui and Elbert, *Hawaiian Language Dictionary*.

42. In Langlas's and Lyon's edited volume and updated translation, featuring a new biographical essay by Noelani Arista, the authors describe Malo's *Ka Moʻolelo Hawaiʻi* as the most important and most-cited "scholarly work concerning pre-Christian Hawaiian culture" (1). However, Arista adds, "It may be a singular irony that . . . [the book was only] first published in 1903, fifty years after his death" (23). Davida Malo, *The Moʻolelo Hawaiʻi of Davida Malo, Volume 2: Hawaiian Text and Translation,* ed. and trans. Charles Langlas and Jeffrey Paul Lyon (Honolulu: University of Hawaiʻi Press, 2020). Malo did not work alone, however, as he and other students at Lahainaluna Seminary in the 1830s compiled much of the research that would be used in the work. See Noenoe K. Silva, *The Power of the Steel-Tipped Pen: Reconstructing Native Hawaiian Intellectual History* (Durham, N.C., and London: Duke University Press, 2017).

43. Malo, *The Moʻolelo Hawaiʻi of Davida Malo, Vol. 2,* 70. Brackets are those of Langlas and Lyon.

44. The ancestor deity known as Papanuihānaumoku, which is commonly shortened to Papahānaumoku and often translated as "Papa who gives birth to islands," is personified in the earth. Wākea is personified in the "expanse of the sky." See Kikiloi, "Kūkulu Manamana," 42.

45. Also Hoʻohōkū and, as noted previously, spelled without the kahakō in Pukui and Korn, *The Echo of Our Song* and Langlas and Lyon, *The Moʻolelo of Hawaiʻi of Davida Malo, Vol. 2.*

46. Kikiloi, "Kūkulu Manamana: Ritual Power and Religious Expansion in Hawaiʻi," 72.

47. Kikiloi adds, "Hoʻomanamana literally means to impart mana (power), as to idols or objects; to deify (Pukui and Elbert 1986) . . . [and] was the formalization of rituals, prayers, and rites in an attempt to connect high-born chiefs to the realm of the afterlife, and to the major gods cosmologically located in the northwest [islands]. When these formalized rituals were conducted at specific times and in exact locations, the connection with ancestral gods was amplified and a transfer of power occurred." See Kikiloi, "Kūkulu Manamana: Ritual Power and Religious Expansion in Hawaiʻi," 73–74.

48. Silva, *The Power of the Steel-Tipped Pen,* 191.

49. Malo's *Ka Moʻolelo Hawaiʻi* was translated in 1892–1893 by Nathaniel B. Emerson, edited by W. A. Alexander, and first published in English only in 1903 by Emerson under the title *Hawaiian Antiquities,* fifty years after Malo's death. See Langlas and Lyon *The Moʻolelo of Hawaiʻi of Davida Malo, Vol. 2*; Davida Malo, *The Moʻolelo of Hawaiʻi of Davida Malo*; See in particular, Noelani Arista, "Davida Malo, a Hawaiian Life," a new biographical essay in Malo, *The Moʻolelo Hawaiʻi of Davida Malo,* 24.

50. Malo, *The Moʻolelo Hawaiʻi of Davida Malo,* 2–3.

51. An earlier draft of this chapter cited Emerson's translation extensively, and I am indebted to one of my reviewers who advised me to review Langlas and Lyon and to revise. Moreover, considering the politics of citational practices, it is not only ethical to cite Kanaka ʻŌiwi scholarship on these topics, but also urgent. This is because, for example, the scope and significance of Emerson's omissions,

distortions, and insertions of words and phrases conveying ideas not in Malo's original reveal how Emerson's own Christian ethnocentrism deny non-Hawaiian language readers as full an understanding as possible of Malo's intended meanings, while providing new meanings Malo did not intend at all. See Malo, *The Mo'olelo Hawai'i of Davida Malo*, 3.

52. A ko'ihonua is a chant that describes the forming of the earth. See Kepā Maly and Onaona Maly, *"Mauna Kea-Ka Piko Kaulana o ka 'Āina" (Mauna Kea-The Famous Summit of the Land): A Collection of Native Traditions, Historical Accounts, and Oral History Interviews for: Mauna Kea, the Lands of Ka'ohe, Humu'ula and the 'Āina Mauna on the Island of Hawai'i*, Prepared for The Office of Mauna Kea Management (Hilo: University of Hawaii-Hilo, 2005), 7.

53. Pō may be translated as "night," "darkness," "realm of the gods."

54. Concerning Malo's use of the word "pō" here, Lyons adds, "This seems to mean that they were forms of pō . . ." (endnote no. 4, 73). See Malo, *The Mo'olelo Hawai'i of Davida Malo*, 72.

55. Malo, *The Mo'olelo Hawai'i of Davida Malo*, 72; See also Martha Warren Beckwith, ed. and trans., *The Kumulipo: A Hawaiian Creation Chant* (Honolulu: University of Hawai'i Press, 1951), 94–106; See also Rubellite K. Johnson, *The Kumulipo Mind: A Global Heritage in the Polynesian Creation Myth* (Honolulu: Rubellite K. Johnson, 2000), 160.

56. Wahine may be translated as "woman," "lady," "wife," "female," and "femininity," among others. As the Hawaiian context does not suggest marriage, "wahine" here likely refers to the woman with whom Kahiko had these children. Personal communication with Noenoe K. Silva; See also Pukui and Elbert, *Hawaiian Language Dictionary*.

57. Malo, *The Mo'olelo Hawai'i of Davida Malo*, 72; Malo, *Hawaiian Antiquities*, 238–39.

58. Malo, *The Mo'olelo Hawai'i of Davida Malo*, 72.

59. Samuel Mānaiakalani Kamakau, *Ka Po'e Kahiko: The People of Old*, trans. Mary Kawena Pukui and ed. Dorothy B. Barrère (Honolulu: Bishop Museum Press, 1991).

60. Kamakau, *Ka Po'e Kahiko: The People of Old*, 3.

61. Kamakau, *Tales and Traditions of the People of Old: Nā Mo'olelo a ka Po'e Kahiko*, trans. Mary Kawena Pukui and ed. Dorothy B. Barrère (Honolulu: Bishop Museum Press, 1991), 32.

62. Kamakau, *Tales and Traditions of the People of Old*, 32.

63. Kamakau, *Tales and Traditions of the People of Old*, 34.

64. According to Jeffrey Lyons, "Pō refers here to the period that came first as a period of primordial darkness, which came before humans, as opposed to ao, the period that came later and in which humankind appeared" (n. 4, 73). See Malo, *The Mo'olelo Hawai'i of Davida Malo*.

65. See Silva, *The Power of the Steel-Tipped Pen*.

66. Mary Kawena Pukui, *'Ōlelo No'eau: Hawaiian Proverbs & Poetical Sayings* (Honolulu: Bishop Museum Press, 1983).

67. Silva, unpublished paper. This phrase is borrowed from Kepā Maly and Onaona Maly, "*Mauna Kea-Ka Piko Kaulana o ka 'Āina" (Mauna Kea-The Famous Summit of the Land): A Collection of Native Traditions, Historical Accounts, and Oral History Interviews for: Mauna Kea, the Lands of Ka'ohe, Humu'ula and the 'Āina Mauna on the Island of Hawai'i,* Prepared for The Office of Mauna Kea Management (Hilo: University of Hawaii-Hilo, 2005), 8.

68. A kapu is a "taboo" or a prohibition, as well as a privilege or an exemption from such. It also means to set apart to prohibit from use, and to make sacred.

69. Kanaka'ole Kanahele and Kanahele translate Kahikikū as "upper horizon" and Kahikimoe as "lower horizon." See Pualani Kanaka'ole Kanahele and Edward L. H. Kanahele, *A Social Impact Assessment—Indigenous Hawaiian Cultural Values of the Proposed Saddle Road Alignments,* Project A-AD-6 (1), Hilo, 1997; as cited in Kepā Maly, *Mauna Kea Science Reserve and Hale Pōhaku Complex Development Plan Update: Oral History and Consultation Study, and Archival Literature Research: Ahupua'a of–Ka'ohe (Hāmākua District) and Humu'ula (Hilo District), Island of Hawia'i (various TMK),* Appendix D, Prepared for Group 70 International by Kumu Pono Associates. Hilo, Hawai'i. 1999, D-20.

70. Kamakau, *Tales and Traditions,* 126.

71. Kanaka'ole Kanahele and Kanahele, *A Social Impact Assessment,* 16.

72. Kekuewa Kikiloi, "Rebirth of an Archipelago: Sustaining a Hawaiian Cultural Identity for People and Homeland," in *Hūlili Journal* 6 (Honolulu: Kamehameha Publishing, 2010), 81.

73. Kikiloi, "Rebirth of an Archipelago," 81.

74. Kikiloi, "Rebirth of an Archipelago," 76.

75. Some accounts have it that the mythical first ocean navigator, Hawai'i Loa—also known as Hawai'i Nui and Hawai'inuiakea—who journeyed from the southern Tahitian group named these islands after his children, which are those names still in use today. See Kepā Maly, *Mauna Kea Science Reserve and Hale Pōhaku Complex Development Plan Update: Oral History and consultation Study, and Archival Literature Research,* Appendix E: Limited Overview of the Hawai'i Loa Traditions (Honolulu: Prepared for Group 70 International, 1999), E1–E5.

76. Kame'eleihiwa, *Native Land, Foreign Desires,* 24. According to Malo, the kalo leaf that sprouted was named laukapalili, or "quivering leaf." Hāloanaka is also known as Hāloanakalaukapalili. See Malo, *Hawaiian Antiquities,* 244.

77. Kame'eleihiwa, *Native Land, Foreign Desires,* 25.

78. An example of a punalua relationship is one in which two women both share a male or two men share a female partner, each in a long-term relationship with the other enjoying privileges and responsibilities. Each spouse was a punalua to the other through the common spouse.

79. David Malo, *Hawaiian Antiquities: Mo'olelo Hawai'i,* Special Publication 2, 2nd ed., trans. Nathaniel B. Emerson (Honolulu: Bernice Pauahi Bishop Museum, 1997), 243. Additional orthography is mine.

80. The temporal approximation was Kalākaua's. See His Hawaiian Majesty King David Kalākaua, *The Legends and Myths of Hawaii: The Fables and Folk-Lore*

of a Strange People, ed. R. M. Daggett (Rutland and Tokyo: Charles E. Tuttle Company 1972), 22.

81. Marie Alohalani Brown, "Mauna Kea: Hoʻomana Hawaiʻi and Protecting the Sacred," *JSRNC* 10, no. 2 (2016): 150–69.

82. Following the death of Kamehameha I in 1819, Kamehameha I's wives, Keōpūolani and Kaʻahumanu, persuaded Liholiho (Kamehameha II) to eat with them and to eat foods forbidden to men in a symbolic and revolutionary gesture. Brown, "Mauna Kea: Hoʻomana Hawaiʻi and Protecting the Sacred," 159–60.

83. According to Marie Alohalani Brown, Hoʻomana Hawaiʻi was the "set of beliefs and belief-related practices indigenous to Hawaiʻi" that constitute what might be called "Hawaiian religion." See Brown, "Mauna Kea: Hoʻomana Hawaiʻi and Protecting the Sacred," 162.

84. The kūpuna i ka pō are those who have passed into pō, that is, our deceased ancestors now in the realm of the akua (gods).

85. Jamaica Heolimeleikalani Osorio, *Remembering Our Intimacies: Moʻolelo, Aloha ʻĀina, and Ea* (Minneapolis and London: University of Minnesota Press, 2021), 15.

86. Pukui and Elbert, *Hawaiian Language Dictionary,* 328.

87. Though not as sexy, the tips of the ears are also listed as piko in the dictionary (Mahalo Noenoe K. Silva). See Pukui and Elbert, *Hawaiian Language Dictionary,* 328.

88. This is according to the Lindsey family of Waimea as recorded by Kepā Maly. See Kepā Maly, *Mauna Kea Science Reserve and Hale Pōhaku Complex Development Plan Update: Oral History and consultation Study, and Archival Literature Research, Appendix E: Limited Overview of the Hawaiʻi Loa Traditions* (Honolulu: Prepared for Group 70 International, 1999), B-14.

89. Maly, Mauna Kea Science Reserve and Hale Pōhaku Complex Development Plan Update (1999), B-15 (emphasis added).

90. For an account of this election, see Jonathan Kamakawiwoʻole Osorio, *Dismembering Lāhui: A History of the Hawaiian Nation to 1887* (Honolulu: University of Hawaiʻi Press, 2002). See also George Kanahele, *Emma: Hawaiʻi's Remarkable Queen* (Honolulu: Queen Emma Foundation & University of Hawaiʻi Press, 1999).

91. Kīhei and Māpuana de Silva provide a useful analysis of over two dozen mele associated with ka Moku o Keawe, or Hawaiʻi Island, that once appeared in Kamehameha Schools' Kaʻiwakīloumoku Hawaiian Cultural Center's online literary archive, Kaleinamanu. While the archive has been removed, "E Hoʻi ka Nani i Mānā" appears to still be available at Kaʻiwakīloumoku: Pacific Indigenous Institute, https://kaiwakiloumoku.ksbe.edu/article/mele-e-hoi-ka-nani-i -mana, accessed on April 10, 2025. For more information about Queen Emma and the mele composed to commemorate her journey to the summit, see Puakea Nogelmeier, *He Lei no ʻEmalani: Chants for Queen Emma Kaleleonalani* (Honolulu: Bishop Museum Press and Queen Emma Foundation, 2001).

92. Maly, *Mauna Kea Science Reserve and Hale Pōhaku Complex Development Plan Update* (1999), B-19. Barbara Robertson quoted from a testimony

given at a Mauna Kea Advisory Council community hearing in Hilo, on December 22, 1998.

93. Larry Kimura, interview by author, June 7, 2013, Hilo, digital recording.

94. Kimura, interview.

95. Pualani Kanaka'ole Kanahele, interview by author, December 14, 2013, Hilo, digital recording.

96. Kanahele, interview.

97. Pualani Kanaka'ole Kanahele, interview by author, December 14, 2013, Hilo, digital recording.

98. A luakini is a type of temple. A ki'i is an image of an akua, generally carved from a wood specific to that akua's kino lau (or, "many bodily" forms taken by a supernatural). A wahi pana is a storied or legendary place.

99. Pualani Kanaka'ole Kanahele, interview by author, December 14, 2013, Hilo, digital recording.

100. Pualani Kanaka'ole Kanahele, interview by author, December 14, 2013, Hilo, digital recording.

101. Pualani Kanaka'ole Kanahele, interview by author, December 14, 2013, Hilo, digital recording.

102. Maly and Maly, "Mauna Kea–Ka Piko Kaulana o ka 'Āina," 10.

103. Kanahele, interview.

104. Kanahele, interview.

105. Kanahele, interview.

106. Kanahele, interview.

107. Kanahele, interview.

108. Kanahele, interview.

109. E. S. Craighill Handy and Mary Kawena Pukui, The Polynesian Family System in Ka'ū, Hawai'i (Rutland, VT: C. E. Tuttle Co., 1998), 28 (emphasis in original).

110. Pualani Kanaka'ole Kanahele, Ka Honua Ola, 'Eli'eli Kau Mai: The Living Earth Descend, Deepen the Revelation (Honolulu: Kamehameha, 2011), xiv.

111. Kikiloi, "Rebirth of an Archipelago," 75.

112. Goodyear-Ka'ōpua, The Seeds We Planted, 33.

113. Ty P. Kāwika Tengan, Native Men Remade: Gender and Nation in Contemporary Hawai'i (Durham, N.C.: Duke University Press, 2008), 25.

6. A Fictive Kinship

1. That is, the Crown and Government Lands of the Hawaiian kingdom, also known as the "Ceded Lands," to which Native Hawaiians continue to hold claims as legal subjects of an independent country under international law.

2. According to Mauna Kea Anaina Hou and the Royal Order of Kamehameha, as of 2000, when counting the "observatories, antennas, mirrors or light collecting surfaces," there are over twenty-five telescopes. "This number does not include the 'foundations' or 'pads' and support structures of the 'interferometers'

or 'Astronomical Arrays'" (Emphasis in original). They argue that if those were included the number of "telescopes" would exceed fifty. See Kealoha Pisciotta, "Why Mauna Kea Should Be Preserved and Protected," (1999) in *Mauna Kea— The Temple: Protecting the Sacred Resource, a report submitted by The Royal Order of Kamehameha I and Mauna Kea Anaina Hou to be included in the Board of Land and Natural Resources review of the University of Hawaiʻi's 2000 Mauna Kea Master Plan*, 34 (Unpublished report submitted to DLNR in the Keck Outrigger contested case, used by permission of the author). The Keck Outrigger would have increased the number from thirteen to nineteen telescopes according to the university's calculation.

3. I use the "Board of Land and Natural Resources," "BLNR," and "Land Board" interchangeably for the seven-member executive head of the Department of Land and Natural Resources.

4. Keck is considered *a single* "observatory," rather than *two* "telescopes."

5. *KAHEA: The Hawaiian-Environmental Alliance* (Blog), "Mauna Kea Timeline," accessed September 18, 2022, http://kahea.org/issues/sacred-summits/timeline-of-events.

6. Interview with Lea Hong by the author on March 12, 2014.

7. *KAHEA,* "Mauna Kea Timeline."

8. Office of the Auditor, State of Hawaiʻi, *Audit of the Management of Mauna Kea and the Mauna Kea Science Reserve, Summary Report No. 98–6* (1998), accessed September 21, 2022, http://www.state.hi.us/auditor/Overviews/1998/98-6.htm.

9. Office of the Auditor, State of Hawaiʻi, *Audit of the Management of Mauna Kea and the Mauna Kea Science Reserve.*

10. University of Hawaiʻi at Hilo, *Final Environmental Impact Statement, Vol. 2: Thirty Meter Telescope Project, Island of Hawaiʻi* (University of Hawaiʻi at Hilo, May 8, 2010), 392.

11. National Aeronautics and Space Administration, *Final Environmental Impact Statement for the Outrigger Telescopes Project,* Vol. 1, Washington DC (NASA, February 2005), xxi.

12. The sentiment appears frequently across documents, but was used quite a bit during the 2011 contested case hearing, particularly in the testimony of Mike Bolte, closing arguments of the university's lawyer Tim Lui-Kwan, and repeated in BLNR's decision to approve the TMT permit; *State of Hawaiʻi, Department of Land and Natural Resources, DLNR File No. HA-11–05,* "Findings of Fact, Conclusions of Law, and Decision and Order," p. 34.

13. University of Hawaiʻi, *Mauna Kea Comprehensive Management Plan, UH Management Areas* (University of Hawaiʻi, January 2009); University of Hawaiʻi at Hilo, *Final Environmental Impact Statement, Vol. 1: Thirty Meter Telescope Project, Island of Hawaiʻi* (University of Hawaiʻi at Hilo, May 8, 2010).

14. Authors were employed by the University of Hawaiʻi and one of the several consulting firms contracted by UH to produce the CMP, its four subplans, and the EIS. The others include Sustainable Resources Group Int'l, Inc., Pacific Consulting Services, Inc., and Parsons Brinckerhoff.

15. This idea was emphasized in my interview with Kanaka astronomer Paul Coleman, who reasoned that "a kahuna is a guy who learned a lot of science and his craft and he is an expert. And so you leave those things for the experts and the rest of us, normal mortals, we do the things that normal mortals do"; see Paul Coleman, interview by author, May 8, 2013, Mānoa, digital recording. See also Pukui and Elbert, *Hawaiian Language Dictionary.*

16. This idea of "becoming without becoming" is about acquiring or possessing Native-ness, but inhabiting the subjection that Kānaka ʻŌiwi and Native people endure more broadly. Kānaka ʻŌiwi Eve Tuck and K. Wayne Yang, "Decolonization Is Not a Metaphor" in *Decolonization: Indigeneity, Education & Society* 1, no. 1 (2012): 13. In the relevant passage, Tuck and Yang are citing Sara Ahmed, *Strange Encounters: Embodied Others in Postcoloniality* (New York: Routledge, 2000), 32.

17. I employ the concept of *dispossession* with the knowledge that it runs the risk of reifying the capitalist logics of proprietary ownership over land insofar as *dispossession* presupposes *possession* through recursive negation. See Robert Nichols, *Theft Is Property: Dispossession and Critical Theory* (Durham, N.C., and London: Duke University Press, 2020).

18. Fredric Chaffee, quoted in University of Hawaiʻi, "Voices and Visions of Mauna Kea," Mauna Kea Science Reserve Master Plan and Implementation Process Summary (2000).

19. Sandra Harding, *Sciences From Below: Feminisms, Postcolonialities, and Modernities* (Durham, N.C.: Duke University Press, 2008).

20. Indeed, the universal subject is always masculine, that is, "Man."

21. Bruno Latour, *We Have Never Been Modern,* trans. Catherine Porter (Cambridge, Mass.: Harvard University Press, 1991).

22. For a brilliant discussion of the ways in which settler legal and social discourses in Hawaiʻi confine contemporary articulations of Kanaka ʻŌiwi indigeneity to a paradoxical status of inauthenticity by disallowing new cultural expressions and practices the capacity to grow and age—that is, to become "ancient"—the effect of which forecloses opportunities for Kānaka ʻŌiwi to "be modern" on our terms. See Emalani Case, *Everything Ancient Was Once New: Indigenous Persistence from Hawaiʻi to Kahiki* (Honolulu: University of Hawaiʻi Press, 2021).

23. Mōʻī David Kāwika Laʻamea Kalākaua, quoted in University of Hawaiʻi, "Voices and Visions of Mauna Kea."

24. *Pacific Commercial Advertiser,* September 19, 1874, quoted in Michael Chauvin, *Hōkūloa: The British 1874 Transit of Venus Expedition to Hawaiʻi* (Honolulu: Bishop Museum Press, 2004), 198–99.

25. Noenoe K. Silva, *Aloha Betrayed: Native Hawaiian Resistance to American Colonialism* (Durham, N.C.: Duke University Press, 2004), 9.

26. University of Hawaiʻi, prepared by Group 70 International, Inc. "Mauna Kea Science Reserve Master Plan," Jun 16, 2000, ES-4.

27. P. K. Kanahele and E. L. Kanahele, *"A Social Impact Assessment—Indigenous Hawaiian Cultural Values of the Proposed Saddle Road Alignments,"* Project A-AD-6 (1), Hilo, Hawaiʻi (1997).

28. University of Hawai'i, *Mauna Kea Comprehensive Management Plan, UH Management Areas,* January 2009, 1–1.

29. The TMT International Observatory Corporation, also the "TMT International Observatory, LLC," which was renamed as simply the "TMT International Observatory" or "TIO" sometime around 2017.

30. Specifically, HAR section 11-200-17 and 11-200-18. See University of Hawai'i at Hilo, *Final Environmental Impact Statement, Vol. 1: Thirty Meter Telescope Project, Island of Hawai'i* (University of Hawai'i at Hilo, May 8, 2010).

31. University of Hawai'i at Hilo, *Final Environmental Impact Statement, Vol. 1.*

32. University of Hawai'i at Hilo, *Final Environmental Impact Statement, Vol. 1,* S-1.

33. Comprehensive Management Plan quoted in University of Hawai'i at Hilo, *Final Environmental Impact Statement, Vol. 1* (2010), S-4. Emphasis added. I discuss the piko metaphor as well in chapter 5.

34. Comprehensive Management Plan quoted in University of Hawai'i at Hilo, *Final Environmental Impact Statement, Vol. 1,* S-4.

35. University of Hawai'i at Hilo, *Final Environmental Impact Statement, Vol. 1,* 3-1. Emphases added.

36. Kepā Maly is a cultural researcher who conducted numerous oral history studies and archival research for the Office of Mauna Kea Management and other governmental projects. See Kepā Maly, *Mauna Kea Science Reserve and Hale Pōhaku Complex Development Plan Update: Oral History and Consultation Study, and Archival Literature Research: Ahupua'a of Ka'ohe (Hāmākua District) and Humu'ula (Hilo District), Island of Hawai'i (various TMK),* Prepared for Group 70 International by Kumu Pono Associates, Hilo, Hawai'i (1999), A-362–382.

37. Kumu Pono, *Mauna Kea Science Reserve and Hale Pōhaku Complex Development Plan Update: Oral History and Consultation Study, and Archival Literature Research: Ahupua'a of Ka'ohe (Hāmākua District) and Humu'ula (Hilo District), Island of Hawai'i,* February 1999, A-376, quoted in University of Hawai'i at Hilo, *Final Environmental Impact Statement, Vol. 1.*

38. Maly, *Mauna Kea Science Reserve and Hale Pōhaku Complex Development Plan Update,* A-378.

39. Maly, *Mauna Kea Science Reserve and Hale Pōhaku Complex Development Plan Update* A-378-9.

40. UHH, *FEIS, Vol. 1* (2010), 3–23; Chapter 343 Final EIS Summary Sheet, TMT Project.

41. UHH, *FEIS, Vol. 1,* Section 3.16–Cumulative Impacts.

42. University of Hawai'i at Hilo, *Final Environmental Impact Statement, Vol. 1,* 3–243. Emphasis added.

43. Somehow, lawyers found no contradiction also arguing the TMT "will not have a significant impact on *any* biological resources" (emphasis mine). Contested Case Hearing, Transcripts of closing arguments, DLNR No. HA-11–05, Vol. VII, September 30, 2011, 24–30.

44. As ʻŌiwi hid the buried remains of their kūpuna, burials will likely not be found until they are unearthed. The argument is self-serving.

45. Contested Case Hearing, Transcripts of closing arguments, DLNR No. HA-11–05, Vol. VII, September 30, 2011, 24–30.

46. State of Hawaiʻi, Department of Land and Natural Resources, DLNR File No. HA-11–05, *Findings of Fact, Conclusions of Law, and Decision and Order*, 92. Internal quote is from Haw. Rev. Stat. § 183C-1. Emphasis is mine.

47. DLNR, HA-11–05, *Findings of Fact, Conclusions of Law, and Decision and Order*, 35.

48. See Leerom Medovoi, "A Contribution To the Critique of Political Ecology: Sustainability as Disavowal" in *New Formations: A Journal of Culture/Theory/ Politics*, ed. Ashley Dawson, Vol. 69, Imperial Ecologies (2010), 131–32, who argues, "The close parallel between tolerance and sustainability captures an underlying political logic of our era: just as tolerance supplements, and ultimately makes tolerable the hegemony of political liberalism, so sustainability serves to sustain economic liberalism and, ultimately, capitalism itself . . . [H]ow does 'sustainability' stand in as a compensatory substitute for some more profound ethical critique and in lieu of the impulse to a deeper political transformation? . . . The connotation of 'sustainability' as tolerating damage permits it to work in exactly the opposite fashion, as a disavowal of that transformation."

49. DLNR File No. HA-11–05 (CDUA HA-3568); Petitioners' Combined Narrative Exceptions to the Hearing Officer's Findings of Fact, Conclusions of Law, and Decision & Order, 5. Emphasis added.

50. Lowercase *n* denotes Kanaka of 50 percent blood quantum or higher who have distinct rights to eligibility for land and benefits established under the 1920 Hawaiian Homes Commission Act. Capital *N* appeared through subsequent judicial cases and legislation to denote Kānaka of less than 50 percent blood quantum who, despite being ineligible for HHCA benefits, qualify for other benefits through various State and federal programs and Hawaiian-serving institutions. These beneficiaries must trace their genealogies to ancestors living in Hawaiʻi prior to settler arrivals as I survey in this chapter.

51. State of Hawaiʻi, Supreme Court (SC). 1998, *State of Hawaiʻi vs. Alapai Hanapi. Appeal from District Court of the Second Circuit, Molokai* (Case no. CTR2:11/14/95), November 20, 1998. Opinion of the Court by J. Klein (Hanapi), as cited in Ulla Hasager, "Indigenous Rights, Praxis, and Social Institutions," in *Social Process in Hawaiʻi* 39 (Honolulu: University of Hawaiʻi Press, 1999), 155–56.

52. Makaʻāinana may be translated as "populace" and is used in reference to the general or common Native people of Hawaiʻi.

53. Mark ʻUmi Perkins, "Kuleana: A Genealogy of Native Tenant Rights" (Ph.D. diss., University of Hawaiʻi, 2013). Perkins argues that the two most significant land laws of the nineteenth century, the Māhele (1848) and the Kuleana Act (1850), "were not the travesties that contemporary scholars would have us think, nor an example of unmitigated agency on the part of Hawaiians" (see Perkins, "Kuleana: A Genealogy of Native Tenant Rights," 6–7). Instead, Perkins's

analysis recognizes that the "processes of erasure and forgetting that led to alien-ation" were not the result of design, but rather an effect of a seemingly insignifi-cant but hugely consequential redefinition of a key stipulation that was figured into each Royal Patent, or original land title, issued through the Kuleana Act. The provision reads "koe nae na kuleana o na kanaka ma loko," which is generally translated as "reserving the rights of the native tenants" (see Perkins, "Kuleana: A Genealogy of Native Tenant Rights," 157). According to Perkins, this phrase provides for the foundational principle of kuleana, or "native tenant rights." He argues the phrase "ma loko" ("inside") has been insufficiently considered in trans-lations with severe, far-reaching, and lasting implications. Because "ma loko" was assigned to gathering rights exclusively—as in the right to enjoy *access on* private property—the intended *guarantee of universal* "vested rights" of all Kānaka ʻŌiwi to all lands in the kingdom has been all but erased from contemporary histori-ographies and legal and popular discourse. He argues for a reading of "the term 'kuleana' (as) used in kingdom law in the Lockean sense of having property *in* land," rendering, "koe nae na kuleana o na kanaka ma loko" to be read as "reserv-ing the property rights of the kanaka *within* a given parcel of land" (160–61). This vested interest in the land was embedded in the system by design, but purged from the historical record through "financial, procedural, bureaucratic and even discursive practices," which has led to the paradoxical "theft" of Hawaiian lands; or more accurately, their illegal transfer. Whereas historians have miscompre-hended the Māhele and the transition of land tenure, as methods of alienating native land rights, Perkins explains "on the contrary, they *embedded* makaʻāinana ('commoner' or native peoples') rights to land and provided for unencumbered ownership" (203). This was a revolutionary idea considering it protected Indig-enous Hawaiian rights and (non-Hawaiian settler) private landowners' rights simultaneously. The point is foreigners "held land only as proprietary interests, and did not hold vested rights in the dominion of the Kingdom [*sic*]" (172).

54. Melody Kapilialoha MacKenzie, *Native Hawaiian Rights Handbook* (Honolulu: Native Hawaiian Legal Corporation, 1991), 216.

55. See *Public Access Shoreline Hawaiʻi v. Hawaiʻi County Planning Commis-sion*, 79 Haw. 425, 903 P.2d 1246 (1995) ("PASH").

56. DLNR File No. HA-11-05, "Findings of Fact, Conclusions of Law, and Decision and Order." The 1892 date refers to common laws of the Hawaiian kingdom, which were cited in PASH. Of notable importance is the difference between the 1892 reference to "Hawaiian national usage," a phrase quoted in the common law section of the 1978 State of Hawaiʻi Constitution in which the "national" was dropped from an otherwise verbatim section. The date signifies when a practice was rendered "common"; See also, Laws of Her Majesty Liliuo-kalani, Queen of the Hawaiian Islands, 1892, 91; Hawaiʻi Revised Statutes §§ 1–1 and 7–1; PASH.

57. Hawaiʻi Constitution, Article XII, section 7.

58. Hawaiʻi Constitution, Article XII, section 7. Emphasis added. An "ahupuaʻa" is a traditional land division and land system that established the rights, responsibilities, and economics of society in precontact Hawaiʻi.

59. *State of Hawai'i v. Alapai Hanapi,* 89 Hawai'i 177, 970 p. 2d 485 (1998) (Hanapi). Constitution, Art. XII, § 7 cited. Emphases in original.

60. DLNR File No. HA-11–05, *The Applicant University of Hawai'i at Hilo's Proposed Findings of Fact, Conclusions of Law, and Decision and Order,* November 18, 2011, 118.

61. The reason is because they had been qualified in earlier court proceedings regarding the Keck Outriggers and NASA proposal years before.

62. DLNR File No. HA-11–05, *The Applicant University of Hawai'i at Hilo's Proposed Findings of Fact, Conclusions of Law, and Decision and Order,* November 18, 2011, 118.

63. As described in chapter 2, the reason the resource subzone was created was to modify the State Conservation District use law to retroactively permit activities on the summit that already existed for a decade up to that point.

64. Contested Case Hearing, Transcripts of closing arguments, DLNR No. HA-11–05, Vol. VII, September 30, 2011, 27.

7. Constellations of Resistance and Resurgence

1. Paul Coleman, interview by author, May 8, 2013, Mānoa, digital recording.

2. A kahu is also a "regent," "caretaker," or "minister" of Ho'omana Hawai'i (Hawaiian religions).

3. Larry Kimura, interview by author, June 7, 2013.

4. A paniolo is a cowboy and a kama'āina is often translated as "one born of a place." See Pukui and Elbert, *Hawaiian Language Dictionary.* This episode in history is discussed in chapter 5 as well.

5. 'Imiloa is a "$28 million, NASA-sponsored, UH-Hilo-operated venture" whose mission is to "to honor Mauna Kea" by weaving "astronomy and Hawaiian culture into a compelling story of human exploration and voyaging." See, *'Imiloa,* accessed May 13, 2014, http://www.imiloahawaii.org/.

6. Including those beyond the observatory. "Kahu Kū Mauna," *Office of Mauna Kea Management,* accessed May 13, 2014, http://www.malamamaunakea.org/management/kahu-ku-mauna.

7. This payout has been described as a bribe, yet ironically one that does more for securing the scientific community's own future well-being, as the money will be paid to STEM programs rather than Kānaka 'Ōiwi or Native-led land protection efforts. See University of Hawai'i at Hilo, *Final Environmental Impact Statement, Vol. 3: Appendices, Thirty Meter Telescope Project, Island of Hawai'i* (May 8, 2010), 174. The "TIO" is the TMT International Observatory Corporation.

8. Kimura, interview.

9. Kimura, interview.

10. Kimura, interview.

11. Kimura, interview.

12. Kimura, interview.

13. Kimura, interview.

14. Kimura, interview.

15. Kimura, interview.

16. Kimura, interview.

17. Kimura, interview.

18. Kimura, interview.

19. Kimura, interview.

20. See "Our Resident Navigator—Chad Kālepa Baybayan," 'Imiloa, accessed February 15, 2014, http://blog.imiloahawaii.org/our-resident-navigator-kalepa -baybayan/; "Hawaiian Voyaging Traditions," Polynesian Voyaging Society, accessed July 17, 2013, http://pvs.kcc.hawaii.edu/index/founder_and_teachers/chad_baybayan.html.

21. One example was his October 13, 2013 presentation at TEDx Mānoa, entitled "He lani ko luna, a sky above" in which he told of the revitalization of early voyaging traditions and the accomplishments of those activities. Chad Kālepa Baybayan, "He lani ko luna, a sky above: Kalepa Baybayan at TEDx-Manoa," TEDx Talks, YouTube video, 26:08, November 25, 2013, http://www.youtube.com/watch?v=nd-A9qJz3Vc.

22. Chad Kālepa Baybayan, interview by author, July 17, 2013.

23. Baybayan, interview.

24. Baybayan, interview.

25. Baybayan, interview.

26. Baybayan, interview.

27. Baybayan, interview.

28. Chad Kālepa Baybayan, Direct Testimony and Cross-examination, DLNR No. HA-11–05, TMT Contested Case Hearing, August 18, 2011, McManus Court Reporters.

29. Baybayan, Direct Testimony, DLNR No. HA-11–05, 2011, 166.

30. Baybayan, Direct Testimony, DLNR No. HA-11–05, 2011, 166.

31. Chad Kālepa Baybayan, "The Search for Knowledge on the Summit of Mauna Kea Is a Sacred Mission," West Hawaii Today, April 19, 2013, accessed July 17, 2013, http://westhawaiitoday.com/sections/opinion/columns/search-knowledge-summit-maunakea-sacred-mission.html.

32. Baybayan, interview.

33. Baybayan, interview.

34. Baybayan, interview.

35. Baybayan, interview.

36. SETI stands for Search for Extraterrestrial Intelligence and is a program based on the idea that discovery of an Earth-like exoplanet could indicate the existence of life.

37. Baybayan, interview.

38. Baybayan, interview.

39. Baybayan, interview.

40. Baybayan, interview.

41. Baybayan, interview.

42. Baybayan, Direct Testimony, DLNR No. HA-11–05, 2011, 169.

43. Baybayan, interview.

44. Baybayan, interview.

45. John and Ruth Ota, interview by author, September 23, 2012, Hilo, digital recording.

46. John and Ruth Ota, interview.

47. John and Ruth Ota, interview.

48. John and Ruth Ota, interview.

49. John and Ruth Ota, interview.

50. John and Ruth Ota, interview.

51. John and Ruth Ota, interview.

52. John and Ruth Ota, interview.

53. John and Ruth Ota, interview.

54. John and Ruth Ota, interview.

55. John and Ruth Ota, interview.

56. As discussed earlier in the book, pono may be translated as "correct" or "proper" procedure, or "that which is right and just." See Pukui and Elbert, *Hawaiian Language Dictionary*. Like Kameʻeleihiwa, I think of the term as meaning something akin to "balance" or "being in good relation." See Lilikalā Kameʻeleihiwa, *Native Land, Foreign Desires: Pehea Lā Pono Ai? How Shall We Live in Harmony?* (Honolulu: Bishop Museum Press, 1992).

57. ʻIke means "to see," "to know," and "knowledge."

58. For a detailed, though not exhaustive, examination of the myriad forms of oppression and destruction, as well as settler capitalist and military occupation that Kānaka ʻŌiwi continue to endure, see Hōkūlani K. Aikau and Vernadette Vicuña Gonzalez, eds., *Detours: A Decolonial Guide to Hawaiʻi* (Durham, N.C., and London: Duke University Press, 2019); and Noelani Goodyear-Kaʻōpua, Ikaika Hussey, and Erin Kahunawaikaʻala Wright, eds., *A Nation Rising: Hawaiian Movements for Life, Land, and Sovereignty* (Durham, N.C., and London: Duke University Press, 2014).

INDEX

Abercrombie, Neil, 37, 91, 93
aboriginal, 155, 188, 224, 266n4,
    278n34
activists: coalition, 24, 55, 207;
    concerns and critiques of, 234,
    239; interviews with, 198–99;
    state response to, 1
ahu lele, 44
ahupuaʻa, 48, 68, 183, 220; definition
    of, 273n35, 302n58
ʻāina: alienation from, 222, 260;
    responsibility to, 16, 49, 92, 263
Akim, Cecilia, 140
Akiyama, Mitsuo, 77
akua: ancestors, 177, 179–80, 186;
    gods, 45–48; Kealiʻiwahilani, 172;
    natural environment, 174–76;
    ocean, 40
Ala Hulu Kūpuna, 21
alienation, or alienate: ʻāina, 260;
    ancestral lands, 228; humanity, 36;
    land and social relations, 18, 28, 56,
    92–93, 109, 140, 222; legal context,
    54, 57, 74, 124, 301n53
Aliʻi Noʻeau Loa, 39
aloha ʻāina: against construction of
    the TMT, 1, 8; ceremony, 40, 45,
    176; chanting, 4; and collective
    liberation, 261–63; contested case
    hearing (CCH), 84; history of
    activism, 8, 14, 16–17, 63, 174, 199;

Kānaka ʻŌiwi, 16–17, 26, 38, 63,
    86; kiaʻi, 54; patriots, 12, 38, 73;
    stewardship and, 194, 198;
    theorizing of, 9–10, 187–88
alternative knowledge systems, 36–37,
    84
ancestors: and genealogies, 301n50;
    narratives of, 135–36; Papa and
    Wākea, 174; passed, 16, 25, 45, 62;
    remains of, 255, 301n44
ancestral places: alienation from,
    140; claims to, 101, 186; protection
    of, 8, 93, 112, 261–62; sacred pilina
    and collective kuleana, 188; settler
    stewardship, 193; support for, 230;
    trivialization of Kanaka ʻŌiwi
    knowledge, 161
ao, 48, 173, 294n64
Aoki, Paul, 88–89
Arista, Noelani, 171, 173, 293n42
Ariyoshi, George, 130–31
articulation: genealogy and
    activism, 18, 31, 126, 174, 186,
    188; theory of, 111, 163. *See also*
    Hall, Stuart
Arvin, Maile, 98
Asian American, 253
Asian settler colonialism, 102–7
assimilation, or assimilationist, 95–96,
    98, 137, 139
ʻaumākua, 25

Barrére, Dorothy B., 172–73. *See also* Kamakau, Samuel Mānaiakalani
Basham, Leilani, 165–66
Baybayan, Chad Kālepa, 245; analysis of, 253, 259; contested case testimony, 246, 250; interview with, 247–52
Berlant, Lauren, 67
big science: definition of, 35; fetish of, 59; Indigenous resistance to, 54, 93, 224, 230; and settler colonialism, 8, 14, 34, 196; and state authority, 65, 80, 83, 191–92, 200, 260; and state violence, 17, 38; University of Hawaiʻi, 81–82, 116, 141, 195, 237–38
binaries, 110, 205, 227, 229; modernity vs. tradition, 192, 203–4, 207, 225, 247–48; racial, 98; science vs. culture, 58, 61, 234; steward vs. obstructionist, 258
biopower, 275n4
Blaisdell, Richard Kekuni Akana, 146, 289nn54–55
blood quantum, 109, 112; eligibility for land and benefits, 74–75, 220–21, 271n13, 278n37, 301n50
Blount, James H., 72
Boy Scouts, 41, 43–45
Brown, Marie Alohalani, 173, 178, 265n2, 296n83
Burns, John A., 77
Byrd, Jodi, 18

California Institute of Technology (Caltech), 118, 195–96; Caltech Submillimeter Observatory, 70, 79
Canada-France-Hawaii (Telescope), 78
capitalism. *See* settler capitalism
Case, B. Pua, 24–25, 60, 84, 223, 258
ceded lands, 74–75, 297n1
Chamber of Commerce, 37, 77, 279n43

Ching, Clarence Kūkauakahi, 53, 84, 221
Christian converts, 178
civil disobedience direct action, 3 (fig.), 5 (fig.), 6, 11 (fig.), 176, 260; aloha ʻāina and, 40, 185–86; arrests, 288n39, 266n3; critiques of opposition, 123; historical examples, 137, 139, 241; and legal struggle, 128
Cleveland, Grover, 72–73
Clinton, Bill, 73
coexistence: and compromise, 211; conception of, 58; Kānaka ʻŌiwi and Indigenous lifeways, 63, 159, 260; TMT discourse, 205, 210–11
Coleman, Paul, 245, 250–51, 259, 299n15; analysis of power, 234, 237, 253; background, 41; guided tours by, 41–42, 44; interview, 232–37; Maunakea, 43, 49; positionality, 233–36
colonial: and alternative knowledge systems, 37, 155; ambivalence, 121, 225; analysis of power, 31, 42, 152, 163; Asian settlers in Hawaiʻi, 102–4; critique of power, 17, 192–93; education, 126, 133; guilt, 95, 106, 202; hegemony, 88, 90, 96, 179; hierarchy of being, 30, 34, 101, 161, 232; history, 59, 133, 204, 228; law, 8, 88–89, 191, 278n32; liberal multiculturalism and, 9, 94, 107, 113, 121, 155; logics of Native elimination, 75, 98–99, 198, 224, 278n37; police enforcement, 21; positionality, 236–37; racism, 133; relations of power, 14, 110–11; resistance to, 55, 92, 126, 177; settler discourse, 27, 36, 63, 112; settler state, 21, 62, 75, 266n6, 287n28, 287n28; subjectivity, 16; violence, 31, 57, 95, 97. *See also* settler colonialism
colonialism: analysis of, 201, 225; discourse about, 93, 236; dismissal

settler: adoption fantasy, 202; authority, 6, 93; belonging, 92, 122; culture,
227; guilt, 107, 253; hegemony, 30,
64, 94–96, 122, 192, 237; inheritance fantasy, 202; law, 8, 27, 38, 75,
87–88, 90, 92, 111, 162, 193, 196,
218, 222, 224; legitimacy, 96; possession, 92–93, 169; science, 35, 53,
58, 261; victimry, 157, 191
settler capitalism: alienation, 260; big
science, 76, 200; hegemony, 71, 97,
229, 259; knowledge systems, 34;
liberal multiculturalism, 9, 60, 93;
occupation, 35, 260, 262; political
subjugation of Kānaka ʻŌiwi, 117;
racial, x, 9, 15, 29, 35, 93, 100,
268n20; resistance against, 29;
scientific industry, 76; in solidarity
against, 96, 103, 253; TMT, 163;
white, 102, 193
settler colonialism (also settler colonial), 94–97; alienation, 97; Asian,
102–3; critical analysis of power, 57,
101, 113; critique, 107; hegemony,
140; historiography, 154, 228;
Kanaka alterity and indigeneity, 90,
110, 11, 121; liberal ideology, 99; as
liberal multiculturalism, 30, 122;
military occupation of Hawaiʻi,
194; Native elimination, 75, 96,
121, 218, 224, 278n37; Native subjectivity, 96; neoliberal environmental policy, 93; possessive logics
of, 97–98; politics of, 234; and
racial discrimination, 268n20; and
U.S. imperialism, 128; under U.S.
occupation, 30, 62, 124, 189, 192;
violence, 230; white liberal respectability, 6; white supremacy, 98. *See
also* Arvin, Maile; Asian settler
colonialism; colonial; Native;
Trask, Haunani-Kay
settler state, 18, 44, 92, 95, 120, 218,
268n18; scientific, 59, 86, 88, 114,
225, 227

settler violence, 100, 107, 117, 154,
205, 261
Sierra Club, 127, 130, 276n16
Silva, Noenoe, 168, 266n4; on historiography, 133–34, 204; Papa and
Wākea, 171, 173–74; on resistance,
134, 137
Simpson, Audra, 18
Simpson, Leanne Betasamosake, 142,
288n40
slavery, 36, 56, 100
solstice, 39–40, 54
Spanish American War, 73, 136
Standing Rock, 22, 56
Starblanket, Gina, 18
star navigation, 42, 289n47
statehood: and activism, 238; Harlem
Renaissance, 127, 137, 239; land
laws and rights, 218–19; liberal
multicultural citizenship, 104;
narrative of, 135, 203; prior to, 134;
referendum for, 140
Statehood Act, 75, 278n32
State of Hawaiʻi Constitutional
Convention, 72, 76, 220, 289n50,
292n34
State of Hawaiʻi Department of
Land and Natural Resources
(DLNR), 69; Board of Land and
Natural Resources (BLNR), 12,
65, 81, 84, 113, 131, 214–15;
Legislative Audit, 197; Office of
Conservation and Coastal Lands
(OCCL), 89; permits issued, 79, 85,
197; and University of Hawaiʻi, 24,
85
State v. Hanapi decision, 220
Stevens, John L., 72
stewardship, 57, 116, 192–93, 214, 254;
University of Hawaiʻi, 113–14, 194,
206, 211, 217, 224
Stone, Fred, 274n46, 275n11
storytelling, 40
subjection, 100, 230; Asian settlers,
103; militarized, 55, 256; Native

IOKEPA CASUMBAL-SALAZAR is associate professor in the Department of Critical Race and Ethnic Studies at UC Santa Cruz.